Digital Terrestrial Television in Europe

Digital Terrestrial Television in Europe

Edited by

Allan Brown
Griffith Business School
Griffith University, Australia

Robert G. Picard
Jönköping International Business School
Jönköping University, Sweden

LAWRENCE ERLBAUM ASSOCIATES PUBLISHERS
2005   Mahwah, New Jersey   London

Camera ready copy for this book was provided by the author.

Lawrence Erlbaum Associates, Inc., Publishers
10 Industrial Avenue
Mahwah, New Jersey 07430-2262

Cover design by Sean Trane Sciarrone

Library of Congress Cataloging-in-Publication Data

Digital Terrestrial Television in Europe / edited by
Allan Brown, Robert G. Picard

Includes bibliographical reference and index.
 p. cm.
ISBN 0-8058-4770-7 (cloth : alk. paper)
ISBN 0-8058-5387-1 (pbk : alk. paper)

CIP information may be obtained by contacting
the Library of Congress

Books published by Lawrence Erlbaum Associates are printed on
acid-free paper, and their bindings are chosen for strength and durability.

Printed in the United States of America
10 9 8 7 6 5 4 3 2 1

Contents

Foreword

PART 1: THEMES AND ISSUES

PART II: COUNTRY CASE STUDIES

Foreword

Digital terrestrial television is being planned and introduced across Europe because of its advantages in spectrum use, its ability to increasing the number of channels available, its reductions in reducing operating costs, and its linkages to telecommunications infrastructures that provide users a wide range of interactive services. The goal is to replace existing terrestrial television broadcasting in the coming with the digital alternative.

The digitalisation of terrestrial television is the latest in a range of policy, technology, and competition changes that are reshaping European television broadcasting. The changes are modernising and commercialising broadcasting, but also forcing public service broadcasters to rethink their missions and their roles in the new broadcasting environment.

European nations are ahead of others in the implementation of this new technology for terrestrial broadcasting and their experiences are providing crucial lessons for others anticipating the transition in the coming years.

This books explores issues in the development and implementation of digital television in Europe, showing how it is inextricably linked to developments in other forms of digital television provided by cable and satellite services and to government policies designed to promote development and use of information and communication technologies to support European wide and domestic industrial and social policies related to the Information Society.

Digital terrestrial television has now been introduced in the United Kingdom, Sweden, Spain, Finland, and Germany. Italy, France, and Denmark are close to beginning the digitalised form of terrestrial broadcasting and the other European nations will initiate systems in the coming years.

The experience of the initial countries in which digital terrestrial television has appeared reveals that the transition requires a precarious balancing of government, commercial, and consumer interests. Initial efforts to make the transformation have been far from successful and this book explores the difficulties, failures, and challenges that have appeared.

The book is divided into two parts. The first deals with concepts and issues associated with digital terrestrial television. Chapters explore the technological, policy, and financial aspects of this new form of broadcasting. It explores their implications for public service and commercial broadcasters and for television viewers.

The second portion of the book closely examines the processes, developments, and results of the introduction of digital terrestrial television in the individual nations that are in the forefront of the transition. The chapters show that more than a simple substitution of technologies is involved and that many factors are influencing and constraining the transition. Decisions by governments, companies, competitors, and consumers are playing critical roles in the development of digital terrestrial television. Decisions being made by the different stakeholders are often inhibiting as much as promoting the technology.

The book is the result of a coordinated effort by an extraordinary group of contributors with deep knowledge of the European television industry. They focus on the processes, problems, and implications of this contemporary history of broadcasting as a means of identifying challenges that will determine the future of digital terrestrial television and what must be done if it is to become a success in the future.

Allan Brown
Robert G. Picard

I

Themes and Issues

Chapter 1
From Analogue to Digital

Christopher Marsden
Independent Consultant on Broadband Communications, London

Monica Ariño
European University Institute, Florence, Italy

"The multimedia revolution was just hype." (John Malone, 1997)

DIGITISATION AND CONVERGENCE
OF INTERACTIVE PLATFORMS

In the 1990s, communications markets have undergone fundamental changes. Analogue technologies are being progressively replaced by digital communications services. Digitisation involves turning data into binary digits (bits) for storing, processing and transmission purposes. A fundamental feature of digital information is its independence from a specific transportation medium; consequently, it can be conveyed over all available networks, including satellite, coax and fibre-optic cable, high frequency wireless, digital terrestrial television (DTTV), analogue and digital telecommunications networks including digital subscriber lines (DSL), and even power lines. This not only leads to a more efficient use of the existing infrastructure but, because digitisation enables compression and packaging of data, it also reduces the amount of transport capacity needed per data unit. In the future, the digital conversion of all signals, transmitters, networks and equipment is envisaged.

It is easily forgotten, given the enormous losses incurred by pension funds and other investors in the technology-media-telecoms meltdown of 2000-2003, that enormous changes in the manner in which communications are undertaken have indeed taken place. It was not all just hype, although Malone's statement may indicate the extent to which business executives used and were used by the irrational optimism of the 1990s. Writing in early March 2003, we can state that in the European Union (EU)[1] today:

- 80 per cent of citizens have a mobile telephone, though none a third generation video phone;
- 50 per cent of British households have bought digital television (DTV) services;
- 50 per cent of citizens use a personal computer (PC) linked to the Internet;
- approximately 5 per cent of all households have a cable or DSL broadband connection (normally 512 kilobits per second); and
- about 33 per cent have a DVD (digital video disc) player, the same number a video camera and/or a still digital camera.

Europe, North America and developed East Asia are becoming digital (Negroponte, 1995).

A convergence phenomenon has taken place between previously separated communications networks and services. The rates of growth of adoption of broadband, in-home PCs and image recording/playback devices (DVD players, digital still and video cameras) means that the majority of EU homes will soon be digital. Using home media servers or 'WiFi' technologies[2] will enable wireless connectivity to spread from its predominant current use in offices to residential uses in and between homes.

Convergence is indeed blurring the market and regulatory boundaries between broadcasting, telecommunications and information technology (IT). The idea of having all services available in all platforms is hard to achieve in practice, because each platform and network has limits, and consumers do not always embrace what is technologically possible. The benefits will be considerably reinforced with universal digital reception allowing consumers to access services from multiple digital platforms (principally Internet-connected PCs, DTV sets and mobile terminals). Convergence will not be absolute and the

---

[1] By 'EU', we refer to the 15 Member States of the European Union, and by extension the advanced Western European nations which are members of the European Economic Area (EEA) but not full political members of the EU (notably, Norway and Switzerland). When the term 'European' is used, this encompasses the ten Eastern 'accession states' expected to join the EU in 2004, creating a market of 25 full political EU members and the EEA states, and those other Council of Europe states which are signatories to the European Convention of Human Rights (including, for instance, Russia, Ukraine, several southern Balkan new states and Belorus). There were 40 Council of Europe member states in 2003.

[2] WiFi is the commercial name for wireless local area network technologies, which provide multi-megabit portable Internet access from laptop computers.

precise capabilities of each platform mean it is more likely that they act as complements rather than substitutes (Liikanen, 2002).

Information Society and DTV

In Europe, public policy discourse has focussed on the metaphor of networks reinforcing 'Information Society,' not technological development of 'Information Superhighways.' The social, economic and regulatory implications are enormous, affecting the population at large: "The information revolution prompts profound changes in the way we view our societies and also in their organisation and structure" (Bangemann, 1994: 1). Digital technology is a "potential vehicle for achieving a broad distribution of access to, and participation in, the social processes of knowledge production" (Benkler, 1998a: 184). Transition to digital raises entertainment and information costs for consumers, which potentially widens gaps between 'information rich' and 'information poor' (the 'digital divide'). Indeed, digitisation increases public dependence on screen-based media for information, entertainment, education and other public services. The principal threat is the creation of a two-tier society in which, ultimately, only a part of the population has access to the new technology, is comfortable using it, and can fully enjoy its benefits. Preventing a similar outcome is a major challenge for public authorities.

Public authorities therefore are taking an important role in the development of DTV for overall societal benefit. Recently, an EU initiative has reiterated the importance of DTV and new digital interactive services, and the consequent need for public policy to remove obstacles to its development, promoting openness, interoperability and freedom of choice (CEC, 2002h). The reason is that, due to higher penetration of analogue television sets, as compared to PCs or even mobile phones, television platforms have the potential of becoming a central and 'consumer friendly' point of access to a wide range of Information Society services. Indeed, Nobuyuki Idei of Sony has stated that the television set will be at the centre of the future broadband experience (*The Economist*, 2003).

The process by which households will progressively migrate from analogue to DTV reception is called digital switch-over. In DTV the benefits to producers and network owners of the use of digitisation have been significant. Digitisation allows:

- improved efficiency in spectrum usage;
- substantially increased capacity in the number of channels that can be transmitted;
- superior quality of image resolution and audio;
- consistent reception over varying distances;

- reduced costs in transmission and energy consumption;
- interactivity with a return path, either dial-up Internet (DTTV, analogue cable and satellite) or broadband (cable and DSL broadband);
- data transmission;
- better applications for the disabled; and
- greater flexibility of operations in general.

Many of those benefits have already been realised to some degree and will be further enhanced when production and storage are fully digitized. However, consumer adoption of DTV has been slower than for other digital equipment and services. There are numerous long term benefits of an all-digital environment (quality, choice, competition, development); yet there are also considerable obstacles (analogue legacy, uncertainties, potential distortions of competition, market failures and externalities). Television's relatively poor current interactivity will be augmented by more powerful future PCs connected to the television screen, including upgraded set-top boxes (STBs), personal video recorders which will integrate video cassette recorders (VCRs) and DVD players, computer games consoles and home media servers. With half of Western European households expected to have broadband fixed connections to the Internet by 2008, policy for the medium term (around five years) needs to consider both households that will be fully wired to interactive broadband, and the remainder that show little propensity to join the digital age beyond a second generation GSM (global system for mobiles) narrowband mobile telephone. That will be a true digital divide.

The remainder of the introductory chapter is structured as follows:

1. We consider the early development of DTV markets to the end of 2002, focussing on the three dominant platforms – satellite, cable and DTTV – and the market development of a STB subsidy model to encourage consumers to switch from analogue.
2. We address the public interest in DTV, as part of Information Society policy.
3. We assess the path dependency in national television market structure and previous technological switch-overs, discussing particularly the central role of public service broadcasting (PSB) in the European television ecology.[3]

---

[3] Public service broadcasting is financed by taxation in most EU Member States, and provided by a public service broadcaster – normally a statutory corporation. The organisation and funding of PSBs are discussed in Chapter 3, and we here use the term PSB to refer to both the concept and the corporation responsible for such programming. Where we refer to terrestrial FTA broadcasters who

4. We follow with discussion of the analogue switch-off, the release of spectrum that will be enabled by the ending of all terrestrial analogue television signals, and the necessary steps and motives in achieving that goal.

5. Finally, we assess the overall role of government in the switch-over process, and conclude by considering the reasons why convergence between DTV, PCs and mobile is proceeding at a slower pace than predicted by the 'hype' of the 1990s.

This final factor includes the most important policy issue: to what extent should government interfere in the processes of a market that is achieving rapid if uneven growth? Should government concentrate on the wider aim of ensuring a rapid migration of households from 25-28 hours per week of passive television viewing to broadband interactivity via computer-like devices? Is government's role in DTV a maximalist sponsorship as in the 1950s introduction of analogue television, or the minimalist role that it played in the introduction of VCRs in the 1980s? In this introductory chapter, we do not seek definitive answers, but rather raise the pertinent questions. As lawyers researching the interaction of economics with law and policy, we begin by assessing the empirical evidence of market development, before analysing the law and policy which interacts with these dynamic market developments.

OVERVIEW OF THE EUROPEAN DTV MARKET

The EU DTV market has experienced substantially greater growth than that in the United States (US). European digital satellite television was first introduced in March 1996 in France; cable services followed shortly and DTTV was introduced in the United Kingdom (UK) in late 1998. There are other potential delivery mechanisms such as DSL, which so far are relatively little utilised. Currently DTV services, whether pay-TV or free-to-air (FTA), are available in all EU countries.[4] DTV markets have developed in different ways depending on migration paths from analogue television. Consequently, important divergences between EU markets can be observed. DTV take-up proved to be more successful in those countries where the majority of consumers previously only accessed analogue FTA (mainly France, UK, Italy and Spain), as compared to

---

receive no public financing, but whose licenses nevertheless contain public service obligations, we do not refer to 'PSB'. The European Commission has conducted extensive investigations into the legal definition of a PSB under the competition rules of the Treaty of Rome.

[4] In 2002 the number of digital households rose to 32.2 million, as compared to 26.6 million in 2001, and overall penetration increased to 20.8 per cent (CEC, 2002a).

Germany, Austria and the Benelux,[5] where multi-channel existed in analogue either by basic cable or by satellite. (Multi-channel has no exact definition, but our working definition is 12 or more channels.)

Consumers' primary motive appears to be access to premium content on pay-TV whether analogue or digital, so analogue pay-TV subscribers are predictive of DTV subscribers. Even where cable or satellite is used for reception by the main television set in the house, secondary and portable sets still depend on FTA terrestrial reception. EU DTV penetration at the end of 2002 was:

- satellite 21.5 million (13.9 percent of all television households);
- cable 8.1 million (5.2 percent); and
- DTTV 2.6 million (1.7 percent) (CEC, 2002a).

Satellite Television

Satellite distribution offers the possibility of up to 500 extra channels (ten times more than analogue satellite). For operators, it has the technical advantage that, unlike cable for instance, services are immediately available anywhere in the satellite's 'footprint,' including even foreign audiences. Sunk costs are thus relatively small. The principal disadvantage is that satellite does not permit two way communications, relying on a telecoms line with a modem to provide interactivity. This is also the case for DTTV. Neither is a truly interactive platform. The distribution processes of digital satellite television are shown in Figure 1.1.

Cable Television

Cable networks do have bi-directional transmission—hence a return path for sophisticated interactive services—but require long-term investments and substantial sunk costs for digital conversion. Even analogue cable can be unprofitable in areas with low density of population. Cable has rolled out DTV incrementally, with easier DTV upgrade in the newest analogue networks. However, in early 2003 digital cable operators were in or near bankruptcy, as will be examined in the conclusion to the chapter.

In addition to its 500 channel DTV capabilities (like satellite, about ten times more than analogue), cable also allows for the provision of telephone

---

[5] The collective term for the 'Low Countries,' namely, Belgium, Netherlands and Luxembourg.

services and Internet broadband (the so-called 'triple play'). The distribution processes of digital cable television are illustrated in Figure 1.2.

Figure 1.1: Digital Satellite Television

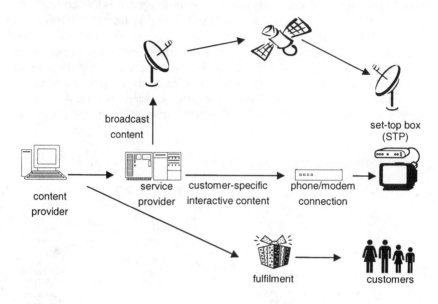

Figure 1.2: Digital Cable Television

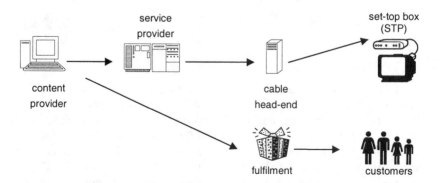

Digital Terrestrial Television

Using a normal television aerial, consumers can receive digital signals in markets where signals are broadcast. They do require a STB to convert the signals back into analogue unless they have an integrated DTV receiver. (By March 2003 there were only a few thousand digital display televisions in Europe.) DTTV offers up to 40 channels, about five to eight times greater than analogue terrestrial. However, this is less than analogue cable or satellite, and far less than digital versions of these platforms. It is therefore an upgrade path for previous viewers of FTA and other terrestrial channels. Its great advantage is portability: there is no requirement for expensive reception dishes or cables, simply a normal aerial and a STB. The distribution processes for DTTV are shown in Figure 1.3.

Figure 1.3: Digital Terrestrial Television

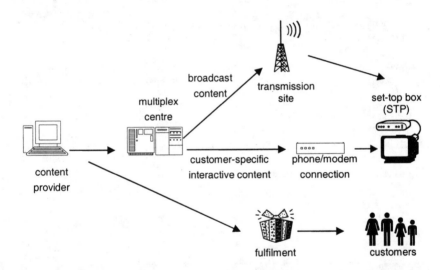

In 1999 most EU States had set rather optimistic deadlines (usually 2000-01) for the launch of DTTV. However, delays and bankruptcies of pioneer DTTV platforms in Spain and the UK mean that in most countries DTTV services have very few or no viewers. To the end of 2002, DTTV had been launched in the UK, Sweden, Finland, Spain and Portugal, and its launch was imminent in France and Italy. In Germany the introduction of DTTV has occurred at different speeds in different regions. In other countries (Ireland, Denmark, Norway and Austria) the launch of DTTV has been postponed or was still subject to ongoing discussions. The specific characteristics of various national markets will be analysed in Part 2 of this book.

Although terrestrial television was historically the main network delivering analogue television reception, DTV markets have so far been driven by satellite and cable (primarily pay-TV) operators, generally using proprietary STB technologies, while DTTV roll-out faces serious problems in most EU Member States, including newly acceding States in 2004, whose DTV markets are typically less developed. This situation makes a uniform migration process throughout the EU highly improbable and subsequently switch-over policies are likely to remain national in scope. There might be an argument for Community action in order to co-ordinate the digital transition, avoiding fragmentation of the internal market in Europe as well as delays in the release of spectrum currently used for analogue FTA services.

Challenges for DTV Broadcasters

Broadcasters encounter three major challenges in the DTV world. First, they must upgrade their infrastructures to support DTV services. As mentioned above, it is DTTV delivery that faces more difficulties in this respect. Nearly all satellite pay-TV platforms now operate exclusively on a digital basis, which is not the case for FTA DTTV channels that must be transmitted ('simulcast') in analogue format until consumers switch over to digital reception for *all* television sets, in the household, tent, and mobile home. More than 80 per cent of EU cable networks have been rapidly upgraded to carry digital, allowing cable operators to offer telephony, Internet access and video services. However, in practice only a relatively small share of connected households have actually been equipped with the STBs that are needed for DTV reception. Because DTV signals must be converted by the consumer's equipment into analogue signals for television display, all DTV reception – whether cable, satellite or DTTV – requires a STB. This box, which also decrypts premium programming for pay-TV households, is the gateway into all DTV households. In consequence, it is regulated as a bottleneck facility. Because it is classified as a telecommunications system, it is regulated by Member States under EU Directive 95/47 (as amended in 2003). Chapter 2, on regulation, deals with this issue (see also Cave & Cowie, 1996), but some general comments may indicate the increased complexity of television reception for the consumer in the DTV era.

The second challenge is the entrance of new players (principally platform operators), which has precipitated a change in organisation and strategies. The DTV industry has been shaped around complex vertically integrated structures, where proprietary systems prevail. Broadcasters are being forced to rethink their roles and business models; in a multi-channel environment this is particularly imperative for PSBs wishing to get access to the increasing number of viewers/voters/taxpayers using non-terrestrial platforms.

Third, a multiplication in the number of channels has boosted demand for television programmes and attractive content has become a highly valued asset. As Cowie and Marsden (1999) remark, the location of constraints in the supply chain of production is reversed. Delivery costs decrease and are no longer an issue; instead, what we now have is a greater number of retail outlets competing for relatively scarce content. Demand for national language audiovisual products remains extremely limited in other linguistic markets, and there is a risk that the already negative trade balance with the US will further increase (Noam, 2000). A stronger demand for 'quality'[6] (and if possible exclusive) programmes implies higher fixed costs for broadcasters (Sutton, 1991). This is because the costs of delivering a programme are the same regardless of the quality of such programme so that fixed costs are not given by exogenous technical considerations but instead by the need to acquire sufficiently attractive content. As Motta and Polo (1997) show, this results in persistent levels of concentration in the media industry and suggests that it is the most likely scenario in the near future. This accentuates pluralism concerns, where concentrated ownership restricts the diversity of media control, and therefore potentially content.

Market Structure and Subsidies for the STB

The analogue installed base of television sets and STBs is an enduring policy issue. Consider Benelux, where almost the entire population receives multi-channel television via analogue cable, using analogue television sets and STBs. A complete transition to DTV will require the replacement of all analogue receivers (including second and third television sets as well as other complementary products such as VCRs) and even some of the current first generation DTV equipment. As with other consumer electronics equipment, initially integrated DTV sets were priced as novelty luxury goods and, therefore, take-up has occurred at a very slow pace. The benefits of digital screens are generally seen in the household only on PCs, leading the consumer to perceive that DTV is essentially more of the same: pay-TV.

STB manufacturers and other consumer electronics producers need to roll out equipment rapidly as mass market volume drives prices in consumer electronics (which is why PCs, DVD players and VCRs are so inexpensive compared to a decade ago). Platform and networks operators also need a fast

---

[6] Here the term 'quality' is understood in an economic sense as referring to 'attractive' or 'popular' programmes that drive demand, but without any moral valuation of the content.

roll-out to achieve a critical mass and the network effects of 'bandwaggoning' – consumers copying early adopter behaviour and creating a virtuous circle of emulation and service development, where supply and demand are mutually reinforced. With the purpose to foster the market for DTV services, platform operators decided to subsidise DTV receivers (effectively giving them away free). In most cases proprietary and non-interoperable standards were adopted in order to 'lock in' the consumer and recoup investments. Boxes for different platforms carry different and incompatible software, which cannot 'talk' to that in other boxes; for example, your DTTV box cannot be used for cable television.

All of this was done in a context of vertical integration, which has proved more effective than retail models in achieving roll-out in initial stages of market development, but where competition is usually restrained. Any rents created by monopoly are justified by cross-subsidies to more competitive segments of the value chain, for instance STB subsidies and new programming and interactive services. Currently, the desire exists, particularly among equipment manufacturers, to migrate towards open standards. A prerequisite, though, is an appropriate regulatory policy with respect to standardisation and interoperability issues. This is discussed further in later chapters, but we identify briefly some concerns here.

Interoperability between proprietary standards is possibly the most critical, controversial and complicated·issue in the DTV environment: "Standardization, compatibility, interoperability and application portability are essential pillars in the erection of a successful and competitive European digital television system" (Nolan, 1997: 610). Mandating standards might not necessarily solve the problem. As the following section illustrates, European television has a strong tradition of *ex ante* standardisation and interoperability that guaranteed certainty in the analogue era, but that differs in the telecommunications sector and is practically absent in the IT industry.

How to reconcile all the different traditions in a digital world is not an easy task. Presently, standardisation difficulties are exacerbated by rapidly changing technologies and by a progressive transition from network based models (hardware), which are relatively easy to standardise, to service based models (software), with more flexible and sophisticated systems. In today's markets there are too many variants, options and interests: A single monolithic concept is almost impossible. Systems present different layers so that standardisation of one of the layers could result in the interoperability problem simply moving up to the next one, if there is an economic incentive to lock in the consumer. Perhaps a more sensible approach might be to concentrate on building bridges between different platforms and layers, to achieve a satisfactory degree of interoperability, understanding it as an evolutionary process more than as a feature.

IDENTIFYING THE PUBLIC INTEREST IN DTV

The regulatory implications of digitisation are many and complex. Before addressing them, some brief considerations about television regulation in general are important. In the analogue tradition there were two major rationales for television broadcasting regulation. The first one was technical: spectrum scarcity. This justified public intervention designed to achieve an efficient distribution of a public resource. The second or 'public interest' rationale referred to the social impact of the media and its centrality in democratic processes (Feintuck, 1999). In practice, greater weight has normally been put on the protection of pluralism, cultural traditions and moral values (democratic rationale), while the technical rationale operated sometimes as an excuse for politically motivated regulation (Humphreys, 1996). In spite of the weakening of the spectrum scarcity rationale (because the introduction of cable and satellite television networks reduced dependence for these networks' viewers on terrestrial television spectrum), the democratic argument remains powerful as an argument for regulatory intervention in the DTV era.

Viewers' commercial and electoral power makes them central to the migration process. First, the digital world empowers the educated consumer, who can personalise his/her media consumption. There is greater freedom to select not only the type of content one wants to watch, but also the time, the conditions (language, with or without advertising, various programmes simultaneously) and the device(s) used. However, greater diversity of content and multiple outlets also implies fragmented and not necessarily better informed audiences. On the contrary "the prospect of individuals knowing of the existence of much of the material more widely available, let alone surveying it, is highly unlikely" (Gibbons, 2000: 311). In addition, a boost in the number of television channels entails an increased difficulty in locating desirable content. For this reason navigation devices (electronic programme guides) become essential tools for viewers and thus have the potential to influence viewing patterns (as Microsoft Windows default settings affect our choice of media player on PCs).

In essence, two fundamental problems can be identified: effectively safeguarding pluralism including access to programming; and avoiding citizen's exclusion from information flows, which includes copyright policy.

Pluralism and Access to DTV Programming

The effect of digitisation on pluralism in television broadcasting markets is twofold. First, it multiplies the number of channels and, hence, the number of potential voices. DTV services are increasingly customised and personalised so that the ability to reach mass audiences is reduced. At the extreme, it could be argued that the need for regulation derived from impact on public opinion disappears. However, the crucial factor is not the hypothetical, but the actual impact of the media on citizens (McGonagle, 2001). This is measured by audience reach, rather than by number of channels. Viewing patterns have certainly not changed enough to suggest that viewers are now emancipated from media manipulation. Television broadcasting remains (and the Internet is emerging) as a means of mass communication of a particularly intrusive nature. Furthermore, there seems to be an inexorable tendency towards globalisation and restrictions on media concentration (structural ownership control) continue to be loosened. This is to accommodate regulation to convergence-oriented conglomerates seeking advantages of complementarities between media and technologies, but has an impact on *ex ante* media specific pluralism and seriously threatens the diversity of opinions required in a democratic state (Marsden, 2000).

Second, digitisation has created new bottlenecks or gateways at the various stages of the value chain; these are facilities without access to which it would be practically impossible for a third party to provide competing services to consumers. This is primary a competition concern, but clearly it has implications from the point of view of pluralism and the 'digital divide' since access to viewers is a fundamental premise for the development of a diversity of views and access to information. Traditional controls are necessary but not sufficient to maintain pluralism in digital services (Marsden, 1999); they need to be combined with greater scrutiny of bottlenecks both under generic competition law and also, when competition rules do not adequately protect pluralism, under specific rules.

Digital Copyright and Peer-to-Peer Networks

Another significant risk of social exclusion is exclusion from copyrighted material, including broadcast material. Convergence, as seen by the extraordinary success of broadband peer-to-peer (P2P) file sharing of media, is increasingly a home-made process. It has overtaken the legal, regulatory and market process. The policy process' major incumbent players increasingly look like their finger-in-the-dyke approach is being overtaken by a broadband digital P2P tidal wave. Content providers are reluctant to produce non-encrypted content in digital forms for various reasons, of which two overriding factors are institutional inertia and disintegration of the vertical value chain, which creates coordination problems (Noam, 2003). The lack of digital programming on the Internet is directly related to the lack of copyright protection, whereas 'closed' television systems protect digital rights holders absolutely from copyright infringement, but could also curtail end-users' legitimate access to the programming for which they have paid.

Copyright was designed as a legal monopoly for a limited period to reward innovators by enabling profitable licensing of their innovation. In a digital network environment there are new challenges in the application of copyright laws (Samuelson, 2000). The numerous advantages of digital technologies (superior quality, lower reproduction and distribution costs) also facilitate copyright infringement (Fallenböck, 2003). Fallenböck proposes a model of regulation through technology as the most effective way to enforce copyright protection, stressing the role of anti-circumvention provisions. Copyright systems are being adapted in order to keep pace with technological change and ensure enough protection for content creators. When doing so, it is crucial to balance copyright protection against the protection of traditional rights like access for public use (US 'doctrine of fair use') or against the protection of the right of freedom of expression.

These tensions between intellectual property rights and their limits have always existed, but are exacerbated in the digital era. As Hugenholtz (1996: 5) states: "In the analogue world, acts of information consumption, for example reading a book or watching TV, are not copyright protected. Arguably, the same should be true for the digital environment". In fact, a potential danger exists of granting copyright owners more protection than they actually had in the analogue world. Such an expansion could hurt the public interest by making digital works less available or less usable (Benkler, 1999) and could eventually be contrary to Articles 8 and 10 of the European Convention of Human Rights, on privacy and freedom of expression. In this context an adequate legal treatment of digital rights management is key. It is widely accepted that functions for managing and protecting digital rights are crucial for a successful distribution of content.

A Multiplatform Approach: DTV and Broadband Policy

It is important to highlight that the achievement of general interest objectives should not be linked to one particular technology only. Overestimating the role of DTV in the convergence process could put at risk developments in other areas. This is why DTV policy should be coordinated with other complementary policies, particularly broadband, which also have the potential to deliver similar social and economic benefits. Forcing DTV as a platform of universal access to a wide range of Information Society services might jeopardise investments in broadband or other platforms in the long term. For this reason it is fundamental to find the appropriate balance between the provision of basic DTV services, affordable and widely available, and the development of other more advanced solutions, so that market players are not faced with excessively heavy obligations that could discourage alternative private initiatives. Recently, the European Commission recognised the necessity of a multi-platform approach and proposed several actions in order to promote widespread availability of broadband networks throughout the EU. Encouraging DTV switch-over is one of them, but by no means the only one; others might include ensuring a wider availability of digital programming on broadband interactive networks.

POLICY SOLUTIONS IN PREVIOUS TELEVISION MARKET DEVELOPMENT

We analyse in this section the specific impact of digital switch-over for the different players and consider the public policy challenges. Special attention is paid to the DTTV market, which is central to the issue of the 'digital divide'.

The vertical value chain between networks and content raises a 'chicken and egg' co-ordination dilemma. It does not make economic sense to invest in digital applications if there are not enough consumers equipped to receive the service. Manufacturers do not want to produce equipment on a large scale (which would increase affordability) if there are no attractive digital services readily available. In the analogue terrestrial environment, this co-ordination problem was solved by integrating manufacture, transmission and production in a licensed oligopoly or monopoly of 'broadcasters.' The British Broadcasting Corporation (BBC), founded in 1924 by equipment manufacturers, produced radio programming initially to incentivise consumers to buy radio receivers. Government periodically regranted the BBC a legal radio monopoly until 1968. This monolithic industrial planning was also the means of introducing monochrome and then colour television in the 1950s and 1960s. Those manufacturers who had gradually withdrawn from the BBC consortium as saturation coverage of radio sets was achieved in the early 1930s, re-invested in the new commercial terrestrial monopolies. The BBC received public funding for colour transmission of its new second channel in 1964, in order to encourage public interest in colour television sets (see Coase, 1950; Briggs & Spicer 1985).

However clumsily monolithic this 'old' approach appears, the continued evolution of an entire broadcasting system in which hardware and programming must make a revolutionary technological and consumer behavioural change in a synchronised manner, does tend towards vertical integration. This is made more difficult in DTV by the increasing number of players in all markets: transmission; production; channel management; multiplex bundling; interactive application development; equipment manufacturing; encryption technology development, and so on. The DTV market more closely resembles the PC market of the 1980s than the analogue television market of the 1970s, when colour television was introduced. The following factors help to identify the coordination problems involved:

- globalisation of manufacturing;
- internationalisation of software production;
- fragmentary evolution paths towards the intended consumer switch-over; and
- government policy favouring the local domestic champion strategy while consumer preference emerges for vertically integrated international system designs.

Consider the 1984 consumer computer buyer: do they buy a PC using the DOS operating system, a legacy of IBM architecture which would develop into the Wintel (Microsoft-Intel) monopoly in associated markets? Or do they plump for a Siemens/Bull/Olivetti/BBC Acorn design running locally designed software? Or do they acquire the user-oriented and technologically advanced Apple that is incompatible with the other systems and creating a ghetto of converts? Those who bought an Apple were fortunate that the software designers created new content and programmes that kept users supplied, and that there was the ability to convert Apple files to DOS. Those who bought the Phillips V2000 or the Sony Betamax VCRs were less fortunate. While programmers could supply computer programming from source code, Hollywood studios and distributors simply stopped supplying Betamax and V2000 format 'software' (cassettes), killing all consumer interest. For the consumer, it is vital to judge which of the rival platforms to purchase.

How to pick a winner? Government has consistently (in VCRs and PCs, but also in multi-channel television) failed to pick the winner. It is impossible to discuss DTV policy without reference to the foreign pirate history of all broadcast innovation. Commercial radio in the UK was the legitimation of a fait accompli, as it emerged due to offshore commercial operators acting entirely outside of national law. The same process resulted from foreign terrestrial television and then satellite television operators achieving commercial success. In DTV, it is again satellite operators who have led technological innovation, with local cable and DTTV operators responding to the 'foreign threat.' It is no accident that the foreign threat is often associated with business interests that are close to government, and which connive to produce the 'foreign invasion', for instance Luxembourg-based foreigner RTL in countries bordering the Rhine River (notably Benelux, France, and Germany) and Luxembourg-based SkyTV in the UK and Ireland (see CEC, 1989).

The Future of Public Service Broadcasters

EU governments have long favoured their domestic television champions to the exclusion of foreign competition. The particular cultural and economic characteristics of television and radio broadcasting demand that the market be supported by publicly directed subsidy to providers of merit goods and public goods: PSBs (Davies & Graham, 1997). Merit goods are those that command no monetary value but which are perceived to contribute to the public welfare, which includes such cultural products as FTA educational programming. Public goods are those that can be consumed by the marginal consumer without degrading the product for the existing consumers, and of course FTA signals do not depend on limiting the number of consumers. In fact, FTA television, because it creates 'water cooler' discussions, is perceived to actually have positive externalities, in that the more viewers, the more non-viewers want to join the 'club' of existing viewers (if only to join the water cooler discussion at work next morning).

The extent to which PSB is marginalised or supported by governments in the interactive multichannel environment determines the degree of non-commercial merit programming that will be broadcast as a public good, and the size of externalities. That also distorts the digital environment, so that the BBC has a position of pre-eminence in British multimedia that AOL-Time Warner cannot imagine in the US. While BBC Worldwide is entrepreneurial in exploiting its properties, US commercial broadcasters such as Walt Disney Co. have made much bigger profits, unfettered by non-commercial merit good (cultural) considerations.

The marginalisation of PSB in the US has acted as a cautionary tale for EU policy-makers in the DTV process. The contrast between the BBC and CNN reporting of the Iraqi disarmament process of 2002-03 is often cited as an example of the 'dumbing down' of US news reporting in the multi-channel era. The bi-media integration of PSB in radio and television in most EU countries has contributed to the strength and independence of PSB, and radio news is a very strong competitor to television as the 'medium of record', most reliable news source. Extremely vigorous lobbying by the BBC has ensured massive increases in resources over the period since the 1996 Broadcasting Act introduced the framework for DTTV, as its commercial competitors were asset stripping through mergers and then suffering the advertising recession of 2001 to date. The Treaty of Amsterdam 1997 addition to the EU 'constitution' included a Protocol on Public Service Broadcasting designed to insulate the sector from normal competition rules. Though individual countries have very culturally specific relations between PSBs and governments, there has been continued support for the non-commercial broadcast sector.

The pact between PSBs and governments revolves around universal availability of programming, within national borders, to all citizens. Politicians receive free political advertising on this medium. The means of providing universal coverage has been terrestrial transmission. In return for providing universal coverage, the French, German and UK governments have imposed a flat rate universal tax on all viewers, backed by criminal sanction for non-payment. The vast majority of this tax is passed on as a public subsidy to the PSBs. The tax is not trivial, and in the UK in 2003 was over 160 Euros. This tax is levied per household, providing reception for all receivers in each household. It is of course quite possible that households have only one television receiver which is connected to a cable or satellite system on which they choose not to view public service channels. Nevertheless, they must pay the license fee, as this tax is called, or go to prison. It is not an idle threat: in the UK there are hundreds of convicted criminals at any one time due to non-payment of the license fee.

The formula for funding PSB is therefore:

$$\begin{array}{c}\text{universal}\\\text{terrestrial}\\\text{availability}\end{array} + \begin{array}{c}\text{meritorious}\\\text{programming}\end{array} + \begin{array}{c}\text{unbiased and}\\\text{copious}\\\text{free political}\\\text{coverage}\end{array} = \begin{array}{c}\text{universal}\\\text{tax}\end{array}$$

Given this grand political settlement of the medium which occupies 70 per cent of leisure hours, reform or abolition of the taxation has been studiously avoided throughout the postwar period. The breaking of the PSB monopoly actually reinforced its values, as the new commercial broadcasters were given access to the medium and concessions to broadcast advertising in return for further political access to the viewing public and further, if slightly less meritorious, programming. The tax was increased with each new entrant to the market, and the number of PSB channels in some EU countries (for instance, Germany, Sweden, Denmark, and France) increased to match those of the terrestrial 'competitors.' The system was therefore reinforced rather than weakened with each innovation. Thus in the UK, the BBC introduced colour television in 1964 just as commercial television reached full penetration, breakfast television in 1982 just as ITV did, independent programming in 1982 just as Channel 4 did, 24 hour news after SkyNews did, all paid for by the tax on television households.

The price paid for this continued expansion of television broadcasting hours was threefold:

• creation of an insatiable public appetite for further programming;

- increased television subsidies to PSB paid from central taxation or a tax on television households to match PSB funding to commercial rivals, apparently in perpetuity, and
- under-pricing of the huge amount of radio spectrum needed for this continued expansion in terrestrial broadcasting.

All three are threatened by cable and satellite entrants, whose viewers use no domestic spectrum, watch non-PSB (often exclusively foreign) programming in abundance, and whose viewers pay significant sums for tangible services, rather than the PSB-politician settlement. Indeed, these viewers' insatiable demand for visual sensual gratification often precludes the viewing of 'serious' merit good programming, and there is evidence that the trivial and superficial news reporting of CNN is favoured over the deeper analysis of the BBC News Directorate. The challenge of these new technologies is therefore to universal coverage, the license tax, and PSB programming.

Unlike in the US, the public service networks have seen relatively slow audience shrinkage. The Hollywood-produced programming of the non-terrestrial broadcasters has proved relatively unattractive to discerning viewers, though children's appetite for cartoons and commercials over factual educational content has resulted in a serious loss of terrestrial viewers. In this particular audience segment (children), the merit goods argument is so overwhelming, in the US as in Europe, that loss of audience actually feeds the moral and political argument for PSB funding. Further, multi-channel households are also voracious consumers of PSB programming via second and third household television sets, and PSBs with even 30 per cent audience share are able in that eight hour exposure each week to convince the audience to continue supporting the license tax. Terrestrial television remains an extraordinarily inexpensive medium to consume.

The current most significant challenges to the PSB model are in two areas: its inefficient use of spectrum and its failure to secure the rights to premium sports, especially football. It is here that the continued domination of broadcasting by terrestrial actors has faced its harshest test. In the case of spectrum, it has been under fire from government; in the case of football the European Commission and national governments have acted to save the terrestrials from pay-TV operators' and football clubs' attempt to raise the cost of viewing football to its real market level. The Competition Directorate General of the European Commission is actively investigating abuses of dominance and cartelisation in both sale and purchase of football rights (Ungerer, 2002a).

Government support for DTTV broadcasters can cynically be viewed as another Olivetti or the BBC or V2000. Is it simply trying to protect its own companies against foreign competition? Is it proportionate for government policy to protect domestic television transmission, production and manufacture from foreign competition? In the case of manufacturing, though the EU attempted in the 1980s to develop a pan-European system for both DTV and high-definition television, its role in the 1990s has been to act as sponsor rather than founder, and therefore to permit a range of proprietary standards to emerge subject to competition policy restraints. Overt government action in the 1980s to develop a single EU high definition standard (incompatible with US or Japanese standards) has been replaced by inaction in the 2000s when the government supported Multimedia Home Platform STB common standard has been rejected by rival platforms in favour of their own incompatible competitive systems. However, STB minimalism policy will be seen to be matched by DTTV maximalism, as the following section demonstrates.

DTTV AND THE SWITCH-OVER PROCESS

DTTV proponents, including governments, argue that availability of DTTV is a pre-requisite for the overall success of the switch-over strategy. Although pay-TV services are available to almost every EU home (be it through cable, satellite or terrestrial transmission), the majority of households has not subscribed yet and most likely will not. In countries where penetration of cable and satellite was already prominent in analogue format, pay-TV models did not provide for a good alternative at sufficiently low prices. This is why it seems reasonable to believe that pay-TV does not constitute the most effective driver to bring DTV into maturity. Rather, a FTA multi-channel offer will be essential for the transition process, particularly in the consolidation phase.

If this is so, the importance of DTTV would become apparent. The collapses of platform owners ITV Digital in the UK and Quiero TV in Spain in 2002 are far from optimistic experiences. If it is believed that DTTV is the best option to achieve universal coverage (a condition without which analogue switch-off would seem unacceptable) to ensure that consumers have access to FTA public service channels, markets alone might not deliver DTTV. Public intervention to sustain DTTV development would be necessary, assuming public interest justification. In fact, there is a policy trend to favour DTTV over other platforms in most Member States.

There are important risks associated with putting in place a policy of rapid implementation of a new technology and services when markets are still in the process of consolidation and when no equipment for reception is available. It might be technologically unjustified and unfair from a competition law perspective. Although it is true that technological differences between platforms may require different regulation, the principle of technological neutrality should prevail when possible. Alternatively, the issue of how other platforms may contribute to deliver public policy objectives could be examined. Digital cable is not widely available yet and might never be, which would mean that, in some areas, if there are no DTTV services, satellite would be the only option available for consumers. This would create not only competition problems, but again give rise to pluralism concerns. It could then be argued that public support for DTTV is justified both from an economic perspective and under media policy considerations. In fact, there are certain limitations (mainly of geographical and physical character) which mean that cable and satellite will not bring universal coverage. Although other platforms can provide for a useful alternative to DTTV, it is unlikely that universality can be achieved without the DTTV platform.

DTTV and Analogue Spectrum Switch-off

For existing terrestrial services provided in analogue format to be widely available to viewers using DTTV sets, simulcast obligations have been enforced. During the simulcast phase the improvement in capacity will be limited because of the need to run analogue and digital in parallel. It is in the interest of governments to switch off the existing analogue network as soon as possible so that the radio spectrum can be released for other uses. Imposing simulcast obligations in order to provide continuity of service to all viewers results in a non-optimum duplicative use of the spectrum, and obliges operators to incur extra costs. Therefore, both governments and operators want a short simulcast period.

DTTV transmission uses the spectrum much more efficiently than analogue so that television broadcasting will require a smaller range of frequencies. Who is to benefit from such efficiency: are broadcasters to retain all the spectrum that they currently exploit or should some spectrum be freed up for public or other uses? Telecommunications operators are eager to employ those frequencies.[7] The perceived benefits of analogue switch-off in terms of recouping switch-off costs with spectrum sale may be limited in the medium term. In highly cabled countries, such as Benelux, the case for rapid analogue switch-off is stronger, dependent on replacement cost for portable terrestrial reception equipment.

---

[7] A competition concern might arise from the fact that, while DTV broadcasting networks represent a potential alternative to 3G networks for the delivery of content to mobile terminals, radio frequencies for television broadcasting have traditionally been available without frequency fees. This would give digital broadcasters a significant cost advantage with respect to mobile operators. The lack of telecoms operator interest in spectrum auctions in the UK in 2001-02 in for instance 2.4, 3.5 or 10GHz bands is an example of the fact that spectrum costs are actually very low (see Cave, 2002).

Where children's bedroom sets must be replaced, it is possible that a games station such as Sony's will be a more desirable option. It can be assumed that in the introduction of DTTV, analogue and digital transmissions will be simulcast for a significant period of time in most EU states.

We have seen that spectrum scarcity was a regulatory justification for intervention in television markets. Television spectrum planning was principally aimed at ensuring universal coverage and at avoiding interference between neighbouring countries. A major issue associated with analogue turn-off is the significant gain in terms of spectrum use that is expected. This has encouraged support for the creation of a private property regime arbitrated by the market. Some (Benkler, 1998b) have gone further and propose an alternative: that of treating the spectrum as a commons, believing that such a model could reduce concentration of ownership and increase the degree of self-governance.

Nevertheless, regulation in some form will certainly continue. The notion of spectrum scarcity and the need to avoid interference was never the sole basis of spectrum regulation. Indeed, spectrum planning was also instrumental to control entry via the licensing of television operators, and some argue that the end of scarcity will undermine the ability of governments to dictate policy outcomes through the control of market entry (Smith, 1999). The role of PSBs was deemed crucial as a cultural rationale, and certain content obligations and quality parameters were extracted from commercial broadcasters in return for the allocation of frequencies. For this reason there are good grounds to believe that statutory regulation will remain.

CONTENT AND NETWORKS: NATIONAL OR EUROPEAN POLICY?

The primary responsibility of public authorities is to protect the public interest, ensuring a clear and consistent regulatory framework. This is extremely complex in the case of multimedia industries because various players with incompatible interests are involved. The European Commission has emphasised the role of national governments in the DTV switch-over process and has recommended that Member States "create transparency as far as the conditions for the envisaged switch-over are concerned" (CEC, 2002h: 18). Although it is generally agreed that the switch-over process should be primarily market led, the role of governments to create the conditions that will make analogue switch-off possible will be crucial in later stages. Public authorities could introduce "a road map, an assessment of market conditions, and possibly a date for the closure of analogue terrestrial television broadcasting which would enable the recovery and refarming of frequencies" (CEC, 2002h: 18). We ext summarize briefly the objectives and options for intervention.

1. *Ensure universal coverage and affordability*: Means that all citizens can at least receive all current terrestrial channels. Access to information services should be ensured for all: a combination of transmission technologies such as DSL, cable, microwave and satellite could be encouraged. The key financial issue is whether there is scope for public subsidy. It is also important that there are no service interruptions. This is why all governments have introduced simulcast obligations.

2. *Guarantee the continuity of PSB*: The dominance of public television in terms of audience is still the most prominent factor in the EU broadcasting market. It is important to ensure that there will be no reduction of the analogue content during the migration phase, particularly of PSB content, which would leave analogue consumers with less choice.

3. *Promote digital content production*: Public financing mechanisms have been devised, generally using extended license fees. For instance, there is an ongoing discussion (particularly in Britain) about the viability of introducing an additional Digital License Fee in order to finance DTV programming and avoid charging analogue households for the development of DTV services that they do not receive. Some argue that such an idea risks slowing down the migration process. However, Creigh-Tyte (2000) considers that the negative effects of a DTV license fee on DTV take-up have been overestimated.

4. *Define flexible and realistic roadmaps*: Some countries have published migration plans describing the tasks to be undertaken, implementation time frames and responsibilities of the different players. Simulcasting is costly and delays lead to competitive advantages for cable and satellite.

5. *Set a switch-off date within a clear spectrum policy*: Switch-off is likely to happen at different dates across Europe. There are clear benefits attached to defining a date for analogue switch-off. This can be inferred from standards switch-off dates in national automobile and domestic electricity markets: the fact that people perceived transitions as necessary accelerated new technology penetration. Berlin's media authority has set a precedent for a major EU market to switch off the terrestrial signal with clearly defined subsidy policies and a switch-off date of November 2003 (Grünwald & Wagner, 2003). BSkyB in the UK switched off the analogue signal for 5 million households in 2001 without any significant market disruption or political interference, though clearly terrestrial switch-off is more problematic.

Governments should also carry out public consultations and studies (UK: Department for Culture, Media and Sports, 2001; Italy: AGCOM, 2000) to get a better idea of how the potential consequences of a DTV switch-over are perceived by consumers and market players. It is also important to generate consumer confidence through information campaigns.

National Content and European Network Regulation

It is important to recall that, while economic regulation rests on fairly straightforward principles, public interest objectives may vary from country to country. This is why, with respect to content issues, regulation will not only continue, but it can be expected that it will primarily remain national in scope, as the belief still exists that the cultural and political impact of broadcasting must be decided according to priorities established in each member state (Levy, 1997). At the EU level several actions have been taken in an attempt to harmonise different regulatory traditions and provide for a coherent approach to the convergence phenomenon. The Convergence Green Paper was meant to launch a discussion about what would be the most appropriate mid-term EU framework for all converging sectors. Yet, in the broadcasting sector, the effectiveness of EU intervention to establish a regulatory framework for DTV broadcasting has been limited and initiatives have been rebuffed by Member States. This could be attributed to differing administrative cultures and political concerns across Europe (Levy, 1999).[8]

The recent adoption of the 'Regulatory Framework for Electronic Communications and Services' is the culmination of the process started in 1997 (Marsden & Verhulst, 1999; CEC, 2002a-g). The New Framework embraces a horizontal and technologically neutral approach to regulation. DTV broadcasting is covered by the New Framework with respect to authorisation of communications networks and services, allocation and assignment of radio spectrum, must-carry obligations and access to networks and associated facilities. Regulation of content remains outside the scope of the new rules, although links between infrastructure and content are to be considered. Such requirement is only mentioned in Recital 7 (that mentions 'broadcasting' content and not general audiovisual content), and it is not to be found in the Directives. Some (Libertus, 2001) consider that the Framework fails to take sufficient account of those interdependencies. Television content regulation remains a national prerogative, but the regulation of the communications networks that deliver the content is subject to Commission scrutiny. This is a political outcome

---

[8] By contrast, competition rules and merger control have had a strong impact in the regulation of the digital media at EU level (Ungerer, 2002b).

that is likely to result in administrative complication. Larouche (2001) remarks that the content/network distinction underlying the Directives is not straightforward; rather, there is a gradation from one end of the chain to the other. This is especially so in the case of associated facilities like electronic programme guides, which lie at the frontier since they present both technical and content related characteristics.

With respect to infrastructure challenges three major regulatory issues arise: access, standardisation and interoperability. Convergence and the transition to DTV may remove some obstacles (for instance market entry due to spectrum scarcity) but they create new ones. While in the analogue world the delivery process was perceived as the principal bottleneck, in the DTV environment a new series of bottlenecks have emerged at different levels of the supply chain. Thus, the focus of regulation has shifted from traditional concerns over natural monopolies towards the issue of gateway control (Veljanovski, 1999). If markets are vertically integrated and standards are proprietary the risks of abuse of dominance are particularly robust. These may be predominantly issues for competition authorities but there is still scope for sector specific regulation, particularly with respect to access regulation.

CONCLUSION: WHERE NEXT AFTER THE CURRENT TELECOMS-MEDIA-TECHNOLOGY DEPRESSION?

From the vantage point of 2003, amongst the dot-bomb wreckage, one can look at previous predictions of the development of DTV with new perspective. Marsden and Verhulst (1999) adopted a deliberately cynical approach towards predictions of the convergence thesis becoming a consumer reality, seeing EU policy being captured by incumbent telecom and broadcast companies whose approach was exceedingly incrementalist by the standards of dot-com euphoria then prevalent. What has changed since then to make even those cynical views appear ludicrously optimistic? Four separate factors: market, technology, consumer behaviour, and government policy.

Market

The market has reacted to the crash by punishing the earliest adopters of convergence strategies, digital cable and DTTV pioneers, notably: cable operators NTL, UPC Chello, and Telewest; DTTV consortia, ITV Digital and Quiero TV; and pay-TV operators Canal Plus (Vivendi Universal) and Kirch. All were bankrupted or bailed out by senior debtholders in the period 2001-03. Arguably BSkyB's survival was not only due to the extremely conservative attitude of its chairman, Rupert Murdoch, but also to the pain it inflicted on its wholesale programming customers, the UK cable and DTTV companies just mentioned. The distress of the entire cable television sector was reflected in the destruction of UPC-Chello's share price jeopardising its entire broadband strategy, the difficulties of Deutsche Telekom's attempts to sell its cable network businesses to Callahan Associates or Liberty Media, and the pain of AOL-Time Warner's attempts to make any effective synergies between audiovisual content and narrow- or broadband access. Broadband roll-out was generally astonishingly slow, with local loop unbundling a disaster for entrants except in Denmark (Jensen, 2002), and it took until 2003 for aggressive incumbent broadband marketing to reinforce their dominance in narrowband access. By contrast, consumers in 2000-2002, without a compelling DSL or cable offer, invested thousand of Euros in widescreen analogue television receivers, digital and analogue video cameras, digital still cameras, and especially DVD players – but not DTV receivers.

Technology

Technological advances towards convergence also slowed in the period, though the huge processing and storage power of PCs began to significantly pressure Hollywood studios and especially record companies to advance digital rights management and streaming technologies, often in alliance with software companies, such as Microsoft, RealNetworks and even Napster, the partial P2P network bought by Bertelsmann in 2002. The Internet has allowed video capability to become a real consumer proposition in 2003, more so in Sweden, Japan, and South Korea where multimegabit rates are available at prices affordable to consumers.[9] DTV is therefore seeking markets in an environment where alternative paths to the home user are becoming a real possibility, at least for early adopters. This potentially splinters the television universe further than in information rich and poor television households, but into post-television households who choose entertainment from the Internet. If the Internet Protocol version 6 (IPv6), the next-generation Internet, is adopted successfully in the next

---

[9] The enormous decrease in costs of transporting and storing very large data files, including movies, will transform the economics of network transmission. Consider: in February 2003, users of the P2P network Direct Connect were sharing over a petabit of data, enough to store 1.5 million full-length films in DivX format; a 2-hour DivX film can be downloaded on a 512Kb/s connection in under an hour and stored on a CD-Rom; a 100Gb hard disk drive, standard issue in top-end PCs for home use, can store 150 movies; and, for MP3 digital music capacity, multiply the number of movies by 200. Sharing video programming over the Internet is no longer a theoretical possibility.

decade, the user experience in the Internet will further approach the quality of television viewing.

Consumer Behaviour

For most users, the choices are satellite, cable, or DTTV, even if the household budget is spent more on 'peripherals' (DVD players, broadband connectivity, PCs, video cameras). The competition is far broader than, say, in the 1960s, when households substituted television viewing for cinema attendance. The temptation to compare DTV with the introduction of colour suffers from too changed an environment, though it does at least permit the cynical observation that colour television took at least 20 years to finally replace monochrome in most states, and that DTV on that basis will entirely replace analogue in 2016-2020. Where governments are taking analogue switch-off seriously, as in Germany and the US, the switchover to DTV is meeting significant obstacles from consumer preferences for either genuinely interactive digital platforms or 'old' analogue systems. The hybrid nature of DTV, with no return path on satellite or DTTV, means that consumers fail to see it as anything significantly advanced over analogue pay-TV.

Government Policy

Given the lack of apparent demand for the spectrum in the current depressed economic environment, there appears to be no overwhelming reason for governments to encourage the market to switchover, except as in Berlin, where only a million Euros will permit complete analogue switch-off, and where the spectrum is densely populated. However, the nationwide case for such a policy, whether in Germany or France or the UK, appears weak currently.

This raises the fundamental set of policy issues for the Information Society:

- if broadband Internet access is not hype for the majority of the population, should government concentrate its resources on DTV or on broadband access?
- given the slow take-up of DTV, is the answer that the 'S' adoption curve will arrive in the next five years or that it is not anticipated?
- is the industry now too fragmented to adopt an integrated path toward DTV, as it did with the transition from monochrome to colour?
- should government encourage competition among platforms and standards, or within those platforms?
- is digital cable, as the only truly interactive platform, the path that should be adopted?

An introductory chapter can only lay out these questions. It should always be remembered that competition policy for most sectors, and even for most sectors of the Information Society is less 'pure' in DTV than elsewhere – all these case studies will illustrate the special case of television. The political power of television and mass media gives special structural and relational power to the broadcaster, which they can be anticipated to use to boost the medium to the exception of more interactive media such as broadband Internet. The oxygen of publicity which broadcasters provide to democratic politicians, whether in commercial or PSB, or some hybrid of the two, is such that policy in this field often appears to be made in a bubble, separated from considerations of the wider Information Society. Rather than use these exceptions to discount policy-making in digital television, readers are encouraged to acknowledge that this uniquely powerful medium is central to the Information Society, whatever its exceptionalism. With consumers spending 70 per cent of leisure time in front of the 'dumb box,' its use is a vital ingredient in analysis of the Information Society generally. The following chapters investigate the extent to which digital television regulation is indeed converging with regulation of other platforms in the Information Society, and in particular whether we can expect digital television to be just hype, or the future of interactive consumer access to the services and products offered in the Digital Age.

REFERENCES

Bangemann Report, 1994. *Europe and the Global Information Society*, Brussels, May, http://www.cyber-rights.org/documents/bangemann.htm (accessed 16.03.03).

Benkler, Yochai, 1998a. Communications infrastructure regulation and the distribution of control over content, *Telecommunications Policy*, vol. 22, no. 3, 183-196, http://www.benkler.org/PolTech.pdf (accessed 16.03.03).

Benkler, Yochai, 1998b. Overcoming agoraphobia: building the commons of the digitally networked environment, *Harvard Journal of Law and Technology*, vol. 11, 287-400, http://www.law.nyu.edu/benklery/agoraphobia.pdf (accessed 16.03.03).

Benkler, Yochai, 1999. Free as the air to common use: First Amendment constraints on enclosure of the public domain, *New York University Law Review*, vol. 74, 354-446, http://www.nyu.edu/pages/lawreview/74/2/benkler.pdf (accessed 16.03.03).

Briggs, Asa, & Joanna Spicer, 1985. *The BBC: The First Fifty Years*, Oxford University Press.

Cave, Martin, 2002. *Radio Spectrum Management Review Consultation* Paper, an independent review for the UK Department of Trade & Industry and H.M. Treasury, March ('The Cave Report'), http://www.spectrumreview.radio.gov. uk/ 2002review/1_whole_job.pdf (accessed 15.03.03).

Cave, Martin & Campbell Cowie, 1996. Regulating conditional access in European pay broadcasting, *Communications and Strategies*, vol.23, no. 3, 119-42.

CEC (Commission of the European Communities), 1989. Council Directive 89/552/EEC of 3 October 1989 on the coordination of certain provisions laid down by law, regulation or administrative action in Member States concerning the pursuit of television broadcasting activities, http://europa.eu.int/eur-lex/en/consleg/main/1989/en_1989L0552_index.html (consolidated version with text of EC/97/33; accessed 16.03.03).

CEC, 2002a. Eighth report on the implementation of the telecommunications regulatory package, COM (2002) 695 final, Brussels, December, http://europa.eu.int/information_society/topics/telecoms/implementation/annual _report/8threport/finalreport/annex2.pdf (accessed 16.03.03).

CEC, 2002b. Directive 2002/21/EC of the European Parliament and of the Council on a common regulatory framework for electronic communications networks and services ('Framework Directive'), OJL 108, 24 April, http://europa.eu.int/information_society/topics/telecoms/regulatory/maindocs/in dex_en.htm (accessed 16.03.03).

CEC, 2002c. Directive 2002/20/EC of the European Parliament and of the Council on the authorisation of electronic communications networks and services ('Authorisation Directive'), OJL 108, 24 April, http://europa.eu.int/ information_society/topics/telecoms/regulatory/maindocs/index_en.htm (accessed 16.03.03).

CEC, 2002d. Directive 2002/19/EC of the European Parliament and of the Council on access to, and interconnection of, electronic communications networks and associated facilities ('Access Directive'), OJL 108, 24 April, http://europa.eu.int/information_society/topics/telecoms/regulatory/maindocs/in dex_en.htm (accessed 16.03.03).

CEC, 2002e. Directive 2002/22/EC of the European Parliament and of the Council on universal service and users' rights relating to electronic communications networks and services ('Universal Service Directive'), OJL 108, 24 April, http://europa.eu.int/information_society/topics/telecoms/ regulatory/maindocs/index_en.htm (accessed 16.03.03).

CEC, 2002f. Directive 2002/58/EC of the European Parliament and of the Council of 12 July 2002 concerning the processing of personal data and the protection of privacy in the electronic communications sector ('Directive on Privacy and Electronic Communications'), OJL 108, 24 April, http://europa.eu.int/information_society/topics/telecoms/regulatory/maindocs/in dex_en.htm (accessed 16.03.03).

CEC, 2002g. Decision no. 676/2002/EC of the European Parliament and of the Council of 7 March 2002 on a regulatory framework for radio spectrum policy in the European Community ('Radio Spectrum Decision'), OJL 108, 24 April, http://europa.eu.int/information_society/topics/telecoms/regulatory/maindocs/in dex_en.htm (accessed 16.03.03).

CEC, 2002h. Communication of the Commission to the European Parliament, the Council, the Economic and Social Committee and the Committee of the Regions, *eEurope 2005: An information society for all.* COM(2002) 263 final, Brussels, May, http://europa.eu.int/information_society/eeurope/news_library/ documents/eeurope2005/eeurope2005_en.pdf (accessed 16.03.03).

Coase, Ronald, 1950. *The BBC: A Study in Monopoly,* Longmans Green, http://coase.org/coasepublications.htm (accessed 16.03.03).

Cowie, Campbell & Christopher T. Marsden, 1999. Convergence, competition and regulation, *INFO,* no. 1, 53-66.

Creigh-Tyte, Stephen W., 2000. *The Impact of a Digital License Fee on Digital TV Adoption: An Assessment,* Department of Culture, Media and Sport, Technical Paper no. 1, London, February, http://www.culture.gov.uk/ pdf/dlic.pdf (accessed 16.03.03).

Davies, Gavyn & Andrew Graham, 1997. *Broadcasting, Society and Policy in the Multimedia Age,* University of Luton Press.

Economist, The, 2003. The complete home entertainer? 1 March, 64-66.

Fallenböck, Markus, 2003. On the technical protection of copyright: The Digital Millennium Copyright Act, the European Community Copyright Directive and their anticircumvention provisions, *International Journal of Communications Law and Policy*, no. 7, http://www.ijclp.org/ 7_2003/ijclp_webdoc_ 4_7_2003.htm (accessed 16.03.03).

Feintuck, Mike, 1999. *Media Regulation, Public Interest and the Law*, Edinburgh University Press.

Gibbons, Thomas, 2000. Pluralism, guidance and the new media, in Christopher T. Marsden (Ed.), *Regulating the Global Information Society*, Routledge, 304-15.

Grünwald, Andreas & Christoph Wagner, 2003. DTV update: Berlin area completes switch-over by mid 2003, *International Journal of Communications Law and Policy*, issue 7, http://www.ijclp.org/7_2003/ijclp_webdoc_ 11_7_2003.htm (accessed 16.03.03).

Hugenholtz, Bernt, 1996. Copyright and multimedia: licensing in the digital era, in Santiago Muñoz Machado (Ed.), *Derecho Europeo del Audiovisual*, ELE, 1393-1404.

Humphreys, Peter, 1996. *Mass Media and Media Policy in Western Europe*, Manchester University Press.

Italy: AGCOM, 2000. *Il libro bianco sulla TV digitale terrestre*, http://www.agcom.it/provv/libro_b_00/librobianco00.htm (accessed 15.03.03).

Jensen, Neils Erik, 2002. Interview with Martin Sims, *Intermedia*, http://www.iicom.org/intermedia/login.html (accessed 15.03.03).

Larouche, Pierre, 2001. Communications convergence and public service broadcasting, http://infolab.kub.nl/uvtweb/bin.php3?id=00011353&mime= application/pdf&file=/tilec/publications/larouche2.pdf (accessed 15.03.03).

Levy. David A., 1997. Regulating digital broadcasting in Europe: the limits of policy convergence, *West European Politics,* vol. 20, no. 4, 24-42.

Levy, David A., 1999. *Europe's Digital Revolution: Broadcasting Regulation, the EU and the Nation State*, Routledge.

Libertus, Michael, 2001. The EU regulatory framework for electronic communications and the Commission's proposal for a decision on a regulatory framework for radio spectrum policy in the Community, *International Journal of Communications Law and Policy*, no. 6, http://www.ijclp.org/ 6_2001/pdf/ijclp_webdoc_10_6_2001.pdf (accessed 16.03.03).

Liikanen, Erkki, 2002. "Convergence and the information society," speech at the Conference on Media Convergence: Opportunities for a Closer Relationship between Europe and the Americas, Madrid, 13 May, http://europa.eu.int/comm/commissioners/liikanen/media/speeches/text_en.htm (accessed 16.03.03).

Malone, John, 1997. The multimedia revolution was just hype, *Broadcast Magazine*, London, 2 January, 10.

Marsden, Christopher T., 1999. Pluralism in the multi-channel market: suggestions for regulatory scrutiny, *International Journal of Communications Law and Policy*, no. 4, http://www.ijclp.org/4_2000/pdf/ijclp_webdoc_ 5_4_2000.pdf (accessed 16.03.03).

Marsden, Christopher T., 2000. Not so special? merging media pluralism with competition and industrial policy, *INFO*, vol.2, no. 1, 5-13.

Marsden, Christopher T., & Stefaan G. Verhulst, 1999. *Convergence in European Digital TV Regulation*, Blackstone Press.

McGonagle, Tarlach, 2001. Changing aspects of broadcasting: new territory and new challenges, *IRIS plus*, no. 10, December, http://www.obs.coe.int/oea_publ/iris/iris_plus/iplus10_2001.pdf.en (accessed 16.03.03).

Motta, Massimo, and Michele Polo, 1997. Concentration and public policies in the broadcasting industry: the future of TV, *Economic Policy*, no. 25, 295-334.

Negroponte Nicholas, 1995. *Being Digital*, Hodder and Stoughton.

Noam, Eli M., 2000. Future cyber trade wars, in Erik Bohlin *et al.* (Eds.), *Convergence in Communications and Beyond*, Elsevier Science.

Noam, Eli M., (Ed.), 2003. *Television over the Internet: Implications for Networks, Infrastructures, Strategy, Policy and Content*, Lawrence Erlbaum.

Nolan, Dermot, 1997. Bottlenecks in pay TV: impact on market development in Europe, *Telecommunications Policy*, vol. 21, no. 7, 597-610.

Samuelson, Pamela, 2000. Five challenges for regulating the global information society, in Christopher T. Marsden (Ed.), *Regulating the Global Information Society*, Routledge, 316-30.

Smith, P., 1999. The politics of UK TV policy: the introduction of digital TV, presentation at Workshop 24, Regulating Communications in the 'Multimedia Age', European Consortium of Political Research, March.

Sutton, John, 1991. *Sunk Costs and Market Structure: Price Competition, Advertising, and the Evolution of Concentration*, MIT Press.

United Kingdom: Department for Culture, Media and Sports, 2001. *Digital TV Action Plan*, http://www.digitalTV.gov.uk/pdfs/draft_digital_TV_action_plan.pdf (accessed 15.03.03).

Ungerer, Herbert, 2002a. Converging technologies and regulations: broadcasting, datacasting, communications', speech at 23rd ETP Plenary Session, Brussels, 19 September, http://europa.eu.int/comm/competition/speeches/text/sp2002_031_en.pdf (accessed 16.03.03).

Ungerer, Herbert, 2002b. Media in Europe: media and EU competition law, speech at the Conference on Media in Poland, Polish Confederation of Private Employers, Warsaw, 13 February, http://europa.eu.int/comm/competition/speeches/text/sp2002_006_en.pdf (accessed 16.03.03).

Veljanovski, Cento, 1999. Competitive regulation of digital pay TV in John Grayston (Ed.), *European Economics and Law*, Palladian Law Publishing, 53-85.

Chapter 2
European Regulation
of Digit al Television

Pertti Näränen
University of Tampere

To understand European regulation of digital television (DTV) it is useful to start with two notions. First, European DTV regulation is not a separate policy field, but is formulated, intertwined and in interaction with regulation and policy in many other fields. In the new converged media environment, audiovisual policy, telecommunications policy, Information Society policy, competition policy and standardisation policy have all affected the emergence of DTV. Secondly, there have been several policy makers involved in European DTV regulation, namely, the European Union (EU) itself, and the governments of the EU Member States. Overall, European communications policy is far from stable and coherent. The policy goals have been constantly on the move for the past two decades, partly because of changes in political trends and partly because of changes in media technologies. There have also been conflicting interests in the various areas of policy.

In this chapter, European DTV regulation is examined with reference to the political and economic developments of the 1980s to the present. The chapter focuses mainly on the EU, for the simple reason that it has gradually become the most important forum for media policy formulation in Europe. The fifteen Member States today develop their national media regulation more in dialogue with the EU than separately from it: They take part in the formulation of EU policy goals, and then implement EU directives into national legislation. While regulation at the EU level will gain more importance with the integration of ten new Member States in 2004, the ability of the EU to harmonise media regulation is likely to become more difficult because of the enlargement.[1]

---

[1] Hungary, Poland, the Czech Republic, Slovenia, Estonia, Latvia, Lithuania, Slovakia, Cyprus, and Malta are due to join the EU in 2004, Romania and Bulgaria in 2007, and negotiations for membership are underway with Turkey and Norway. The ten new countries joining in 2004 will increase the population of the EU to more than 450 million (easily surpassing that of the North

The next section considers audiovisual policy over the past two decades within the context of the trend towards the neo-liberal philosophy in Europe. DTV standards regulation and EU initiatives relating to public service broadcasting are then analysed. The chapter then examines the European regulation of interactive television. The promises of more efficient spectrum use are then considered, and the final section outlines the future challenges facing European DTV regulation.

AUDIOVISUAL POLICY
AND THE NEO-LIBERAL TREND

Since the 1957 Treaty of Rome the ideas of free trade and efficient market competition in the common market area have been fundamental to European co-operation. The EU was founded in 1992 on the basis of the original European 'communities,' namely, the European Coal and Steel Community, the European Atomic Energy Community and the European Economic Community.[2] Following the expansion and integration of the Union, European economic co-operation extended to a broader range of concerns, including foreign policy, social policy and cultural issues. It is against this background that media issues have been handled within the EU mainly from an economic 'cultural industry' (rather than social policy) perspective. Within this framework, public service broadcasting in the EU Member States has usually been treated as an 'exception' to the free trade rule (Harrison & Woods, 2001)

The formulation of industrial audiovisual policy by the EU commenced in the 1980s in the form of support for European co-operation in content production, innovation and distribution (media programmes), and in efforts to build a common European standard for analogue high definition television

---

American Free Trade Area). The new Member States, however, will contribute less than 5 percent to the EU's gross domestic product. Differences in their political and cultural traditions are likely to cause difficulties in media policy harmonisation.

[2] The EU today has a complex organisational and operational structure. It includes European Council meetings, where at least twice a year the Heads of Member States agree upon the primary political goals. The Council of the EU is the institution where ministers meet more regularly with different agendas. The European Parliament, with 626 representatives elected every five years, has steadily acquired greater political influence and has an important role in passing directives for national implementation. The Commission of the European Communities (CEC) is a powerful executive organ, responsible for the preparation of legislative proposals, with 20 Commissioners appointed every five years by the governments of the EU Member States. The CEC Commissioners act as heads of the Directorates-General with the help of approximately 20,000 officials. Together with the European Court of Justice, the CEC ensures that the Treaties and other Community laws are properly and uniformly applied (see European Union, 2003).

(HDTV) for satellite and cable broadcasting with the so-called MAC Directives. The HDTV initiative was based on the assumption that the European television industry – including set manufacturers – could best compete with American and Japanese HDTV by the development of a common pan-European standard. In practice, the analogue MAC HDTV standard was never commercialised, mainly because of the lack of interest by the major satellite players and the rapid development of digital technology (Levy, 1997).

The mid-1980s witnessed an international neo-liberal trend towards deregulation in many areas of public policy. In media policy this trend developed mainly through national decisions, which opened broadcasting markets to commercial competition and ended the public service broadcasting monopoly in most Western European countries. The EU did not initiate this trend of deregulation, but was prepared to support the principle of free trade in the form of pan-European satellite broadcasting. Already in 1982 the Hahn Report (European Parliament, 1982) had declared that the control of mass media at national levels was a barrier to European political integration. The same tone was echoed in the 1984 European Commission Green Paper on 'Television Without Frontiers' – the early version of a later directive (European Parliament, 1997) – which supported the idea of a pan-European television market based on private content production and competition (Levy, 1999).

The neo-liberal model came to Europe primarily from the United States (US) during the Reagan administration. Tunstall and Machin (1999) argue that the American media influence was imported to Europe via Italy and Luxembourg, followed by France and Germany. Others (Collins, 1998; Papathanassopoulos, 2002) emphasise that, considering the prominence of the United Kingdom (UK) in the EU's media and communication economy and its public service broadcasting tradition as a successful role model, the British example of deregulation and liberalisation was highly influential in Europe. At any rate, a wide political consensus emerged regarding the need to open nationally regulated broadcasting markets to increased domestic and international competition.

In its 1977 examination of the future of broadcasting in the UK, the Annan Committee stated that the traditional objective of broadcasting was to "provide entertainment, information and education for large audiences" and to "enlarge people's interests." A decade later, the Peacock Committee talked in rather different terms: "The fundamental aim of broadcasting policy should in our view be to enlarge both the freedom of choice of the consumer and opportunities available to programme makers to offer alternative wares to the public" (cited in Hutchison, 1999: 83). These quotations from UK policy documents reflect the wider change in European media policy rhetoric during the 1980s – from the enrichment of *citizens* to the free choice of *consumers*.

In 1989 the EU took an active part in the move towards a neo-liberal agenda by publishing the Television Without Frontiers (TWF) Directive (European Parliament, 1997) which remains the cornerstone of European television policy. TWF is in line with the principles both of free trade and freedom of expression.[3] The Directive restricts *national protectionism* by forbidding Member States to prevent reception of a television channel licensed anywhere in the EU. However, the TWF also embodies cultural regulation and *European protectionism*: it prohibits incitement to hatred on grounds of race, gender, religion, or nationality in broadcasting, and regulates the slot placement, duration and content of advertising. The famous 'European content quotas' of the Directive oblige broadcasters to reserve a majority proportion of their transmission time for programmes of European origin. The effectiveness of this requirement, however, is diminished by a provision (article 4) specifying that Member States need only apply the quotas "where practicable and by appropriate means." The national implementation of content quotas has also been quite irregular. Levy (1999) argues that rather than the overall competitiveness of the European television industry, the TWF Directive has supported UK based pan-European satellite services and the widespread distribution of American programming.

While in the 1980s the EU had only a secondary role in the liberalisation of the 'content industry' (audiovisual), in the 1990s it was a strong promoter of marketisation in the 'conversation industry' (telecommunications). Overall, telecommunications has gained more attention in the EU than the audiovisual sector (European Commission, 2000). One reason for this is that the economic value of the telecom market is much higher than that of the audiovisual market (Michalis, 2002). Telecommunications has also been perceived as a key factor in the development of the Information Society (IS), in contrast to 'old-fashioned' television.

The early IS strategies of the EU were interwoven with the idea of media *convergence* – the technological and economic integration of telecommunications with broadcasting and other media networks. The concept of convergence came to the fore with the Bangemann Report (1994), which was prepared by a group of key figures from the ICT (information and communications technology) industry under the aegis of the EU Directorate-General for telecommunications. The report emphasised the urgent need to increase competitiveness in the European audiovisual and telecommunications industries. It stated that technological convergence was moving these sectors closer together, freeing the audiovisual industry from spectrum scarcity and

---

[3] The Convention on Human Rights and Fundamental Freedoms signed in 1950 states (article 10) that the right of freedom of expression includes the freedom to receive and impart information without interference by public authority and regardless of frontiers. This principle also guides the current revision of the TWF Directive (European Commission, 2002).

bringing a new industrial revolution. To seize this opportunity, and to build the Information Society, the report called for deregulation, large scale commercial initiatives, and support for broadband and satellite infrastructure to develop trans-European networks. The role of public service broadcasting was not even mentioned. Similar rhetoric later filtered into the EU Green Paper on convergence (European Commission, 1997). Also within the IS framework, the Green Paper supported liberalisation of both the audiovisual and telecom industries, as well as more technologically-neutral (rather than the traditional sector-specific) regulation of these industries (Levy, 1999; Murdock, 2000).

The Bangemann report stressed the interconnection of European networks and the interoperability of services and applications. The first EU policy document to deal specifically with DTV (European Council, 1994) similarly considered a common European standard to be an essential precondition for the harmonious pan-European market evolution of DTV. In spite of all this 'common market and common standard' rhetoric, the actual EU regulation of DTV standardisation took quite a different course.

DTV STANDARDS

The first directive tailored to digital broadcasting, the Advanced Television Standards Directive (European Parliament, 1995), was prepared hurriedly and barely before the start of digital broadcasting in Europe. Regrettably, it was drafted in a way that did little to facilitate the emergence of a single European DTV market supported by common standards. The directive stipulated (article 1) that Member States should promote the accelerated development of DTV but allowed DTV operators to use proprietary 'middleware standards' – conditional access (CA) and application programme interface (API) standards – needed for pay-TV and interactive services. It required only that operators should licence their technology to other operators "on fair, reasonable and non-discriminatory terms" (article 3c). With great variation in the national implementation of the Directive and difficulty in the regulation of the 'reasonable terms' provision, it was soon apparent that access by viewers to all digital channels available to them with a single set-top box (STB) would not be possible (Levy, 1999; Galperin, 2002)

DTV was first broadcast in Europe in 1996 by DF1 in Germany, DStv (Telepiú) in Italy and Canal Plus in France. These vertically integrated operators used the same European transmission signal standard but different proprietary middleware standards. The DTV operators were thus able to restrict customers' access to competing digital channels and services. This created competition problems and obstacles to the development of a pan-European DTV market.

Already linguistically segmented European television markets started to fragment into rival blocks operating with incompatible STBs, even within the same national and/or linguistic markets (Levy, 1997; Näränen, 2003).

What was the reason for this 'light touch' regulation of DTV standards? Firstly, DTV represents *digital* technology, the use of which in the European environment of IS hype was seen not only as a natural step in the direction of 'technical progress,' but also as an unavoidable step which must be taken quickly. The national governments were reluctant to slow the pace of DTV development with standardisation issues, and were keen to get the DTV industry started in their territories, partly because of perceived national prestige from the early adoption of digital technology (van Lente, 2000; Goodwin & Spittle, 2002). Secondly, the TWF directive left no room for national regulatory authorities to impose requirements on satellite operators licensed in other countries. For example, the Spanish government tried to force the Canal Plus subsidiary, Canal Satéllite Digital, to use the same CA technology as the partly state-owned Vía Digital. However, this action was prohibited by the Commission, which understandably saw it as a violation of Treaty rules (Llorens-Maluquer, 1998). (In the event, these competing platforms merged in 2002 after it became clear that the Spanish market could not support them both.) Thirdly, as indicated earlier, the EU-led efforts to build a common European standard for analogue HDTV had resulted in failure. Ever since this failure was acknowledged in the early 1990s the guiding principle of EU technology policy has been to go with the flow of the market rather than to try to steer it.

In practice, standardisation for DTV has been consigned to the Digital Video Broadcasting Project, an industry-led European consortium of over 300 broadcasters, manufacturers and operators, with only one (non-voting) Commission representative. By 1995 the DVB Group had succeeded in creating common *transmission* standards for digital terrestrial (DVB-T), satellite (DVB-S) and cable (DVB-C) television broadcasting. It has faced difficulties, however, with middleware standards where there are conflicting interests among the different commercial players. Notably, in the transition from analogue to digital, it has been in the interest of pay-TV satellite broadcasters to extend control over their existing customers rather than allow the market to be opened to new competitors via common standards solutions (Levy, 1997; Galperin, 2002). The creation of uniform DTV 'gateways' has thus been seriously delayed.

Notwithstanding the fading prospect of voluntary industry consensus within the DVB Group on API and CA systems, the Commission has refused to intervene. Within the developing DTV markets, expensive bidding wars over premium content erupted, as well as hardware wars when the DTV operators attempted to win market shares with subsidised, incompatible STBs. The uncertainty created by the lack of interoperability in digital reception equipment is at least partly responsible for the generally poor reputation of DTV among viewers. And because each application must be specifically tailored to fit each proprietary STB platform, multiple standards has made the production of DTV interactive applications both expensive and risky. This has retarded the development of interactive DTV (see chap. 5).

In 2000, after several delays, the DVB group succeeded in the development of a common API standard for DTV broadcasting called Multimedia Home Platform (MHP), based on the Java code. In principle, MHP could be used as an open multi-platform pan-European standard for interactive DTV services, including Internet browsing, but it does not prevent a pay-TV operator from using a proprietary CA system if so desired. MHP is now widely supported in the EU states as a common market solution. It has taken too long, however, for the Commission to formulate specific proposals for the implementation of this open standard in second generation STBs. Problems related to different middleware standards in digital STBs were noted by the Commission in the late 1990s, but it failed to propose specific action "at this early stage, when market and technological developments are highly unpredictable" (European Commission, 1999: 15). The refusal of the Commission to specify middleware standards was a major reason for that unpredictability!

There are signs, however, that European open access principles may gradually be coming clearer and more concrete. A recent EU regulatory framework package, encompassing six directives, aims to make competition rules the prime instruments for the regulation of all electronic communications (European Parliament, 2002a), and the separate 'Access Directive' (European Parliament, 2002b) now gives Member States permission to regulate DTV access and interoperability issues more specifically than previously.

COMPETITION AND
PUBLIC SERVICE BROADCASTING

In the economics of broadcasting, high initial production costs ('first copy costs') and low reproduction and distribution costs ('marginal costs') create economies of scale. Another important feature is economies of scope, which refer to economies achieved through multi-product publishing with the option of extensive re-editing. Economies of scale and scope allow large multimedia conglomerates to gain economic advantage in competition. Unregulated media markets thus have an inherent tendency towards dominance by large scale commercial players – oligopolies or even monopolies (Doyle, 2002; Blevins, 2002).

In the 1990s the widespread adoption of the Internet and the commencement of DTV broadcasting increased the prospect of economic convergence and raised concerns over media concentration, new commercial and technical bottlenecks and the declining role of public service broadcasting (PSB). These concerns, together with mounting criticism of neo-liberal audiovisual policy in Europe, were evident in June 1997 at the Amsterdam summit meeting where the heads of Member States accepted the 'Amsterdam Protocol' (European Council, 1997). The document, annexed as a protocol to the Treaty establishing the European Community, recognised the importance of PSB in Europe and approved its funding by national governments for the promotion of democratic, social, and cultural values. The provision left room for implementation problems, however, by noting that the financing of PSB should "not affect trading conditions and competition in the Community to an extent which would be contrary to the common interest". Also in 1997 a 'listed events' policy was introduced in a revision of the TWF Directive (European Parliament, 1997: article 3a), which allowed Member States to prevent pay-TV channels from acquiring exclusive rights to certain broadcasts (e.g., sports events) regarded as being of major national importance.

These 're-regulation' policy shifts have resulted partly from the increased political power of the European Parliament and partly from political changes in the governments of the Member States. The year 1997 can thus be seen as a turning point in the liberalisation trend of EU media policy. Since then, issues such as harmful content, interoperability and affordable access have been more prominent in telecommunications and audiovisual policies, even if minimisation and harmonisation of regulation have remained important goals. Each Member State is now in principle free to define the extent of PSB in their countries and the way it is financed and organised. They are, however, required to develop a clear statement of the PSB remit and to put in place an appropriate authority to monitor its fulfilment (European Commission, 1999; 2001).

Although the EU has endeavoured to simplify media regulation, and to shift the emphasis from sector-specific to general competition regulation, harmonisation of competition regulation has been difficult to achieve. A major goal of EU audiovisual policy has been to strengthen European competitiveness in global markets. This has resulted in support for the emergence of large European-wide multimedia conglomerates to compete with imported American content and exploit the opportunities created by technological convergence. At the same time, there have been efforts to regulate anti-competitive behaviour in national media markets, which has resulted in a contradiction in policy goals. In particular, competition regulation is inadequate in addressing cross-media ownership where, for example, a large corporation may have accumulated substantial media power across a number of countries, but under competition regulation is deemed not to have excessive market power in any single national market.[4] In practice, only major mergers have been 'negatively regulated', while media ownership across Europe overall has been allowed to become more concentrated (Iosifidis, 2002; Papathanassopoulos, 2002). There is mounting theoretical and empirical evidence that competition policy alone cannot guarantee increased choice, media pluralism or lower consumer prices in broadcasting markets (Humphreys, 2000; Blevins, 2002).

The European Commission has played an important role in global trade negotiations within the World Trade Organisation. Contrary to the wishes of the US, the Commission, together with Canada, has so far been able to prevent total liberalisation of trade in audiovisual content (Simpson & Wilkinson, 2002). In the current (2000-2004) round of GATS (General Agreement on Trade in Services) negotiations, the EC is maintaining this position and making no commitments to further liberalise the audiovisual sector (European Commission, 2003a).

Although the status and importance of PSB is currently protected in the EU, some problems remain. The remit of public service broadcasters with dual funding sources (licence fees and advertising) may be difficult to formulate. There are also no strategies in place for the further development of the dual broadcasting system (where broadcasting markets comprise both public service broadcasters and commercial operators). This is of particular concern in certain new Member States where the role of PSB has been diminished to a marginal position (see chap. 3).

INTERACTIVE TELEVISION

One of the problems with the regulation of interactive television services in Europe is that EU legislation makes a distinction between television broadcasting services and IS services. The TWF Directive is the instrument for the regulation of DTV programmes, while DTV interactive services fall under the 'Information Society services' regulation in the 'E-commerce Directive' (European Parliament, 2000). IS services are defined as "any service normally provided for remuneration, at a distance, by electronic means and at the individual request of a recipient of services" (European Commission, 2002: 30-31). In the EU framework, IS services can therefore refer to on-demand services

---

[4] Since its establishment in 1990, the Merger Task Force, working under the DG Competition, has examined more than 2000 notified mergers, of which only 18 have been prohibited. With the forthcoming EU enlargement likely to increase the workload of the competition regulator significantly, the Commission has decided to reorganise the DG Competition to make it more efficient in the handling of its tasks (European Commission, 2003c).

such as downloading computer games, but not, for example, television news or educational programmes.[5]

In a working paper published in early 2003 the European Commission again identifies the problems associated with proprietary API standards in DTV and, more forcefully than before, reiterates its power to mandate a common standard when "strictly necessary to ensure interoperability" (European Commission, 2003b: 8). No compulsion is yet proposed, however, as the Commission is still encouraging voluntary migration by the industry to the open MHP standard. Following a period of public consultation on the working paper, the publication of a further Commission document on the issue is expected by the end of 2003. Strategies to achieve interoperability have also been developed in a separate study commissioned by the Commission (OXERA Consulting, 2003).

It is usual for commentators on media policy to emphasise the need for regulators to enforce standards and procedures that allow for open access and interoperability between rival technologies. Cuilenburg and McQuail (2000) take this point further by proposing that the main policy goal in the age of convergence should be free and equal access to a communications system that provides for the diverse information and communication needs of society. They argue that there are three dimensions to such a system – market structure, market conduct of participants, and media content – and access issues are important in each of these dimensions. Where power relations and control are at stake, open access is an important democratic issue. To consider access only in terms of access to media consumption reflects the way in which *citizens* are increasingly viewed as *consumers* (see also Gandy, 2002).

Within the EU, the broadcasting issues that attract most attention relate mainly to technical and commercial interoperability, and access of new entrants to media markets. Access regulation has not always been effective, as was demonstrated by the lack of interoperability of the first generation DTV STBs. Access regulation is inherently problematic because the issue is both technically difficult and commercially contentious. This implies that sole reliance on 'technologically-neutral' competition principles may need to give way to the adoption of sector-specific regulation (Levy, 1997; Bittlingmayer & Hazlett, 2002).

One of the features identified with the new media is the possible erosion of mass audiences resulting from audience fragmentation and the use of interactive applications. In DTV, personal video recorders may offer the user the ability to bypass conventional commercial breaks altogether. New forms of advertising and alternative revenue models are thus of great interest to broadcasters and

---

[5] It seems that the commercial interests of the telecommunications sector lie behind this technocratic IS service definition, rather than ideals of 'informed citizens' or the 'knowledge society.'

advertisers. These include 'infomercials,' shopping channels, split screen advertising, virtual advertising, programme sponsorship, and cross-promotion among brands.

Some new advertising techniques give more options for 'forced advertising' in which commercial information is presented as an integral part of the programmes. The TWF Directive requires, however, clear separation of advertising from programme content. While consumer groups have expressed concerns in this area, the advertising industry is lobbying for self-regulation of interactive advertising. The European Commission has somehow to balance these contending interests.

Currently, the only Member State with specific regulation for interactive advertising is the UK. Virtual advertising is banned in Italy, France, Portugal and Norway. Split-screen advertising is authorised in the UK and Germany, but prohibited in the Netherlands, Portugal, Sweden and France (European Commission, 2002). Clarification and harmonisation of advertising regulation are clearly needed.

EFFICIENT SPECTRUM USE AS A POLICY PROMISE

DTV promises different options and benefits to different stakeholders. In the European media policy context, the promise of more efficient radio spectrum use has been the most important (Liikanen 2003). The promise has two dimensions. First, digital compression and more efficient use of the frequency spectrum give increased channel space for broadcasters and facilitate pay-TV services in the terrestrial platform. This new space can also be used for interactive services and/or to improve technical quality. Second, after analogue switch-off, some UHF frequencies below 1 GHz, currently reserved for television broadcasting, could be reallocated to allow for the growth of UMTS (Universal Mobile Telecommunications Services) and other third generation (3G) wireless services. This represents an opportunity to encourage growth of the mobile industry, provide financial resources for governments, and to implement spectrum allocation policy based on market principles (Serafini, 2001).

In relation to the first promise, pay-TV's share of the total European television market increased substantially in the 1990s. Given its pro-competitive and growth oriented objectives, the EU can now be expected to endeavour to graft that growth factor onto the terrestrial platform, even though pay-TV on digital terrestrial has not yet been financially successful. Improvements in picture quality from digital transmissions are still only minimal, since spectrum-hungry HDTV is not yet transmitted anywhere in Europe. The development of interactive services has been delayed by the lack of a common standard, although this remains an essential part of European DTV policy (European Commission, 2003b).

Fulfilment of the second promise is questionable. A major goal of EU radio spectrum policy is to achieve a more efficient use of the radio spectrum to make room for new services (European Parliament, 2002c). However, the need for additional television frequencies is not as great as previously anticipated. At its May 2000 conference in Istambul, the International Telecommunication Union reserved new frequencies for European 3G mobile networks in the 2520-2670 MHz band, which is technically most suitable for UMTS and still little used in Europe. This new space will satisfy the spectrum needs of mobile operators for some years. It is also now evident that the UMTS spectrum requirements calculated in the late 1990s were grossly overestimated. A recent study conducted for the European Commission commented that mobile telecom operators "have already secured and paid for the bandwidth they are going to need for UMTS in mid-term, and they also have already taken official positions in order to access additional frequencies, in higher bands, for their longer term needs" (BIPE Consulting, 2002: 89). The overheated market expectations for the 3G mobile industry increased the hype and encouraged the rush to introduce DTV. Some Member States have maintained their policy to use spectrum auctions, largely in response to the US experience where, between 1993 and 1998, spectrum auctions generated more than $US23 billion. The shortcomings of the spectrum auction policy for Europe can now be seen, however, after major telecoms hugely overpaid for 3G licences for central European markets, causing serious difficulties in their financing the development of the services (Collins, 1998; Grünwald, 2001).

All things considered, the promise that DTV has best fulfilled so far has been the increase in the number of channels, first on satellite (pay-TV) and then on terrestrial. The number of television channels in Europe doubled every three years between 1985 and 2000, and this rate of increase has continued with digital transmission. In 1989 there were 47 channels available in Europe; by 2002 the number had increased to more than 1500, over 600 of which were digital (BIPE Consulting, 2002: 5). A greater number of channels does increase consumer choice. However, because most channels are bundled into vertically integrated satellite pay-TV packages, the choice offered to individual consumers has not increased as much as the expansion of channel numbers implies. The rapid increase in the quantity of channels also creates problems for European broadcasters. Fragmentation of audiences decreases per channel income, at least for free-to-air broadcasters (see chap. 4). If each television channel has to be filled with cheaper programming, broadcasters may be forced to reduce their own production levels and increase imports of content, leading in turn to a worsening audiovisual trade imbalance with the US (Doyle, 2002; Papathanassopoulos, 2002).[6]

This is not to say that DTV is failing altogether. However, the Information Society goals originally attached to DTV are proving to be over-optimistic, and the target dates for the switch-off of analogue terrestrial broadcasting are likely to be postponed in most countries. A prolonged period of simulcasting, where both analogue and digital signals are transmitted, is both expensive for broadcasters and an inefficient use of the spectrum.

FUTURE CHALLENGES

The development of DTV is an area where the challenges for regulation are increasing, and where many directives and regulatory principles intersect. The Commission has promised, by the end of 2003, to present its long awaited review of the TWF Directive. However, it seems reluctant to undertake a fundamental reform of the Directive, maintaining its position that regulation must be kept to the minimum necessary to achieve public interest objectives. The Commission is willing to reinforce the coherence of European audiovisual regulation, but the policy goals are likely to comprise an uneasy combination of liberalism and cultural protectionism (European Commission, 2002; Rosenthal, 2003).

What is problematic is not so much the lack of coherence in policy goals, but inertia in taking decisive action when regulation is clearly failing. In particular, much faster regulatory procedures are required to prevent anti-competitive behaviour. This problem is often voiced by representatives of private corporations (Birchall, 2000; Prebble, 2002). European case law tradition in competition regulation is frequently too slow a tool, which makes it difficult for firms to anticipate regulatory decisions. This was demonstrated in October 2002 when the Court of Justice of the European Communities annulled the exemption the Commission had granted to the European Broadcasting Union for the joint acquisition of broadcasting rights for certain sporting events (European Court of Justice, 2002). Complaints and disputes regarding 'Eurovision rights' have been unresolved since 1987.

In the past few years the European Commission and the European Parliament have made serious efforts to assist DTV development, especially by supporting the principles of open access and open standards. Full interoperability for DTV may be difficult to achieve however. There is a legacy

---

[6] The European trade deficit with the US in television rights for 2000 was 4.1 billion Euros (a 17.5 per cent increase on 1999), while the total audiovisual trade deficit was 8.2 billion Euros (European Commission, 2002: 5).

of 32 million STBs across Europe, of which it is feasible to upgrade only 1.7 million to the MHP standard (OXERA Consulting, 2003).

While there remains a need for additional regulation, excessive regulation can stifle innovation. 'Regulatory risk' refers to the potential of regulatory intervention to raise a regulated firm's cost of capital, and to bring about inefficient investment. But, as the case of DTV standards demonstrates, there are also risks in non-regulation. 'Non-regulatory risk' is most obvious in intensive new market competition where dominant firms may use underpricing and other anti-competitive practices to gain strategic advantages over competitors and where consumers face incompatibility between rival technologies and services (OXERA Consulting, 2003: Wright et al., 2003). Greater cooperation is needed between the Commission, the national regulatory authorities, the television industry and consumer organisations to avoid further risks in the difficult transition from analogue to digital.

REFERENCES

Bangemann Report, 1994. *Europe and the Global Information Society*, Brussels, May, http://www.cyber-rights.org/documents/bangemann.htm (accessed 28.12.01).

Birchall, Andrew, 2000. Digital: The end of television as we know it? in Tim Lees et al. (Eds.), *Is Regulation Still an Option in a Digital Universe? Papers from the 30th University of Manchester International Broadcasting Conference*, University of Luton Press, 4-19.

Blevins, Jeffrey Layne, 2002. Source diversity after the Telecommunications Act of 1996: Media oligarchs begin to colonize cyberspace, *Television & New Media*, vol. 3, no. 1, 95-112.

BIPE Consulting, 2002. *Digital Switchover in Broadcasting*, Final Report, April, europa.eu.int/information_society/topics/telecoms/regulatory/studies/documents/digital_switchover_in_broadcasting_executive_summary_120402_en.pdf (accessed 20.08.02).

Bittlingmayer, George & Thomas W. Hazlett, 2002. Open access: the ideal and the real, *Telecommunications Policy*, vol. 26, 295-310.

Collins, Richard, 1998. Back to the future: digital television and convergence in the United Kingdom, *Telecommunication Policy*, vol. 22(4/5), 383-396.

Cuilenburg, Jan van & Denis McQuail, 2000. Media policy paradigm shifts: In search of a new communications policy paradigm, in Bart Cammaerts and Jean-Claude Burgelman (Eds.), *Beyond Competition: Broadening the Scope of Telecommunications Policy*, Brussels, VUB University Press, 111-130.

Doyle, Gillian, 2002. *Understanding Media Economics*, London, Sage.

European Commission, 1997. COM(97) 623, Green paper on the convergence of the telecommunications, media and information technology sectors, and the implications for regulation: Towards an information society approach, Brussels, December.

European Commission, 1999. COM(1999) 657, Communication from the Commission on the principles and guidelines for the community's audiovisual policy in the digital age, Brussels, December.

European Commission, 2000. COM(2000) 814, Sixth report on the implementation of the telecommunications regulatory package, Brussels, December.

European Commission, 2001. Communication from the Commission on the application of state aid rules to public service broadcasting, Brussels, Official Journal 2001/C 320/04, November.

European Commission, 2002. COM(2002) 778 final, Fourth report from the Commission on the application of directive 89/552/EEC 'Television Without Frontiers,' Brussels.

European Commission, 2003a. WTO services: Commission submits draft offer to Council and Parliament–public services fully defended, press release, IP/03/186, Brussels, February, europa.eu.int/rapid/start/cgi/guesten.ksh?p_action.gettxt=gt&doc=IP/03/186|0|RAPID&lg=EN (accessed 17.03.03).

European Commission, 2003b. Commission staff working document on barriers to widespread access to new services and applications of the Information Society through open platforms in digital television and third generation mobile communications, February, europa.eu.int/information_society/topics/telecoms/regulatory/publiconsult/documents/211_29_en.pdf (accessed 17.03.03).

European Commission, 2003c. Commission reorganises its Competition Department in advance of enlargement, press release, IP/03/603, Brussels, April, http://europa.eu.int/rapid/start/cgi/guesten.ksh?p_action.gettxt=gt&doc=IP/03/60 3|0|RAPID&lg=EN (accessed 02.05.03).

European Council, 1994. Council resolution of 27 June 1994 on a framework for Community policy on digital video broadcasting, Official Journal C 181, July. European Council, 1997, Protocol on the system of public broadcasting in the member states, ('Amsterdam Protocol'), europa.eu.int/comm/avpolicy/legis/ key_doc/amsprot_en.htm, accessed 28.12.01).

European Court of Justice, 2002. Rules governing the acquisition by third parties of television rights for sporting events under Eurovision lead to restrictions on competition in breach of the provisions of the Treaty, Press release no. 80/02, October, curia.eu.int/en/actu/communiques/index.htm (accessed 25.03.02).

European Parliament, 1982. *Report on Radio and Television Broadcasting in the European Community* ('Hahn Report'), Official Journal C87, April.

European Parliament, 1995. Directive 95/47/EC of the European Parliament and of the Council on the use of standards for the transmission of television signals, Official Journal L 281, November.

European Parliament, 1997. Directive 97/36/EC, amending Council Directive 89/552/EEC on the coordination of certain provisions laid down by law, regulation or administrative action in Member States concerning the pursuit of television broadcasting activities ('Television Without Frontiers Directive'), Official Journal L 202, July.

European Parliament, 2000. Directive 2000/31/EC on certain legal aspects of Information Society services, in particular electronic commerce, in the Internal market ('E-commerce Directive'), Official Journal L178, July.

European Parliament, 2002a. Directive 2002/21/EC on a common regulatory framework for electronic communications networks and services ('Framework Directive'), Official Journal L108/33, April.

European Parliament, 2002b. Directive 2002/19/EC of the European Parliament and of the Council on access to, and interconnection of, electronic communications networks and associated facilities ('Access Directive'), Official Journal L108/7, April.

European Parliament, 2002c. Decision 676/2002/EC of the European Parliament and of the Council of 7 March 2002 on a regulatory framework for radio spectrum policy in the European Community ('Radio Spectrum Decision'), Official Journal L108/1, April.

European Union, 2003. Institutions of the European Union, http://www.europa.eu.int/inst-en.htm (accessed 23.04.03).

Galperin, Hernan, 2002. Can the US transition to digital TV be fixed? Some lessons from two European Union cases, Telecommunications Policy, vol. 26, no. 1-2, 3-15.

Gandy, Oscar H., 2002. The real digital divide: Citizens versus consumers, in Leah Lievrouw & Sonia Livingstone (Eds.), The Handbook of New Media, Sage, 448-460.

Goodwin, Ian & Steve Spittle, 2002. The European Union and the information society: Discourse, power and policy, New Media & Society, vol. 2, 225-249.

Grünwald, Andreas, 2001. Riding the US wave: spectrum auctions in the digital age, Telecommunications Policy, vol. 25, no. 10/11, 719-728.

Harrison, Jackie & Lorna Woods, 2001. Defining European public service broadcasting, European Journal of Communication, vol. 4, 477-504.

Humphreys, Peter, 2000. Regulating for pluralism in the digital age, in Tim Lees et al. (Eds.), Is Regulation Still an Option in a Digital Universe?, University of Luton Press, 87-98.

Hutchison, David, 1999. Media Policy: An Introduction, Oxford, Blackwell Publishers.

Iosifidis, Petros, 2002. Digital convergence: challenges for European regulation, Javnost: The Public, vol. 9, no. 3, 27-47.

Lente, Harro van, 2000. Forceful futures: from promise to requirement, in Nik Brown et al. (Eds.), *Contested Futures: A Sociology of Prospective Techno-Science*, Aldershot, Ashgate Publishing.

Levy, David, 1997. The regulation of digital conditional access systems: A case study in European policymaking, *Telecommunications Policy*, vol. 21, 661-76.

Levy, David, 1999. *Europe's Digital Revolution: Broadcasting Regulation, the EU and the Nation State*, Routledge.

Liikanen, Erkki, 2003. Is digital TV a priority for Europe?, European Parliament, February, speech/03/72, europa.eu.int/comm/commissioners/liikanen/media/speeches/text_en.htm (accessed 20.03.03).

Llorens-Maluquer, Carles, 1998. European responses to bottlenecks in digital pay-TV: Impacts on pluralism and competition policy, *Cardozo Arts and Entertainment Law Journal*, 2-3, 557-586.

Michalis, Maria, 2002. The debate over universal service in the European Union, *Convergence*, vol. 8, no. 2, 80-98.

Murdock, Graham, 2000. Digital futures: European television in the age of convergence, in Jan Wieten, Graham Murdock & Peter Dahlgren (Eds.), *Television Across Europe: A Comparative Introduction*, Sage, 35-57.

Näränen, Pertti, 2003. The opportunity lost and found? European regulation of digital television, in Greg Lowe & Taisto Hujanen (Eds.), *Broadcasting & Convergence: New Articulations of the Public Remit*, Nordicom (forthcoming).

OXERA Consulting Limited, 2003. *Study on Interoperability, Service Diversity and Business Models in Digital Broadcasting Markets*, report for the European Commission, February, europa.eu.int/information_society/topics/telecoms/regulatory/studies/documents/oxera_final_report_volume_1_report1.pdf (accessed 15.04.03).

Papathanassopoulos, Stylianos, 2002. *European Television in the Digital Age: Issues, Dynamics and Realities*, Polity Press.

Prebble, Stuart, 2002. History will judge us harshly, *Digital News*, no. 25, 24.

Rosenthal, Michael, 2003. Open access from the EU perspective, *International Journal of Communications Law and Policy*, Winter 2002/2003, www.ijclp.org/7_2003/ijclp_webdoc_5_7_2003.htm (accessed 17.03.03).

Serafini, Dom, 2001. For how long will broadcast be an over-the-air TV biz?, *InterMedia*, vol. 28, no. 4.

Simpson, Seamus & Rorden Wilkinson, 2002. Regulatory change and telecommunications governance: A neo-Gramscian analysis, *Convergence*, vol. 2, 30-51.

Tunstall, Jeremy & David Machin, 1999. *The Anglo-American Media Connection*, Oxford University Press.

Wright, Stephen, Robin Mason & David Miles, 2003. A study into certain aspects of the cost of capital for regulated utilities in the UK, a report commissioned the Office of Fair Trading, February, www.oftel.gov.uk/publications/pricing/2003/cofk0203.htm (accessed 17.03.03).

Chapter 3
Implications for Public Service Broadcasters

Taisto Hujanen

University of Tampere

Although public service broadcasting (PSB) in international comparison easily turns up as the European model of broadcasting, the notion is historically more specific. The concept of PSB is of British origin and characterises the social ethos of the British Broadcasting Corporation (BBC) as expressed by the first Director General of the corporation, Lord Reith (Scannell & Cardiff, 1991: 3-19). In other European countries this tradition of broadcasting was more often identified as 'public broadcasting' describing the status of broadcasting as a public or state institution. As is well known, these institutions typically had a monopoly position in their respective home countries.

Through deregulation and the consequent commercialisation of European broadcasting since the late 1970s, the notion of 'public service' became a means of making a distinction in relation to private, commercial broadcasting. In this process of adaptation towards a more competitive broadcasting environment, the idea of public service symbolised the new audience orientation of public broadcasters. Competition not only forced public broadcasters to become more aware of their mission, but it also made them more directly accountable to their audiences. In the atmosphere of economic liberalism, this kind of accountability became, in fact, essential in the political legitimation of PSB. At the same time, it favoured the editorial independence of public service broadcasters (PSBers), a condition which was central to their future credibility but which was easily harmed by their reputation as state broadcasters.

Despite efforts towards unification, Europe remains characterised by political, cultural and linguistic heterogeneity. One should remember that not so long ago Europe was divided by an iron curtain which did not encourage dreaming of joint European values. In the East–West dimension of Europe, PSB clearly represents Western values. In the near future ten former Eastern-bloc countries will join the European Union (EU) and become integrated into joint political decision making and a common economy. It remains to be seen whether integration increases the relevance of the public service model in these countries. After decades of one-party domination of both government and broadcasting, the people of these countries remain suspicious of any state form of media, and seem to think that money is the only democratic and neutral political factor in society (Jakubowicz, 2001; Bajomi-Lázár, 2002; Vartanova & Zassoursky, 2003).

As demonstrated by a recent comparison of their mission statements (Coppens, 2002), one can compile a list of factors common to all European PSBers. The list would include:

- a universal service to all on equal terms;
- a broad range of programme genres;
- diversity in programming;
- a striving for quality, with a particular emphasis on reliable and accurate information;
- provision of education;
- promotion of national and regional cultures; and
- support for democratic debate and decision making (Avery, 1993; Collins, 1998: 51-74; Wieten et al., 2000: 8-10; Hujanen & Lowe, 2003: 20-21).

In other words, there is a range of factors which forms a common value basis for European PSB, although it might be hard to find a universal definition of the concept. Such common values form the background to the Protocol on Public Service Broadcasting which was added to the Treaty of Rome, the 'constitution' of the EU, in Amsterdam in 1997 (European Council, 1997). Together with free trade and the market economy, PSB now represents joint European values.

The Amsterdam Protocol represents a solution to the conflict between the competition rules of the EU and the form of state aid incorporated into the structure and operation of PSB. This conflict has led to a series of complaints from commercial broadcasters to the European Court of Justice which challenged the particular status of PSBers (Ward, 2003). The point of the Protocol is (as explained in chap. 1 of this volume) to insulate PSB from normal competition rules. This kind of insulation means that in the case of PSB the Union will apply the so called principle of 'subsidiarity.' In other words, the definition of PSB, as well as its organisation and funding, remain to be decided by the individual member states. In this way the EU acknowledges the national history and character of PSB. Therefore, in spite of efforts for unification, national policies dominate over Union policy in this respect.

National variation of PSB is demonstrated by differences in organisation and funding. Some PSBers operate as state institutions which are more or less directly controlled by their respective national parliament or government, while others act as public corporations whose link with the state is more indirect. As to funding, the BBC and the Swedish SVT represent what a document from the EU's Competition Directorate calls the 'pure funding model' (cited in Ward, 2003: 242). Such broadcasters traditionally earn almost all of their revenues from viewers' licence fees, which could be characterised as a special kind of flat-rate taxation (see chap. 1). This kind of universal tax is problematic from the consumer point of view, and the end of the licence fee system has been predicted. Who would have believed in the late 1980s that a major part of the BBC's operations are still financed by the licence fee? Even more amazing is that the BBC, like a few other PSBers, has been able to increase the licence fee to pay for the costs of digitisation.

PSBers prefer licence fee funding over direct state subsidy. The broadcasters saw that although the level of the licence fee was decided by politicians, it guaranteed them more independence than did direct state aid (see Public Service Broadcasting and Editorial Independence, 1998). In relation to their competition with commercial broadcasters, it could also be used as a measure to articulate a special kind of relationship with audiences, based upon more direct accountability between PSBers as 'service providers' and licence fee payers as their 'customers'. The competition over shares is linked with the future of the licence fee system. In my own country, Finland, it was generally thought ten years ago, at the start of channel competition between public service and commercial television, that continuation of the licence fee system required a 50 per cent audience share (Hellman, 1999: 101-103). Public service television never reached that limit and, for a while, even dropped below the 40 per cent level. However, that did not prevent the government recently from raising the level of the licence fee to enable the PSBer to cover the increased costs of digitisation (see chap. 10). At the same time, both broadcasters and politicians are certainly aware that the more marginal the share of PSB becomes, the more difficult it will be to support the licence fee system. Table 3.1 sets out PSB audience shares in Western European countries from 1995 to 2001.

In case PSBers want to avoid business models of funding, the only feasible alternative to licence fees is direct state subsidy. The finances of PSB institutions would certainly collapse and their role marginalised if funding were changed from the licence fee system to a kind of voluntary membership fee. In 2000 the Netherlands substituted licence fees with a public contribution, which is collected as part of income tax (Papathanassopoulos, 2002: 70). Belgium is another country where a major part of PSB financing is based on public funds (SIS Briefings, 2003). In addition, only two post-socialist countries of East

Table 3.1: Public Service Broadcasting Audience Shares in Western European
Countries: 1995-2001

	1995	1996	1997	1998	1999	2000	2001
Large Markets							
Germany	39.0	39.3	40.1	41.3	40.0	40.3	40.3
United Kingdom	43.2	43.9	42.3	40.7	39.1	37.9	38.0
France	41.4	41.9	40.8	39.5	40.4	40.8	40.0
Italy	47.9	47.9	48.1	48.1	47.6	47.3	47.1
Spain	36.8	36.0	34.1	34.4	33.0	32.4	32.6
Medium Markets							
The Netherlands	39.3	35.6	35.1	36.6	34.5	39.0	37.0
Belgium (Flemish)	22.6	25.0	27.8	30.3	30.6	31.6	33.5
Belgium (French)	na	na	19.1	19.8	20.9	na	20.5
Austria	63.0	61.0	61.0	62.0	58.1	56.5	55.4
Portugal	44.9	39.1	38.6	37.7	32.6	na	32.0
Switzerland (German)	32.6	33.4	32.4	33.8	33.2	32.5	32.9
Switzerland (French)	32.1	32.7	32.2	33.8	32.9	32.2	31.1
Switzerland (Italian)	27.3	30.2	32.2	31.9	32.4	31.3	31.5
Ireland	53.5	53.7	53.7	52.4	49.7	47.3	43.4
Nordic/Scandinavian Markets						-	
Sweden	51.4	48.9	47.6	48.2	46.9	43.8	42.0
Denmark	28.0	27.0	29.0	31.0	31.0	32.0	30.0
Finland	46.7	48.2	48.4	45.7	43.1	42.2	43.2
Norway	45.0	43.0	43.0	41.0	39.0	41.0	41.0
Iceland	53.0	51.0	52.0	48.0	43.0	46.0	na

Note: na = not available.
Source: EBU, 2002.

Central Europe – Hungary and Lithuania – adopt public funding or special state
grants in the financing of PSB. Otherwise, licensee fees are still the dominant
form of PSB funding in Europe.

There are, however, a few countries – Luxembourg, Portugal, Spain –
where licence fees do not exist and where public funding is used only marginally
for PSB. These countries use advertising revenues to substitute or complement
licence fees. As well, Austria, Ireland, and Poland are countries where
advertising revenues are either dominant or equal to other forms of PSB funding.
Among the big traditional PSBers, the Italian RAI is most dependent on
advertising revenues (about 40 per cent). For the two German networks, ARD
and ZDF, advertising remains much less important (ARD about 3 per cent, ZDF

10 per cent). In the UK, Channel 4 is a new PSBer which operates on a wholly commercial basis. Similarly, the new Danish PSBer, TV2, is dependent on commercial funding, the share of advertising revenues being about two-thirds of the total. The BBC is the only major PSBer in Europe whose funding is considerably complemented by the sale of programme rights, merchandising etc.

This mixed nature of financing is one reason why PSB continuously appears on the agenda of the EU's competition policy. It seems that the Amsterdam Protocol has not fully succeeded in 'insulating' PSB from competition issues, although it clearly has favoured the competence of member states in this field. Commentators and evaluators of the impact of the Protocol point to three recent EU documents which have relevance in the discussion on PSB (Harrison & Woods, 2001; Ward, 2003; Jakubowicz, 2003). These are a new *Communication on Services of General Interest* (European Commission, 2000a), the amended 'Transparency Directive' (European Commission, 2000b), and a *Communication on the Application of State Aid Rules to Public Service Broadcasting* (European Commission, 2001).

There is manifest pressure from the European Commission, as expressed in these documents, towards a clear and precise definition of public service in broadcasting by the public authorities of the member states. The Commission anticipates that formal entrustment of the public service mission to one or more undertakings should be based on an official act; and, furthermore, that public funding should be limited to what is necessary for the fulfilment of the public service mission (Jakubowicz, 2003). This last point refers to the principle of 'proportionality' which was one of the central features of the revisions to the Transparency Directive from 1980. The new directive aims at guaranteeing transparency in the financial relations between the state and public undertakings, and at ensuring that public funding is proportionate to the public service remit. This is complemented by the objective to ensure transparency and a clear division, including separate accounting systems, by the different activities of the public undertakings in terms of public and non-public service activities (Ward, 2003).

The intention of this kind of pressure is to create and implement what Jakubowicz (2003) calls a two-tier system of accountability. In such a system, PSB organisations are accountable to their respective public authorities in the EU member states, and the member states themselves are accountable to the European Commission for the way they confer, define, organise and finance the public service remit. The problem with the intended accountability is that in order to function it requires a clear statement of what constitutes the public service remit of the PSBers in the EU countries and more or less explicit criteria regarding how to distinguish public service from other types of programming. But again EU documents do not offer any solution on how to define PSB. One can therefore conclude that a clear and precise definition of PSB is needed. It is thus easy to agree with the conclusions which Ward (2003: 248-49) draws on the basis of the recent EU debate:

> It is the West European nation states and the broadcasters themselves to whom we must turn in order to understand the source of the recent changes in broadcasting …. the Commission has generally been supportive of public broadcasters and their perceived role in public and democratic life. It would be no bad thing for the Member States and public broadcasters to take a leaf out of the Commission book and reiterate a commitment to principles of public service broadcasting, stating exactly what these principles are, at a time when they appear to be struggling with the whole issue of the role of broadcasting in society.

The only thing to be added to Ward's definition of priorities is to say that in the frame of the new EU the reference to West European nation states and broadcasters is not enough. One should add the new member states in East Central Europe as well.

DIGITISATION AND THE FUTURE
OF BROADCAST TELEVISION

When speaking about digital television (DTV) as a strategic option for public service broadcasters one should keep in mind that these broadcasters represent the tradition of terrestrial broadcast television, together with commercial free-to-air (FTA) television. Against that background one can say, as hinted in the above quotation from Ward, that the whole issue of broadcasting in society is at stake when considering DTV and PSB. As to the history of broadcast television, one should emphasise that DTV is not the first technological innovation to challenge the role and position of broadcast television. In fact, one of the paradoxes of broadcasting history is that as soon as broadcast television reached maturity as a national institution it was challenged, first by cable and since the 1980s by satellite transmissions. The United States is a prime example of a large market in which cable and satellite successfully challenged the role and position of broadcast television. In Europe these new electronic media were not as successful as alternatives to broadcast television, but through the 'must-carry' rules cable became important and in some markets even dominant as an alternative technology of distribution for broadcast television.

So in terms of the history of European PSB, digitisation, and the consequent technological convergence of broadcasting, telecommunication, and computing, are about the future of FTA broadcast television. As technology, the choice of digital terrestrial television (DTTV) represents for European PSBers the continuation of FTA broadcast television. In this sense, DTTV is a logical and the most natural choice for PSBers when switching from analogue to digital technology. Remaining analogue is not an option considering the central role that digitisation plays in the EU and its member states' policies concerning the 'Information Society.' DTTV is not only about the image of PSBers as terrestrial FTA broadcasters, but is also about power and competition between converging platforms of media and communication. Without DTTV, PSBers would be totally dependent on cable and satellite operators for distribution of their services, or, as emerging future options, on internet and telephone operators. Currently, about 50 per cent of European households receive television only through terrestrial reception, while 30 per cent receive it through cable and 20 per cent through satellite dishes (BIPE Consulting, 2002: 3).

Even DTTV does not guarantee PSBers full control over distribution. In the time of monopoly, the PSBers were the only users of the national terrestrial network and could control its use independent of whether they owned it or rented it from the state telecommunication authority. Deregulation and the consequent development of a multichannel environment created the need to open terrestrial networks to all operators on an equal basis. The result was that distribution was separated from the PSB institutions and organised as an independent function for the service of the whole broadcasting sector. Considering the strong national tradition of PSB, it is remarkable that large PSBers, such as the BBC; today operate within a distribution network which is owned by foreign capital. In Finland, a small EU country, the terrestrial network is now 90 per cent owned by the former French public telecommunications company, TDF.

The history of deregulation is a reminder that the traditional integration of production, programming and distribution in broadcasting started to change character prior to digitisation. Technological convergence continues to renegotiate the functional divisions in broadcasting as well as between broadcasting, telecommunication and the emerging new forms of information technology. The former division of work and power between broadcasting and other technologies is 'disaggregated' in the form of the new media 'value chain', which reduces the role of broadcasters to content production and the packaging of services – a role which makes them dependent on numerous gatekeepers in distribution as well as in user conduit and reception technology (Küng-Shankleman, 2000: 42; EBU Digital Strategy Group 2001a; Alm & Lowe, 2003). The problems in the manufacture of set-top boxes (STBs, 'digiboxes') demonstrate effectively how difficult it may now be for broadcasters to control the whole value chain from production to reception.

What makes the new media value chain so powerful a conception is its central role in the articulation of the EU's convergence policy. The disaggregation of media forms is most effectively expressed in the principle of 'technological neutrality,' informing the EU approach to convergence (on this debate see chap. 2 in this volume; also European Commission, 1997; 1999a; 1999b). This means that in the future construction of the Information Society, EU policy and, consequently, that of the member states will adopt a neutral view regarding the desirability and use of different technologies of media and communication. In other words, as to the future of broadcast television as technology, broadcasting is not a priority in terms of EU policy. Whether broadcasting will survive in the form of terrestrial FTA distribution will depend upon open competition between different forms of distribution. As is well known, this has not hindered some countries from using state aid to subsidise the spread of set-top boxes.

It is useful to consider the principle of technological neutrality in relation to what was said in the introduction to this chapter about the special status of PSB in EU regulation. In relation to convergence, one should emphasise that if PSB has any special status, it is in terms of values and functions, not technology. This is one of the reasons why the question of the remit is so important in the future development of PSB. Another important consequence of technological neutrality is that, if applied consistently, it should open up the possibility for member states and PSBers to deliver public service in all available platforms including the internet. As Steemers pointed out when summarising the visions of digital television, broadcast television is supposed to become less significant, and television will become a "random access medium" alongside other forms of audio-visual and text-based content (Steemers, 1998: 2). Accordingly, she also presumed that in the future debate on public provision and public service there might be a need to focus more on the audio-visual media as a whole and less on PSB. Since then, many PSBers have adopted an active role in the development of multimedia services through the internet. More often now, these services not only complement broadcasting but represent genuine new types of platforms for public service. Similarly, DTTV has been constructed as 'enhanced television' which gradually develops to a multimedia platform of public services. (On the notion of enhanced television see van Tassel, 1996; Owen, 1999.)

As documented by Ward (2003), the EU Commission has already confirmed, in relation to complaints concerning the satellite channels of the BBC and the German PSBers, that the public service nature of a service cannot be judged on the basis of the distribution platform. Once the governments of member states define a certain service as being a public service, such a service remains a public service regardless of the delivery platform. Such a conclusion would most probably apply to new media platforms as well. A recent law in

Finland concerning the regulation of the telecommunications market gives an example of this logic by stating explicitly that the public service remit of the PSBer, the YLE, applies also to its multimedia services on the internet. The YLE is one of those PSBers which are prohibited from advertising, and that applies also to its new internet services. The German authorities have decided, in relation to the ARD and ZDF, that although they otherwise have the right to advertise, that does not apply to their online services (Steemers, 2003).

Knowing the consequences of disaggregation of media forms and the availability of so many new opportunities, one may reasonably wonder why PSBers in general should invest in the development of DTTV. However, there are only a few markets in Europe in which one could guarantee universal access to services without the continuation of terrestrial distribution. These few cases represent countries with an exceptionally high penetration of cable. Cable delivery can be substituted or complemented by the internet, which is not, however, a realistic alternative for distribution of broadcast programming without the implementation of broadband (ADSL) capacity. Even in highly wired markets there remain people who are outside these networks and need to be reached through on-air solutions. Without DTTV, the most feasible way to reach these people is by direct satellite distribution. (Whether third generation mobile phones is an alternative, and to what extent, remains to be seen, but in the foreseeable future its potential seems marginal for broadcasters.)

Now and in the future, technology offers increased opportunities of delivery. Nevertheless, it seems that most European PSBers, with the active support from their governments, have selected to invest in DTTV as their gateway to digital transfer. The argument is that television, as the most common user interface in homes, should be used to connect people with the new digital infrastructure of the Information Society. Making that transformation possible requires the conversion of the old terrestrial networks to digital.

For broadcasters, DTTV is an investment in continuity. Most people are used to receive television through FTA delivery. One should, however, remember that technically there is nothing to hinder the use of DTTV as a pay-TV (or even pay-per-view) service (for example, the British ITV Digital and the Spanish Quiero). Continuity is marked also in the sense that DTTV makes it possible for broadcasters to continue operating in the 'free' electromagnetic spectrum, a platform on which they have historically most experience. This experience, connected with the availability of DTTV in general, increases their relative power in competition with other service providers and the gatekeepers of technical platforms. The active government support for DTTV implies that broadcasting and broadcasters are supposed to play an important role also in the new media ecology of European information societies. Accordingly, as expressed in the European Broadcasting Union's (EBU) digital strategy, the

European PSBers should remain true to their mission as broadcasters and concentrate on guaranteeing basic broadcast services in the new digital environment (EBU Digital Strategy Group, 2001b).

From the public interest point of view, terrestrial broadcast networks remain a cost-effective way to access public services in a digital environment. National security is an additional reason which makes DTTV preferable to other forms of FTA distribution. Even if the terrestrial network is owned by a foreign operator, it is hardly likely that in a crisis situation the operator would remove all the links and masts out of the country. This argument was recently used by the Director General of the Finnish public service broadcaster, the YLE, in the debate concerning the sale of the Finnish DTTV network to a French operator.

Whatever the economic calculations or political motivations for DTTV, it is hard to imagine that any single technology could guarantee universal access to public services in a digital media environment (Thomass, 2003). User preferences alone make such an approach problematic. A multi-platform approach, combining DTTV with cable and satellite delivery, and secondarily with the internet, is probably the most realistic way to implement the digital transition in broadcasting. The Swedish SVT and the British BBC are examples of European PSBers which have adopted such a multi-platform policy (see chaps. 7 and 9). This approach involves the re-articulation of the traditional universal service obligation with respect to geographical coverage of DTTV. In other words, 100 per cent coverage of the terrestrial network is not required if one can guarantee universal access through multiple platforms.

DTTV IN THE HISTORY
OF PUBLIC SERVICE TELEVISION

The aforementioned technology-oriented consideration of DTTV is complemented in this section by a historical contextualisation of public service television. The aim is to discuss the continuities and eventual discontinuities of public service television as a particular cultural form. As pointed in the previous paragraphs, public service television represents the tradition of broadcast television which reached maturity in the 1970s. That matured form of television is described by Umberto Eco (1984) as the phase of *paleo television*, a notion which refers to universalism and the national character of such television. In Table 3.2, paleo television is contrasted with two other phases of television, *multichannel television* and *digital television*. The focus in each case is to point out what happened to the role and position of public service television. A few remarks concerning the overall development of television are added for comparison.

Table 3.2 presents an ideal-type contextualisation of television history. It should not be understood as a periodisation of history but rather a theory to discuss the social and cultural impact of digitisation. The model incorporates the lessons of my own recent research on the Finnish YLE (Hujanen, 2002; 2003), and a few related aspects from Küng-Shankleman (2000) and Ellis (2000b). The model identifies three themes for discussion on the challenges of digitisation: the first, 'role and identity,' concerns the social and cultural role of public service television as well as its institutional and organisational identity; the second theme is entitled 'service orientation;' and the third refers to the market 'position' of public service television. These themes will structure the following discussion on the impact of digitisation. This discussion, along with earlier parts of the chapter, draws heavily on the experiences from the *RIPE Initiative*, a joint scholarly and professional discussion forum reported in Lowe and Hujanen (2003).

Table 3.2: Public Service Television in Context

Paleo Television	Multichannel Television	Digital Television
Role and identity		
cultural institution	cultural industry	content provider
programmes	schedule	contents
production	programming	content production & packaging
Service orientation		
universalism	audience orientation	fragmented public service(?)
information, education, entertainment	public service	branded public service
Position		
monopoly or dominance	competition & co-existence	co-existence or marginalisation
Compare with development of television in general		
broadcasting	electronic media	digital convergence
broadcasting	narrowcasting	customisation & individualisation
universal access	choice	conditional access

Source: compiled by author

The New Identity of PSBers as Content Providers

As to the role and identity of public service television, the model offers PSBers a new role as content providers. This kind of identification points directly to what was earlier called the new media 'value chain.' This identification is a key conclusion in the strategic analysis which the EBU recently conducted with respect to digitisation (EBU Digital Strategy Group, 2001a; 2001b). The premise of the analysis is that technological convergence will essentially change the role and position of PSB. It is forecast that, because of new platforms and operators, content supply (including television programming) will continue to grow, and as a consequence competition will intensify. The increasing supply will threaten the visibility of PSB and make it necessary to maintain the relative volume of public service programming at a satisfactory level. The search for greater cost effectiveness must therefore continue. That can be reached through a matrix-structured organisation which puts content production and packaging at the strategic centre of operation.

What does this kind of content orientation mean in relation to earlier phases of public service television? Does it imply anything more than adopting a new language to describe the role and identity of broadcasting? Or could that language imply major changes in the role and practices of PSBers? As to the last question, one might point to what Born (2003) writes in relation to DTV in Britain: Broadcasters' projections for the future are not innocent but an important aspect of the construction of the digital future. The notion of content itself may arouse both positive and negative connotations depending on the perspective of the commentator. Those who are worried about the continual commercialisation and industrialisation of broadcasting, and the consequent fixation on the form, might greet the term very positively: "Excellent! We are finally back to content!" For others, including particularly those producers in PSB institutions who consider themselves as programme makers, the term may sound suspect and detrimental to craftsmanship and the quality of public service.

The EBU Digital Strategy Group's discussion on convergence links content orientation in broadcasting to administrative and policy discourse typical of the EU's approach to cultural industries. That approach characterises the EU's audiovisual policy, for example, in the form of the European Television Directive (European Parliament, 1997). But similarly, the dominance of industrial logic is typical of later discussions on convergence policy as well as of visions of the European Information Society. In a comparative study concerning the content production industry in Finland, Sweden and Ireland (Kallio et al., 2001), the authors point out that the discourse of content has a technological background. Accordingly, content is something which refers to the 'software' aspect of technology as distinct from 'hardware.' Although content can be used to refer to media contents such as newspapers, radio and television programmes, it now relates typically to new digital, consumer- and customer-oriented contents. As the authors comment, the notion of content expands to entertainment and commerce, particularly in relation to, for example, web content and games on the Internet.

Considering the technological and industrial background of content orientation it seems logical to conclude that the new identity as content providers continues to distance European PSBers from their traditional role as unique cultural institutions. What the new identity projects is that PSBers will be an integral part of the future content producing and providing industries. The industrial approach to broadcasting is not in itself new to PSBers. It characterised their response to intensified competition in the 1990s multichannel environment. In the longer term, the more critical question for all broadcasters is whether broadcast content maintains its role among the even more customised and individualised services. Could counteracting these trends form a strong enough 'brand' for PSBers to guarantee them visibility in the ocean of alternatives, and thus safeguard the popular support and political legitimacy necessary for their continued economic viability?

This is to say that content orientation mainly represents continuity in PSB if contrasted with adaptation to the earlier multichannel environment. But similarly, it probably strengthens discontinuity if contrasted with the old tradition of PSB. No doubt the new technological landscape threatens new discontinuities concerning the basics of broadcasting itself and of PSB in particular. As to the latter aspect, one should emphasise that the technical potential of any technology is different from its social application and use. For example, how the new media technology is applied and used will depend also on broadcasters and, not least, their old and potential new audiences. It seems also that the pace of change is slower than forecasted, as demonstrated by recent problems in the information technology sector. This will give more time and space for broadcasters to accommodate.

As pointed out earlier, the old PSB institutions formed an integrated whole of programming, production and distribution. Distribution was then organisationally separated to an independent function to serve the whole broadcasting sector in the new multichannel environment. Another major change concerned the relationship between programming and production. As with the example of the BBC, PSBers started separating broadcasting from production – the former referring to programming operations including scheduling. As suggested by Table 3.2, programming and scheduling formed the strategic centre of operations in the adaptation of PSBers to the multichannel environment. In the organisational hierarchy this meant that production became more clearly submitted to programming operations. In other words, as concluded by Ellis

(2000a; 2000b; see also Hujanen, 2002), the schedule became the power centre of television.

Packaging as an element of the new media value chain also makes scheduling and programming functions in general a priority in the emerging new content orientation in the digital environment. However, the former scheduling of an individual channel or a number of channels changes character to a more overall branding of services in which, as expressed by Ytreberg (2002), the continuity of environments becomes an issue. In other words, independent of platform, the operator is supposed to maintain a consistent identity; or (as formulated by the EBU Digital Strategy Group) to create the identity of a trusted agent. Such an overall branding will most probably require more centralised control over programming operations which reduces the relative power of individual channels. Channels and similar service entities remain, however, important actors in at least two ways: in construction of audiences to content production; and as commissioners of programming.

The new matrix organisation retains the separation of broadcasting and production and, in fact, makes it stronger. In concrete terms, a matrix organisation means that the traditional link between television channels and their production is broken and substituted by commissioning of production across the borders of channels and, gradually, even of media (Alm & Lowe, 2003; Hujanen, 2002: 148-158). In this structure, channels become pure packagers and commissioners of programming and lose their production identity. As a strategy towards a digital future, it means that whatever number of channels or services, and whatever media or platform they use, they will be served by the same more or less centralised production machine.

This kind of matrix organisation represents both continuity and discontinuity in relation to earlier PSB. The introduction of producer choice and cross-commissioning practices, complemented by outsourcing of production, represent examples of matrix logic which have already characterised the response of many PSBers to the earlier multichannel environment. Some key areas of production may have been organised to serve the whole organisation in terms of matrix logic. Accordingly, it seems that the new content-oriented matrix organisation of PSB will predominantly apply to certain generic traditions, particularly in relation to news and current affairs, education, drama, documentary etc. (Hujanen, 2003).

The most radical aspect of discontinuity in the content-oriented matrix organisation is the way it cuts across the media-based divisions. Whether it leads to the dominance of general 'content competences,' over media-specific competences, remains to be seen. But in the idea of content production there is the potential for the identity of a television or radio producer to gradually become secondary. Certainly the digital transition requires investment in general content and media know-how by PSBers. This becomes increasingly important as PSBers get more involved in multimedia platforms, and is probably a necessity in terms of cost effectiveness in certain areas of production, such as news, when versioning contents to different platforms.

The risk of too much emphasis on general content or media competences is that PSBers become weaker in their strongest area, namely broadcasting. Broadcasters who neglect developing the media-specific skills of radio and television production and programming risk falling into the trap which is set for them by the most radical visions of media convergence – the death of broadcasting (Given, 1999). One should, however, emphasise that matrix organisation as such does not hinder the nurture of media-specific skills. But to succeed in that requires intensive and long-term co-operation between production and packaging units (that is, channels and other service entities). This need, however, together with the requirement of continuity in audience relations, easily conflicts with the striving for more flexibility implicit in the new organisation.

The separation of broadcasting and production in PSB organisations opened up a process known as outsourcing (or externalisation) of production. Nevertheless, European PSBers retained what Küng-Shankleman (2000) called the 'integrated factory' model, referring to vertically integrated broadcasters which make the bulk of their programmes themselves in their own studios, assemble these into a schedule and transmit this via a national network over which they have control. As discussed earlier, however, that form of distribution is no longer part of the traditional integration. The British Channel 4 is an example of another kind of broadcaster which applies the 'publisher' model, that is, it assembles and transmits programming commissioned and acquired from producers outside the organisation.

When breaking the traditional link between channels and production in the new content-oriented matrix organisation, the channels will have more freedom from the organisation, namely, in commissioning programmes. In addition, their potential to negotiate deals with outside independent producers will also probably increase. Küng-Shankleman concludes that the publisher model is growing in popularity since it enables organisations to offer a broad spectrum of programming with maximum flexibility and creativity, while minimising the fixed cost base. This kind of cost effectiveness might tempt channels to increase outsourcing of production in case they are not able to reach satisfactory deals internally. From the management point of view flexibility is certainly one of the important potentials of the new organisation. Concretely, it will be easier to decide on resourcing of production without the immediate consent of channels. All these changes together imply that outsourcing will remain an issue in the corporate economy of PSBers.

Born (2003) notes in relation to Channel 4 that its position in the new 'value chain' is vulnerable. She explains that its identity is focused on 'aggregating content' (or channels), and this is considered a relatively powerless position in comparison with platform owners and rights-owning production companies. Similarly, one could argue that the old PSB organisations, such as the BBC, will weaken their relative power the more they continue outsourcing their production. This demonstrates that outsourcing is not only a matter of cost effectiveness or flexibility, but crucially concerns the whole position and institutional character of PSB organisations. Alm and Lowe (2003) connect the discussion on outsourcing with the questions of competences and know-how. Their conclusion is that value-competence is the key competence for PSBers, and that can be best nurtured through their own content production.

This conclusion by Alm and Lowe is particularly relevant if one connects it with the EU discussion on how to confer, define, organise and finance PSB (see introduction to this chapter). If public service competence is, broadly, on sale in the independent market of production, how to argue for the continuation of the old PSB institutions in the future media ecology? If they would reduce their role to pure publishers of public service contents, should not the market then be open to other publishers to do the same? Such questions point out that outsourcing is a risky way for PSBers to manage the digital transfer. If not handled carefully, it may lead to a situation which is certainly a nightmare for most PSB institutions, namely, the auctioning of public service in the form of tenders open to anyone to produce the service. Such a system was included in the models which the EU's Competition Directorate circulated for discussion in 1998 (compare with the notion of disaggregated public service in Jakubowicz, 2003: 158-160). As documented by Ward (2003), the discussion paper received rather a hostile response from both PSBers and member states.

With regard to outsourcing one should note that original domestic programming, be it in-house or independent production, normally comprises half or less of the output of European PSBers (Wieten et al., 2000: 17-20). The rest is covered by programme imports and international co-productions. The role of domestic programming is clearly more important in the PSB supply than in commercial television and, in that sense, outsourcing is a more serious issue for PSBers. One should also remember that outsourcing does not always mean commissioning a full package of programmes, but may represent a co-operative venture between the broadcaster and one or more independent producers. Internationally, co-productions with other PSBers and, secondarily, with private partners are of growing relevance for PSBers. The harsh competition over programme rights requires similar search for alliances, for example, in the frame of the EBU.

The more DTTV develops into a multimedia platform which connects television viewers with other digital services, the more European PSBers must pay attention to co-operation with the whole public sector. I recently attended a seminar in the headquarters of the YLE in Helsinki, where public authorities and semi-public organisations in the so called 'third sector' were urged to get involved in DTTV. The seminar took place a few months after the several times delayed delivery of STBs with interactive capacity (based on the Multimedia Home Platform, MHP, standard) into the market. Interactivity is a prerequisite for the individualised use of public services – such as taxation, social security, health care etc. – through DTTV.

The idea of using DTTV as a gateway to public services of the Information Society is nothing new. Finland is one of those countries where the 'internet to every home' vision was important to the political legitimation of DTTV in the principal government decision in 1996. Instead, the most interesting aspect of the YLE seminar was how DTTV was characterised as a unique platform different from the internet. It was claimed that DTTV is interactive and enables individual navigation similar to the internet, even though DTTV does not offer a return channel. But because of the user interface – the television set – DTTV is essentially different, not only in terms of social context but also technically (Raudaskoski & Rasmussen, 2003). A particularly important conclusion was that the differences in the technical resolution of the screen make it difficult to use web-based materials as such in DTTV. Therefore, the solution to simply link web pages with the DTTV platform will not work. This seems an important conclusion considering the original visions of how DTTV and the internet would converge, and a further reminder that broadcasters need find their own path to digital transition.

Universalism and the Position of PSB

The traditional service orientation of PSBers is based on what Table 3.2 identifies as universalism, or what sometimes is called *universal service obligation* (Collins, 1998: 64-65; Harrison & Woods, 2001). Universalism can be understood as a question of access – where, how, and on what terms one can receive the broadcast signal. In this sense, universalism means that PSB should be available for all on equal conditions independent of place of residence or of social class. In addition, one can say that the traditional three-point mission to inform, educate and entertain is part of PSB's universalism. When considering the impact of DTTV on the service orientation of PSBers, one can hardly avoid the question of universalism and the consequent questions of access and composition of contents.

As to the effects of the multichannel environment, one should emphasise that universalism remained central to PSB, but its implementation was affected by the new competitive environment. That change is expressed by reference to audience orientation in the frame of multichannel television which indicates that PSBers now articulate their traditional service mission in terms of their audience construction. As formulated in the 1980s critique of paternalism and authoritarianism of PSB, the normative mission of PSBers was earlier motivated on the basis of more general concerns related to social responsibility (Rowland & Tracey, 1990; Ang, 1991). The traditional mission could be called 'sender-oriented', but the terms 'society-oriented' and 'public interest-oriented' better capture the historical essence of that approach. The now popular dichotomy of sender/audience orientation remains too media-centric to characterise the historical background of PSB. However, such media-centrism probably better describes the social and cultural atmosphere of multichannel television. That is why 'audience orientation' is used in Table 3.2 to describe the re-articulation of PSBers' service orientation in the new multichannel environment.

Considering the continuous growth of supply and intensification of competition, audience orientation and the related question of the public service mission remain pertinent issues for PSB in the digital environment. As discussed in the introduction to this chapter, the questions concerning definition and content of public service are central for pure regulatory reasons. In other words, there is a clear continuity from multichannel to digital television with regard to service orientation. One might, however, point out that audience orientation in the digital environment is not the same as in earlier periods. This is implied in the notion of *branded public service*, adopted from the documents of the EBU Digital Strategy Group (discussed previously). In a way, branding complements and in part substitutes the earlier reference to scheduling in the management discourse of broadcasters. My own research on the so called 'management by schedule' in Finnish public service television in the 1990s (Hujanen, 2002) showed that one of the major questions in this approach was how to make producers (programme makers) aware of their audiences in all that they did. To learn to be aware of their audience was central to the development of programme competences.

Scheduling is by definition an intermediate process between production, programming and audiences. As the above example from one PSB organisation shows, it has a particularly important role in the internal transformation of PSB institutions in the context of multichannel television (see examples from other Nordic countries in Ytreberg, 2001; 2002). In comparison with that impact, branding orientation is more about overall image construction of PSBers in relation to their audiences and, naturally, about how to incorporate the brand in the entire PSB programme supply. Compared with scheduling, the strategic emphasis on branding turns the attention towards the competition environment of PSBers. In management this means that the importance of marketing increases in relation to scheduling.

The question of the remit is unavoidably linked with branding and the consequent construction of audiences. Should PSBers develop their services in accordance with the general trends of increased customisation and individualisation, or remain true to the aspect of 'broad' in their tradition as broadcasters (Hujanen & Lowe, 2003)? In the former multichannel environment the new audience orientation of European PSBers resulted in a kind of narrowcasting approach in relation to a portion of the audience. The view of broad general audiences was complemented by more targeted audiences based on age, sex, interest orientation, life style and even on programme tastes and preferences (Schulz, 2000). In addition, serving linguistic, ethnic, and other minorities has been an important element of the public service mission. One should remember that targeting special audiences took place mainly in the frame of channels which could be called 'general interest' or 'full-service' channels. Or if one preferred to characterise the generic mix of these channels, they could be called 'mixed-genre' channels.

The notion of *fragmented public service* (notice, with a question mark in Table 3.2) refers to a model of service orientation which was seriously discussed by the BBC in the winter of 2000 (Born, 2003). The question was whether or not to thematise all BBC channels according to the niche logic typical of cable and satellite. The plan raised heavy criticism inside and outside the organisation and was not implemented as such. A newspaper comment in Finland on this British debate illustrates how strongly the generalist approach is connected with the public service tradition. An article in the *Helsingin Sanomat*, a leading Finnish newspaper, commenting on a speech by the BBC's Director General proposing a reduction in the generalist nature of BBC1 and BBC2, had the dramatic heading, "BBC will skip public service channel!" (Hämäläinen, 2000).

The BBC's decision to retain the position of generalist mixed-genre channels seems to be, until now, the dominant model of service orientation in the frame of DTTV. The combination of broad mixed-genre channels complemented by new specialised or niche channels is the typical point of departure for the digital transition of PSBers (in addition to BBC, e.g., the German ARD, the Swedish SVT, and the Finnish YLE). The new PSB digital channels are either targeted to special audiences such as youth and children, or represent core areas of public service programming such as news, arts and culture, education and science. Born (2003) describes the BBC's orientation as a "portfolio approach," which is based on a particular kind of projection of future consumer behaviour:

The BBC is not assuming a universal shift from viewing mixed genre to niche channels; nor is it assuming that pay services will become near-universally acceptable. Instead, BBC strategists stress the need not to alienate analogue and free-to-air consumers during the transition to digital. The BBC's 'future proofing' thus aims to prepare the portfolio for a fully digital world, but without knowing precisely when that will occur, what form it will take, or how consumers will respond.

The rationale for this portfolio approach is that it gives time for broadcasters to wait and see when and how quickly the transition to digital takes place. The collapse in 2002 of ITV Digital in the UK and Quiero TV in Spain demonstrates that forecasts of the pay-TV option have been too optimistic. It seems that even the BBC believes that DTTV should represent a continuation of FTA television. The UK Freeview service, launched in October 2002, offers a total of nine digital FTA channels. As pointed out in chapter 7 of this volume, despite the apparent success of Freeview, at the end of 2002 DTTV covered only just over 1.3 million of the total 10.2 million UK digital households. Not only in the UK but in Europe generally, the pay-TV option through satellite continues to be the dominant form of DTV. At the end of 2001, 27 million European households were receiving television in digital format, representing 18 per cent of all television households. Of these, 19 million (70 per cent) accessed DTV through satellite and the rest mainly by cable (BIPE Consulting, 2002).

The need to maintain visibility in relation to increasing competitive services makes this portfolio approach necessary for PSBers in most markets. One could also wonder how to convince audiences to change to DTTV, if that meant investing in a new technology without receiving additional services. There is evidence that what people most anticipate with DTV is more television (Theodoropoulou, 2003). Another surplus element of DTV relates to *interactive services* which characterise the visions of enhanced or advanced television (see chap. 5). As pointed out earlier, these visions have characterised digital television as a multimedia platform comparable to the internet. However, in the marketing of DTTV, the difference between the interactive services that were promised and those actually available has been confusing to viewers and harmful to the launch of the DTTV project. Therefore, it seems that interactivity is hardly the primary feature with which to convince current PSB audiences to convert to DTTV.

In common with digital satellite, DTTV does not include a return channel. By using STBs or digital receivers with an interactive capacity (for example, the MHP standard) it is, however, possible to offer a return connection through the telephone. The disadvantage of such a system from the consumer point of view is that it means higher telephone bills. Without a broadband capacity (ADSL) such a return line is slow and complicated to use, especially compared with television remote control devices. Not least for technical reasons, PSBers must remain cautious when making promises about interactivity. At the same time, however, there seems no technical reason why interactivity could not in the long term develop as a standard feature of DTTV.

In case European PSBers select some form of portfolio approach in the transition to digital, the critical question is how to guarantee the funding of additional services. Will increased supply lead to the same solution as that which developed for the multichannel environment of television, namely a proliferation of low-cost production? (Caldwell, 1995); or to an alternative solution which were even more devastating to European PSBers, namely, the neglect of domestic production and increased importation of foreign (American) programming? My own research on the YLE (a PSBer in a small EU country) points out that digitisation means pressure toward more cost effectiveness and continued reduction in average funding per programme hour (Hujanen, 2002). The question is how to maintain the traditional PSB quality of programming in such conditions. Born's (2003) description of the BBC (a PSBer in a large EU country) demonstrates that BBC strategists paint a more positive view of the future. The BBC3 and BBC4 digital channels are intended to avoid low budgets for digital and cable by adopting two main measures, namely, restricted schedules (6-8 hours a day), and repeat programming (within each schedule and between channels – notice that this policy also concerns the relationship between new and old channels). In general, the aim is to keep budgets close to terrestrial norms and remain committed to original programming on digital channels.

The way BBC strategists refer to repeats within schedules and between channels distances PSB from its high-culture tradition whereby programming, especially art, implied a unique experience unsuitable for repetition. In that tradition even serialisation of production was considered a deterioration of standards. In commercial television repetition represented a cost-saving practice typical of summer schedules. But today repetition is widely applied by all broadcasters and not only for reasons of cost. According to one programmer from the YLE, repetition is an essential aspect of service in the multichannel environment – a way of offering people a greater choice of when to watch a programme. On the basis of letters to the editor in newspapers, however, one easily gets the impression that many people consider repeats to be a nuisance rather than a service.

In addition to repetition, one might include versioning as an important practice between channels. A typical example from arts and culture or sport would be to offer an event in full on a specialised channel and then version the highlights on a generalist channel. In the production of digital content, versioning also refers to cross-media practices such as the synchronisation of radio and television productions. For example, since 1998 the YLE has offered a digital radio channel which is based on versioning audio productions from various channels including television. Repetition of programmes from new digital channels on the main channel or channels gives them a function of a 'show window' in relation to the PSB digital portfolio. In this sense, they not only represent tradition but play a role in the promotion of the new digital services. Supposing that repetitions from new digital channels represent the best of their programme offerings, the generalist channels might also have an opportunity to maintain their quality profile despite the relative decline of their production budgets.

These conclusions concerning the role of generalist channels in the digital portfolio demonstrate that they have a key role to play in the promotion of new digital services. Moreover, they represent a continuation from analogue to digital television. A fully fragmented public service, brought about by the transition to a bouquet of pure niche or specialised services, would certainly alienate the analogue audience from DTTV (as suggested by the BBC's projections). Should that happen, the way would be open to the marginalisation of PSB's social and cultural position (see the options in Table 3.2).

However, the future of generalist channels in a digital environment is not only a strategic concern of PSBers as organisations or institutions. A fragmented public service would most probably strengthen the segmentation and individualisation of media culture, and in that sense the selection of the PSB strategy is of public concern. According to Harrison and Woods (2001), generalist channels are crucial parts of the universal service obligation of PSB. Their broad mixture of content and audiences is necessary if one wants to maintain the minimum amount of social coherence in the increasingly fragmented public sphere of modern society (see also Wieten et al., 2000: 16-17). As Harrison and Woods point out, the market position of PSB and universalism are connected. Marginalisation of PSBers in the market would destroy their ability to act as forums of social coherence and ruin the basics of universalism. In other words, as far as universalism is constitutive of PSB, generalist channels should remain an essential feature of the PSB digital supply.

CONCLUSION

When discussing DTV or DTTV one should remember that these notions refer to television in a very particular sense. In technologically developed countries television *production* has been digital for a decade. It is notable that this transition has taken place with little of the public concern evident in the recent discussion on digital *transmission*. One could conclude that DTV has become an issue only after the focus of technological development switched from production to distribution. There are several reasons why digital distribution of television has become a hot issue in media and communication policy as well as in the broader debate on the Information Society.

First, through digitisation of distribution television was put on the agenda of technological convergence and became comparable to other digital networks. In a way, television lost its particularity as technology and, as shown above, that started to affect its institutional character and social and cultural identity. Convergence created the discussion about enhanced television and even raised the question of whether 'television' would remain 'television' at all. From the broadcasters' point of view, convergence opened up the question concerning the multi-platform approach – whether to remain true to FTA broadcasting, or complement it with other forms of distribution, or even substitute it with new forms.

Another reason why digitisation of distribution is an issue is the way it affects the use of the electromagnetic spectrum for broadcasting and other purposes. As is well known, digitisation multiplies the information capacity of electromagnetic networks, thus making it possible to licence more operators in these networks and to offer more services through either new or old operators. From the broadcasters point of view this means more competition and, to ensure visibility among multiple operators, the proliferation of production and services.

All of these changes affect us all more or less directly – as television viewers and as citizens and consumers. In this context DTV becomes an issue not only because of the increased options for choice, but also because of changes of user interface. Reception·of digital signals requires a new kind of receiver, or a STB to transform the signal. Antennas may require updating to ensure continuous reception, and with digital new VCRs or DVDs are preferred. The total bill for digital conversion for an individual consumer or household is considerable (see chap. 6). In addition, the implementation of digital distribution may also create the need to raise the licence fee for the funding of PSB.

This financial effect of digitisation upon individuals and households makes it particularly important for PSBers to listen to their audiences when considering DTTV or any other digital option. This is also the central reason why no broadcaster should see DTV as purely a change of technology. Digital television, be it DTTV or something else, is more than a switchover from one technology to another. For PSBers in particular, digital television requires building and maintaining a trust, a social and cultural relationship, which may take a long time to develop but may collapse overnight.

REFERENCES

Alm, Ari & Gregory Ferrel Lowe, 2003. Outsourcing core competencies?, in Gregory Ferrel Lowe & Taisto Hujanen (Eds.), *Broadcasting & Convergence: New Articulations of the Public Service Remit*, Nordicom, Gothenburg, 223-235.

Ang, Ien, 1991. *Desperately Seeking the Audience*, Routledge, London.

Avery, Robert K. (Ed.). 1993, *Public Service Broadcasting in a Multichannel Environment*, Longman, New York.

Bajomi-Lázár, Péter, 2002. Public Service Television in East Central Europe, IFJ International Federation of Journalists, January 2002.

BIPE Consulting, 2002. *Digital Switchover in Broadcasting: Final Report*, A study for the European Commission, Executive Summary, April.

Born, Georgina, 2003. Public service broadcasting and digital television in the UK: politics of positioning, in Gregory Ferrel Lowe & Taisto Hujanen (Eds.), *Broadcasting & Convergence: New Articulations of the Public Service Remit*, Nordicom, Gothenburg, 205-221.

Caldwell, John Thornton, 1995. *Televisuality: Style, Crisis and Authority in American Television*, Rutgers University Press, New Brunswick.

Collins, Richard, 1998. *From Satellite to Single Market: New Communication Technology and European Public Service Television*, Routledge: London.

Coppens, Tomas, 2002. A tour of duties: A comparative study of PSB mission statements in 13 European countries, paper presented at the 23rd Conference and General Assembly of the IAMCR (Working Group Broadcasting in Europe), Barcelona, July 2002.

EBU (European Broadcasting Union), 2002. *EBU Members' Audience Trends 1990-2001*, SIS Guides, vol. 2, GEAR-EBU Information and Statistics Network, Strategic Information Service, July.

EBU Digital Strategy Group, 2001a. *Media With a Progressive Purpose, Conclusions of the EBU Digital Strategy Group, Part 1: New Maps of Media Space*, European Broadcasting Union, May.

EBU Digital Strategy Group, 2001b. *Media With a Progressive Purpose, Conclusions of the EBU Digital Strategy Group, Part 2: Managing Digital Evolution*, For 111th Meeting of the Administrative Council, Geneva, November.

Eco, Umberto, 1984. *Semiologia Quotidiana*, Gruppo Editoriale Fabbri-Bompiana, Milan.

Ellis, John, 2000a. Scheduling: the last creative act in television?, *Media, Culture & Society*, vol. 22, no. 1, 25-38.

Ellis, John, 2000b. *Seeing Things: Television in the Age of Uncertainty*, Tauris, London.

European Commission, 1997. *Green paper on the convergence of the telecommunications, media and information technology sectors, and the implications for regulation: Towards an information society approach*, COM(97) 623, Brussels, December.

European Commission, 1999a. *Results of the public consultation on the Convergence Green Paper: communication to the European Parliament, the Council, the Economic and Social Committee and the Committee of the Regions*, COM(1999)108, Brussels.

European Commission, 1999b. *Communication from the Commission on the principles and guidelines for the community's audiovisual policy in the digital age*, COM(1999) 657, Brussels, December.

European Commission, 2000a. *Communication from the Commission — Services of general interest in Europe* (COM/2000/0580 final), The European Union: Brussels.

European Commission, 2000b. Commission Directive 2000/52/EC of 26 July 2000 amending Directive 80/723/EEC on the transparency of financial relations between Member States and public undertakings, *Official Journal of the European Communities*, July.

European Commission, 2001. Communication from the Commission on the application of state aid rules to public service broadcasting, *Official Journal*, 2001/C 320/04, November.

European Council, 1997. Protocol on the system of public broadcasting in the member states, ('Amsterdam Protocol'), europa.eu.int/comm/avpolicy/legis/ key_doc/amsprot_en.htm (accessed 28.12.2001).

European Parliament, 1997. Directive 97/36/EC, amending Council Directive 89/552/EEC on the coordination of certain provisions laid down by law, regulation or administrative action in Member States concerning the pursuit of television broadcasting activities ('Television Without Frontiers Directive'), Official Journal L 202, July.

Given, Jock, 1999. *The Death of Broadcasting: Media's Digital Future*, University of New South Wales Press, Sydney.

Hämäläinen, Timo, 2000. Kutistuvan vahemmiston ohjelmaa [Programming for a shrinking minority], *Helsingin Sanomat*, 26 June, p. D13.

Harrison, J. & L. M. Woods, 2001. Defining European public service broadcasting, *European Journal of Communication*, vol. 16, no. 4 , 477-504.

Hellman, Heikki, 1999. *From Companions to Competitors: The Changing Broadcasting Market and Television Programming in Finland*, University of Tampere.

Hujanen, Taisto, 2002. *The Power of Schedule: Programme Management in the Transformation of Finnish Public Service Television*, Tampere University Press.

Hujanen, Taisto, 2003. Public service strategy in digital television: From schedule to content, in Ib Bondebjerg & Peter Golding (Eds.), *Media Cultures in a Changing Europe*, Intellect Books, Bristol.

Hujanen, Taisto & Gregory Ferrel Lowe, 2003. Broadcasting and convergence: rearticulating the future past, in Gregory Ferrel Lowe & Taisto Hujanen (Eds.), *Broadcasting & Convergence: New Articulations of the Public Service Remit*, Nordicom, Gothenburg, 9-25.

Jakubowicz, Karol, 2001. Rude awakening: social and media change in central and Eastern Europe, *Javnost-The Public*, vol. 8, no. 4, 59-80.

Jakubowicz, Karol, 2003. Bringing public service broadcasting to account, in Gregory Ferrel Lowe & Taisto Hujanen (Eds.), *Broadcasting & Convergence: New Articulations of the Public Service Remit*, Nordicom, Gothenburg, 147-165.

Kallio, Jukka et al., 2001. *Sisällöntuotannon kilpailukyky* [Competition Power of Content Production Industry], LTT Research, Helsinki.

Küng-Shankleman, Lucy, 2000. *Inside the BBC and CNN: Managing Media Organizations*, Routledge, London.

Lowe, Gregory Ferrel & Taisto Hujanen (Eds.), 2003. *Broadcasting & Convergence: New Articulations of the Public Service Remit*, Nordicom, Gothenburg.

Owen, Bruce, 1999. *The Internet Challenge to Television*, Harvard University Press, Cambridge, Massachusetts.

Papathanassopoulos, Stylianos, 2002. *European Television in the Digital Age: Issues, Dynamics and Realities*, Polity Press, Bodmin.

Public Service Broadcasting and Editorial Independence, 1998. Report of the International Seminar, Tampere, June 1997, Finnish National Commission for UNESCO and UNESCO, Keuruu.

Raudaskoski, Pirkko & Tove Arendt Rasmussen, 2003. Cross media and (inter)active media use: a situated perspective, in Gregory Ferrel Lowe & Taisto Hujanen (Eds.), *Broadcasting & Convergence: New Articulations of the Public Service Remit*, Nordicom, Gothenburg, 313-325.

Rowland, Willard D. Jr. & Michael Tracey, 1990. Worldwide challenges to public service broadcasting, *Journal of Communication*, vol. 40, no. 2, 8-27.

Scannell, Paddy & David Cardiff, 1991. *A Social History of British Broadcasting: Volume One 1922-1939*, Basil Blackwell, Padstow.

Schulz, Winfried, 2000. Television audiences, in Jan Wieten, Graham Murdock & Peter Dahlgren (Eds.), 2000, *Television Across Europe: A Comparative Introduction*, Sage, London.

SIS Briefings (The), 2003. A Monthly Bulletin of the EBU Strategic Information Service, December-January 2003, no. 54.

Steemers, Jeanette (Ed.), 1998. *Changing Channels: The Prospects for Television in a Digital World*, University of Luton Press.

Steemers, Jeanette, 2003. Public service broadcasting is not dead yet: Strategies in the 21st century, in Gregory Ferrel Lowe & Taisto Hujanen (Eds.), *Broadcasting & Convergence: New Articulations of the Public Service Remit,* Nordicom, Gothenburg, 123-136.

Theodoropoulou, Vivi, 2003. Consumer convergence: digital television and the early interactive audience in the UK, in Gregory Ferrel Lowe & Taisto Hujanen (Eds.), *Broadcasting & Convergence: New Articulations of the Public Service Remit,* Nordicom, Gothenburg, 285-299.

Thomass, Barbara, 2003. Knowledge society and public sphere, in Gregory Ferrel Lowe & Taisto Hujanen (Eds.), *Broadcasting & Convergence: New Articulations of the Public Service Remit,* Nordicom, Gothenburg, 29-39.

Ward, David, 2003. State aid or band aid? An evaluation of the European Commission's approach to public service broadcasting, *Media, Culture and Society,* vol. 25, 233-250.

Vartanova, Elena & Yassen N. Zassoursky, 2003. Television in Russia: is the concept of PSB relevant?, in Gregory Ferrel Lowe & Taisto Hujanen (Eds.), *Broadcasting & Convergence: New Articulations of the Public Service Remit,* Nordicom, Gothenburg, 93-108.

Van Tassel, Joan, 1996. *Advanced Television Systems: Brave New TV,* Focal Press, Boston.

Wieten, Jan, Graham Murdock & Peter Dahlgren (Eds.), 2000. *Television Across Europe: A Comparative Introduction,* Sage, London.

Ytreberg, Espen, 2001. *Programskjemaarbeid i NRK Fjernsynet: Beslutningsprosesser i et maktsentrum* [Scheduling in NRK Television: Decision Processes in a Power Centre], National report for a joint Nordic study "Scheduling in Nordic public service television", Media Studies, Department of Media and Communication, Publications, No. 40, University of Oslo.

Ytreberg, Espen, 2002. Continuity in environments: The evolution of basic practices and dilemmas in Nordic television scheduling, *European Journal of Communication,* vol. 17, no. 3, 283-304.

Chapter 4
Implications for
Commercial Broadcasters

Allan Brown
Griffith Business School, Griffith University

The technical superiority of digital over analogue television broadcasting is widely recognised. Digital is much less susceptible to distortion and atmospheric interference. Digital broadcasters can transmit 'enhanced' programming, that is, additional content relating to a broadcast programme—for example, information concerning a player or choice of camera angles during a sports telecast. There is also far more scope with digital than analogue for on-screen display of programming information (electronic programme guide), and for 'interactivity' between viewers and broadcasters thus allowing the provision of a range of 'interactive' services (see chap. 5). In terms of the structure of the commercial television broadcasting industry, however, the most important feature of digital is that it facilitates the transmission of a much greater number of channels than analogue. This is largely due to the ability to 'compress' the digital signal. As well, for terrestrial transmissions, the spectrum currently used for 'buffer' channels between analogue signals and for 'shadow infill' in areas of hilly terrain is either not required or is greatly reduced. Ongoing developments in compression technologies are likely to increase further the number of channels that can be transmitted by each of the three main digital 'platforms'—satellite, cable and terrestrial.

For European Union (EU) countries the transition from analogue to digital television represents a continuance of the transformation of the industry which has been underway since the 1980s. The past two decades has seen the introduction of commercial satellite and cable television services in Europe, and policy liberalisation in terrestrial broadcasting that has removed the monopolies previously held in many countries by public service broadcasters. The pace of liberalisation has varied from nation to nation, but most have experienced a radical change from zero or very few commercial channels to multiple commercial channels. Citing European Commission figures, Picard (2001) reports that in five years alone, from 1996 to 2000, the total number of television channels rose from 220 to 580, practically entirely all new commercial services.

Another source (BIPE Consulting, 2002) estimates that by 2001 there were more than 600 *digital* channels available across Europe, many of them still also broadcast in analogue. BIPE Consulting points out that, contrary to the history of analogue which was launched and transmitted for a long period solely via terrestrial broadcasting, digital television is now being developed simultaneously over three distribution platforms. This is adding another dimension to competition within the commercial television broadcasting industry across Europe.

The chapter is structured as follows: The next section briefly discusses issues related to the conversion from analogue to digital of the three main television delivery platforms. Then follows an examination of the financial implications, for commercial terrestrial advertiser-supported broadcasters, of the transition from a restricted number of channels with analogue to unrestricted channel numbers made possible by digital. The policy options available to national governments relating to the licensing of digital terrestrial television channels are then set out. The chapter then considers whether or not the switch from analogue to digital television will increase the diversity of ownership within the television broadcasting industry. In the final section the main issues and arguments of the chapter are summarised.[1]

DIGITAL TELEVISION PLATFORMS

Satellite

New equipment is required to send (uplink) digital signals to a satellite, and its transponders need to be converted from analogue to retransmit digital signals. Once a satellite is converted, however, digital signals can immediately be transmitted anywhere in the satellite's 'footprint.' Digital television was introduced to Europe in 1996, firstly via satellite, then by cable and finally through terrestrial broadcasting.[2] At the end of 2002 there was an estimated 32 million digital households in EU countries (around 21 per cent of the total). The overwhelming proportion of these digital households subscribed to a pay-TV service, in two-thirds of cases transmitted by satellite. Most European satellite operators, offering mainly pay-TV channels, had by the end of 2002 turned off their analogue transponders and completed digital switchover. These 'private'

---

[1] The chapter draws heavily from Brown (2003).
[2] The main reason for the relatively late start by terrestrial is that the terrestrial digital broadcasting standard was defined later than that for satellite and cable systems.

analogue turn-offs were undertaken by the satellite operators in the expectation of increasing their ARPU (average revenue per user) and profits from increased channel offerings (BIPE Consulting, 2002).

As explained in chapter 2, a major problem with digital satellite is the incompatibility of set-top boxes (STBs) deployed by rival operators, arising from the failure of the EU regulators to mandate common standards for digital terminals. A major part of the cost of digital conversion for European satellite operators has been the cost to them of providing proprietary digital STBs to subscribers, either free of charge or at heavily subsidised prices, so as to maintain their customer base.

Cable

Whereas the satellite platform allows for the speediest and least expensive conversion to digital, digital broadband cable offers the largest potential bandwidth, the greatest diversity of services and the highest interactive capacity. Digital cable, unlike both satellite and terrestrial, has a 'built-in' back channel capability for two-way (non-telecom) communication between the operator and subscriber. In addition to video services, digital cable operators can offer telephony and Internet access—the so-called 'triple play'.

The major problem with upgrading cable networks to carry digital signals is the very high cost per (potential) subscriber. The same cable can be used for the distribution of both analogue and digital signals, but the central unit at the cable head-end needs to be converted for digital distribution. For interactivity, amplifiers are needed in the coaxial cable, both from the operator to subscriber and from subscriber to operator. Old cable networks need to be upgraded with amplifiers to carry signals from subscribers to the operator (Swedish Radio & Television Authority, 2000).

At the end of 2002, more than 80 per cent of EU cable networks had been upgraded to carry digital. In contrast to satellite broadcasters, however, cable operators have opted to maintain analogue 'simulcasts' on their networks, and only a small proportion of cable subscribers (around 17 percent) are equipped with STBs capable of digital reception.[3] This is because many cable subscribers pay a basic fee for a basic cable service, and are not (yet) prepared to pay more for premium channels. Conversely, operators of digital-ready cable networks consider it economical to provide digital STBs only to pay-TV, high ARPU subscribers, but not to basic subscribers who continue to receive analogue signals. This situation may change in time as the price of digital converters falls,

---

[3] The United Kingdom is the only EU country where a significant proportion of cable subscribers are 'digitised' (see chap. 7).

and if basic cable subscribers are prepared to pay a premium for the additional video and other broadband services on offer (BIPE Consulting, 2002).

Terrestrial

In general terms, digital television via satellite and cable has been driven by commercial forces, whereas digital terrestrial television (DTTV) is driven by government policy. National governments have decided to introduce DTTV for various reasons. They have seen the transition to digital as inevitable, and have considered it advantageous for their broadcasting, programme production and manufacturing industries to make the transition sooner rather than later. Some governments see DTTV as an opportunity to 'democratise' access to multichannel television and to pre-empt further inroads into their markets by foreign owned satellite broadcasters.

In 2001 across all EU countries around 50 per cent of households received television only through terrestrial reception, 30 per cent by cable and 20 per cent through satellite dishes.[4] There is a desire by at least some governments to maintain the prominent role of terrestrial into the digital era. Terrestrial broadcasters operate at the national level, through national facilities, and require licences allocated by national governments to use the radio spectrum. It is thus easier for national governments to regulate the number of terrestrial channels and their programming than those of channels distributed by satellite or cable (BIPE Consulting, 2002).

To provide for DTTV broadcasting existing analogue transmission towers need to be upgraded. Viewers generally do not need to purchase new aerials, but do require a digital STB (unless they have an integrated digital receiver). Digital STBs are relatively easy to install and can be bought off-the-shelf on a 'plug and play' basis. One of the features of DTTV (and digital television transmission generally) is that substantially less power is required, so the energy consumption for each programme service is much lower than for analogue. Similar to satellite, DTTV relies on a telecoms line with a modem to provide for interactivity between viewer and broadcaster.

---

[4] These figures refer to the delivery mechanism for the primary set in the house. Many households using cable or satellite for their primary set use terrestrial reception for their secondary and tertiary sets.

MULTICHANNEL TERRESTRIAL TELEVISION

As already mentioned, a major feature of digital over analogue is its capacity to provide many more channels of programmes within a given amount of broadcast spectrum. Currently, DTTV can offer around five to eight times the number of channels provided on analogue terrestrial. This is still a much smaller number of channels than can be provided on digital satellite or cable. After analogue turn-off, however, and with the use of single frequency instead of multi-frequency networks, it will be theoretically possible to broadcast up to 300 channels via digital terrestrial. This would make DTTV as attractive to viewers in terms of channel supply as satellite or cable (BIPE Consulting, 2002).

Historically, the number of commercial advertiser-supported terrestrial channels has been restricted. Part of the reason for this has been the policy of governments to protect incumbent broadcasters. However, the limited spectrum space available for television broadcasting has imposed severe limitations on the number of analogue channels that could be licensed. DTTV thus provides the potential for the number of commercial channels in any market to be determined by market forces rather than by governments.

Although digital transmissions allow subscriber-supported television (pay-TV) on the terrestrial platform, in this section the analysis is confined to commercial advertiser-supported, free-to-air (FTA) television broadcasting. It considers a hypothetical situation where, with the introduction of DTTV, a government decides to no longer restrict the number of channels, but to allow as many FTA licences to be granted as are applied for by incumbent and new broadcasters. Such an arrangement would have substantial implications for the commercial television broadcasting industry. In general:

- an increase in the number of competing channels would bring about a reduction in the size of the average audience for each programme broadcast;
- as average audience numbers decline, the programming cost per audience member will increase; and
- without a corresponding increase in advertising revenues, the average profit of television channels will be reduced.

These consequences are due to certain features relating to television audiences and the economics of commercial FTA television broadcasting, in particular:

- the overall size of the viewing audience;

- the nature of audience fragmentation with increased channel numbers;
- advertising rates and revenues; and
- programming costs.

Each of these is now considered in turn.

The Size of the Viewing Audience

Unlike many other industries, increased 'supply' of programming from an increased number of television channels is unlikely to bring forth much by way of an increase in 'demand' for those programmes in terms of aggregate viewing time. This is due in part to relative stability in the overall population of most markets, at least in the medium term, and to natural limitations on individuals' viewing time.

Empirical evidence suggests that total viewing time increases only slightly with increased channel numbers. Picard (2001) reports that in EU countries between 1990 and 2000 the number of terrestrial channels rose by a substantial 44 per cent, but that average daily viewing time rose by only 13.7 per cent, a total of 22 minutes for each viewer over the decade (about 2 minutes a year). He concludes (p. 9) that:

... when additional channels are added, it typically does not alter overall audience size and overall demand remains relatively constant. Additionally, time spent on television remains relatively constant in the short term, so providing more channels and hours of programming does not significantly increase consumption of television programming.

Competing claims on viewers' discretionary time from the Internet, interactive services and prerecorded digital video disks may, in the future, further limit the time spent viewing FTA television programmes.

Nature of Audience Fragmentation

A distinction must be made here between national television *networks* and independent non-network channels. Networks act as intermediaries between programme producers (who have programming content to sell), television channels (that seek programming to fill air time), and advertisers (who desire to expose their messages to viewing audiences). Networks have substantial economic advantages over television channels confined to single (or only a few) market areas. The financial advantages of networking include reduced transaction costs in the acquisition and scheduling of programmes, savings to advertisers in the distribution of advertising budgets and, because of simultaneous transmission of programmes to network stations, efficiencies in transmission costs. National television networks are also likely to have a programming 'quality' advantage, as single-market channels will generally be unable to invest the same level of funds in programmes for local transmission as networks can for programmes distributed nationally. Finally, viewers generally favour national (and international) programmes to local programming, especially for entertainment (Owen & Wildman, 1992).

For these reasons it is very difficult for independent single-market channels to set up in competition with incumbent networks. They will be able to do so only in very large markets with one or more minority audience segments that are large enough to support the cost of providing their preferred programmes. An alternative strategy is for new entrants in terrestrial television to try to establish new networks to take advantage of network economies. New networks will have the choice of competing head-to-head with incumbent networks by providing 'all-round' general interest programming, or directing their programming at special interest 'niche' audiences.

Although the advertiser-supported networks face strong competition from satellite and cable pay-TV, within most European national markets they are the dominant force in television broadcasting in terms of audiences, advertising revenue and profitability. With the introduction of digital transmissions they will have strong incumbency advantages over new entrants with programme acquisition experience, as well as established relationships with advertisers and viewers. Many incumbent networks also have a considerable degree of vertical integration in programme production.

There is a tendency for individual viewers to focus most of their viewing on relatively few channels even when multiple channels are available. There is also a bias by viewers in favour of larger channels and against smaller channels: "Smaller channels not only have fewer viewers but also attract less of these viewers' viewing time than the larger channels" (Barwise & Ehrenberg, 1988: 63). There is still strong advertiser demand for the kind of broad appeal programming that only the incumbent advertiser-supported networks can efficiently provide: "... the more the market fragments, the greater the value to advertisers of any outlet that can offer such a mass audience" (Pedder, 2002).

All of this suggests that the incumbent advertiser-supported networks should be able to retain a disproportionate share of the viewing audience after the commencement of new commercial DTTV channels. It is unlikely that most new entrants into advertiser-supported television will compete head-to-head with the existing networks. Instead, they will seek to become niche players in the market by directing their programming toward relatively small, differentiated audience segments whose viewing preferences are not adequately catered for by the existing networks. The strategy of targeting niche audiences will tend to result in *unequal* audience shares between, on the one hand, the existing terrestrial networks with relatively large audiences and, on the other hand, new niche networks and independent channels with smaller audiences.

Advertising Rates and Revenues

The amount of advertising revenue available to television broadcasters will obviously limit the number of commercial FTA channels any market can support. If average advertising rates rise with an increase in channel numbers a market will support a greater number of channels, while if average rates decline, fewer channels will be financially viable. For incumbent channels the rates charged for advertising per audience member will need to increase by the same percentage as the per audience programme costs for channel profitability to be maintained.

It is difficult *a priori* to predict accurately the level of advertising rates and aggregate television advertising revenues with increased channel numbers. Orthodox economic theory suggests that an increase in supply of advertising time will cause the price to fall. However, it may be that with new channels providing special interest programming, advertisers may be prepared to pay premium advertising rates for better targeted, niche audiences. Indeed, there will be a tendency for new broadcasters to identify potential audience segments with above average disposable incomes and/or an interest in specific products that will enhance their value to advertisers. But even if new niche channels could command a higher per viewer rate from advertisers, it seems improbable that *average* advertising rates for all channels would rise at all, let alone significantly. Incumbent channels would face downward pressures on their aggregate advertising revenues because of their declining audience numbers.

It seems more likely that increased channel numbers will cause aggregate advertising revenues to rise, but at a lower rate than the increase in channel numbers. This accords with the recent experience in EU countries. Picard (2001: 14) found that over the 1990s aggregate advertising revenues rose with an increase in channel numbers, but at a lower rate than the rate of channel expansion. This was "... having the effect of reducing income per channel, thus putting significant financial pressures on channels."

Programming Costs

Programming is by far the largest cost component for FTA television broadcasters, usually accounting for well over half of total costs. As with advertising, the effect of increased channel numbers on television programming costs is unclear, with contrary forces operating. The greater demand for programming material resulting from increased channels will tend to raise the cost of programming content. Incumbent channels may also endeavour to minimise their loss of audience share to new entrants by increasing their spending on 'higher quality' programming. At the same time, as average per channel audiences fall the level of programming expenditure that channels can support will also fall.

Programme investment strategies may involve channels endeavouring to maximise audiences during the most profitable 'peak' viewing hours (early evening) and minimise programming costs during off-peak periods. Programming costs can be reduced by an emphasis on lower-cost programme types such as 'talk,' game shows, and 'reality' programmes, and by increased repetition of programmes (Picard, 2001; Owen & Wildman, 1992).

Summary

The above analysis suggests that with an increased number of advertiser-supported channel made possible by the introduction of DTTV the average audience size for programmes and channels will decline; advertising revenue per channel will decline; programme costs per audience member will increase; aggregate advertising revenues will increase, but by a smaller proportion than the rate of increase in channel numbers; and the average profit per channel will decline.

The digital transmission of signals and entry and exit into the industry unimpeded by government regulation would allow the number of commercial FTA television channels in any broadcast area to be determined by market forces. Some channels may incur losses and exit the market, while declining channel profits will tend to deter further entry. The number of channels that can be supported by any given market will depend on various factors. The most important of these is population size. In common with most industries, an advertiser-supported television market with a larger population will generally support more outlets than a smaller market.

The number of channels in any television market will also depend on the nature of the population in that market. It is argued that new channels will tend not to compete directly with established channels, but will seek out profitable audience segments whose programming preferences are not already catered for. By this analysis there will be niche channels for as many audience segments that are large enough to support the cost of providing their preferred programmes.

THE ROLE OF GOVERNMENT

As elsewhere, television broadcasting in Europe is one of the most heavily regulated of all industries. This situation will continue with the transition to digital (see chap. 2). National governments have the responsibility to determine, among other things, the timing of the switch to digital, the means to ensure that viewers can receive terrestrial FTA programming with existing analogue receivers, and arrangements for the eventual 'switch-off' of the analogue transmission system. Most crucially, while digital transmission makes it technically possible to expand greatly the number of terrestrial television channels, the actual number of channels and the number of competing broadcasters will continue to be determined by national governments.

A common strategy adopted to date for the introduction of DTTV has been for national governments to make additional spectrum available to existing analogue broadcasters and require them to 'simulcast' their programming in both analogue and digital during an interim period until such time as the analogue system can be switched off and returned to the government.[5]

Although it is possible for a government to decide on digital conversion for *existing* analogue channels only with no increase in the number of advertiser-supported channels (for example, Australia: see Brown, 2002), this has not so far been the practice in Europe. With the introduction of DTTV, European national governments have decided to increase the number of commercial television channels by means of multiplexing (or 'multichannelling'). As explained in chapter 1, multiplexing is a technical device that allows the broadcast of multiple programmes simultaneously on a single transmission. Different streams of programming are funnelled into a single data stream for transmission, and at the reception end the stream is split back into the original multiple programme streams. Significantly, the various programming streams can be originated by *different broadcasters*.

National governments are faced with a wide range of policy options regarding multiplexing for terrestrial commercial television broadcasting. Considering, firstly, the licensing of advertiser-supported channels (only), a government can decide:

1. to license one or more new advertiser-supported channels to *existing* broadcasters only;

---

[5] Germany and Italy provide exceptions to the simulcast model (see chaps. 13 and 14).

2. to license one or more new advertiser-supported channels to *new* broadcasters only; or
3. to license new advertiser-supported channels to both *existing and new* broadcasters.

Option 1 would impose additional programming costs on incumbent broadcasters who would be likely to set up new niche channels in addition to their established mass audience channels. This would result in some fragmentation of the advertiser-supported audience, but total television advertising revenues would continue to be shared among the incumbent broadcasters. There would be no increased competition from new players. Programming diversity to audiences would be increased, while diversity of broadcast ownership would be unchanged.

Option 2 would represent a greater threat to incumbent broadcasters by allowing the introduction of new advertiser-supported players and increased competition. New channels would result in a diversion of audiences and advertising revenues from the existing broadcasters. With this option both programming diversity and ownership diversity would be increased.

Option 3 is similar to option 2, but also provides for existing broadcasters to be licensed with new channels. For the same number of new channels, this would likely result in a smaller diversion of audience and advertising revenues from the incumbents than option 2.

As mentioned earlier, it is also possible with digital transmission for terrestrial broadcasters to operate pay-TV services. Pay-TV gives a government a further set of policy options in relation to the licensing of new commercial DTTV channels. It can decide:

4. to license one or more pay-TV channels to *existing* broadcasters only;
5. to license one or more pay-TV channels to *new* broadcasters only; or
6. to license pay-TV channels to both *existing and new* broadcasters.

Option 4 would be a means to increase the number of commercial channels in a market with minimum impact on the advertiser-supported television industry and existing broadcasters. This is because terrestrial pay channels can be expected to result in less diversion of audiences and revenues from existing FTA channels than additional advertiser-supported channels. Incumbent commercial broadcasters may also welcome the opportunity to have access to the additional source of revenue provided by pay-TV.[6] Option 5 would introduce

---

[6] Owen and Wildman (1992: 204) suggest that some broadcasters may decide to transmit the *same* programming on pay-TV without advertisements, and on FTA with advertisements.

new players into commercial broadcasting, but would reserve advertiser-supported television for the incumbents. Option 6 incorporates options 4 and 5.

Finally, national governments could decide to issue new DTTV licences for both advertiser-supported *and* pay-TV services. This would give them a further set of options:

7. to license advertiser-supported and pay-TV channels to *existing* broadcasters only;
8. to license advertiser-supported and pay-TV channels to *new* broadcasters only; or
9. to license advertiser-supported and pay-TV channels to both *existing and new* broadcasters.

With option 7, new DTTV licences would be issued only to existing commercial broadcasters, but viewers would have access to new digital FTA and pay channels. Programming diversity would be increased, but diversity of broadcast ownership would be unchanged. Options 8 and 9 represent the most liberal licensing options for DTTV. They would increase both diversity of programming and diversity of broadcasting ownership.

The nine options available to governments for the licensing of new DTTV channels are summarised in Table 4.1.

Table 4.1: Government Policy Options for New Commercial DTTV Channels

Advertiser-Supported Channels Only	Pay-TV Channels Only	Advertiser-Supported and Pay-TV Channels
1. to existing broadcasters only	4. to existing broadcasters only	7. to existing broadcasters only
2. to new broadcasters only	5. to new broadcasters only	8. to new broadcasters only
3. to both existing & new broadcasters	6. to both existing & new broadcasters	9. to both existing & new broadcasters

This discussion of the policy options available to governments presupposes that new digital licences will be issued in the same way as traditionally employed for analogue licences, that is, on a channel-by-channel basis. It is possible, however, for national governments to licence *multiplexes* rather than channels, and for multiplex licensees to operate all channels transmitted on their respective multiplexes. In practice, both methods have been adopted in European countries. DTTV licences have been granted on a channel-by-channel basis in Sweden (chap. 9) and Finland (chap. 10); in the United Kingdom (chap.

7) licences for multiplexes have been granted; and in Spain (chap. 8) both schemes have been implemented, one multiplex licence plus a number of licences for individual channels.

PROLIFERATION OR CONCENTRATION?

It is evident that because digital transmission greatly increases the channel carrying capacity of the spectrum and provides scope for a substantial increase in the number of channels, it has the potential to alter radically the structure and level of competition in terrestrial advertiser-supported television (and pay-TV). This potential has provoked some writers to suggest that digitisation will bring about a large increase in the number of channels and broadcasters. Jones (1998: 526), for example, claims that "... digitisation would allow numerous [commercial] free-to-air networks". Negroponte (1995: 57-58) goes further and argues that "the monolithic empires of mass media are dissolving into an array of cottage industries [and the] media barons of today will be grasping to hold on to their centralized empires tomorrow."

It is not at all clear, however, that this predicted proliferation of new channels and broadcasters will in fact eventuate. The ability of governments to allow the number of commercial television channels to be determined by market forces will not ensure that they will give up their power to restrict channel numbers. National governments will be mindful of the turbulent period incumbent terrestrial broadcasters have experienced in recent years and the competition they face from satellite and cable services. European commercial FTA terrestrial broadcasters have been reluctant adopters of digital, recognising that for them it involves new equipment costs and, particularly, the threat of increased competition. National governments can generally be expected to be cautious in their DTTV licensing decisions and so avoid exposing incumbent commercial terrestrial broadcasters to further severe financial hardships.[7]

Moreover, the examination of the economics of commercial FTA television broadcasting in this chapter suggests that the digitisation of transmissions, even if accompanied by liberalisation of government licensing policy, may not result in a very great increase in the number of new channels, new networks or new broadcasters. As with most industries that experience significant scale economies, advertiser-supported television broadcasting is likely to be a natural

---

[7] This is evident in the licensing decisions in Sweden (chap. 9), Finland (chap. 10), and France (chap. 12), where many of the new DTTV licenses have been granted to incumbent commercial FTA broadcasters.

oligopoly. The inherent competitive advantages of incumbent networks will make it hard for new entrants to become successfully established. As Humphreys and Lang (1998: 31) have commented:

> Digital technology may in theory present the opportunity to target new, smaller niche markets, thus leading to greater choice for the viewer ... In practice, however, economic circumstances will ensure that it will mainly be the established commercial media players which will further consolidate their position in their respective national media markets.

SUMMARY AND CONCLUSIONS

Historically, with analogue terrestrial advertiser-supported television broadcasting the number of channels and broadcasters has been restricted by both a shortage of available broadcast spectrum and protective government licensing policy. A major feature of the transition to digital transmission is that it largely solves the problem of spectrum scarcity. A liberalisation of television licensing policy by governments would therefore allow the number of channels and broadcasters to be determined by market forces.

Some scholars have claimed that digital transmission will result in a proliferation in the number of channels and broadcasters, and a diminution in the role of the incumbent commercial television networks. This chapter argues that neither of these outcomes is probable. The number of new channels licensed will continue to be subject to government regulatory decisions, and even with liberalisation of licensing policy, the economics of advertiser-supported television broadcasting will impose severe limitations on the number of new channels that any market can support.

For the foreseeable future advertiser-supported television will continue to be dominated by the existing national commercial networks providing programming to mass audiences. DTTV may allow the establishment of niche audience channels, the number depending on the population size and characteristics of broadcasting markets in different European countries. Where incumbent FTA networks are granted multiple new DTTV licences they will be likely themselves to operate niche channels, thus narrowing the scope for entry by new competitors.

Digital technology facilitates the provision of pay-TV services by DTTV. This may divert some of the audience from advertiser-supported television as well as intensify competition among the various transmission platforms — terrestrial, cable, and satellite. Digital also allows broadcasters to provide interactive television services. These potentially provide a new revenue source for commercial television broadcasters, but it is not yet clear there will be sufficient consumer demand for these services to make them profitable.

The transition from analogue to digital transmission is the major development in broadcasting since the commencement of television half a century ago. It will have wide-ranging effects on commercial television *viewing*, but probably not on the structure and ownership of the commercial television broadcasting industry. The switch to digital will not alter the fundamental economic characteristics of advertiser-supported television broadcasting, which is likely to remain a natural oligopoly.

REFERENCES

Barwise, Patrick & Andrew Ehrenberg, 1988. *Television and its Audience*, Sage Publications, Newbury Park, California.

BIPE Consulting, 2002. *Digital Switchover in Broadcasting: Final Report*, http://Europa.eu.int/information_society/topics/telecoms/regulatory/studies/docu ments/final_report_120402.pdf (accessed 24.07.02).

Brown, Allan, 2002. From analogue to digital television broadcasting: A case study of Australia and Australian firm experiences, pp. 27-39 in Robert G. Picard (Ed.), *Media Firms: Structures, Operations, and Performance*, Lawrence Erlbaum Associates, Mahwah, New Jersey.

Brown, Allan, 2003. The digital future of terrestrial advertiser-supported television, *Prometheus*, vol. 21, no. 1, 41-57.

Humphreys, Peter & Matthias Lang, 1998. Digital television between the economy and pluralism, pp. 9-35 in Jeanette Steemers (Ed.), *Changing Channels: The Prospects for Television in a Digital World*, Luton University Press.

Jones, Ross, 1998. Australia's digital TV giveaway, *Agenda*, vol. 5, no. 4.

Negroponte, Nicholas, 1995. *Being Digital*, Hodder, Sydney.

Owen, Bruce M. & Steven S. Wildman, 1992. *Video Economics*, Harvard University Press, Cambridge, Massachusetts.

Pedder, Sophie, 2002. Power in your hand, *The Economist*, 11 April, on-line version, www.economist.com (accessed 01.05.02).

Picard, Robert G., 2001. Expansion and limits in EU television markets: audience, advertising and competition issues, Turku School of Economics and Business Administration, Discussion Paper C2.

Swedish Radio & Television Authority, 2000. *A Guide to Digital Television*, Haninge

Chapter 5
Interactive Content, Applications, and Services

Jens F. Jensen

Aalborg University

An aura of magic and mysterious power seems to surround the concept of 'content.' Media publishers, software companies, telecommunications companies, and film and television industries are pursuing 'content' as the Holy Grail of the information age. Everyone wants to team up with the 'content owners' – the copyright holders of the big media archives and libraries. And, at the many conferences, trade shows and seminars around the world dealing with new media technology, the saying "Content is King!" has already become a cliché.

If 'content' as a concept is endowed with magic, the concept of 'interactive content' is even more magical. 'Interactive media' are grabbing the headlines and there is no limit to the hype. 'Interactive content' has become the more or less authoritative and official gospel in the converging industries. 'Interactivity,' so the story goes, will put the world at your fingertips; 'interactivity' will transform what used to be boring, passive experiences into something much more full, vivid and engaging. 'Interactivity' will give birth to a new epoch in commerce, entertainment, education, and forever change the ways you shop, play, and learn. The ultimate promise of 'interactive content' is, just to quote one example (Kantrowitz et al, 1993):

A huge amount of information available to anyone at the touch of a button, everything from airline schedules to esoteric scientific journals to video versions of off-off-off Broadway. Watching a movie won't be a passive experience. At various points, you'll click on alternative story lines and create your individualized version of *Terminator XII*. Consumers will send as well as receive all kinds of data. Say you shoot a video that you think is particularly artsy. Beam it out and make a small fortune by charging an untold number of viewers a fee for watching. ... Video-camera owners could record news they see and put it on the universal network. On the receiving end, the era of the no-brainer will have finally arrived. An electronic device called an 'intelligent agent' would be programmed to know each viewer's preferences and make selections from the endless stream of data. Viewers could select whatever they wanted just by pushing a button ... Instead of playing rented tapes on their VCRs, they may be able to call up a movie from a library of thousands through a menu displayed on the TV. Game fanatics may be able to do the same from another electronic library filled with realistic video versions of arcade shoot 'em-ups'... at-home shoppers may watch video catalogues with models demonstrating front and rear views of the latest gear. Some cable companies are also testing other interactive models that allow viewers to choose their own news or select camera angles for sporting events.

This is the utopian vision of the brave new world of interactive television and new media.

Although the potential of 'interactivity' is widely recognised, and despite the fact that 'interactive content' and 'interactive applications' have been subject to this kind of hype and media attention, it has received remarkably little attention within the research community. The concept of 'interactivity' remains poorly defined (Jensen, 1998; 1999a; 1999b; 2001) and 'interactive content' as a product and as a business is still not well understood. Interactivity, interactive content, and applications are clearly areas in need of theoretical and analytical work.

The aim of this chapter is to introduce and discuss some of the main issues associated with interactive content, applications and services in the context of interactive digital television (iDTV). First, the concept of interactive television (iTV) will be described and defined. Second, a set of new categorisations or typologies of iTV applications will be presented. And thirdly, the suite of interactive application and services that currently constitutes iTV will be introduced and discussed.

BASIC DEFINITIONS

Television is one of the most successful technological consumer products ever produced and has spread to virtually every household in Western society. Television sets are often located in a central part of the main living room. Television viewing is a dominant part of most people's leisure activities and daily lives, and, for many, television has become their most important source of information and entertainment. To say that television has a central place in our culture, or that television over the past decades has thoroughly changed our society and our daily lives is, therefore, an understatement that barely begins to describe reality.

Television, however, is not a static medium, neither as a technology nor as a service. Game consoles, video cassette recorders (VCRs), cable, and satellite systems have already begun to change the image of what television is and what it can be as a medium. In the years ahead, television faces even more radical developments and changes. Terms like interactivity, digitisation, convergence, integrated full service networks, content-on-demand, two-way cables, direct broadcast satellites, the mixture of televisions and computers, of broadcast and Internet etc. point out some of the aspects involved in this process of change. Briefly, what is at stake here is the delivery of iDTV services to the home.

But what is 'interactive digital television' anyway? The first problem in describing iDTV is the abundance of differing concepts and understandings currently in circulation. The various industrial players in the iDTV field – cable operators, telcos, computer companies, broadcast networks, movie studios, etc. – all seem to have different notions of the concept of iTV as a technology. Furthermore, the players have differing philosophies about what interactivity is and what it means to 'interact' with television, as well as varying perspectives on what services and content the consumer will want and be willing to pay for. As a result, during the past decades a broad spectrum of content, services and applications has laid claim to the terms 'interactive' or 'digital television.' Some of them include: Multi-channel systems with several hundreds of channels to select from; on-demand access to movies, videos, news, sports; customisation of and control over content; interactive news; local storage of programming; real time interaction and communication between users of the system, such as text messaging, voice telephony or video phone; access to database and online information; voting in (real-time) opinion polls; control over choice of camera angles in the transmission of sports events and the like; interactive games based on stand alone or networked applications; participation in game shows; user created content; electronic town meetings, etc. As should be apparent, iTV is many different things, just as the degree of interactivity varies widely.

An analysis from eMarketer (Macklin, 2002) points out that one of the main reasons why iTV has not been adopted as fast as some marketers may have hoped, and some experts have predicted, is exactly because there is a great deal of confusion about what iTV is in the first place. When viewers and consumers cannot even define and understand the concept of iTV, why should they demand it? eMarketer presents the following fictive dialogue between a consumer and an iTV expert, which in an ironic mode highlights the challenges in explaining the concept of iTV to the ordinary consumer.

Table 5.1: The Mystery of iTV

Consumer	iTV Expert
Is it the Internet on TV?	It can be, sort of.
You can change camera angles while watching the football, right?	Sometimes.
Is it video-on-demand?	Yes, and no.
You can do e-mail and instant messaging on the TV?	Maybe.
Is it like having multi-screens on your TV and being able to 'click onto' some parts of it to get information?	It can be.
Is it playing games and shopping on the TV?	If you like.
It is like a new program guide where you can set preferences and record shows and fast forward ads?	Yes, but ...
What has a garden got to do with it, and who put the wall around it?	Ummm....

Source: Macklin (2002: 4).

Among the variety of challenges confronting iDTV, one of the most urgent is therefore to educate media consumers about what iDTV is, and what kinds of content, services and applications it currently offers and may carry in the future. The following is an attempt at working definitions of the concepts of 'interactive television' and 'digital television', as well as of concepts such as 'content' and 'interactivity'.

'Content' as a concept refers to the media material available to the consumer via the media system, that is, information, entertainment, services, etc. On the one hand, this consists of the audio-visual material that characterises the interface or programme, and on the other hand, the interaction design. In other words, 'content' is what the user of a media system actually accesses, uses, or consumes. In the specific context of this chapter the terms content, application, service, and programme will be used more or less synonymously.

'Content' has established itself as a sort of 'compromise term' among the very different industries involved in the new media technologies, covering the media material that appears on the consumer's screen. Thus, it seems as if the converging industries are converting all the creative people – directors, programmers, writers, musicians, artists, producers, etc. – into 'content producers'; and consequently all the individual industries – broadcasters, publishers, film studios, computer companies, telcos, software houses, entertainment companies, and even the users – into 'content' providers (Van Tassel, 1996).

As already indicated, one of the most significant and unique features of new media, compared to the old, is their interactive character. 'Interactivity' in this context signifies the active participation of the user in directing the flow of content. Consequently, interactive content designates content types that exchange information with the user, that is, in addition to conventional media's output to the user, this type of content allows various kinds and amounts of input from the user to the media system, which can significantly influence the form, order, length, or structure of the message – the content of the media text (Jensen, 1998; 1999a; 1999b; 2001).

Media researchers, especially those from reception research, media ethnography, and media and cultural studies, have in recent years denied the perception of television as a passive medium and have instead pointed out that the viewer's reading of television texts is always active (and interactive). Practically and technically, however, traditional television claims very little activity from the users. Naturally, the viewers decide what to watch, just as they must cognitively and socially deal with, interpret, and make sense of what they watch on the screen. But apart from this, strictly speaking, the only physical requirements involve turning on the set, (perhaps) changing the channel, and turning it off again (and on the odd occasion making small adjustments to the sound and picture).

In a negatively defined demarcation, iTV can be understood as television which, aside from the traditional turn-on-zap-and-turn-off interaction, and cognitive (and social) interaction between the presented text and the viewer's ability to make sense of what is seen – that is, the purely interpretative interaction – also relies on an actual, physical interaction in the form of choices, decisions and communicative input to the system. In a shorter, more positive version iTV can be considered a new form of television that makes it possible for the viewer to interact with the medium in such a way that he gains control over what to watch, when to watch, and how to watch, or directly opens up for active participation in a programme.

Understood in this way, iTV can be considered a fairly broadly defined concept. The organising committee for a 1996 world conference on interactive television, *The Superhighway Through the Home?*, used the term 'interactive television':

> rhetorically to suggest the provision of interactive multimedia services to domestic spaces. At its most general this can mean services accessed through a variety of platforms and infrastructures. At its most specific it relates to services and content specifically designed to be used through television, relating strongly in appearance with broadcast style displays and

presentation and even co-existing and augmenting existing broadcast programming.

Correspondingly, the *Interactive TV News* website (no longer available) defined the term 'interactive television' as:

> the meeting of television with new interactive technology. ITV is domestic television with interactive facilities usually facilitated through a 'back channel' and/or an advanced terminal. Equally important, interactive television is content that users and viewers can interact with via the technical system ... There are many delivery systems, technical standards, possible uses and content. These range from the WWW to home shopping, Digital Video Broadcasting to Internet, movies on demand to video telephony. The unifying factor is that television is central to the entertainment, education, information, leisure and social life of millions of homes all over the world.

In other words, iTV can be defined as interactive services designed for the television, that is, traditional television broadcast combined and coupled with enhancements and extensions, that provide viewers with the opportunity to participate in and interact with the content.

There is no necessary correlation between interactive television and digital television (DTV), except for the fact that interactive television services have been available for many years over analogue television signals. To mention but two obvious examples, European teletext services have been around for over 20 years and Two Way TV offered analogue interactive gaming services in the United Kingdom as early as 1996. So then what, exactly, is digital television as opposed to interactive television? DTV is first and foremost a technical term that refers to the transition of formerly analogue television technologies to digital technologies. This provides better picture and sound quality and more channels to choose from due to technological and cost-effective advantages (see chap. 1). However, except for the fact that the possibility of broadcasting digital data alongside traditional television picture and programming enables a range of new interactive features, the digitisation of television also, to a considerable degree, expands the potential for interactive services on the television. Thus, with the growing demand for DTV in Europe and around the world, an increasing number of iTV applications are also emerging.

Although iTV over the past two or three decades has been subject to several false starts, many analysts and observers expect that interactive digital television will experience a breakthrough in the near future. Jim Stroud of The Carmel Group, to mention but one example, gives the following outline of the iTV viewing (r)evolution over the next couple of years.

Table 5.2: The iTV Viewing (Re)volution

	1930-2000	**2001-2005**	**2005-?**
Viewing pattern	passive viewing	passive/interactive viewing	interactive viewing
Programming	Operator based programming	operator based programming	user driven programming
Form of advertising	shotgun advertising	targeted advertising	customised advertising
Interaction style	lean back style	lean up style	lean forward style
Channels	basic/premium channels	basic/premium/video-on-demand channels	premium channels
Applications/ services	basic programme guide	advanced programme guide Internet connectivity hard drive capability home network	entertainment on demand hi-speed fibre net connectivity hard drive standard capability video telephony standard capability home network standard capability

Source: Stroud, 2001.

Several of these applications and services are discussed next.. The interactive and digital aspects raise a number of questions having to do with the technology, but they also raise questions relating to the users and the content. New communication technologies and media always make new types of communication possible – new content, new applications, new services. So, obviously, new technologies, interactivity, and the new convergence of media will naturally change the premises for *how content* can be made available and *for the kinds of content* that can be made available. Furthermore, each of the multitudinous new technologies will produce its own language, and each will colour content in its own way.

The questions then arise: What differences will these new technologies make in terms of content, applications and services? What will digitisation, convergence, and interactivity, etc. mean with respect to the kinds of services that can be offered? How can interactivity enhance or change current entertainment and information programmes? Can interactivity, for example, increase the massive cultural and commercial success which traditional broadcasting has already achieved? And what, exactly, is novel, entertaining, and informative about interactivity and interactive content? Do average viewers actually want interactive media and services, and to what extent will they be willing to pay for them?

The complex and many-sided processes of change that the television medium is currently involved in thus create a whirlwind of questions. The following discussion outlines only a handful of them, with special reference to interactive content, applications and services.

TYPOLOGIES OF INTERACTIVE CONTENT, APPLICATIONS, AND SERVICES

This radical transformation of television as a medium and the extreme complexity of the new applications and services supported by iTV necessitates, among other things, new typologies or classifications of information services that can provide us with a general view of the modes of communication in the new media form. The purpose of this section is to give a short sketch of such cognitive or conceptual maps of interactive content, applications, and services.

There have been numerous attempts to categorise and typologise new communication and media technologies. The most common classifications have been based on application domains or types of content. So far, in the context of iDTV, developers and analysts have recognised the following types of content:

- information (emergency service, tourist information, local government information, customised electronic newspapers, database access, library, and electronic guides);
- navigation (electronic programming guides, search engines);
- entertainment (broadcast television and radio, video-on-demand (VOD), near-video-on-demand (NVOD), music-on-demand, etc.);
- transactions (Electronic High Street: travel, real estate agents, banking, financial services, electronic commerce, home shopping);
- commercials (Adland: electronic catalogues, electronic yellow pages, product information);
- games (games-on-demand, downloadable games, multi-player network games, play-along, and pay-per-play);
- education (tele-learning, libraries, help with homework);
- tele-working (tele-commuting, SOHO: Small Office/Home Office, computer-supported co-operative work, groupware);
- communication services (e-mail, voice and video telephony, video conferencing);
- Internet connectivity (Web@TV, webcasting);

- communities (chat, news groups, dating services, inhabited virtual worlds);
- social services (health care information, tele-consulting, health care requests or prescription ordering);
- control and security (meter reading, domestic appliances, theft prevention).

These types of content make up the suite of iDTV elements. However, the above categorisations are more or less adapted from traditional content genres in ordinary non-interactive television and media and they do not illuminate the specific and significant features of interactive content.

But there are numerous other typologies, which are not based on elementary non-interactive content types. Other common classifications have been based on technological characteristics, forms of representation, or information and media types (see e.g., Jeffcoate, 1995; Purchase, 1998; 1999). However, as different media technologies merge in digitisation and media convergence, classification based on technological criteria becomes increasingly less distinctive; as different forms of information types melt together into multimedia, classifications based on forms of representation become increasingly less revealing; and as various content melts with multi-functional networks, classification based on content or service types become increasingly less instructive or satisfying. They simply do not seem to catch the significant features in new media development and the significant differences in the new services. Therefore, interactive digital media often require their own particular conceptualisations, classification format, and typologies.

Some of the new typologies are based on information traffic patterns. According to Vinay Kumar (1996), information access and distribution mechanisms can basically be divided into two models:

- *the information source comes to you*, and
- *you go to the information source*.

In *the information source comes to you* model, information and entertainment are beamed to consumers. Consequently, consumers "… do not have to try hard (with the exception of changing channels) to access the information – the information is delivered directly to the home (or is it the couch?)" (Kumar, 1996: 29). Typical examples would of course be terrestrial broadcast, cable television, or satellite broadcast. In the *you go to the information source* model, the initiative and the responsibility for finding and accessing the information is located at the consumer end of the creator/consumer opposition. The creators of the information just wait for consumers to request or access the desired information. Typical examples of this model would be the world wide web (WWW), magazines, and bookstores.

In recent years, these information traffic patterns have frequently been described in terms of the buzzwords: *'push media'* and *'pull media.'* Kelly et al. (1997) describe *push media*, typical examples of which are radio, television and film, as follows: "Content is pushed to you ... Push media arrive automatically – on your desktop, in your e-mail, via your pager ... The distinguishing characteristic of the new push media is that it finds you, rather than you finding it. That means the content knows where you are and what you are seeing" (1997: 14, 23). These media correspond in many ways to the information traffic pattern, which Kumar calls *the information source comes to you. Pull media*, on the other hand, get their name from "the invitational pull you make when you click on the Web" (1997: 14). In other words, *pull media* are media that you (interactively) steer. In many respects, they correspond to what Kumar terms *you go to the information source.*

A similar, but slightly more complicated and sophisticated way of classifying interactive content and services, is the media typology originally developed by Bordewijk and Kaam (1986; see also Jensen, 1996, 1999a, 1999b, 2001). The distinctive mark of this typology is that it is defined independently of the technical design of the media, the form of presentation, and the content of information, and is instead based on social power relations and power positions, which constitute different 'communication patterns' or 'information traffic patterns'. These patterns are described here in relation to who delivers the information and who controls the access to and use of the information (where the latter primarily refers to the choice of the content of information as well as the time that it is to be received). By cross-tabulating these two aspects in relation to whether ownership and selection are performed by a centralised information source or by a decentralised information user, Bordewijk and Kaam arrive at a four-field matrix of fundamentally distinct media, or as they are called, 'idealized information traffic patterns' (see table 5.3):

- *transmission*: If the information content is produced and owned by a central information provider and this centre also controls the selection of and time for the information content distributed to the information user, we have a case of transmission. Typical examples of the transmission pattern are, of course, classical broadcast media such as television and radio, where the principal mode of use is relatively passive reception. In other words, this is the type of communication which has often been labelled as one-way communication, one-to-many communication, mass communication, or mass media. This corresponds to Kumar's *the information source comes to you* model and to the concept of *push media*.

- *consultation*: If the information content is produced and owned by a central information provider, but the individual information user controls which information content is delivered and when, we have a case of consultation. In this case, the information centre delivers only information on demand from the individual information user and the information user receives only that information content which has been requested, at the time that it is requested. The characteristic mode of behaviour on the part of the user is active choice among several alternatives. Exemplary representatives of consultation media can be found in various forms of on-demand services, on-line information resources, WWW, electronic memories such as electronic reference works on CD-ROMs or online databases. This corresponds to Kumar's *you go to the information source* model, or the concept of *pull media*.

- *conversation*: If the information content is produced and owned by an individual information user, and if control of the means of distribution and handling of the information content also lies with the user, we have a case of conversation. In this instance, the information flows both ways between individual information users. Prototypical examples of this communication pattern are therefore the telephone, e-mail, fax and letters. In other words, this is the type of communication that is often labelled one-to-one communication (or many-to-many communication), conversation, dialogue, etc.

- *registration*: Finally, if the information content is produced by an individual information user, but the actual use of the information content is handled and controlled by a central information service, we have a case of registration. Here it is no longer the centre's job to transmit information, but to collect it. In this case, the information collected can in turn be treated, calculated, (re)arranged, etc. by the centre. This pattern type could be called many-to-one communication. Examples of registration media are: opinion polling, television monitoring, electronic surveillance system, registration system, but also various kinds of adaptive media, programmable software agents, intelligent interfaces, personalised and customised services. (For a full account of Bordewijk and Kaam's media typology and an elaboration of their matrix see Jensen, 1996; 1998; 1999a; 1999b; 2001).

Table 5.3: Matrix for the Four Information Traffic Patterns

	Information content issued by centre	Information content issued by user
Content controlled by centre	transmission	registration
Content controlled by user	consultation	conversation

Table 5.4: Matrix with Examples of Services and Content as Prototypical Representatives of the Various Information Traffic Patterns

	Information content issued by centre	Information content issued by user
Content controlled by centre	broadcast television and radio, MBone / multicasting, push media	home shopping & banking, ticketing, voting, polling, security systems
Content controlled by user	content-on-demand: (VOD, NVOD, music-on-demand, news-on-demand, etc.), pull media, WWW	e-mail, videophone & -conference, IRC, MUDs, online games, 3D-virtual worlds

Table 5.4 indicates some examples of content, applications and services within the two-dimensional matrix and its four information traffic patterns. As should be clear, this typology can be used for significant categorisation and meaningful description of various forms of iDTV services, using the information pattern that the specific service is primarily based on, as illustrated in Table 5.3.

If you consider the actual and future trends of television's development from the perspective of the matrix, they are best described as a relative movement from the top left position towards the other positions, that is, from the traditional transmission information pattern toward the consultation, registration, and conversation patterns. So, one way to conceptualise and describe interactive television is as the television medium's transformation from a solely transmitting medium to a complex transmission, consultation, registration, and perhaps even conversation medium.

Another alternative way of classifying interactive content, applications and services (somewhat similar to that just mentioned) is the media typology developed by Joan M. Van Tassel. Van Tassel (1996) points out four types of content based on discrimination criteria such as transient versus permanent and pre-packaged versus user-created:

- *pre-packaged evergreen:* Pre-packaged content is text, graphics, audio, video, etc. that users may access. If the material is relatively permanent, it is called 'evergreen,' meaning it will be of common interest over some length of time;

- *pre-packaged transient:* If pre-packaged material is replaced regularly, for example each week, it is called 'pre-package transient;'
- *user-created added data:* If the pre-packaged content is structured in a way so that the users can add to the material and thereby create a user-based database it is called 'user-created added data;'
- *user-created content:* If the content is created entirely by users, as for example in online 'chat rooms' or telephone conversations, it is called 'user-created content.'

These criteria and categories can be elaborated in a matrix as shown in Table 5.5 below.

Table 5.5: Matrix Based on Van Tassel's Typology

	Pre-packaged	User created
Evergreen	classical film	user reviews
Transient	news, weather forecasts	chat rooms, telephone, etc.

Finally, Interactive Television International (iTVi) has proposed a set of new definitions of interactive television content, allegedly with the view of harmonising the various circulating definitions and thereby helping the world-wide dialogue. ITVi proposes a classification of iTV content in four categories:

- *Category 1: television programmes that are not modified by the interactivity.* This category comprises all television programmes where the interactive elements run parallel to the show but does not influence any of the content of the programme, for example, because the programmes are taped. Examples are television shows with a web site running in parallel during the broadcast or later, such as *Who Wants to be a Millionaire?* with its web site. In this case, the web site can supply more information, initiate sales, contests, or present other shows.
- *Category 2: television programmes that are modified by the interactivity.* This category consists of live shows where the anchor or the participants can receive input from the viewers and interact with their messages. The concept is in no way new but widely used by radio programmes with call-ins. Typical examples in the television context are television games where answers can be supplied live by the viewers, reality shows or contests such as *Big Brother* where viewers decide the fate of the candidates, or *Hugo the Troll* where selected

viewers play a video game live on the screen by pushing the keys of their telephone keypad. Often the interactive device is simply the telephone used as a regular calling instrument or the back channel takes the form of a short message service (SMS), e-mails, or a dedicated web site. In some cases, television shows use what might be termed 'delayed interactivity,' that is, viewers interact with the show but there is a delay between the viewers' input and the effect on the show.

- *Category 3: television programmes assembled by the viewer from several broadcast signals.* In this category the content is transmitted by the broadcaster, but the viewer makes the choices to select some of the content elements and reassemble them as he or she wishes. As can be seen, this category has some affinity to the concept of 'personalisation' (see below). Examples are 'be your own editor' or 'choose your own camera angle' in sports events, interactive fiction using several channels etc.
- *Category 4: interactive services that can eventually become television shows.* This (rather odd) category covers various services offered on television, which at the moment cannot be called television shows, but in iTV might appear more and more like television programmes to many viewers and eventually be transformed into television shows. Examples are weather reports, traffic information, stock quotes, betting information, and personalised services.

INTERACTIVE TV CONTENT, APPLICATIONS, AND SERVICES

Although the terms interactive television and digital television today cover a wide range of content, applications and services, it is possible to group the variety of interactive television elements into a number of major categories or interactive genres. The next section of this chapter is a brief overview of different types of iDTV applications, reflected through some of the typologies mentioned earlier. The issues dealt with include electronic programme guides (EPGs), Enhanced TV, content-on-demand, Personalised TV, Internet@TV, interactive advertising, t-commerce, games and betting, cross media consumption, and SMS TV. This group of applications, services and content types currently makes up the suite of iDTV categories. Thus, in a more concrete way, iDTV can be defined as one, or a combination, of these iDTV elements.

Electronic Programme Guides

As channel choices in cable television and satellite television expand to literally hundreds of channels, surfing or zapping as the dominant way of navigating and accessing content – not to mention reading print based television guides – will become unmanageable. With, for example, 500 channels on a cable system, a complete 'channel surf' using the remote control would take so long (even just stopping to see a few seconds of each cablecast channel) that most of the scanned programmes would be over before the entire system is checked. In principle, the viewer could then start from the beginning and spend his or her entire time in front of the television just zapping. Therefore, viewers will demand more comfortable, effective and sophisticated navigation tools and interfaces to the television content. These new interfaces and navigation tools are often called electronic programme guides (or interchangeably interactive programme guides, iPGs).

EPGs are onscreen programme guides, that is, new computer based techniques or advanced interfaces that use various menus and quick scanning of current and upcoming programmes to aid navigation through the channels and to identify content that the viewer may want to see. EPGs thus allow the viewer to get a set of programme listings on their screen searched and organised by time, channel, category, genre, topic, actors, etc., or view a description of the individual programme, for example, by activating the programme name on the screen, and in that way navigate through the content using their remote controls.

An advanced EPG may contain:

- *search engines* that support interactive searches to explore more detailed programme information in a reservoir of deep, searchable content;
- *reminders* that prompt the viewer when favourite programmes are on;
- *automatic recordings* that automatically record previously selected choices;
- *customisation facilities* including customised 'homepages' for individual family members; and
- *intelligent personal agents*, that is, software with pre-programmed guidelines, that regularly checks for certain types of programmes or registers and 'remembers' a viewer's preferences, so that it can point out when and where something of probable interest will turn up and alternatively exclude channels or programmes that the particular viewer never watches.

The EPG has the potential to become something of a web portal on television. It is also likely that advertising and even commerce will be conducted via the EPG so a substantial part of the iTV advertising revenue will come from the EPG (see below). All in all, EPGs strengthen the consultation aspects (navigation, search) and the registration aspects (intelligent agent etc.) of the television media.

Enhanced TV

Enhanced TV refers to any type of content – whether it be text, graphics, or video – which is overlaid on regularly displayed video content and is accessed interactively. Hence, enhanced TV may also be conceived as a refined tele-text service, a sort of super-text television. The enhanced content may be synchronised with the programme stream, so that viewers can access data during the programme or at different points in the programming, or it may be available on demand from the consumer independent of the given programme. Enhanced content linked with the programme stream might typically include statistics in sports programming, or information about favourite actors in television shows and films. Enhanced content independent of the programme includes services such as weather reports, up-to-date news bulletins and interactive product catalogues. This corresponds to iTV's category 4 above, *interactive services that can eventually become television shows*. Similarly, enhanced TV may either be based on so-called local interactivity, that is, interaction between the viewer and content downloaded to the individual set-top box or based on user requests through a return channel (Macklin, 2002). In both cases the viewer simply browses the desired information, possibly displayed along with the programme.

Recent examples of enhanced TV include *Big Brother* (where viewers can link directly from the show to enhancements associated with the programme, viewing additional content and information) and *Wimbledon 2003* (where BBC viewers could choose between individual games and multiple camera angles as well as statistics and results). In these cases enhanced TV has leveraged existing entertainment formats and values of traditional broadcast and extended them further.

Content-on-Demand

The media of yesterday were based almost without exception on the transmission pattern, that is, in Kumar's terms, *the information source comes to you* model. Among the four information traffic patterns enumerated in Bordewijk and Kaam's (1986) media matrix, this is the only one that does not have a return or back-channel that makes an information flow possible from the information user to the media system. However, current media developments including the arrival of new media such as iTV have been more or less singularly characterised by a movement away from the transmission pattern toward the three other media patterns, especially toward the consultation pattern. The media of tomorrow will thus most likely have much more to do with consultation, that is, requests, content-on-demand, or *you go to the information source* models. There are several different types of content-on-demand systems as well as genres.

Concerning the information traffic patterns of content-on-demand systems there is a decisive difference between *video-on-demand* and *near-video-on-demand* systems. *Video-on-demand* (also *called true video-on-demand* or *movies-on-demand*) is the reception of content according to individual orders, which enables television viewers to access video content whenever they wish. In this case, the content is delivered directly to each individual home without a wait. Hence, this type of service corresponds to Kumar's *you go to the information* model and Bordewijk and Kaam's request or consultation pattern. *Near-video-on-demand* (or *multicasting*), on the other hand, is the continuous transmission of the same programme, for example, a movie on multiple channels at alternative time slots, so that the individual viewer only has to wait a short time (thus the name 'near') between ordering the programme and receiving it on the home television set. If, for example, a 100-minutes long movie is aired at staggered times by ten channels the viewer would end up waiting a maximum of ten minutes from the time the movie is ordered until it is delivered. In services of this type, you might say that television as a transmitting medium is actually used consultatively. In reality *the information source comes to you* – the signals are in the air (or in the cables) all the time – but the user will experience it as if he requests the information, that is, according to the *you go to the information source* model.

Likewise, content-on-demand covers a wide range of content types or genres. Most often the programmes are movies. In this case, the service can be considered a network version of video rental or sales. Similar services can be found in the music field, that is, *music-on-demand*. In the same way, *news-on-demand* is a news service, which is updated continuously, where the consumer interactively selects and retrieves news items and may even choose the level of detail and type of presentation (text, graphics, narration, photos, or video). Parallel services can also be found for sports (*sports-on-demand*), weather etc. Finally, *games-on-demand* is the network distribution of video, television or computer games (replacing diskettes, cartridges, and CD-ROMs), where the consumer either downloads the desired game from a cable network to a computer, game machine or set-top box, and is given online access to the game on a pay-per-play basis, or is able to compete against other players connected to the network (see below).

Personalised TV

The new interactive media not only represent a shift in information traffic patterns from transmission to consultation, from *the information source comes to you* model to the *you go to the information source* model, or from *push media* to *pull media*; they also mean new combinations and the convergence of familiar patterns. One of the groups of applications or interactive genres that can be conceptualised as a combination or convergence of traffic patterns is personalised TV.

Personalised, customised, or individualised TV takes on many forms. In its most simple model, personalised TV is television with Personal Video Recorder (PVR) – interchangeably called Digital Video Recorder (DVR) – functionality. This functionality can come from a 'stand alone' PVR device such as TiVo or Replay TV, or it can be contained within a digital set-top box. With full PVR functionality the user can pause during a broadcast as content is cached on the disk and take up viewing later. Likewise, PVR functions enable the user to rewind and fast-forward television content using the remote control. In this way, viewers can time shift the broadcast during a sports event to see a goal again, skip over commercials and so on. A PVR can also be programmed to automatically record episodes and programmes by title, timeslot, actor, theme, rating etc., and even adjust to changes in the schedule. Thus PVRs empower viewers to watch what they want, when they want.

Other versions of personalised TV allow users to modify a programme such as calling up instant replays in sports and live news, guiding the plot in dramas or comedies, or choosing their own camera angels in a sports event (Macklin, 2002). This last kind of service, *be your own editor* or *choose your own camera angle*, is based on the principle that the same event, for example, a live transmission of a sports event, is transmitted on several parallel channels where each channel represents a certain camera angle. This way the viewer can 'zap' from channel to channel and 'edit' his own coverage of the event. So again, this is a service of the 'push' type – the information actually comes to you – that from the user's point of view is experienced as a pull-service, you choose which information you want to receive.

On a more general level, personalisation and customisation can be conceived as ways of managing information. Both relate to the information traffic pattern Bordewijk & Kaam call *registration*, that is, they are both based on the media system's registration of the individual user's choice, behaviour or preferences. However, there is a significant difference concerning the *location* of the agency of this registration.

Personalisation is driven by the media system, which tries to serve up individualised information to the user based on some model of that user's need. This form is also called adaptation or adaptive systems, that is, systems and interfaces that seem intelligently to adapt themselves to the user by noticing patterns of interaction or responding to user idiosyncrasies or desires according to expectations. Thus, personalisation requires the system to have some sort of information about the user. This form of service can be conceptualised as the combination of registration and transmission.

Customisation is driven by the user, that is, is under direct user control. The user explicitly selects from certain options and thereby tailors the information. An example is the setting up of a personal television home page on an EPG service that presents the user with a set of favourites, a variety of options or preferences concerning topics of interest, news channel, etc. This service can therefore, in contrast to personalisation, be conceptualised as a combination of consultation, registration and transmission.

Personalised or customised TV is thus a new kind of hybrid media form, a sort of 'push-pull media', that allows you "to move seamlessly between media you steer (interactive) and media that steer you (passive)" (Kelly et al., 1997: 12). There are several reasons for this media development. One of them, according to Kelly et al. (1997: 19) is a more or less explicit demand from the users of the media:

> What ... [people] want ... are more ways to zap. More ways to interrupt flow, more varieties ... of things done together with other people and things done alone. More states that flit between steering the media and being steered by it. More ability to tweak the dial, between twirling and being twirled, so that finally you can dance with the media. Networked media offer nothing more and nothing less than this: an expanding set of possible in-between states, combinations of push and pull and the means to slide between them.

The promise of push-pull media is, in other words, "... to marry the programmed experience of television with two key yearnings: navigating information and experience, and connecting to other people" (Kelly et al., 1997: 18). Using Bordewijk and Kaam's concepts, the promise of push-pull media is therefore a complex combination of transmission ('programmed experience of television'), consultation ('navigating information') and conversation ('connecting to other people'). This point is elaborated again in the following from Kelly et al. (1997: 18):

With networked media you get TV's high production values along with the intense communal experience of watching something together – virtual communities. You also get the ability to address small self-organizing audiences that broadcast could never afford to find. And you get well-crafted stories seamlessly integrated into other media, such as on-line conversations. This heightened ability to extract meaning, experience, or community – rare with content pushed by broadcast – is almost the rule with content pushed on a network.

Thus, one of the most significant consequences of these networked push media (compared to media known from the era of broadcasting) may be:

the creation of a whole universe of small-scale (and not-so-small-scale) broadcast networks. Until now, broadcast networks had to be huge to be ubiquitous. Smaller ones were proprietary and fixed. Really small ones were called mailing lists or videoconferences. Networked media, on the other hand, can create broadcasting networks of any size and shape, especially the intermediate size between TV and, say, personal mailing lists. You can push-pull broadcast to llama keepers or home scholars, reconfiguring the shape of the network on the fly. Until now, the Net has been a place of pull-laden networks; now it will also be a Net of push-laden networks, a world of nichecasting – thousands of mini-networks, ranging from micro TV stations to totally customized personal programming (Kelly et al, 1997: 21).

These new mini-networked media will – so predict Kelly et al., 1997: 21 – fill the entire media continuum, taking us " ... one more step toward closing the gaps between existing media, toward one seamless media continuum, viewable in an infinite number of ingenious ways". So far, in the context of traditional media, *push* is better developed than *pull*. On the other hand, in the context of the web, *pull* is better developed than *push*. But that may be changing fast, and conceivably the trend is towards a combination – or a re-balancing – of *push* and *pull* or, using Bordewijk & Kaam's concepts, toward a complex combination of transmission and consultation patterns. This combination of broadcast and networked media patterns has several similarities to the merging of television and the Internet.

Internet@TV

Internet on TV, or television-based Internet access, enables users to carry out many of the activities normally performed on a personal computer (PC) connected to the Internet through the television set, for example, to read and write e-mail and instant messaging, to participate in chat and discussion groups, to surf the web or search the Internet by keyword or category etc.

The web, as well as being a way of transferring files on the Internet using a hyperlink system to connect computer files or pages, has become a huge collection of interlinked information and entertainment including tens of millions of web sites. However, the content of the web is not restricted to being delivered over the Internet, it can be selected and distributed in other ways as well. There have been many experiments with broadcasting web pages to computers or television sets. One way is to upload selected popular web sites to a data carousel. This can provide a much faster response time than is usually available over a telephone line to the Internet. Another way is to download specific pages through an on-line communication channel upon user request.

In this case, the iDTV operators' general strategy is to transfer the web from the PC in the study to the television in the family room. The argument goes like this: the Internet is the killer application, and you just have to bring it to the unwired majority where they already are – on the couch.

There are several important trends that bring broadcasting and the web together at this moment. At first many broadcasters feared that the rapid growth of the Internet and the web would draw audiences away from traditional broadcasting and lead to its eventual demise. This fear has now more or less been substituted by a vision that sees broadcasters and content providers as perhaps those best positioned to turn Internet growth to their advantage. On one hand, the web is no longer seen simply as a shop window where broadcasters must have a site in order to keep up with competitors. Instead, many believe that the emergence of packaging and 'channel' concepts on the web means that broadcasters can now use the Internet as a valuable extra resource through which to reach new consumers of their products. On the other hand, if it proves correct that the real mass market for Internet access is through the television, then broadcasters are surely the best positioned to exploit this medium. In both cases, the emerging digital television markets – where video and audio are converted to digital data – provide the most obvious framework through which an Internet business can be fully integrated into a broadcasting strategy.

Besides the web, Internet @ TV is also closely related to and sometimes identical with communication, chat and messaging services on the iDTV platform.

Chat and messaging offer the viewer the opportunity to interact with and respond to their television programmes. The most common form is so-called event chat, that is, chat that runs with existing programming, and is planned and executed as an integrated part of the programme. This allows the viewer to engage in conversation with the host of the programme, with participants and guests in the show, or simply with other viewers on topics relevant to the programming. Comments are usually entered into an on-screen text box using the remote control or a keypad, or simply drawn from a list of commonly used phrases, and the chat stream is normally displayed beside or underneath the broadcast. Seen from the point of view of the user, this extends the viewing experience beyond the passive into a truly embedded interactive form. Furthermore, chat and messaging are perhaps the most simple, intuitive, and engaging ways of interacting with a medium. Seen from the point of view of the programmer, it makes it possible to produce programmes in the form of live chat-based events where content, to a certain extent, is based on direct viewer input, that is, user produced (and therefore cheap) content.

It is expected that chat functions will increase the viewer's loyalty to the programme, so that he or she stays with the programme and even returns to the channel or programme for the next event. Thus, in a situation with increasing viewer fragmentation, chat can be a way of producing the 'stickiness' that make viewers stay with the programme, and in this way maintaining and increasing viewership.

To summarise, from a general perspective, Internet access from the television screen can be conceptualised as television's transformation from an exclusively transmissional service into a complex combination of transmissional services (POTV: plain old television), consultational services (web browsing and searching, television-based home pages, interactive television links that connect programmes or commercials with web pages), conversational services (e-mail, chat, messaging, discussion groups, page builder) and registrational services (surfwatch, parental control, etc.). Or, to use van Tassel's concepts, television's transition from a carrier of purely pre-packaged content to a hybrid medium for pre-packaged content combined with user-created added data and user-created content. At the same time, the viewer undergoes a metamorphosis from a television viewer or receiver into a producer and sender of messages and content.

Clearly, one aspect of this development is the convergence of *push* and *pull* technologies, of broadcasting and the Internet, and consequently the merger of television and the computer, and more specifically, television's universal market acceptance and the web's anarchic multimedia content.

iTV Advertising

iTV advertising—also known as interactive advertising, personalised or customised advertising, targeted advertising, addressable advertising, one-to-one advertising, or nichecasting—are terms broadly used to signify the communication of marketing and brand messages using the expanded functionality supported by interactive television and digital broadcast (Online ITV Dictionary, 2003).

In traditional television advertising, broadcasters and companies subject viewers to commercials during standard commercial breaks whether they have asked for it or not, in the expectation that the viewers will notice their television presence, remember the brand and eventually buy the product. This is the exemplary model of *push*, the advertisers push the information to the passive, non-(inter)active viewers. Conversely, when the viewer or user actively accesses and pulls information about commercial products and services, we have the prototypical *pull* model. Hence, interactive advertising has a strong affinity towards the *pull* pattern.

There are numerous forms of interactive advertising, that is, many ways of attracting the viewer's attention and generating specific responses by means of ads extended with interactivity. NDS Business Consulting lists the following aspects:

- *jump*: go to a specific interactive site, for example, a product catalogue (consultation);
- *tag*: mark a specific interactive site for later access (consultation);
- *response*: order a brochure or sales call (consultation);
- targeted: display a different message to different viewers depending on the viewer profile, that is, target specialised market cross sections (registration, transmission);
- *incentive*: reward the viewer for watching or interacting with an advertisement, for example, in the form of product coupons, discounts, special offers, an entry to a lottery, etc.;
- *quiz and interactive contests*: reward the viewer for providing the right answers to questions relating to ads;
- *viewer response*: collect viewer responses and register them in a database (registration);
- *impulse purchase*: allow the viewer to purchase a product directly, that is, while viewing the ad (consultation, registration).

Often interactive advertising simply takes the form of conventional television commercials with additional overlaid information offering various interactive options to the user or additional links—often called triggers, hot spots, or rollovers—that are displayed along with or on top of the existing video content. If the interactive user 'clicks' on one of these links or presses a button on the remote control he can experience more of the commercial than the ordinary viewer. The overlaid information or the links can, for example, make it possible for the user to request more information concerning a specific product, to express an opinion, to order a brochure, to buy a product, or simply lead to the advertiser's web site containing extra information. Thus, interactive advertising allows the commercial messages to be expanded and supplemented beyond the 30-second slot.

One of the significant potentials of iTV advertising is the ability accurately to target messages to specific market cross sections or even individuals—or rather to each individual set-top box—with personalised messages based on their customer profiles. This specific kind of advertising is also called targeted advertising, addressable advertising, personalised advertising, one-to-one advertising, or nichecasting. iDTV has the potential to gather information about the personal demographics of television viewers, the programme preference, the viewer interaction, the individual responses to the advertising, etc. On the basis of this kind of information it is possible to create customer profiles, and these profiles can in turn be used to direct specific adverts toward the expected interests of specific audiences or individual users. The term narrowcast hints specifically at the targeting of the interests of smaller and smaller segments, even down to the individual viewer. In this respect, as can be seen from the above, iTV advertising has a strong affinity to personalised TV (Online ITV Dictionary, 2003).

However, there are also some serious challenges to interactive advertising. One of the most important of these is the personal video recorder (PVR). With the emergence of the PVR the way people watch television is basically changing. First and foremost, there is an increasing amount of time-shifted television viewing, that is, television watched asynchronously outside the scheduled programme time slots (the way people check their e-mail). Furthermore, some PVRs give the user the ability to record shows without ads. Other challenges are concerns about privacy, the problem of who owns the customer data, and who is going to sort and analyse it, technological incompatibility, etc. (Macklin, 2002).

As it has been demonstrated, interactive advertising not only allows the user to request more information about the product, but in some cases even allows the viewer to purchase the product directly from the ad. In this aspect iTV advertising borders on T-commerce.

T-Commerce

T-commerce – also known as television commerce, T-com, home shopping, iTV-based Retail, TRetail, Real Time Merchandising, or transactional TV – is simply the e-commerce phenomenon known from the Internet transferred to the medium of television. While traditional television monetised creative content by putting commercials between content segments, the television world of T-commerce monetises creative content by supporting sales during the content (Gelles, 2001). In other words, T-commerce allows the viewer to purchase products and services that he or she views on the television screen. In this way, viewers become consumers as they transact through television content. This new mingling of content and commerce will be realised in a variety of ways. Among other things, T-commerce includes shopping and banking.

Home shopping turns the television set into a 'virtual shopping mall.' The combination of the set-top box interactivity and home shopping channels (and advertising) allows the viewer to purchase products interactively. One of the advantages of T-commerce is the ability to target niche markets that are almost impossible to reach through traditional channels. Home shopping includes the sale of books, CDs, clothing, travel, food, and similar goods and services one usually also finds on the Internet. Furthermore, home shopping will be used in a variety of new and creative ways: music shows will let you buy the new CD; 'handy man' programmes will have product placement with direct purchase available from local retailers; television film will let you order pizza through sponsorship, and so on.

While home shopping turns the television set into a shopping mall, home banking turns the set into a simple ATM machine. iTV viewers can check their balance and account status, pay monthly bills, and perhaps download cash to their cash card. Clearly, such sensitive transactions – both in the form of home banking and home shopping – must be based on a highly secure system for sending information to and from the viewers.

As seen above, the new generation of interactive services will, among other things, allow access to the Internet through iTV. At the same time, however, open Internet access will permit users to engage in transactions outside the controlled environment of the local service provider (broadcaster/cable operator/Internet provider, etc.). In the short term, this may even cause service providers to be reluctant to offer access to the Internet to consumers. In the long term, however, market forces and user demand will force service providers to differentiate their service offerings and, for example, offer Internet access. For this reason, the British based analysis institute, Ovum, predicts that service providers will have to think of new ways to minimise the user's engagement in transactions outside the controlled environment of the service provider and, conversely, to keep subscribers in their own environment, thereby maximising revenues from their own interactive services (Ovum, 1998).

One way of doing this is to ensure that the content is more attractive than similar offerings delivered on the web. For instance, service providers may choose to reinforce the thematic content of a channel; or they may seek to establish alliances with content owners to develop attractive interactive content or to offer additional services to subscribers. That is, to develop what Ovum calls a 'walled garden:' "By 'walled garden' we mean the areas of interactive service revenues that digital broadcasters and Internet portal services develop within their own environment" (Ovum, 1998). A 'walled garden' is thus a portal-like suite of iTV applications and additional services, a discreet area of a television service that the user can access with the press of a button. Walled garden services normally incorporate communications, entertainment, gaming, commercials, shopping, banking, and customer care applications. The metaphor of the 'wall' around the garden implies that only the content and the applications provided and included by the platform operator are available to the user. In this way, the service is secured from the wider Internet and potential competitors, and consumers can in principle only move between the services as defined by the content provider and the broadcaster.

In that way, the concept of 'walled garden' may be considered iTV's counterpart to traditional broadcast television's concept of 'station design' and 'programme flow,' since the general purpose of station design and programme flow is, precisely, to keep the viewers from zapping to other channels. The user experience of a walled garden in an iTV environment is often more or less like another channel on the television. However, within the walled garden the user can access the available interactive applications with the press of a button on the remote control.

Games and Betting

Interactive television games have become the surprise hit on iDTV platforms around the world. They come in a variety of forms and flavours:

- *Play-along interactive games* are driven by a broadcast main event, such as a quiz show or sports event. The game set-up allows the viewers to become active participants in the show or contest by interactively responding to questions associated with the event from their homes. Their competitors may be in the television studio or be other television viewers at home. The correct answers are either securely transmitted over the iTV channel (terrestrial, satellite or cable) and stored locally in the set-top box memory for local interactivity, or sent to the broadcaster via a two-way interactive system or a cross media return path (such a mobile phone, SMS, e-mail, etc.). Correct answers from the viewers are often rewarded in some way.
- *Pay-per-play* are game services that charge the user on a 'taxi' payment principle, so that the player pays for the games that are actually played. Gaming content in this case includes trivia quizzes, simple platform games, and classics such as *Tetris* and *Trivial Pursuit*.

- *Downloadable games* are games you download to the set-top box. These kinds of services take advantage of the power and storage capacity of the set-top box to provide a veritable stand-alone game console. Many of these games can be played with the familiar remote control. A wide range of game providers is currently converting their conventional computer games to the set-top box platform. Other services offer download to conventional game consoles and PCs. In this way downloadable games are effectively the game version of on-demand services
- Finally, *multi-player network games* are games that allow the viewer to compete against other players connected to the iDTV network.

A service related to games is *betting* or *wagering*, that is, gambling services, that make it possible to play the lottery, place bets, etc. using the television. Sometimes this is done in real time, that is, while the event being bet on is taking place.

Cross Media Interaction

Since most places still do not have comprehensive, interactive, two-way television systems, a kind of 'two-channel' interaction is often used to produce interactive programmes or interactive features. This means that another medium acts as a 'return path' or 'feedback channel' from the television viewer to the media sender. A suitable name for this hybrid form of medium practise might be cross media interaction. Or, depending on your perspective on the services, cross media production, or cross media consumption.

There is a long, and apparently growing, list of interactive programme forms or features with considerable variations between the national television channels, television systems, and programme formats that in this way establish a simple and temporary interactive two-way and two-channel communication system by supplementing the television's one-way communication with for example, the telephone, e-mail, web chat, fax, SMS, MMS (multimedia messaging service), etc. as a return channel from the viewer to the media sender.

Compared to fully integrated interactive television systems the obvious advantage with this kind of cross media interaction is that the so-called 'terminal barrier' is already broken down. Today most Western households have a television set and a phone, and to some extent also a computer with Internet access, a mobile phone with SMS and possibly MMS, fax etc. Cross media interaction thus does not imply large investments in hardware and software on the part of the service provider, distributor, or viewer. Therefore, it is to be expected that these kinds of interactive programmes, with two-channel cross media interactivity, will have a much larger distribution in the short term – a fact already indicated by current trends. It is also to be expected that primarily the phone and mobile phone with SMS, MMS etc., but also the modem equipped computer (also using phone lines or cable) will provide the return channel. Finally, it is obvious that interactive cross media television programmes are at a comparatively primitive and preliminary stage today. No doubt far more advanced formats will be developed in the future.

As indicated above, one currently very popular instance of cross media is the use of SMS services via mobile phones as a return path to live television programming. In a newly published research report with the significant title, *SMS TV: Interactive Television Reinvented,* Van Dusseldorp and Partners (2003) point out that one of the most unexpected developments in the field of iTV is, precisely, that television broadcasters have embraced SMS text messaging as a new return channel to enhance their programmes with interactive features, now commonly called SMS TV.

According to Van Dusseldorp and Partners, broadcasters use SMS for television interactivity because the mobile phone, aside from television and radio, has become the only other true mass medium in Western Europe. Furthermore, SMS TV is more cost effective than most iTV solutions and is available to a larger potential audience, since mobile phone penetration is considerably higher than the penetration of true interactivity, that is, subscribers to DTV with a return path. Finally, SMS technology is familiar and very popular among consumers, since for most people, the use of the mobile phone for text messaging is as intuitive as using the remote control.

This kind of interactivity enables broadcasters to increase customer loyalty and to learn more about their audience. Viewer participation in votes or other forms of SMS interactivity generates valuable information for future marketing campaigns, but it also, in a very direct way, helps to generate additional revenues from viewers who pay to send messages via their mobile phones. During recent years, SMS TV applications have achieved considerable commercial success. Dusseldorp and Partners (2003) write:

> SMS messaging is no longer a gimmick—and Europe's leading television players aren't about to miss out on its benefits ... This trend transcends the lofty high tech promises that accompanied the dot.com boom – because broadcasters, producers and telecom operators can actually make money out of SMS.

It is especially game shows, reality television (such as *Big Brother*), sports, and channels or programmes dedicated to teenagers and young adults that are currently using SMS text messaging to enable their viewers to interact with the programme content, influence programming, publish messages, and communicate with each other. The most popular formats for SMS TV are voting, gaming, and chat. The successor to SMS TV will most likely be television combined with MMS TV, that is, which supplements the text based SMS service with audio, pictures and video.

CONCLUSION

Contrary to traditional prejudice against television viewers as passive couch potatoes, there are strong indications that they are in fact willing to be very active. iTV programmers can derive advantage from this trend. However, according to many observers (e.g., Bernhoff et al., 1998; NDS Business Consulting), it will not be the flavour of interactivity known from the computer with complex applications that require concentration, long attention spans, etc. Instead, they point out that made-for-television applications will have to live up to a new mode of interactivity particularly designed for television: the principle of 'lazy interactivity.' Lazy interactivity is a so-called 'low-attention-span paradigm designed for television viewers,' that is, interactive applications intended for quick decisions, short attention spans, handheld remotes, and instant gratification.

Lazy interactivity thus requires a simpler interface, involving minimal consumer effort that can attract couch potatoes (presumably with the remote in one hand and a pizza or a beer in the other). For example, Bernhoff et al. expect that the first instances of lazy interactivity applications for iTV, and generally, the most typical interactive applications for television in the long view will be:

- *electronic programme guides*;
- *interactive commercials*: adds are seen as well suited for lazy interactive content and are assumed to be effective because advertisers, for example, by adding web links to television spots can drive self-selecting consumers to a web page offering further information or transactions (see earlier discussion). Short attention span 'lazy interactivity' is therefore perfect for interactive advertisements;
- *shopping*: quick-hit applications like buy-the-CD on *MTV* or buy-the-t-shirt on *Baywatch* are well suited for 'lazy interactive' television;
- *news and weather programming*: news and weather programming are inherently non-linear, random access content and as such appropriate for interactivity and iTV;
- *sportscasts*: television producers are looking for ways to retain viewers during slow moments in sports transmissions or between plays.

Sportscasts are thus in need of interactivity in the form of additional information, statistics, betting, games, chat, etc.;

- *talk and game shows:* it will be relatively easy to supplement talk and game shows with interactive elements and participatory events like real-time polling, play-along, chat, etc. This will engage viewers, retain viewer loyalty, and fit well into television viewers' presumed biases toward effortless entertainment.

All in all, Ovum (1999) expects that interactivity will bring television viewers or iTV users into more direct relationship with networks, programmers, and advertisers. Likewise, it is expected that interactivity will be most appropriate for non-linear content or random access content like news, weather programmes, ads and sports. These types of programmes or genres are immanently well suited to being viewed by hyper-jumps, selective choices or browsing. On the other hand, it can be expected that drama or narrative storytelling will be much more difficult to enhance through interactive services.

Another general point is that iTV may also refocus consumer attention on the television screen and thus function as a remedy for the current fragmentation of audience attention (Bernhoff et al., 1998). Children and young people already watch television and simultaneously engage in several other media activities. In Michael J. Wolf's book, *The Entertainment* Economy, the new generation is portrayed in the following way (Wolf, 1999: 24):

As children of the media—actually multimedia—this generation more than any other has learned to multitask, or *time stack*, its media experience. In the same way that their computers can be opened to multiple applications, today's young consumers can be watching something on TV, have a CD playing in the background, and be surfing the Net.

iTV has the potential of addressing these kinds of consumers. By communicating with the consumers on multiple levels and by connecting to several parts of the consumer's activities and needs, iTV can prevent the viewers from zapping and leaving the channel.

In many respects, content, applications, and services are the least developed, least explored aspect of the new media. New forms of expression, new genres, formats, and products, will, of course, evolve. When the PC was first introduced, word processing and the spreadsheets were just about the only software applications envisaged. However, once the technology was in place, applications proliferated at a previously unimagined pace. The same will surely occur in the case of interactive media such as interactive television.

Although the potential of interactivity is widely recognised, and despite the fact that interactivity, as indicated, has been the subject of a considerable amount of hype and media attention, it has received remarkably little attention within the research community. The field of media and communication research still lacks a comprehensive theory of the phenomenon, let alone a consensus definition of it. Likewise, 'interactive content' and audience demand for this interactivity is still not well understood. Interactivity and interactive content, applications, and services are clearly areas in need of theoretical and analytical work.

REFERENCES

Bernhoff, Josh, (1998). *Lazy Interactive TV*, Forrester Research.

Bordewijk, L. & van Kaam, B. (1986). Towards a new classification of tele-information services, *Intermedia*, 14.

Gelles, Adam (2001). *Myers Mediaenomics: T-Commerce Business Models*. New York: Jack Meyers Reports.

Interactive Television International.

Jeffcoate, Judith (1995). *Multimedia in Practice. Technology and Applications*, Prentice-Hall.

Jensen, Jens F. (1996). Mapping the web: a media typology for information traffic patterns on the internet highway, in Herman Mauer (Ed.), *Proceedings of WebNet 96. World Conference of the Web Society*, San Francisco, AACE.

Jensen, Jens F. (1998). Interactivity: tracking a new concept in media and communication studies, *Nordicom Review*, vol. 19.

Jensen, Jens F. (1999a). Interactivity: tracking a new concept, in P. Mayer (Ed.), *Computer Media and Communication*, Oxford University Press.

Jensen, Jens F. (1999b). The concept of interactivity in interactive television and interactive media, in Jens F. Jensen & Cathy Toscan (Eds.), *Interactive Television: The TV of the Future or the Future of TV?*, Aalborg University Press.

Jensen, Jens F. (2001). So, what do you think, Linda? media typologies for interactive television, in Gunhild Agger & Jens F. Jensen (Eds.), *The Aesthetics of Television*, Media & Cultural Studies 2, Aalborg University Press.

Kantrowitz, Barbara (1993). An interactive life, *Newsweek*, 31 May.

Kelly, Kevin (1997). PUSH! Kiss your browser goodbye: The radical future of media beyond the Web, *Wired*, 5.03.

Kumar, Vinay (1996). *Mbone. Interactive Multimedia on the Internet*, New Riders.

Macklin, Ben (2002). *What every marketer needs to know about iTV*, eMarketer.

NDS Business Consulting

Online ITV Dictionary (2003), Definitions, www.itvdictionary.com/itv.html.

Ovum (1998). *Digital Television: How to Survive and Make Money*, Ovum White Paper.

Ovum (1999). *Digital Television Global Forecast Report*, Ovum Consultancy Limited in association with DVB Project Office.

Purchase, Helen (1998). Defining Multimedia, *Multimedia*.

Purchase, Helen (1999), A semiotic definition of multimedia communication, *Semiotica*, 123 2/3.

Stroud, Jim (2001). The Carmel Group.

Van Dusseldorp & Partners (2003). *SMS TV: Interactive Television Reinvented.* Amsterdam.

Van Tassel, J. (1996). *Advanced Television Systems. Brave New TV*, Focal Press.

Wolf, Michael (1999). *The Entertainment Economy: How Mega-media Forces are Transforming our Lives*, Random House.

Chapter 6
A Consumer Perspective
on Digital Terrestrial
and Interactive Television

Robert G. Picard
Jönköping International Business School, Jönköping University

Perhaps the most fundamental impact of digital communications on consumers is its ability to improve the quality of video and audio signals and to transform one-way communications that has traditionally been received in a relative passive manner into two-way communications in which users can play a more active role. These changes have led policymakers and broadcasters of various types to promote opportunities in digital television (DTV), digital terrestrial television (DTTV) and interactive television (iTV). Digital television is being offered to many consumers through cable and satellite systems, and broadcasters in some European nations are beginning to offer basic DTTV broadcasts. Simple interactive services are appearing in some markets as a prelude to future more extensive interactive operations.

The introduction of DTTV and iTV, however, is being far more affected by the marketplace than were the introduction of analogue television and cable television, both of which tended to receive significant financial support and market protection from European governments. Because these newer broadcast services are being developed within a consumer-oriented commercial context, consumers are at the centre of decisions that will determine their success or failure. Although public service broadcasters are among the strongest supporters or DTTV and offering many of the new channels and services (as shown in chap. 3), they are doing so in a market-based environment that requires significant consumer spending for set-top boxes (STBs) and in which consumers have choices of other digital television services. DTTV and iTV are not alone in this regard as choices involving many information and communications technologies and services today are now being left to consumers and the marketplace (Picard, 2003).

Issues of consumer acceptance and use are important because it is the choices of consumers in markets that determine how much of their financial resources are devoted to various media and those choices influence decisions of sources of capital, marketers, and advertisers (Albarran, 2000; Picard, 2002).

The development of linking communications such as the Internet and other telecommunications-based systems has made it possible to combine content availability with a high degree of user selectivity, filtering and participation. The greatest developments in this regard to date are currently seen in the World Wide Web, which at the beginning of 2003 provided users more than 171 million hosts to chose among (Internet Software Corporation, 2003). It is browsed with software that permits users to be both audiences and content providers, to search for specific material and to exclude others, to collect and reorganise information, and to obtain and react to material.

The underlying technologies that have created these Internet opportunities are now being transferred to the television environment because the digitalisation of television signals uses technologies that are compatible with linkages to telecommunications systems such as the Internet and will permit users to easily play more active roles in determining what material they receive and when and how they receive it. The technologies also allow them greater control over what they do with the material received and provide opportunities to react to it and otherwise interact with the content.

Interactive television and digital television (whether terrestrial, cable, or satellite) are inextricably combined because iTV can be added to the technology of the digital platform easily and cost effectively.

ISSUES IN CONSUMER DEMAND

Consumer demand for digital and interactive television is affected by a number of factors. Demand for and acceptance of new media products and services as a whole are dictated by a variety of factors including the uniqueness of the content and services, the improvements they provide over existing media, the amount of use expected, their belief in the success of the technologies, and — of course — price (Picard, 2002 and 2003). The extent to which DTTV and iTV provide sufficient incentives to large number of consumers in these regards remains uncertain.

Wide individual differences in demand for other media and communications products and services have produced highly different patterns of acquisition (Figure 6.1). DTTV and iTV are being introduced in an environment of unclear demand and with political wishes for universal acceptance in a relatively short time. Given the patterns of acquisition for other media and communication products and services, the desire seems highly problematic because even terrestrial television is not acquired in all households and other interactive media are used in far less than half of all households.

Figure 6.1: Penetration of Selected Media and Communication Products/ Services in European Households, 2000

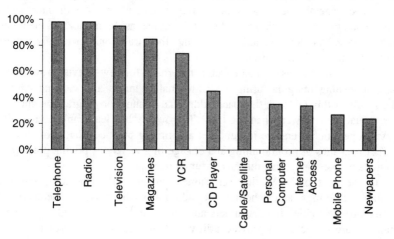

Source: Eurostat, 2001

The difficulties of achieving household acquisition of DTTV are illustrated in the countries where it is currently being offered. For example, one year after its introduction digital terrestrial television reaches less than 1 per cent of households in Spain and 3 per cent in Finland. Three years after its introduction in the United Kingdom DTTV serves only about 5 per cent of households.

Cost issues associated with digital and interactive television present a significant challenge because acquisition of signals and services requires significant consumer investment in STBs. Basic boxes to receive digital signals but not including a feedback loop for interactivity require consumer expenditures of €300 to €500, and advanced STBs that support interactive services are €1,000 or more. In some households additional expenditures to upgrade reception antennas will be required as well.

These costs to consumers represent significant household expenditures and will require a significant transfer of discretionary income given that the European average household spending for all media is currently under €1,000 per annum. As a result costs of acquiring hardware will clearly influence choices of consumers to acquire the technologies in the market.

Consumer demand for digital television is also highly affected by the number of new channels provided and the pre-existence of channels via terrestrial and other means. It is affected by the number of free channels, basic paid channels, and premium channels available. It is affected by the amount of original, syndicated, and repeat programming provided. It is affect by whether programming is provided for general or niche audiences. It is affected by the number of movies broadcast, and the number of specialised channels provided. Demand changes because the audience fragments and becomes disinterested in some available content (Picard, 2000) and because as the number of media and content providers increase, audiences change their traditional media use patterns (Becker & Schoenbach, 1999).

This occurs because a major factor in demand for new television services is the diminishing marginal utility of additional channels and viewing choices. The result of this factor is that each additional channel or programme choice is less valuable to viewers than the last. This reality has lead cable and satellite system operators to engage in bundling and tiering practices that allow them to market packages of programming and engage in a variety of pricing practices in attempts to overcome this limit on consumer demand.

In the case of DTV, then, consumer demand will depend on currently available offerings and whether the additional channels are perceived as sufficiently desirable, that consumers anticipate viewing them, and that the new channels are expected to provide utility that justifies expenditures to acquire them.

Both DTTV and iTV, then, are less likely to appeal to viewers who choose not to have cable, satellite or Internet services because their benefits are similar to those provided by those technologies. Bruce Owen (1999) has noted that an important factor in consumer demand for television is a desire for passive entertainment, but that newer technological opportunities tend to satisfy different demands. As a result, they are not fully substitutable and are unlikely to gain equal consumer interest.

Digital television in its various forms presents consumers with a number of choices through which to satisfy their viewing desires. To date, DTTV has not provided a sufficiently desirable proposition to consumers to induce them to choose DTTV over cable or satellite, or to reject analogue terrestrial broadcasting. In situations with many choices and mixed advantages, consumers tend toward inertia and the avoidance of choice making, to continue pre-existing behaviours, and to wait for market clarity to reduce uncertainty before reconsideration. These behaviours present a significant challenge to the rapid uptake of DTTV.

In addition to these consumer issues, concerns over the use and usability of STBs and interactive systems also will affect demand. Many consumers are currently confused by basic videocassette recorders (VCRs) and computers, which limits their acquisition and use. The perception of complexity will have to be overcome for iTV services, in particular, to become attractive.

A use issue also exists because most current DTTV and iTV services require households to acquire a STB for each television set in the home, thus requiring higher expenditures for full use of the technologies.

Demand issues also exist among the second set of consumers involved in DTTV and iTV—advertisers. Uncertainty about viewer acceptance of the technologies and the audiences that will become available, as well as a prolonged downturn in their advertising expenditures, is limiting their interest in the potential of these developments.

In addition, the high costs of establishing and operating iTV advertising systems and difficulties in integrating advertising and sales processes to make effective use of iTV are also constraining advertiser activities in iTV (European Commission, 2002).

INTERACTIVITY, iTV, AND CONSUMERS

The key characteristic of iTV is interactivity that permits the users more influence over the content than the mere traditional choice of whether to watch or not watch what has been provided by a broadcaster. In interactive television, the user gains greater control and becomes the driver of the process. Interactive media are not defined by technology used in delivering content but by the ability of users to act and determine the course of the interaction between themselves and the content provider.

Interactive television is based on the reception of a broadcast signal with a link back to the broadcast organisation or service provider via a communication system that allows the user to exert influence over the content provided or to link to other communication systems.

The concept is not completely new. Cable television, for example, has provided interactive television capabilities using analogue technologies for more than two decades by allowing viewers to place telephone orders for pay-per-view programming and, more recently, to use Internet-based ordering systems.

What is new regarding interactive television, however, is that it acquires greater potential and features with digital television—whether terrestrial, cable, or satellite—because it allows creation of content in formats and provides the underlying infrastructure that creates enhanced usability and greater interactivity. It is the improvements that digitalised content, content management systems, and distribution systems provide that create natural linkage between some digital television activities and iTV.

Digital television combined with interactive functions allows users to choice among video and audio signals; it creates the ability for viewers to opt out of programme streams though time shifting; and it allow individuals to make unique free and fee-based programme selections. It also gives users digital recording and playback ability and the potential for data transmission in the form of e-mail, messaging, Internet, and e-commerce.

In understanding the potential interactivity, one must consider the functional differences and use difference for various types of interactive activities proposed for iTV. The primary types of activities proposed involve transactions, communication, information/news, entertainment and advertising (Fig. 6.2).

Figure 6.2: Communication Functions and Use in Static and Interactive Formats

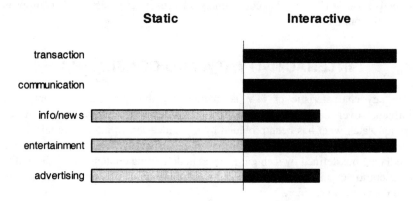

In traditional broadcasting—whether analogue or digital—users can only use information/news, advertising, and entertainment in a static way, that is, they can only passively receive the content. Because of the technological limitations, they are not able to use the system for communications or transactions. With iTV, the ability to interact is heightened, although somewhat less for information/news and advertising where interaction is primarily search and selection rather than fuller participation.

For marketers, including broadcasters themselves, iTV offers the ability to communicate with persons actively engaged in media use, to communicate with a single audience member and consumer rather than an amorphous audience, and to communicate with an identifiable receiver of an advertiser's message. These factors all increase the effectiveness of marketing messages, so interactivity appeals to those wishing to engage the audience for commercial purposes. Even general advertising becomes more effective because iTV allows some interactivity that can be used to establish channels for personal marketing, and hopefully, for transactions.

Because gaining new capabilities and communications opportunities is a central component in consumer demand for media products and services, it is important to understand exactly what they gain by iTV.

Important functions provided by iTV include recording and playback. These functions allow users to view materials that were offered in a broadcast stream by a broadcaster but missed by the viewer. Thus, a viewer who missed last night's episode of *The Sopranos* can use the broadcast channels interactive system to see it today.

This function is not new and has been provided for three decades by VCRs and more recently by digital recording devises such as TVRO. Such recording and playback functions are popular among consumers. VCRs, for example, cost only about €150 and are found in about three-quarters of European homes.

Newer digital recording and playback systems, such as TiVO, record available DTV programming. These consumer electronic systems are separate units like VCRs, but they also require payment for services that operate the equipment, and made so that users avoid the necessity of planning by specifying genres of programmes, directors, actors, types of sports, etc. that should be recorded or specific programme titles. The hardware for the systems currently costs about €300 and service cost about €150 per year.

Plans for the full-blown iTV systems in the future would replace the need for consumers to acquire separate devices and incorporate the functions at the broadcaster level or within the system. Interactive television playback also has advantages over VCRs in that users do not have to plan ahead, do not have to set their equipment to record the programme, and are able view the programme in digital quality.

Some limited, poor resolution playback capability of television content is now available on computer screens via the Internet. They are primarily limited to news and public affairs content because of copyright limitations, and broadcasters supplying this service provide video files which can be downloaded or streamed with user-friendly point-and-click technology. As iTV develops, these same functions will be transferred to the television environment bringing the quality up to DTV standards and—when copyright payment issues are resolved—availability will be extended to the entire range of broadcast content.

Another significant function involves information seeking, in which iTV users can access programme archives and the Internet to seek information and news. The systems will allow them to use search capabilities to seek out text, audio, and video clips containing information and news from a wide variety of local, domestic, and global sources.

This function will thus permit television users to acquire information not currently in the broadcast stream, not available from local broadcasters, not currently being broadcast, and will meet the unique informational requirements of the user. These capabilities have been widely used in policy debates as a justification for DTTV, iTV, and public policies supporting their development.

Another capability of iTV is the accessing of information about products and services in the market in which the user is interested. A viewer who is planning to purchase a new automobile might be attracted by an advertisement for Volkswagen in a broadcast stream and then use the interactive system to find out additional information about specific models and features or to view models in preferred colours.

Interactive television also presents the opportunity for users to play and take part in games and gaming activities. Users can play videogames without having to purchase game devises such as PlayStation or Xbox, and play with individuals at other locations through the Internet connection.

The gaming opportunities allow users to take part in gambling activities, including live casino games and betting on sport events. Not only could wagers be placed on the outcomes of events such as horse races or hockey matches, but wagers could be made in real time. During a football match, for example, a viewer could place a wager on the outcome of a penalty kick.

Transactional functions of iTV make it attractive for e-commerce, banking, and other transactional activities. Viewers watching a movie, for example, might like it so much that they choose to purchase a DVD copy that can be shipped to their home or to order takeout pizza from a local shop to consume while viewing the motion picture. Both these functions can be accommodated using the iTV system.

Similarly, viewers wishing to receive a pay-per-view broadcast of a boxing match or motion picture could use the system to make the financial transaction and begin receiving the content.

Interactive television also provides the communication capabilities available through the Internet such as e-mail, messaging, chatting, and voice transmission.

The additional programming and enhanced functions provided by DTV and iTV provide users content and services not previously available in the broadcast format. The increased content and functionality are a factor in the demand for communication products, but they alone do not determine consumer acceptance.

THE CONTEXT OF DTTV AND iTV

Comprehending the potential for DTTV and iTV also requires that the context in which these technologies have been introduced be well understood. Throughout Europe, DTTV has been promoted by governments and major firms, not by consumer demand. Although consumers will enjoy the primary benefits of clearer signals, increases in the number of channels available, and the potential for interactivity, these have not driven developments in DTTV. Instead, the aspirations of the European Commission and national governments to be world leaders in information and communication technologies and to free existing analogue television frequencies that can be potentially auctioned for other uses have been the primary impetus toward DTTV. The governmental initiative has been supported by major technology manufacturing and service firms that stand to gain financially by the transition to digital broadcasting.

Existing terrestrial broadcasters have not been wholly supportive because DTTV makes it necessary for them to acquire new studio technology—a capital cost factor—and the policy requirements and transition time for consumer switchover requires them to maintain both analogue and digital broadcasts, which have operating cost implications. Nevertheless, the longer term potential for existing broadcasters to provide additional channels and services through multiplexes make DTTV strategically interesting.

Public service broadcasters have shown the greatest interest in DTTV because it allows them to increase niche offerings and provide more localised services. The infrastructure and operating costs remain a concern, however, because most have not been provided additional financial resources with which to provide DTTV services. In some markets, potential income from supplemental services based on digital infrastructure and revenue-generating interactive services may provide resources to help pay for the additional costs.

Commercial broadcasters typically have been less supportive of DTTV because of the relatively short history of advertising-supported television in many nations, the relatively short time many have had to depreciate analogue equipment purchased in the 1990s, and because new channels and broadcast competitors created by DTTV are coming just as television market stability is developing after the upheaval caused by the rapid increase in analogue channels in the late 1980s and 1990s.

Market questions today are creating great uncertainty about DTTV and iTV developments and the issues are primarily related to consumer choices and behaviour, rather than technology and supply side questions The basic technologies and infrastructures necessary for iTV exist today, but companies are moving slowly toward integrating systems and content because of concerns over the ability and willingness of consumers to accept these new systems.

The concern revolves around consumer cost issues. The willingness of consumers to pay additional costs for the services and the necessity for consumers to purchase STBs with capabilities far beyond mere acquisition of DTTV signals are slowing iTV development. The uncertain business potential and high financial risks involved, and current limitations on available capital, are all slowing the movement of firms into DTTV and iTV services.

These issues are compounded because consumer knowledge about DTTV and iTV is generally limited, because current DTTV and iTV offerings are limited as those on the supply side await more consumer take-up before investing in more services, because development and performance of DTTV and iTV have not lived up to the promoted vision and expectations of policymakers and digital broadcast firms in markets where they have been introduced, and because issues involving technologies and standards of STBs have created consumer and industry uncertainty.

DTTV and iTV clearly offer consumers additional services to those they currently receive. Consumer research on DTTV and iTV shows audiences welcome improvements in picture quality, increased choices among content, electronic programme guides, and supplemental audio programming that is provided. Where interactive systems actually exist, consumers show great willingness to use the new capabilities to access programme guides, online games, gambling, and pornography. When it comes to the communications capabilities for e-mail, messaging, and internet activities, however, limited interest is shown.

Market data show that only a few consumers acquiring STBs for DTV are acquiring the advanced boxes needed for significant interactivity, and most of the few consumers acquiring DTTV boxes are purchasing low-end boxes with little interactivity capabilities.

The most advanced existing iTV systems, such as those offered by BSkyB through its satellite-based digital television operations in the United Kingdom, only provide very rudimentary interactivity in which viewers can make highly limited, pre-established choices using their remote control device. These allow viewers the ability to select among various cameras at sporting events and to respond to viewer polls, for example.

Part of the difficulty with the entire process of introducing digital and interactive television to consumers is that it has relied primarily on market funding. Policy makers and companies have assumed that there would be strong consumer demand for DTTV and rapid, widespread adoption. This approach has brought the entire funding methods of DTTV and iTV to a crisis point. It has been a remarkable failure because it was based on policy and technology triumphing over the marketplace.

For the most part, the movement to DTTV and iTV have been designed to support frequency reallocation, designed to support the information and communication technology sectors, and designed to promote images of European and national leadership in technology. Consumer interest and demand were never seriously a factor in past policy decisions regarding DTTV and iTV.

The result is that across Europe, we are currently seeing resistance to and rejection of DTTV and iTV costs by consumers. Market failures of ONdigital in the United Kingdom and Quiero TV in Spain and consumer disinterest in Germany and elsewhere are hampering development of DTTV and iTV services.

As a result, some European governments are floating the idea of free or subsidised distribution of digital TV boxes and considering the approach of the Federal Communications Commission in the United States to force television set manufacturers to install digital receivers in sets. Many are making efforts to delay implementation of DTTV broadcasting and moving to postponing planned switch-offs of analogue broadcasting.

The necessity for slowing development of DTTV and iTV underscores two major problems with the view of consumers in the planning of the systems: the assumption that there would be universal interest in DTV services and the assumption that there would be universal take-up at some point.

Both of these views are extremely problematic. The first is problematic even if one considers existing services beyond basic terrestrial broadcasting. Only about half of Europeans make use of cable and satellite services to obtain addition channels and programming (a major advantage of DTTV) and only about one-quarter access premium services, even though basic and premium cable and satellite services are widely available (Cable and Satellite Europe, 2000). These take-up numbers present difficulties for iTV because, as Owen (1999) has observed, interactive television is unlikely to appeal to television viewers that do not currently have cable or satellite services.

DISCUSSION

The consumer perspective on DTTV and iTV produces an evaluation that is more negative than evaluations emanating from technical or policy perspectives. Serious consumer impediments exist to the adoption and use of the related technologies that must be overcome if the technologies are to be successful. The need to overcome these constraints is critical because introduction is based on market financing.

The limited introduction of DTTV and iTV to date appears to present classic cases of failures, or at least false starts, in the introduction of new technologies. Consumer disinterest and resistance have been particularly strong. Many of the primary benefits of DTTV and iTV are related to political/social goals sought by policymakers and to commercial gain sought by hardware and service providers. As a result, individual consumers do not directly accumulate the greatest benefits and have less desire to pay the price for them. It should not be surprising that they are not rushing to embrace the opportunities of these new technologies. For this situation to be overcome, a better accommodation of consumer behaviour and a balancing of producer and consumer funding will need to emerge, perhaps through public policies that deal with the failure.

Part of the problem is that DTTV is being introduced simultaneously, and in some cases after, the introduction of cable and satellite digital services. Cable and satellite in analogue form are well understood by consumers and digital offerings have been introduced as enhancements by the marketing arms of industry firms and federations. A number of operators also provided subsidised digital STBs that did not increase subscription costs to users or did so in an inconsequential way.

The introduction of DTTV, digital cable and satellite services, and iTV are occurring within the context of the wholesale transformation of European broadcasting of the last 15 years, and the industry is beginning to reach the limits of potential market expansion (Picard, 2001). It should not be surprising that consumers are evidencing technology fatigue, reduced willingness to invest, and perceiving fewer benefits in additional services.

It must be recognised, however, that the consumer demand issues vary widely across Europe because of wide differences in the markets based on size of nation, pre-existing terrestrial cable and satellite channels and their use, and household incomes. Because many of the interactive television services use telecommunications and Internet feedback loops, current infrastructure supporting those technologies and computer and Internet adoption and use patterns will also affect demand for iTV.

Such issues are important because consumers who do not wish to interact online are not likely to significantly interact with television, and because persons who have access to cable and satellite services but choose not acquire and use them are unlikely to find DTTV and iTV attractive.

The introduction of the technologies also faces significant challenges because of language. Because use of services requires the ability to view and interact in the language in which content and services are provided, the technologies are being introduced at the national rather than European level. Although limited market adoption in highly populous nations might provide sufficient number of consumers to maintain commercial operations, limited adoption in the many smaller nations of Europe will lead to commercial failures. Limited adoption in smaller nations can be overcome by aggregating audiences across those nations but linguistic limitations make that impractical.

In recent years, information and communication technology advocates and policy makers have regularly used the adoption curve (Fig. 6.3) to project take-up of new products and services. They assume that the curve represents widespread or universal adoption of the technologies. The curve, however, does not represent the entire population but only those who ultimately adopt the new product or service. In many cases, projections are based only on the first half of the curve and its "S" curve. These approaches are problematic because the number of adopters and the time and capital required to reach the lower thresholds of adoption for continued operations may halt the spread and acceptance of the technology altogether.

Figure 6.3: The Adoption Curve

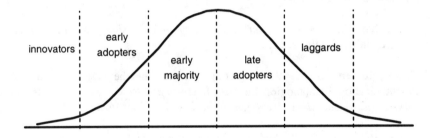

Many proponents of DTV and iTV have seemed to assume that because they provide some benefits, they would be automatically embraced by consumers. The current situation shows that there are a range of impediments to success within the broadcasting industry and from choices of consumers. The difficulties in the introduction of digital and interactive television underscore the fact that good technologies can be rejected or delayed when consumer desires and choices do not coincide with those of policymakers, technology firms, infrastructure firms, content providers and other interested parties (Picard, 1998).

A consumer perspective thus shows that the introduction of digital terrestrial television and interactive television face significant challenges and that their success in the market is uncertain. Only if and when the consumer-related impediments are overcome can these technologies survive and begin to achieve the social and individual benefits they are asserted to provide.

REFERENCES

Albarran, Alan B. 2000. *Media Economics: Understanding Markets, Industries and Concepts*. Mahwah, NJ: Lawrence Erlbaum Associates.

Becker, Lee, & Klaus Schoenbach 1999. *Audience Responses to Media Diversification*. Mahwah, NJ: Lawrence Erlbaum Associates.

Cable and Satellite Europe 2000.

European Commission 2002. *ACTIVE-AD: Analysis of Success Criteria for Interactive Advertising Formats*, Public Final Report. Luxembourg: Office for Official Publications of the European Communities, 2002

Internet Software Corporation. Host Survey Data. Accessible at www.isc.org Accessed 6 May 2003.

Owen, Bruce M. 1999. *The Internet Challenge to Television*. Cambridge, MA: Harvard University Press, 1999.

Picard, Robert G. 1998 Interacting Forces in the Development of Communication Technologies: Business Interests and New Media Products and Services, *European Media Management Review* No. 1, pp. 16-22.

Picard, Robert G. 2000. Audience Fragmentation and Structural Limits on Media Innovation and Diversity, pp. 180-191 in Jan van Cuilenburg & Richard van der Wurff (Eds.), *Media and Open Societies: Cultural, Economic and Policy Foundations for Media Openness and Diversity in East and West*. Amsterdam: Het Spinhuis, 2000.

Picard, Robert G. 2001. *Expansion and Limits in EU Television Markets: Audience, Advertising, and Competition Issues*. Discussion Papers C2/2001, Business Research and Development Centre, Turku School of Economics and Business Administration.

Picard, Robert G. 2002. *The Economics and Financing of Media Companies*. New York: Fordham University Press.

Picard, Robert G. 2003. Business Issues Facing New Media, in Jan Servaes (Ed.), *The European Information Society: A Reality Check*. Bristol, UK: Intellect Publishing.

II
Country Case Studies

Chapter 7
United Kingdom: Never Mind the Policy, Feel the Growth

Peter Goodwin
Communication and Media Research Institute
University of Westminster

The story of Digital Terrestrial Television in the UK effectively starts in August 1995 with the publication of the White Paper, *Digital Terrestrial Broadcasting: The Government's Proposals* (DNH, 1995). The 1995 White Paper is of crucial importance to the story of UK DTTV in two ways. It laid down for the first time the general outlines of the regulatory framework under which DTTV in the UK was to be launched nearly three and a half years later. And it advanced a set of policy objectives which DTTV might be expected to deliver—policy objectives which, although formulated by the Conservative administration of John Major, have been enthusiastically embraced by the New Labour administrations of Tony Blair, and, as we shall discuss, persist to this day. So each of these aspects of the government's 1995 DTTV proposals is worth looking at in some detail, both in terms of its historical context and in terms of its logic for subsequent developments.

First the regulatory framework. The 1995 White Paper anticipated that "for digital terrestrial television, it is likely that six frequency channels will be available initially, with potential coverage in the medium term ranging from 60-70 per cent to over 90 per cent of the UK population. Each frequency channel will be able to carry at least three television channels, and at times possibly many more. These will need to be 'multiplexed' into a single digital signal before transmission." (DNH, 1995, p. 1). Licences for these multiplexes would be allocated by, and the multiplexes regulated by, the Independent Television Commission (ITC). In other words they would be allocated to commercial operators in a, by historical UK standards, lightly regulated but, by many international standards, still quite highly regulated context. The ITC had been established by the 1990 Broadcasting Act to license and regulate all television services in the UK other than the BBC. By 1995 the ITC had already conducted licence allocations for the old analogue terrestrial Channel 3 (ITV) and the new analogue terrestrial Channel 5 on the basis of a highly qualified cash bid system. (Goodwin, 1998, chap. 8.)

DTTV was therefore placed firmly in the more commercially-oriented and "lighter touch" regulated framework of television broadcasting established during the last years of the Thatcher administrations by the 1988 White Paper *Broadcasting in the '90s: Competition, Quality and Choice* (Home Office, 1998) and the 1990 Broadcasting Act (Goodwin, 1998, chap. 7).

In two important respects, however, in its treatment of DTTV the 1995 White Paper departed from the more extreme rigours of the Conservative Government's recent deregulatory thrust.

First, space on the frequencies allocated to DTTV was to be given as of right to the existing analogue terrestrial channels including the BBC. The 1995 White Paper explained:

> The Government believes in the merits of public service broadcasting and wishes to safeguard it into the digital age. The Government therefore believes that it is essential to give public service broadcasters the opportunity of a place in the new technology. This will enable them to offer an improved service, for example through widescreen television, and will be in the interests of digital terrestrial television as a whole, since the involvement of the existing broadcasters is likely to encourage consumers to move to digital.

So each of the following channels, BBC1, BBC2, Channel 3 (ITV), Channel 4/S4C and Channel 5 would have about a third of a multiplex reserved for it (DNH, 1995, pp. 11-12). In practice that would mean ability both to simulcast and to provide an additional channel.

Second, the ITC would not employ (even a heavily qualified) cash bid in its allocation of DTTV multiplexes. Instead the ITC would assess applications "according to three main criteria:"

a)   investment in infrastructure over time in order to provide services as quickly and as widely as possible across the UK;

b)   investment additional to a) to promote the early take-up of digital television, including investment to encourage take-up of receivers; and

c)   the variety of programme services to be transmitted" (DNH, 1995, p. 9).

These two elements of the proposed regulatory regime for DTTV might have seemed surprising to observers of Conservative broadcasting policy at the end of the 1980s, but by the mid-1990s they were not unexpected. In 1994 John

Major's government had produced a White Paper on the BBC (DNH, 1994) which both endorsed its established domestic position and enthusiastically embraced the corporation's new international ambitions (Goodwin, 1998, chap. 9). And the operations of the cash bid system for Channels 3 and 5 had been so creatively interpreted by the ITC and so sceptically or hostilely received by media commentators that it was hardly surprising that the Government did choose not to repeat the exercise for DTTV (Goodwin, 1998, chap. 8).

The second important aspect of the 1995 White Paper was the policy objectives it advanced for DTTV. The central elements of these are crisply summed up in the very first paragraph of the document:

> Digital broadcasting could mean many more television channels and radio stations. For many people, it will provide their first experience of the full potential of the information superhighways. It will provide significant opportunities for the British manufacturing and programme production industries. In the longer term it may be possible to switch off analogue transmissions of terrestrial broadcast services, releasing significant amounts of valuable spectrum for further broadcast or other use (DNH, 1995, p. 1).

Before we examine these policy objectives further one crucial ambiguity in their formulation should be noted. This opening paragraph of the White Paper quoted above, made its claims not for digital *terrestrial* broadcasting in particular but for digital broadcasting (presumably) in general, including not only digital terrestrial, but also digital satellite and digital cable. The White Paper rapidly moved from these bold pronouncements about digital broadcasting in general to proposals almost exclusively about digital terrestrial. Satellite and cable were almost wholly ignored in the rest of the document with the one significant exception (to which we shall return shortly) that digital terrestrial broadcasting would "give terrestrial broadcasters the opportunity to compete with those on satellite and cable" (DNH, 1995, p. 1).

This slippage from digital broadcasting in general to digital terrestrial was to prove of crucial importance not merely because of its theoretical sloppiness but because of the particular features of the UK television market into which DTTV was to be launched.

The theoretical issue is easy to clarify. Digital broadcasting could indeed "mean more television channels" than analogue. Exactly how many more was a technical question (involving compression technology, frequency allocation, etc). But that multiplication in channels applied not simply to terrestrial television, but also to satellite and cable, each of which could (and did) already deliver, in their analogue format several times the number of channels delivered by analogue terrestrial television. Two conclusions result from this:

1. DTTV would deliver no more (and probably less) channels than were already delivered by analogue satellite and analogue cable.
2. Digital satellite and digital cable would deliver several times the number of channels delivered by DTTV, thereby enabling them to offer a qualitatively superior service in terms of channel choice and services like near-video-on-demand.

Both these points were of crucial practical importance in the UK case, because, in 1995 the UK already had an established and substantial multi-channel pay television subscriber base delivered by (most importantly) analogue satellite and (less importantly but still significantly) by analogue cable.

By 1995 multi-channel television in the UK already had a significant history. In the early 1980s the Conservative government had proposed an ambitious plan (of which more later) to bring broadband cable to the UK. But for most of the rest of the decade build had been slow, programme offer unattractive and take-up consequently very low (Goodwin, 1998, chap. 5). Things changed dramatically with the start of specifically UK-directed DTH satellite television broadcasting by Rupert Murdoch's Sky in March 1989 and (less importantly) British Satellite Broadcasting (BSB) in May 1990. The two merged (very much on Murdoch and Sky's terms) to form British Sky Broadcasting (BSkyB) in November 1990. BSkyB grew steadily, and cable emerged from its earlier lethargy. By January 1995 there were estimated to be over 4 million subscribers to multi-channel pay television in the UK (more than 3 million by satellite, nearly 1 million by cable) and by January 1996 that had increased to nearly 5 million (BARB). This meant, respectively, 16 per cent and 20 per cent, of UK television households, and (because satellite and cable households were generally significantly bigger than average) somewhat larger percentages of the UK population. So, in August 1995 at the time that the White Paper was pronouncing that digital television would deliver more channels, and using this as a justification for its proposals on DTTV, probably 20 per cent of the UK population lived in households subscribing to analogue multi-channel pay television, delivered by either satellite or cable, each of which already delivered significantly more than the 18 channels which the White Paper flagged up for DTTV.

That raised a quite fundamental practical problem for any prospective DTTV service.

Simply on the basis of providing more channels, DTTV faced a huge and possibly crippling disadvantage. It would be launched into an environment in which more than 20 per cent of the population (the early and not-so-early adopters) already had multi-channel television via satellite or cable platforms which, in their even in their analogue format already offered more channels than DTTV would. So what distinguishing and attractive features would enable DTTV to find a market?

The problem was made even more serious by one other feature of the UK television market. Multi-channel pay television in the UK in 1995 was overwhelmingly dominated by BSkyB. Three quarters of subscribers received their service via satellite, almost all from BSkyB, which, over the previous six years had built up very effective systems of marketing and subscriber management. BSkyB's dominance of multi-channel content in the UK extended even further. The cable companies had not managed to establish a substantially independent programming offer. What they offered to their subscribers was effectively the same programming mix that BSkyB offered its DTH satellite subscribers, in many cases wholesaled from BSkyB. BSkyB had the most popular general entertainment channel on multi-channel television, Sky One, the most popular 24-hour news channel, Sky News; it had done the deals with the Hollywood studios to feed its premium movie channels and it already owned the most important sports rights (most notably Premier League football) to support its popular premium sports channels.

This fundamental problem for the prospects of DTTV was in no way addressed by the 1995 White Paper. Nor was it seriously addressed by the Government in the period between the White Paper and the eventual launch of DTTV. But it certainly did not escape contemporary observers. To give just one example, reviewing the prospects for DTTV in the leading UK television trade weekly *Broadcast* at the beginning of 1997, Martin Jackson referred to the "widespread scepticism" about the prospects for DTTV and "the spectre overshadowing" it:

> ... a spectre whose name is Rupert Murdoch. Already dominating pay-TV through satellite broadcaster BSkyB, Murdoch has more than just a head start on his land-locked rivals in the journey beyond analogue (*Broadcast*, 1 January 1997).

The BSkyB spectre haunting DTTV had obvious implications for the rest of the policy objectives for digital terrestrial television advanced by the White Paper. For, of course, if DTTV failed to gain a significant new market, then its contribution to British industry, to alternative routes to the information superhighway and to analogue switch-off would all be negligible.

But, even with a more optimistic prognosis about prospects for DTTV take-up, these other policy objectives each had their own problems. 'Opportunities for British manufacturing and programming industries' had been a familiar mantra in previous Conservative Government plans for new broadcasting technologies—cable and satellite—in the first half of the 1980s, yet the outcome on this score for both these industries had turned out disappointing (Goodwin, 1998, pp. 52-53 and 67-68).

Providing the "first experience of the full potential of the information superhighways" was, it might seem a particularly (early) 1990s policy goal. But, to anyone with a memory of UK broadcasting policy, it also had a distinct echo of the claims advanced for cable in the UK in the early 1980s. In 1982 the Cabinet Office's Information Technology Advisory Panel (ITAP) had argued:

> The initial attraction for home subscribers [to cable PG] would be the extra television entertainment channels. However the main role of cable systems eventually will be the delivery of many information, financial and other services to the home (ITAP, 1982, p. 7).

As we have already mentioned, the roll-out of cable in the UK was painfully slow until the nineties. It did however eventually happen. Between the end of 1990 and April 1997 homes passed by cable increased from just over 800,000 to nearly 9 million, and cable television subscribers from less than 150,000 to nearly 2 million. But these very considerable advances by the cable industry were exclusively confined to delivery of cable television and voice telephony. They produced absolutely nothing in terms of the interactive services that the Government had originally anticipated (Goodwin, 1998, p. 68) So, at the time when the White Paper was published, the strategy of using multi-channel television to leverage take-up of interactive services (which was what the jargon of the time meant by "the information superhighways") had already been demonstrated to be highly problematic.

The fourth policy goal behind DTTV – "releasing significant amounts of valuable spectrum for further broadcasting or other use" by analogue switch-off – was an altogether newer issue, without the parallels in previous Conservative Government broadcasting policy which I have identified for the last two. Unlike the other policy goals it had one particular – and particularly problematic – feature. The supposed benefits of the other policy goals could all in principle be achieved incrementally – as DTTV rolled out so would the number of extra multi-channel viewers and (assuming things worked out as hoped) so would be benefits to UK industry and new entrants to the "information superhighways". But there was no such incremental aspect to the benefits of analogue switch-off. These benefits would only come once analogue was switched off. And it could only be switched off once a very substantial proportion of the population had digital reception. Understandably in 1995 the Government was unwilling to set any targets for this. Once targets were set by a Labour Government in September 1999 the difficulties in reaching them became all too apparent.

One last possible policy objective for DTTV can be found in the 1995 White Paper, in addition to the four contained in its opening paragraph that we have already discussed. DTTV would, claimed the White Paper, "give terrestrial broadcasters the opportunity to compete with those on satellite and cable" (DNH, 1995, p. 1). In other words, DTTV was expected to provide platform competition in the multi-channel television market. Given the dominant position of BSkyB in that market this might be thought a highly desirable objective. But precisely because of BSkyB's dominant position, it was also a hugely challenging one. Again, the White Paper paid very little attention to examining those challenges.

In summary, in launching its plans for DTTV in 1995 the Conservative Government advanced five policy objectives for (or justifications for) the new service:

1. Extending viewer choice;
2. Providing benefits for UK industry;
3. Extending take up of interactive services;
4. More efficient use of spectrum via analogue switch-off;
5. Platform competition in multi-channel television.

The framework the Government advanced for DTTV to achieve these objectives, although it allowed some space for public service and abandoned a cash-bid system of licence allocation, was essentially the framework of the Conservative's 1988–1990 broadcasting reform, namely licence allocation to commercial operators, "lightly regulated" by the ITC.

At the level of high politics both this framework and these policy goals for DTTV went largely unchallenged. Although formulated by a Conservative Government, and treated with much scepticism by many contemporary commentators, they were enthusiastically embraced in their essentials by the Labour Party both in opposition and (after May 1997) in office.

HOW DID POLICY OBJECTIVES FARE IN PRACTICE?

The 1995 White Paper proposals on DTTV were fairly rapidly fleshed out into legislation in the 1996 Broadcasting Act. By the time that Act came into force in July the ITC had already established a frequency plan which designated six national multiplexes. One was mandated for use by the BBC; a second was to be shared by Channel 3 (ITV) and Channel 4; a third (labelled multiplex A) was to have dedicated space for Channel 5 and S4C (the Welsh language channel) plus some extra capacity which could be commercially allocated. This left three multiplexes (B, C, and D) without any mandated use. It was over these three that the DTTV license allocation battle was to be fought. The ITC could, if it wanted, allocate each of these three multiplexes to different companies. But it could also, if it so decided, allocate all three to the same company, for the ownership regulations in the 1996 Act set three as the maximum number of multiplexes that could be owned by one company. Given the priority that the ITC would set (and was required to set by the 1996 Act) on maximising the long-term commercial viability of the new service, it was always likely that it would choose to allocate all three of these non-mandated multiplexes to a single winner.

The licence for each multiplex gave the licensee the right to operate multiple television and audio channels, plus additional (data or interactive) services, on each multiplex. Exactly how many television channels could be carried by each multiplex was a matter for the licensee, their decisions on transmission mode and advances in statistical multiplexing. The ITC made its indicative calculations of coverage on the basis of a transmission mode of 64-QAM, although it made it clear that 16-QAM mode would give greater coverage at the expense of lower channel capacity (ITC, 1996). With 64-QAM mode, licensees might expect to start broadcasting with five television channels per multiplex, rapidly rising to seven and eventually perhaps more.

At the end of October 1996 the ITC issued an invitation to apply for the multiplex licences, with a deadline of January 31, 1997. By the time the deadline came round there were just three contenders. One of these (from S4C Digital Network, owned by S4C) was for the half-mandated Multiplex A. The real contest was between the two contenders for all three of the completely non-mandated multiplexes B, C and D: Digital Television Network (DTN) (wholly owned by the cable and transmission company CableTel) and British Digital Broadcasting (BDB) (a joint venture of the two biggest players in ITV, Carlton and Granada, and BSkyB).

Although the ITC invitation had left it open to propose a purely free-to-air offer, the two bids for the three wholly commercial multiplexes were both formulated as pay television propositions, with both a basic package and premium services. However, beyond that, they proposed radically different solutions to the fundamental problem of how to build a DTTV market in the face of the already established position of satellite and cable. DTN was particularly explicit about the challenge.

> DTN will launch its services ... into one of the most competitive and dynamic television markets in the world. The British consumer will be able to choose between three successful analogue media (cable,

satellite and terrestrial), all of which plan to launch digital offerings during the next two years. BSkyB's position in the market for analogue pay-tv is commanding, established through a combination of its unprecedented freedom of operation and its marketing effectiveness. It dominates the marketing for premium programming and can build on this dominance to launch digital satellite services, probably in the next twelve months (DTN, 1997, A3.4).

However, DTN pointed out, "over three-quarters of UK households have not so far subscribed to multi-channel television." On the basis of its own market research it suggested two reasons for this:

The first reason is price-related: 18 per cent of respondents believe that they could not afford to subscribe; another 17 per cent consider that multi-channel television is not worth the money. The second reason is the lack of perceived need for more than four channels. Almost half the population (46 per cent) believe that four channels are enough for anybody.... The British feel that their television is already the best in the world, with a wide range of genres and high quality programmes on offer.... However, on probing further, it is clear that many people would welcome more *high quality* television (DTN, 1997, A3.4-5).

DTN presented a threefold strategy to appeal to these so-far non-takers of multichannel pay-television.

1. A qualitatively distinct (and presumably "high quality") programme offer including "four brand new channels that are not available on satellite." These would be: the Money Channel, bringing "light and colour to a traditionally sombre subject"; the Knowledge Network "for every parent who's ever worried about their children's education, every employee who's ever worried about being left behind"; the British Sports Channel "for the viewer who know's there is more to British Sport than Premier League Football"; and Metro TV which would "exploit the capabilities of digital technology to bring a new sort of city-based service". Alongside these would be more familiar multi-channel fare like the Cartoon Network (DTN, 1997, A3.8-9). The DTN offer included none of BSkyB's basic or premium channels.
2. A range of "innovative new data services." It would provide "simple access via the TV to data services including internet and internet services" (DTN, 1997, A 3.5 and 2.1).

3. A qualitatively distinct pricing policy to that of satellite and cable.
    'We will make digital terrestrial television affordable to a mass
    audience by offering a low entry price and by not requiring
    customers to buy a broader package of channels than they actually
    want' (DTN, 1997, A3.2).

In contrast BDB offered (at least in its publicly available part A) rather less
precise market research, a far less clear commitment to compete on the basis of
price and a very different offer on programmes and services. On programmes, it
proposed a basic package which contained little that was qualitatively different
from that already provided on satellite and cable, and it included in its
prospective basic offer BSkyB's most popular basic channel, Sky One. On top
of that it offered three premium channels, all from BSkyB: Sky Movies, Sky
Sports and the Movie Channel' (BDB, 1997, p. 159). BDB explicitly rejected
initial provision of local or regional services as too costly and of little attraction
to the younger viewers who loomed larger in its target demographic. And it
similarly explicitly rejected any early provision of 'additional' services (data or
interactive) "British digital Broadcasting strongly believes that digital terrestrial
television should concentrate initially on a broad range of family
entertainment... There is a danger that a preponderance of new service concepts
that are poorly understood would provide something of a barrier, rather than a
driver of early take-up" (BDB, 1997, p. 66 and 250).

The ITC was therefore presented with a choice between very two different
pay propositions for DTTV. One (DTN) offered competition with BSkyB on
programming, data and interactive services, and pricing. The other offered no
data or interactive services, no clear pricing alternative and a programme offer
that was essentially BSkyB-lite. There was one other crucial difference between
the two bidders. DTN's backers, Cable Tel had limited programming experience
in the UK market (although they were to be joined in their bid, after it was
submitted, by the third player in ITV, United News and Media). In contrast
BDB's backers consisted of the two biggest players in ITV plus the dominant
player in existing multi-channel television in the UK, BSkyB. Particularly in
view of the widespread scepticism in and around the industry that had greeted
DTTV, Granada, Carlton, and BSkyB could understandably be viewed as the
one "dream ticket" that could make it work.

Not everyone shared this view: some commentators were impressed by
DTN's interactive proposals, OFTEL favoured DTN on competition grounds.
But most contemporary observers grudgingly took the view that BDB was the
most viable option. So too, when it came to a decision, did the ITC. In June
1997 the commission announced the award of all three multiplexes B, C and D
to BDB. It offered the following explanation of its decision:

The ITC considered that BDB's application offered a greater degree of assurance than that of DTN that the proposed services could be established and maintained throughout the period of the licences. The ITC considered that the revenue assumptions in BDB's business plan were more cautious than those of DTN.... Funding for BDB is to be provided from the internal resources of the shareholders, both of whom are substantial FTSE 100 companies. In the case of DTN, the business plan was dependant upon its parent company raising further debt....

The ITC's conclusion was that, on the basis of each applicant's business plan and funding proposals and the further information supplied by each applicant, there would be a higher degree of confidence in the ability of BDB to establish and maintain its services throughout the licence period.

Each applicant put forward acceptable proposals for appealing to a variety of tastes and interests but of a different character. BDB put forward proposals for programme services generally intended to appeal to broad audiences. On balance the ITC was more attracted by the innovative programme proposals (supported by additional services) designed to appeal principally to a wide range of different audiences which were put forward by DTN.

Each applicant proposed substantial expenditure on the promotion of DTTV, both in respect of the subsidy of domestic receiving equipment and in advertising and marketing costs. Although DTN proposed a higher level of expenditure on receiving equipment than BDB, this expenditure was dependant on a more optimistic estimate of subscriber numbers (ITC, 1997).

It would be not unfair to conclude that the ITC saw BDB as the duller, but altogether stronger and safer option.

There was, however, one big problem in the BDB bid. The presence of BSkyB, already the dominant player in UK multi-channel television, as a one third equity-holder had obvious attractions; but on competition grounds, it had obvious and very serious drawbacks. These were raised initially by the European Commission and then accepted by the ITC. So a condition of the ITC's award of the multiplex licences to BDB was that BSkyB withdraw as a shareholder, although it was required to remain as a guaranteed programme provider. The withdrawal robbed BDB of established pay television expertise and turned BSkyB from a potentially benevolent stake-holder in the DTTV enterprise, into a potentially aggressive platform competitor.

Rebranded as ONdigital, BDB launched its service (a few months later than originally planned) on November 15, 1998. By the time of the launch the multi-channel television market in the UK had moved on from 1995 in two important respects.

First, the numbers of subscribers to the established analogue multi-channel television had continued to grow, with most of the growth over the previous three years having come from cable (a key factor in cable's growth in this period being its competitive telephony offer). By the end of 1998 there were nearly 6.4 million cable and satellite subscribers in the UK (over 3.6 million satellite—virtually all analogue, and over 2.8 million cable—all analogue). This constituted over 25 per cent of UK households.

Second, BSkyB had gained a six-week advantage over ONdigital by launching its own digital satellite television service, Sky Digital, on October 1. ONdigital was therefore faced from the outset with an aggressive digital platform war.

The two digital platforms both offered a range of basic packages, plus premium channels. ONdigital's fullest basic package, priced at £9.99 a month, initially consisted of 12 television channels (the majority already carried by Sky, plus some thematic channels supplied by Carlton and Granada which were eventually replaced by more popular channels also carried by Sky). On top of that ONdigital had three premium channels, one sport and two movie, again all provided by Sky. Sky Digital's fullest basic package, the 'Family Package', offered 40 television channels for £11.99 a month, plus a far wider range of premium channels and near-video-on-demand pay-per-view movies. Both platforms offered alternative, lower-priced points of entry for more limited basic packages. ONdigital's lowest priced package (with six channels) cost £7.99. At £6.99, Sky Digital's "Value Pack" undercut that by a pound per month.

Both digital platforms made a modest but significant starts. By the end of June 1999 ONdigital had just over 200,000 subscriptions and SkyDigital 750,000 (Flynn, 2003) SkyDigital's apparently far more impressive figures, look rather less impressive when one looks at the whole BSkyB satellite subscription base (analogue plus digital). This remained almost completely flat in the nine months that followed BSkyB's digital launch. Any new customers that SkyDigital was getting were only just compensating BSkyB for loss of its analogue satellite customers.

Things changed in the middle of 1999. In their first few months both ONdigital and Sky Digital had charged new subscribers (and conversions from analogue) a one-off (although subsidised) price for their set-top boxes. In May 1999 Sky announced that it would provide free set-top boxes from June 1. ONdigital immediately followed suit. After that the rate of take-up of both digital platforms increased significantly.

By the end of 1999 ONdigital had well over 500,000 subscribers and by the end of 2000 nearly one million. By that time, however, ONdigital's rate of growth was already slowing significantly. And it slowed further the following year. During 2001 the digital terrestrial platform (now rebranded ITV Digital) added only a further quarter of a million subscribers to reach nearly 1.25 million by the end of that year. In retrospect, the last two quarters of 1999 turned out to be ONdigital's period of fastest net growth.

Sky Digital's take-off after the introduction of free set top boxes was both more dramatic than ONdigital's and longer lasting. By the end of 1999 Sky Digital had nearly 2.1 million subscribers, and by the end of 2000 nearly 4.7 million. By that stage BSkyB had been so successful in converting its analogue satellite subscriber base to digital that it could switch off its analogue DTH service in the middle of the following year. Also, from the time that it began offering free-set top boxes, BSkyB resumed overall growth in its total (analogue plus digital) satellite subscriber base. By the end of 2001 (after the BSkyB's analogue satellite service had been switched off) Sky Digital had more than 5.7 million subscribers, compared with the 3.4 million satellite subscribers BSkyB had just before the digital service was launched.

So, in simple numbers terms, just over three years after the launch of both platforms, by the end of 2001 Sky Digital had clearly roundly beaten ONdigital/ITV Digital in the platform war. Viewed in isolation, one and a quarter subscribers to ITV Digital after three years might look impressive (this was, after all, 5 per cent of UK households and on an international basis, easily the biggest DTTV platform in the world at the time). But in the same period BSkyB had, in net terms, not only successfully converted the whole of its analogue satellite subscriber base to digital, but had additionally recruited nearly twice as many new subscribers to digital as its terrestrial rival.

Looking beyond comparisons between the two platforms, ITV Digital's position at the end of 2001 was even bleaker. In its early days ONdigital's ITV owners had declared 2 million subscribers to be the break even point. 1.25 million was still well short of that. And, as we have seen, the rebranding to ITV Digital in mid 2001, though entertaining viewers and winning plaudits from the advertising industry with its expensive "monkey" promotional campaign, had not even succeeded in restoring the terrestrial platform to its earlier levels of growth. So ITV's digital terrestrial operation continued to generate large losses for its parents.

In awarding the digital terrestrial franchise to Carlton and Granada in 1997 the ITC had, as we have mentioned, seen it has a positive factor that "funding for BDB is to be provided from the internal resources of the shareholders, both of whom are substantial FTSE 100 companies." But what had looked a plus in 1997 had become a distinct minus in 2001. Television advertising revenues in general and ITV's in particular were now in sharp decline, and, with that down turn in their core business, Carlton and Granada were under heavy pressure from their shareholders to end the continued haemorrhage of cash to their digital terrestrial sideline.

The situation was exacerbated by ITV Digital's expensive purchase (at the height of the sports rights bubble) of rights to Football League (second tier English soccer) matches. Faced with the increased shareholder pressure to reduce the continued losses on their digital operation Carlton and Granada sought to renegotiate the deal. Faced with the prospect of their own financial melt-down the Football League clubs resisted. At the end of March 2002 ITV Digital went into receivership, and at the end of April 2002 the receivers closed it down. The world's first experiment in Digital Terrestrial Television had gone bust.

WHAT WENT WRONG?

Former Chief Executive of ONdigital/ITV Digital (from July 1999 until its demise), Stuart Prebble offers the following overall verdict: "There were probably half a dozen major problems. We could have survived any three or four of them, but not all six" (Prebble, 2003).

The biggest of those problems, according to Prebble and many other observers, was the transmission technology:

> This was the first launch of the DTTV system anywhere in the world.... There were no textbooks to look up.... It said in the laboratory that we would start with 70 per cent of coverage. But it is only by trial and error that you know what your coverage is. We were getting something like 30 per cent of the boxes coming back because people couldn't get the signal.... Our initial coverage was closer to 40 per cent. And, of those 40 per cent, many needed aerial upgrades.
>
> The bottom line was that the signal was not powerful enough... We started at a very early stage trying to lobby the regulatory authorities to increase the power of the signal. We never really made any headway (Prebble, 2003).

A second major problem was pricing. The programme supply deal struck by BSkyB with (what was to become) ONdigital, after BSkyB had been forced to pull out of an equity stake in the terrestrial platform, was a tough one. According to Prebble, "Sky charged ONdigital a higher wholesale price than the retail price it charged its own customers. This meant that from Day One our business lost money on every customer that was taking premium channels" (Prebble, 2003).

Added to these were substantial problems with piracy, regulatory limits on the amount of on-screen cross-promotion that could be done for ONdigital by its ITV parents and, and the Football League deal. "But probably all of these," argues Prebble, "might have been sustainable were it not for the fact that at the same moment ITV went into the most serious advertising recession in its history." This latter, Prebble argues, helps to explain the apparent miscalculation of the Football League deal. ONdigital had, he says, entered into it, on the premise that it could wholesale the rights to BSkyB, which would have a compelling reason to match the terrestrial platform's football offer. But BSkyB, realising Carlton and Granada's financial problems, held out against taking the Football League coverage, thereby turning the deal into the financial disaster that finally sunk ITV Digital (Prebble, 2003).

Prebble is undoubtedly right that ONdigital/ITV Digital's eventual failure was a result of a combination of a number of unfavourable factors. And, given that combination, ONdigital/ITV Digital's 1.25 million subscribers after little more than three years should certainly not be sneered at. But this set of unfavourable factors was neither totally accidental nor totally unpredictable. To a considerable it resulted from the basically flawed premises under which DTTV had been launched in the UK. As I have emphasised, DTTV faced the basic problem of being a technology which, at best, could offer less than its already well-established satellite and cable rivals. Government strategy ignored this, and invited commercial operators to bid for this new platform. The two bidders both proposed a pay model. The ITC chose the bidder with the safest programme offer (a cut down version of that already offered by BSkyB) because it was backed by the two largest ITV companies. A platform war was inevitable (and, from the perspective of the fifth of the policy objectives we have identified for DTTV, positively desirable). In such a war it was entirely predictable that BSkyB would set the wholesale price of its programming (which the DTTV platform rightly considered essential to its programme offer) so as to avoid its own satellite platform being undercut.

It was also undeniably the case that DTTV transmission was underpowered, because of the (as it turned out, undue) concern of the regulators about interfering with analogue transmissions. But, placed in a situation of having to directly compete with the far higher capacity digital satellite platform, the terrestrial licensees understandably, but mistakenly, tried to maximise the number of channels they could carry on their multiplexes, and therefore substantially increased the difficulties potential subscribers would have with successful reception.

The ill-fated Football League deal was also, in part, a product of ONdigital/ITV Digital seeing itself as competing directly, as a pay television platform with BSkyB. Given that perspective, and given the enormous importance of sports rights in BSkyB's success, it was natural that the terrestrial platform should seek to get its own slice of the sports action, and therefore take risks and over-bid in order to do so.

Finally, the downturn in advertising revenue for ITV, and the consequences for ITV Digital that would stem from it, were also neither accidental nor unpredictable. Advertising funded commercial television was already well-known to be a business highly sensitive to the general business cycle at the time that the ITC portrayed ownership by Carlton and Granada as a guarantee of ON Digital/ITV Digital's long term financial security.

In this head-to-head platform competition with BSkyB did ONdigital/ITV Digital have any potential advantages?

Price, as we have seen, was ruled out—and not just for premium services. Even for the most basic package, BSkyB maintained a lower entry point than its terrestrial rival.

Cross promotion by ITV might have seemed a powerful asset but was greatly inhibited by regulation. And during its first years of operation ONdigital was unable to exploit the powerful ITV brand because of the fragmentation of ownership of the ITV network. It was only late in the day, after United News and Media had exited from ITV, leaving the network dominated by Carlton and Granada, that ONdigital could be rebranded as ITV Digital. But, by that stage, the results were, as we have noted, disappointing.

Which left one other potential advantage for the DTTV platform. For some of the market, perhaps DTTV's lower channel capacity might be an advantage rather than a liability. Stuart Prebble explains:

> The research told us that the satellite dish was a barrier to entry for a lot of people…. But also there was a positive resistance to what was seen as too much choice. 200 channels was actually a turn-off for a lot of people…. The notion of 20 was potentially manageable, but the research told you, and I suspect still tells you, that with 200 channels, and 190 channels of junk, people perceived that they were paying for all of this but did not really want it…. We tried, not in a very overt way, to make our marketing appeal to Middle England (Prebble, 2003).

It might plausibly be argued that the 1.25 million subscribers that ITV Digital eventually secured were an indication that this type of market existed. But the nearly double that number of additional subscribers to multi-channel pay television that BSkyB achieved during the same period would suggest that hostility to a satellite dish and reluctance to spend on large numbers of extra channels were less fixed than is often supposed. But if there really was a significant satellite-hostile and hyper-multi-channel-hostile Middle England audience available, the fact remained that it was not big enough to sustain a commercial pay television digital terrestrial platform.

After the collapse of ITV Digital the ITC moved rapidly to appoint a successor to occupy the three DTTV multiplexes it had vacated. In May the commission invited applications for the three multiplex licences, with a closing date of 13 June 2002.

The established analogue broadcasters, BBC, ITV and Channel 4, all showed considerable interest in rapidly reviving a full DTTV service and engaged in serious negotiations between themselves to put forward a joint bid for the three vacant multiplexes. The negotiations indicated considerable elements of consensus about what would be needed to create a viable new operation.

First reception would have to be made far more robust and coverage greater. There were two ways in which this could be done – increase in signal power and change in the mode of transmission. Before the demise of ITV Digital the ITC had already authorised an experimental 3dB power increase programme on some digital transmitters. The BBC eventually made its bid for licences conditional on making this power increase permanent and extending it to all transmitters. The BBC and ITV were also agreed that it was necessary to change the transmission mode from 64-QAM (that originally chosen by ONdigital) to 16-QAM, giving less channels, in return for a far more robust reception.

Secondly, the BBC, ITV and Channel 4 were all now agreed that the DTTV service should deliver a core of approximately 20 free-to-air channels, rather than a subscription basic package.

But negotiations foundered on whether this free-to-air service should be supplemented by a small number of pay channels. ITV and Channel 4 saw this as essential, while the BBC favoured a completely free-to-air service. So, in June, the BBC on the one hand, and ITV and Channel 4, on the other, submitted separate and competing applications.

In total there were six applications for one or more of the three vacated multiplexes. But the contest was essentially two way – between the bids backed by the established analogue terrestrial broadcasters. One of these main contenders centred on the former ITV Digital owners, Carlton and Granada, now joined by Channel 4 under the banner of Digital Terrestrial Alliance (DTA). DTA bid for two of the multiplexes and made its bid conditional upon a bid for the third multiplex by Freeview Plus, which was led by two former BSkyB executives. The DTA/Freeview Plus proposition was for "a strong core of around 20 free-to-air channels built around the services provided by the five analogue terrestrial channels," supplemented by what DTA/Freeview Plus called a light (or in Freeview Plus's perhaps unfortunate terminology "lite") pay service of up to seven pay channels 'targeting homes prepared to pay £10–15 a month over and above the BBC licence fee' (as opposed to the 'mid/high' Average Revenue Per User of £20 to £30 per month then typical of Sky Digital and cable subscribers.) (DTA, 2002, and Freeview Plus, 2002).

DTA gave the following reasoning for tying their free-to-air service to Freeview Plus's pay offer:

> Further free-to air channels [on top of the 20 DTA proposed PG] will attract only marginal incremental viewing... The proposed pay package is the best way to add attractive channels and to increase overall viewing to the platform beyond the free-to-air saturation point. Based on historic viewing behaviour, we believe that viewing to a light pay package ... would be ten times the viewing of the more marginal free-to-air channels that would form the alternative. For these reasons, customer research concludes that over 60% of potential DTTV viewers would wish the service to be upgradeable to pay (DTA, 2002, p. 4).

The second main contender, applying under the banner of the "The Consortium," was led by the BBC, bidding for one multiplex, in alliance with Crown Castle, bidding for the other two.

The BBC/Crown Castle bid, assertively proposed an even more radical break from the ITV Digital model.

"ITV Digital," argued the BBC/Crown Castle application, "was last into a crowded market and used the same business plan as existing pay television operators: high cost, premium value content aimed at the multi-channel heartland." Not only did the platform have fewer channels, at a similar price to its competitors, but DTTV's only content differentiators—the *Nationwide Football League* and the *Champions League*—failed to draw sufficient viewers and their high costs increased the pressures already faced by ITV Digital.

> It is our contention that, after the experiences of ITV Digital, a new pay operator would struggle to make the platform a viable and profitable success. No platform operator could afford to offer enough pay channels to create a real consumer alternative. The best alternative to the ITV model is to make DTTV services available free-to view, differentiating DTTV from cable and satellite and offering analogue consumers something they recognise as an exciting improvement to their familiar television experience. Simply put it is more, better, free-to-view television. *DTTV needs to be free-to-view* (Consortium, 2002, p. 3-4).

The ITC seems to have accepted this case for a more radical break from the recently failed ITV Digital model. On July 4 it announced that it was awarding the three multiplexes to the BBC/Crown Castle consortium, citing, as one of the factors in its decision, 'the opportunity provided by the consortium for a fresh start for DTTV by offering a distinctive new proposition to consumers.' (ITC,

2002) The Commission was also, one may suspect, also reluctant to effectively hand back DTTV to the former owners of a failed operation.

Rebranded as Freeview, the BBC/Crown Castle consortium launched its service on 31 October 2002. The launch was generally credited with being a very considerable success, with, according to one estimate, half a million DTTV adaptors being sold in the first four months after launch (Ewington, 2003). And, thanks to the reconfigured transmission technology, few of those boxes went back. The free-to-air model plus cheap adaptors seemed to have revived DTTV's fortunes.

THE CURRENT SITUATION

Where does this leave the UK digital television? What are its prospects after the new start for DTTV? And how do these measure up to the policy objectives for digital television so boldly outlined in 1995?

We can usefully start answering these questions by looking at the most recent full statistical snapshot of UK television available at the time of going to press, that taken at the end of June 2003. This pictures the situation just over a year after the demise of ITV Digital and includes the first eight months after Freeview's very successful launch. On June 30, 2003 there were, according to the ITC, nearly 11.3 million households with digital television in the UK. At 45.5 percent of UK households, that meant that the UK was, as it had been for at least three years previously, the country with easily the highest penetration of digital television in the world. So, if there is a digital television "revolution," the UK could, quite reasonably be seen as at its forefront.

But once those figures are broken down a more complex picture emerges. Of those 11.3 million digital television households the great majority, more than 6.5 million, were DTH subscribers to Sky Digital. The next biggest chunk (nearly 2.2 million) were digital cable subscribers, while DTTV (now, after the demise of ITV Digital, all free-to-air) came in third, at just under 1.8 million. The remaining, 0.7 million, digital television households, were made up of free-to-air satellite (ITC, 2003).

So, if the UK led the digital television "revolution" in mid 2003, it did so not primarily (or even secondarily) because of digital *terrestrial* television (which made up just under 16 percent of UK digital television homes), but because of pay digital *satellite* (Sky Digital subscribers counting for nearly 58 percent of digital television homes).

Of course, what had gone for the past does not necessarily go for the future. And, after the launch of Freeview, digital terrestrial television was already showing that it will figure more prominently than in its former pay television incarnation. But how much more? And with what bearing on the policy objectives set out for it?

Prognoses for the future development of digital television in the UK have been most concerned with one of those policy objectives—progress toward the conditions which would permit analogue switch-off. In September 1999 the New Labour Government set criteria for analogue switch-off which included most importantly an "accessibility" criterion that "95 per cent of consumers have access to digital equipment." The goal for switch-over was set at 2006-2010. So in what way, and how rapidly, might 45.5 percent of UK households having digital television grow to 95 percent? This was the central question that the ITC and the BBC addressed in their joint report on 'Progress Towards Digital Switchover' published in April 2003 (ITC/BBC, 2003).

In assessing the prospects for growth of the three major digital platforms we need to recognise that each presents a very different range of dynamics (we will not discuss a fourth platform—digital television over the phone-line via DSL—which is, and looks likely to remain, in the immediate future, quite marginal in the UK).

Digital pay satellite, offered in the UK effectively exclusively by BSkyB, has, as we have stressed, been to date the main driver of the UK's digital television development. BSkyB's rapid conversion of its existing analogue base had been dramatic and its acquisition of new digital customers impressive, but the rate of acquisition had slowed. For many observers that slow down is an indication of some sort of plateau' for pay television. However, it should be noted, first that the notion of such a "plateau" has been around ever since the start of (analogue) Sky, but the supposed plateau always seems to have been getting higher. Secondly in the second quarter of 2003 Sky Digital added another 126,000 subscribers in the UK, held its churn below ten percent for the fourth quarter in a row and was on the verge of reaching its long-announced goal of 7 million (UK and Ireland) DTH subscribers by the end of 2003.

But, alongside growth in numbers, BSkyB has another, probably more important, goal – squeezing more money out of its existing DTH customers. Its declared aim was to raise ARPU (Average Revenue Per User) to £400 per year by the end of 2005. In mid 2003 BSkyB's DTH annualised ARPU stood at £366 and had increased by 5.5 percent over the previous year, so that target looks stiff but achievable. However, there is clearly at least some trade-off between maximising revenue from each subscriber, and attracting new ones. If BSkyB's strategy of increasing ARPU prevails, then it may well turn the notion of a 'plateau' for digital pay television into a self fulfilling prophecy.

Cable, the second largest digital television platform in mid 2003, looked distinctly less dynamic than its satellite rival. It had been slow to convert its analogue networks to digital. By the end of June 2003 more than one million of the nearly 3.3 million cable television subscribers were still analogue. And over the previous year the total number of cable television subscribers in the UK had actually fallen. Both the major cable operators, NTL and Telewest had suffered severe financial difficulties (a legacy of the debts incurred in building their infrastructure) and their efforts were focussed on financial restructuring rather than growth. So the immediate prospects for cable television were of slow conversion of its remaining analogue subscribers to digital, but little overall growth of its television subscriber base. Successful financial restructuring and the possible consolidation of the two cable operators into one, might lead to more effective marketing and a resumption of overall subscriber growth, but seems unlikely to dramatically change the picture.

So, even on the most optimistic prognoses, the two biggest digital television platforms, both operating on a pay television model, were by themselves in no way set to convert anything like the required numbers of remaining analogue UK television households to digital in anything remotely like the Government's 2006-2010 time frame for analogue-switch off.

So, from the view-point of analogue switch-off, the prospects for the new free-to-air DTTV become crucial. Because of the newness of the free-to-air DTTV offer they are even more difficult to predict than the prospects for the other two major digital television platforms. In mid 2003 the ITC estimated that some 1.8 million UK households received free-to-air DTTV—600,000 (a rough estimate) of them through the legacy of ITV Digital's set top boxes, nearly 400,000 via integrated digital television (iDTV) sets and nearly 800,000 via 'Freeview' boxes (some purchased before Freeview's official launch, but most purchased since the October 31, 2002 launch). With the surviving ITV Digital boxes being a one-off inheritance, and very slow take up of iDTV sets, the immediate and medium term prospects of DTTV growth are almost entirely dependent on the sale of Freeview boxes. And early figures here have certainly been impressive. "In the first eight weeks of the service Freeview boxes... were selling at approximately 33,000 per week," ITC observers estimated, a figure they rightly remarked "eclipsed" the early (and indeed any PG) performance of ONdigital/ITV Digital (ITC, 2003, p. 4). This initial rate of take-up slowed slightly, but it continued to be impressive, with another 400,000 Freeview boxes bought in the first six months of 2003. A one-off payment of £99 (now falling to £80), in order to get a significant number of extra channels, does appear to be an attractive option to significant numbers of UK viewers who have so far resisted the lure of pay television (including pay-DTTV).

However it would be dangerous to project these figures into an indefinite future. In July 2002 one consumer survey found that 58 percent of those currently without digital television said that they would never switch to it (ITC/BBC, 2003, p. 26). Coming so soon after the collapse of ITV Digital and before the beginning of the Freeview offer this may be an exceptionally high figure, but it does indicate the potential level of consumer resistance even free-to-air DTTV has to overcome. The programme offer of Freeview has some very obvious gaps (The Freeview digital offerings as at August 2003 are listed in Table 7.1). Unlike ONdigital/ITV Digital, Freeview does *not* carry the most popular non-analogue-terrestrial general entertainment channel Sky One; the popular children's channels Cartoon Network or Nickelodeon; the most popular music channel MTV; or the popular "golden oldies" channel, UK Gold, which might be expected to be one of the most appealing channels to the most "digitally resistant"—the elderly. And even with the greatly improved DTTV transmission coverage, a significant proportion of the UK population will be unable to access it (perhaps 20 percent), and a further significant proportion only able to access it with the extra cost and trouble of aerial upgrade (another 20 percent).

Taking these, and other factors, into consideration, and starting from end of 2002 data, in April 2003 the ITC/BBC report on 'Progress Towards Digital Switchover' made what it called "upper case scenario" and "lower case scenario" projections of digital television take-up in the UK to 2007. Its "upper case scenario" projected 78 percent of UK households having digital television by 2007; its "lower case scenario" envisaged only 58 percent. On that basis the report concluded that: "Notwithstanding the optimism surrounding the early data for Freeview, it is unlikely that the Government's current criteria will be met to enable a nationwide switchover in the early part of the 2006-2010 'target window'".

It added, rather awkwardly, that "continued progress according to the upper case scenario within the take-up range suggests that 95 per cent take-up might be approached around the end of the target window" (ITC/BBC, 2003, p. 6).

In rather plainer language, that meant that, given the most optimistic combination of the most optimistic projections for the various different digital television platforms, 95 percent household take-up of digital television might just about be achieved by 2010 (and on any less optimistic projection it certainly would not be).

But even this self-confessedly "upper case scenario" for the conditions for analogue switch off in the UK being achieved by 2010 contains two big problems. First the ITC/BBC "upper case scenario" stretches optimism to its limits. It assumes a combination of *all* of the following factors to 2010, each of which, as we have seen, is distinctly questionable:

    I.   Continued successful take-up of Freeview.
    II. A recapitalised, dynamic cable sector which both builds out networks and achieves a higher conversion rate of homes passed.

III. Ongoing net subscriber acquisition .... By BSkyB.
IV. DSL technology taking off as a platform for digital TV distribution (ITC/BBC, 2003, p. 6).

Table 7.1: Digital channels available on Freeview

Generalist channels (also available on analogue)	BBC 1
	BBC 2
	ITV 1
	Channel 4
	Five
Entertainment	BBC 3
	ITV 2
	Sky Travel
	UK Bright Ideas
	F tn
News & Sports News	BBC News 24
	ITV News
	Sky News
	Sky Sports News
Documentaries	BBC 4
	UK History
Children's	CBeebies
	CBBC
Shopping & Travel	QVC
	TV Travel Shop
	Bid-up tv (interactive auction channel)
Music	TFM
	The hits
Special interest	BBC Parliament
	BBCi (interactive)
	Community Channel
	Free Play (interactive games)
	Teletext
Welsh language (Wales only)	S4C
	S4C2
Radio	BBC: 11 channels
	Commercial: 8 channels

Source: www.freeview.co.uk

But even if this highly optimistic scenario turns out to be the case that would mean 95 percent of households with *their first sets* converted to digital. Yet, as the report recognises three quarters of UK households have more than one television set. Converting these may give an added impulse to extra purchases of cheap adaptors for free-to-air DTTV, but it also adds another massive obstacle to analogue switch-off.

In an immediate Government response of the to the ITC/BBC report Culture Secretary, Tessa Jowell's, commented: "Doomsayers may suggest we won't meet the target. I would say to them that if industry can make this much progress on its own, anything is possible. The strong take-up since the launch of Freeview shows digital television is a product the public wants" (DCMS, 2003).

In view of the evidence presented in the report by two organisations far from unsympathetic to the Government's aims, this response seems both tetchy and complacently over-optimistic.

In contrast, but probably far more realistically, David Elstein, a long-term critic of the UK Government's DTTV policy, dryly observed about the report: "Analogue switch-off may arrive—eventually. The most intelligent analysis of the issue sees the first million homes being switched off by 2014. But failure to achieve the switch-off would not be a disaster..." (Elstein, 2003).

If progress towards analogue switch-off looks both slower and more problematic than Government policy envisaged, what of the other goal for digital television set by the Conservatives back in 1995, that "for many people, it will provide their first experience of the full potential of the information superhighways"? With suitable shift in jargon, this goal is still firmly propounded by New Labour, eight years later. Trade Secretary, Patricia Hewitt and Culture Secretary, Tessa Jowell now maintain:

> We want every home to be able to enjoy the present and future benefits of digital television. The future is even brighter—today's cutting edge and pilot services already offer health advice, shopping, education, holidays, text messages, email, auctions, games and food delivered to your home. Interactive television can put control into the hands of viewers instead of broadcasters. Combined with a phone line, digital TV can open up access to the Internet through a familiar and trusted medium, broadening the opportunities for education, information, shopping and games (Hewitt/Jowell 2003).

In assessing whether the experience to date supports this vision, we again need to stress, that so far, in this respect too, digital *terrestrial* television has proved far less important than digital *satellite*. As we have already noted, when Carlton and Granada won the DTTV licences in 1997 their proposals explicitly rejected the provision of any additional interactive services. In the autumn of 2000, ONdigital launched ONnet, an internet access service based on a "sidecar" coupled to the set-top box, containing an internet browser and modem. Stuart Prebble explains the motivation behind the launch.

> Comparative analysis in newspapers between the three digital platforms labelled DTTV as having no interactivity to speak of, which was why we went for the internet proposition. It was never really going to be a serious piece of business, but it did enable us to say that we are the only platform that gives you full access to the internet. It was something we wanted to be able to say we had as a way of levelling the playing field in terms of perception by customers (Prebble, 2003).

It probably made little difference. Subscriptions to ONnet peaked at around 100,000 (roughly 10 percent of ONdigital/ITV Digital subscribers) and the service ceased with the collapse of ITV Digital.

The free-to-air revival in DTTV's fortunes, seems unlikely (at least in the immediate term) to produce a major expansion in any similar DTTV-related internet service for the simple reason that of the nine different DTTV adaptors currently being marketed in the UK only one (Netgem) contains a modem and internet browser (ITC/BBC, 2003).

Altogether more important in scope, but different in type, have been the interactive services provided to Sky Digital's subscribers. Sky Digital adopted the model of a "walled garden" portal, originally in partnership with a number of high street names, under the brand name Open. Open provided a range of services including shopping, banking, games, e-mail, betting, and information services. Since the end of 2000 it has been wholly owned by BSkyB and rebranded as Sky Active.

The availability of such a large range of interactive services via the television to such a large number of households is undoubtedly a significant and interesting development. But both the qualitative and quantitative research that has been done on subscribers' use of and attitude to these services, strongly suggests that, while they may produce important changes to the television viewing experience, they hardly amount to any alternative television route to the interactivity proved by the internet-connected PC.

In the summer of 2001 Oftel commissioned Counterpoint Research to undertake a small number of in-depth individual and household interviews and peer group discussions on consumer use and perception of digital television services. A major aspect of this study was use and perception of digital interactive services. The study concluded that:

There were mixed to lukewarm reactions to interactive services, with some subscribers unsure whether they had any interactive services at all as part of their package. All argued that it was difficult to get an overview of what was available... Such services were generally seen as "an interesting extra" and were not part of the justification for, and value in, their digital subscription (Counterpoint, 2001, pp. 10-11).

One big obstacle to all interactive services via the television was the widespread feeling that they "tended to 'take over' the television when being used and were consistently criticised for doing so. Respondents argued that this was a 'selfish' use of the television when others were watching." On particular services:

> Respondents were confused indeed about the home shopping offer... On-line banking was almost universally rejected. Those who wanted to bank remotely already did so (via telephone and internet banking), and those who did not already have "remote" accounts were extremely uncomfortable with the idea of managing their account on a large TV screen in the middle of the living room....
>   Email had very limited appeal, and those who had tried it once or twice had experienced technical difficulties and had simply given up. In any case most already had at least one email address and they were extremely concerned about the lack of compatibility with their PCs (Counterpoint, 2001, p. 11).

This picture of the rather marginal use of digital television interactive services given by qualitative research is reinforced by quantitative research. The ITC has for many years commissioned an annual survey (of about a thousand individuals) of viewers' attitudes to television, results of which have been published under the title 'Television: The Public's View.' In both 2001 and 2002 the survey asked all those in the sample who subscribed to a digital television service how often they used an interactive television service. The responses to the 2002 survey (2001 figures in brackets) were as follows: "Of those with such services 66 percent said they never used them (62% in 2001), while just 15% said they used them at least once a week (19 in 2001)" (ITC/BSC, 2003, p. 5).

One partial explanation of this continued poor response to interactive television services may be the dramatic rise of home internet access via computer. When UK DTTV policy was formulated in 1995, home computer internet access in the UK was tiny. The year digital television was launched in the UK in 1998 only 8 percent of respondents to the ITC 'Public' View' survey had home computer internet access. By 2002 that figure had risen to 43 percent (up from 35 percent in 2001) (ITC/BSC, 2003, p. 15). Of course the demographics of (particularly satellite) digital television and home computer internet access are in a number of respects markedly different: home internet access via computer being heavily up market, satellite subscribers traditionally down market. But there is now a large overlap between the two. It seems scarcely surprising that those with experience of and ready access to internet access via a computer are likely to find many of the interactive services offered by digital television (apart from those which are directly and immediately programme related) distinctly second best.

But the 'Public's View' survey provides only slight indication that those digital subscribers without home computer internet access are any more interested in its interactive services. And, as we have seen, if Freeview boxes do reach out to the so far "digitally resistant" (and also internet resistant) poor and elderly demographics, it will, for the most part, be doing so without any return path, and therefore without any serious interactive services even available, never mind used.

The story to date of DTTV in the UK is full of paradoxes, not the least of which is that (as this chapter has argued) the progress and impact of DTTV were inherently going to be dependent on the progress and impact of other potentially more powerful digital television platforms (in the UK case, particularly DTH satellite). Yet UK Government policy on DTTV glossed over this issue and virtually ignored those other platforms. UK policy on DTTV in many ways replicated policy on previous new distribution technologies, without in any serious way drawing lessons from their failures or unintended outcomes. The result, as it had been in the case of both cable and satellite before, was, eventually, "success" in terms of take up of the new technology, but not in the way that that Government had originally anticipated nor with the achievement of the policy objectives on which Government policy was originally premised. In the case of DTTV, the UK did take a lead in the take up of digital, but primarily because of digital *satellite*, not digital *terrestrial*. And, despite the "success" in take-up of the new technology, two of the main policy goals (analogue switch off, and alternative route to interactivity) remain distinctly problematic.

The lesson that free-marketeers might be tempted to draw from this is that, particularly when it comes to new communication technologies, government's can't (and shouldn't try) to pick winners. That conclusion would be wrong. Because in this case, in line with the policy mantra of the times, government policy was precisely not to pick winners. So DTTV was left to commercial operators, who chose a (rather conservative) pay model and were backed in this by the regulators (and by the majority of independent commentators) because they saw this as the strongest commercial option. That pay model, directly competing with stronger platforms, was a (predictable and predicted) failure. The new, initially very successful and much-lauded, free-to-air model for DTTV is essentially led and sustained by a publicly funded broadcaster (which has already come under sustained attack from commercial operators because of its success in this and other areas).

But important as it is to remember the past, particularly when most of the still powerful actors involved are all too happy to forget it, we should also try and look at the future of digital television in the UK from perspectives other than the ONdigital/ ITV Digital disaster, analogue switch-off and alternative routes to full-blown digital interactivity.

If initial successes are anything to go by, the free-to-air model led by a publicly funded broadcaster, gives a new impetus to DTTV as one half of a new digital television age. This age will be split between a modest free-to-air multi-channel offer carried mainly by DTTV and a pay television hyper-multi-channel offer, enhanced by interactivity, and carried by satellite and cable platforms. Such a scenario raises a number of interesting and important questions for the future and for future research. Will the new free-to-air DTTV exert downward cost pressures on the dominant pay television operator? (an argument intriguingly advanced in Ewington 2003). Or will the modest free-to-air multichannel offer simply be a stepping stone for more consumers to take up the full-blown hyper-multi-channel pay offer? How much, and in what ways, will the television viewing experience be changed by majority access to a multiplicity of channels? And (forget about being an alternative to home computer internet access) how much and in what ways will the television viewing experience be changed by widespread experience of interactivity?

These are all questions which have wide international significance. With its lead in overall digital television penetration, and its second wind with DTTV, in the next few years the UK will be an important research lab for answering them.

Acknowledgements
My thanks to Barry Flynn of *Inside Digital TV*, Pam Hanley and Leila Agyeman of the ITC, and Stuart Prebble, former Chief Executive of ONdigital and ITV Digital for help in research for this chapter.

REFERENCES

BARB (British Audience Research Board), www.barb.co.uk .

BDB (British Digital Broadcasting), 1997. *Application to the ITC for Multiplex Service Licences*, Section A.

Broadcast London, weekly.

(The) Consortium, 2002. *Application to the ITC Multiplex Service Licences. Summary of Application.*

Counterpoint, 2001. *Digital Television–Consumers' Use and Perceptions: A Report on a Research Study.*

DCMS (Department of Culture Media and Sport), 2003. News Release 4/4/03.

DNH (Department of National Heritage), 1994. *The Future of the BBC: Serving the Nation, Competing World-wide,* HMSO, Cm.2621.

DNH (Department of National Heritage), 1995. *Digital Terrestrial Broadcasting: The Government's Proposals* HMSO, Cm.2946.

DTA (Digital Terrestrial Alliance), 2002. *Application to the ITC for Multiplex Service Licence for Multiplex C.*

DTN (Digital Terrestrial Network), 1997. *Bid for Multiplex B*, Section A.

Elstein, David, 2003. 'Doomsdaying' on Jowell's Digital Dead Line, *The Guardian*, 8/4/03.

Ewington, Tim, 2003. Freeview alters the picture, *FT Creative Business* 22 April 2003.

Flynn, Barry, 2003. Unpublished data base.

Freeview Plus, 2002. *Application to the ITC for Multiplex Service Licence for Multiplex D.*

Goodwin, Peter, 1998. *Television Under the Tories: Broadcasting Policy 1979-1997.* London: British Film Institute.

Hewitt, Patricia & Jowell, Tessa, 2003. *Forward to Digital Television Action Plan: the Government's Vision* http://www.digitaltv.culture.gov.uk/ministers_fwd.html (accessed 22 April 2003).

Home Office, 1998. Paper *Broadcasting in the '90s: Competition, Quality and Choice,* HMSO Cm. 517.

ITAP (Cabinet Office Information Technology Advisory Panel), 1982. *Cable Systems,* Cabinet Office.

ITC (Independent Television Commission), 1996. *ITC Note for Applicants on Coverage for Digital Television,* 31 October 1996.

ITC, 1997. *News Release 49/97,* 24 June 1997.

ITC, 2002. *News Release 53/02,* 4 July 2002.

ITC, 2003. *ITC Multichannel Quarterly–Q2 2003.*

ITC/BBC, 2003. *A Report on Progress Towards Digital Switchover.*

ITC/BSC (Broadcasting Standards Council), 2003. *The Public's View 2002- An ITC and BSC Research Publication.*

Prebble, Stuart, 2003. Interview with the author, 26/3/03.

Chapter 8
Spain: A Market in Turmoil

Angel Arrese
Mónica Herrero
University of Navarra

The television landscape in Spain has undergone a complete transformation during the last decade of the 20th-century. Between 1990 and 2000, it went from a system of public television monopoly to a system of coexistence between public and private initiatives, with the introduction of private television channels. During that opening process, a series of political and managerial decisions were made, which in theory, turned the Spanish market into one of the most active in Europe.

In this sense, it should be stated that the television market in Spain experienced an authentic boom during the second half of the 1990s and especially since 1997. Undoubtedly, it should be necessary to draw particular attention to three phenomena in order to illustrate this situation.

First of all, after a period of depression, the advertising television market grew extraordinarily, thanks to the good economic situation and to the processes of privatisation and liberalisation, especially in the telecommunications market. Those changes allowed a significant improvement in the balance accounts of both public and private television channels and, at the same time, they revived the debate about the funding system and the nature of television as a public service.

Secondly, the actual starting signal to competitive pay television occurred within the last triennium of the twentieth century. At the same time different distribution systems emerged, mainly cable and digital television.

Finally the relationship between television services and telecommunications services was forged, with the necessary changes which the entrance in the audiovisual market of companies such as Telefónica or Retevisión implied.

Furthermore, together with those circumstances of growth and transformation on the supply side, three significant tendencies could be observed from the viewpoint of demand: 1) The stability of television consumption level by person, regardless of the increase of the offer; 2) The situation of a certain balance and consolidation of the *share* of the various free-to-air channels since the middle years of the decade; 3) The low importance of the new digital pay television offer, which is extremely dependent in the previously existent analogue system, and certain confusion among the viewers with respect to the new services of distribution, whose entrance to the market has also been quite controversial.

The advertising crisis of 2001 and 2002 exacerbated tensions in the sector, which had been trying to introduce all the possible forms of distribution in an accelerated way. During this period, digital television has been immersed in an extraordinarily uncertain environment. Among the three fundamental forms of digital distribution, the great winner has been digital television by satellite. This left the role of being the support for the medium- and long-term for cable, and the hope to become the leading form of free multi-channel television for digital terrestrial television (Arthur Andersen, 2000; Bustamante, 2002).

The following pages analyse the evolution of the main figures of the Spanish television market, taking the introduction of the forms of digital distribution as a starting point. The first part of the research focuses on the description of the main economic parameters of the market and the fundamental changes in the legal framework. The second part examines the specifics of the development of digital satellite television, cable and digital terrestrial television. Finally, the conclusions present an advance on which could be the future keys for development of the sector.

DIGITAL TELEVISION: LEGAL FRAMEWORK AND MARKET CONDITIONS

The Liberalisation of Television Services

The legislation on digital television requires first the setting up of a context for a legal framework related to television in Spain. During the 1990s, an authentic transformation of the Spanish television panorama took place, with the private television law of 1988 as a starting point. This law allowed the management of public service television to three licence holder companies. As a consequence of this legal regulation, there were five channels of national scope in the first years of the 1990s: two state-owned channels (TVE1 and TVE2), two commercial ones (Antena 3 and Telecinco), and a pay television channel, Canal Plus.

Once the state monopoly of television by terrestrial waves ended, the legislation gradually opened television broadcasting for other distribution means, which were rather more in a situation of alegality than one of illegality. In December 1995, the Telecommunications by Satellite Law and the

Telecommunications by Cable Law were approved, as well as a law Local Television by Terrestrial Waves.

The Law 37/1995 of Telecommunications by Satellite of 12 December liberalises the services rendered by use of telecommunications satellites; hence it left the door for satellite television open. At the end of 1992, Canal Plus launched two thematic channels distributed through the Astra satellite, Cinemanía and Documanía, which began their regular broadcasting on 1 March 1993. The new offer's name was Canalsatélite and the signal was sent from Luxembourg, to avoid breaking the Spanish legislation in force. The viewers interested in this offer needed to be subscribed to Canal Plus, as well as to count on a satellite dish oriented towards the Astra satellite. This experience was decisive for the implantation of digital satellite television in 1997, once it was allowed by law.

Simultaneously with satellite transmission, cable operators began to work in Spain as a result of the Law 42/1995 of Telecommunications by Cable of 22 December. The Law 12/1997 of Liberalization of Telecommunications of 24 April later modified this law, especially as far as the changes of the demarcations already constituted are concerned.

Indeed, the regulations established the creation of demarcations with a municipal or regional character. Thus, in a certain way, they prevented the emergence of an operator in the cable television market at a national level. The law imposed limitations on ownership when decreeing that no physical or legal entity could participate or own one or more adjudicated societies that jointly reached more than a million and a half subscribers in Spanish territory. In these demarcations two operators would work, one of them the result of a public competition and the other one Telefónica, the state telecommunications operator, which initiated its operations 16 months after the resolution of the corresponding concession contests. Nevertheless, the General Secretary of Telecommunications decided in December 1998 to extend up to 2 years the moratorium imposed on Telefónica, because it considered that the previous 16 months were insufficient to make sure the newcomers could get established.

On the other hand, the long term of the moratorium gave time to Telefónica to develop ADSL technology, which allows the supply of such services with a much more reduced cost than that of cable. On 31 January 2002, the government, by means of a change of titles, authorized Telefónica to use ADSL for telephone, Internet and television services. Logically, at the same time, the government freed Telefónica from the commitment of investing in cable. The protests of cable operators, which considered these measures as favourable treatment by the government, did not seem enough. In its meeting of 7 January 2003, the Telecommunications Market Commission was in favour of releasing Telefónica from these commitments, although it has not made a definitive decision on that matter. At the moment, the use of this technology is beginning to be considered as an obstacle for the development of the cable and satellite industries.

All these legal measures related to cable and satellite are not specific regulations on digital television; however, they facilitate its implementation. It should not be forgotten that the legislation on cable and satellite coincides at the same moment with the possibilities of applying digital technology to television broadcasting, through these distribution systems.

Specific Regulations on Digital Terrestrial Television

Something different happened with regard to television by terrestrial waves. The first legal regulation specifically referring to digital television came as a result of government efforts to establish digital terrestrial television at the same pace as the rest of Europe. The Real Decree 2169/1998 of 9 October, which approved the National Technical Plan for Digital Terrestrial Television, provided the necessary legal framework for the development of digital technology in terrestrial television. Among other provisions, it set a two-year deadline, starting from the moment of licence renewal, for private televisions to begin to broadcast using digital technology.

Nevertheless, the first project of digital terrestrial television arose thanks to a licence from the Ministry of Public Works on 18 June 1999, which appears totally apart from the regulations on private television. Thus, under the trade name of Onda Digital, which later became Quiero TV, the Ministry entrusted Retevisión with the task of introducing this model of television in Spain. In 1995, Retevisión, the main shareholder of Onda Digital with 49 per cent of the shares, had already signed an agreement with the State Telecommunications Office to develop a project on specifications and tests for the experimental system of digital television. Finally, Quiero TV was launched, under subscription, on 5 May 2000. However, it did not last more than two years, after the company bankruptcy in May 2002.

In parallel with this licence, which was granted with the specific purpose of introducing digital terrestrial television in Spain, the government renewed the private television licences of Antena 3, Telecinco and Canal Plus on 10 March 2000. This renewal imposed on them the obligation to broadcast by means of digital technology within less than two years, as the National Technical Plan for Digital Terrestrial Television of 1998 determined it. With this aim in mind, they were also granted rights for programmes within certain multiple channels. As a consequence, the three private channels began to broadcast the same programming of their analogue channels in digital format in April 2002.

Once the licences were renewed in March 2000, the government approved months later a new measure in order to promote digital terrestrial television. With the Resolution of the General State Secretary of Telecommunications on 13 December, the cabinet meeting decision to award two licences for public service broadcasting on digital terrestrial television, by means of free-to-air broadcasting, was made public. For that reason, it could be stated that the government granted two more private television broadcasting stations, which will broadcast directly with digital technology. The companies are Net TV and Veo TV.

Therefore, regarding digital terrestrial television of national scope, the government has definitely encouraged the implementation of this technology from 1998 to date with its regulations. Nevertheless, the success of these new media remains very different, but this will be addressed in another section of this chapter.

The last legal regulation which deals with digital terrestrial television refers to a local scope and dates from the end of 2002. The Law 53/2002 of Accompaniment of the National Budget modifies the Spanish audiovisual panorama to a great extent. Indeed, it modifies the Law 41/1995 of Local Television by Terrestrial Waves, which established that the local stations would broadcast with digital technology. According to the new law, the approval of the National Technical Plan for Local Digital Television falls to the government. In addition, it also indicates the deadlines for requesting submission and licences. The new law presents an important adjustment concerning participation, which is aimed to preserve pluralism. This way, any physical or legal entity sharing the capital of a company with a licence for a public service of state scope will not be able to participate in any other licence, regardless of its scope of coverage. Hence, a national television company cannot have participation in local channels that are already digital.

The PRISA media group, shareholder of Canal Plus, was already operating a local television network under the trade name of Localia. Moreover, the Correo-Prensa Española media group, with participation in Telecinco, had also started to broadcast through a local television network, mainly in the north of Spain. These legal measures coincide with the government approval to the merging of the digital platforms by satellite, Vía Digital and Canal Satélite Digital, in December 2002, which establishes a monopoly in the digital satellite television market.

The Rapid but Troubled Development of the Market

In Spain, digital television was introduced in 1997 with the launch of the first digital platform by satellite. At first, digital development was in debt with the existing experience with pay television of national scope, which Canal Plus initiated in 1989, but little by little its effects became apparent in the whole television panorama.

In 2001, the television sector in Spain invoiced around 3.5 billion Euros (the figure increases to 4.6 billion if public subventions and financing of public channel deficits are taken into account). Approximately two-thirds of that amount corresponded to free television and one-third to pay television (CMT, 2002). As far as the latter is concerned, at the end of 2001, there were 3.5 million households with pay television in Spain, about 27 per cent of the total households (13 million). These were distributed as follows: 2 million were subscribed to digital satellite television; 0.9 million to terrestrial television (analogue) and 0.6 million to cable television. Figure 8.1 shows the evolution of the penetration of the different types of pay television since 1997.

Figure 8.1: Pay Television in Spain (Percent of Households)

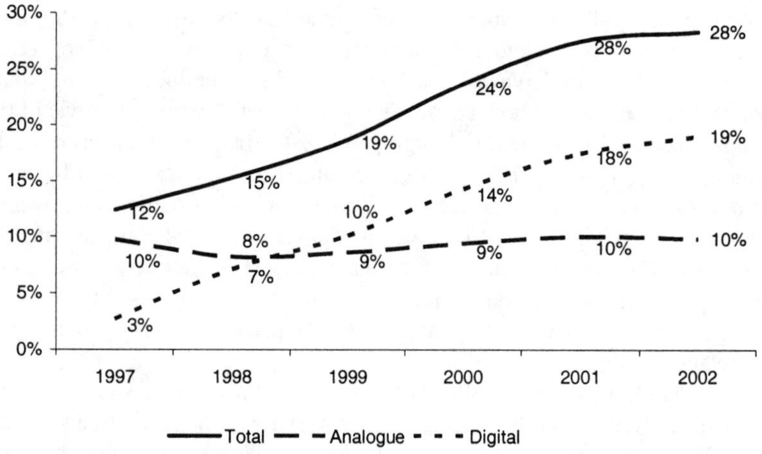

Source: Data from television companies.

Altogether, the audience share of pay channels represented around 7 per cent of the total. In households with pay television, about two-thirds of the total watching time is devoted to free television and one-third corresponds to pay channels (*Sofres*, 2002). Television watching time per household reached an average of 209 minutes in 2001, below the average during the mid 1990s (211 minutes).

In spite of the absence of definitive data for 2002, it certainly can be affirmed that the basic conditions of the market did not change significantly, although the introduction of pay television kept progressing. In Spain, this advance is becoming more and more identified with the digital offer, because the migration from the main analogue pay television channel (Canal Plus) toward its digital brother (Canal Satélite Digital) has continued, together with the commitment of cable to this type of programming offer. Without a doubt, the main novelty of 2002 was the implementation of the different offers of digital terrestrial television, which were introduced already in 2001. After getting almost 300,000 subscribers, the main pay television platform, Quiero TV, ended up in bankruptcy, with an accumulated loss of approximately 400 million Euros.

Nonetheless, as Figure 8.2 shows, the consumption habits for television—at least from the point of view of the time dedicated to the different channels—have changed very slowly during the last years. The audience corresponding to "otros" (other channels), which include the digital channels, is the only one that has grown significantly percentage-wise, but it still entails a very small percentage of the total time devoted to watching television.

From a managerial point of view, several peculiarities have marked the process of introduction and development of digital television in Spain. First, the structure of companies in the sector has been subject to political decisions, which at first tried to avoid monopolistic situations in each one of the distribution forms. Second, these political measures opted to favour the prominence of telecommunications companies—mostly, the key operators, Telefónica and Retevisión—as the main promoters of the sector together with the traditional television services suppliers. Third, there has been fierce competition for the most attractive pay contents of payment, mainly soccer and films, which has extraordinarily eroded the balance accounts of the companies and has toughened the circumstances of competition in the sector. Fourth, a practically direct identification between digital television and pay television has taken place, which is especially problematic for the development of digital terrestrial television.

DIGITAL TELEVISION BY SATELLITE

The Advantage of Being First

The introduction of digital television in Spain came by way of, and is very related to, the development of the first pay television channel, Canal Plus. The licence of private television awarded to Canal Plus allowed it to enjoy a monopoly in pay television until 1997. Since September 1990, it was the only national television channel in Spain which demanded a direct payment from its audience. This way, it benefited from the monopoly of exploitation of the pay "window" for films. Regarding the other mainstay of its programming, soccer,

Figure 8.2: Distribution of Share among Television Channels (1990-2002)

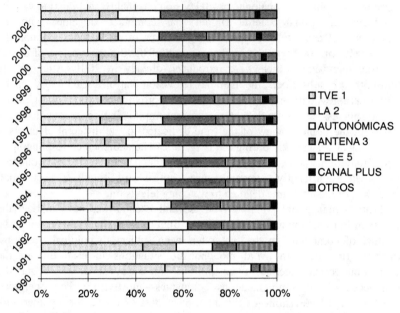

Source: Sofres.

Canal Plus began to experience some difficulties in preserving the exclusiveness of this service in 1994 because of its conflicts with other commercial channels.

Despite the challenges to the exclusiveness in the mid 1990s, Canal Plus was not forced by law to yield rights of transmission to other pay channels until after 1997, however.

The liberalisation measures of the different means of distribution contributed to the end of the monopoly of Canal Plus. The first pay television offers that arose in this new context came as a result of the regulations which made possible the competition in the pay television market. It should not be ignored that the new pay television offers emerged within a different technological context, distinguished by the advance of digital technology. In this sense, any new pay television channel was a consequence of the liberalisation of the distribution sector in which it operated as well as an effect of the development of digital technology, which made possible a multi-channel supply service together with better-quality reception. Therefore, there is a close relation between the development of pay television and the implementation of digital television.

The launch of a television platform by satellite, using digital technology, did not arrive until January 1997, and this was largely due to the failure of the ambitious project between PRISA and Telefónica of national cable television: Cablevisión (Lopez-Escobar, 1996). When the law restrained this project at the end of 1996, Sogecable, the company that owns Canal Plus, undertook the implementation of digital television by satellite. In order to understand all this, it is necessary to clarify the relation between Canal Plus, Sogecable and PRISA Group. In March 1996, the Society of Television Canal Plus changed its name and became Sogecable, a new society which included all the audiovisual activities of PRISA Group. Since 1997, Sogecable is the proper name of the audiovisual division of the group (PRISA, 1997).

In order to launch digital television by satellite, Sogecable for a time counted on the experience of the analogue service supply of thematic channels under the name of Canalsatélite and, moreover, with the precedent of its French homonym which had been commercialising Canalsatellite Numérique, the first platform of digital television by satellite in France (Alonso, 1998).

In January 1997, Sogecable's platform of digital television by satellite began broadcasting under the commercial name of Canal Satélite Digital, and counted on Canal Plus as the driving force for its service supply. In fact, the promotional offer mainly targeted Canal Plus' subscribers, offering them special discount prices. As a result, during 1997, the migrations from Canal Plus to Canal Satélite Digital represented 90.3 per cent of the platform subscriptions. Nevertheless, these discounts do not seem as decisive for the migration as the extension of the same type of contents and the brand image that Canal Plus had consolidated during the seven previous years. This process of migration continued rapidly, as Figure 8.3 shows.

From that moment on, *Canal Plus* continued commercialising its analogue version and began to do it with its digital version through the Canal Satélite Digital offer. Since the launch of the platform, it is possible to subscribe to Canal Plus Digital, which in addition to the analogue channel includes two more channels, Canal Plus Rojo and Canal Plus Azul, its multiplexed channels, which air the main channel programming in different hours.

A Duopoly in Trouble

Nevertheless, the launch of the first service of digital television confronted many legal obstacles related to its competitor, Vía Digital, and to the signal decoders and the soccer broadcasting rights. Vía Digital, the digital television platform led by Telefónica and transmitted through the Hispasat satellite, was the direct competitor to Canal Satélite Digital, even though it began its transmissions months later, in September 1997. The legal battles which the two platforms

Figure 8.3: Canal Plus and CSD: Migration from Analogue to Digital

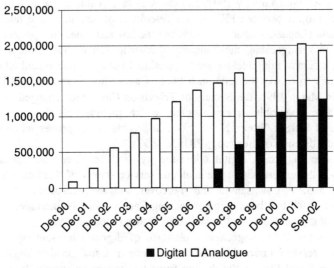

■ Digital □ Analogue

Source: Sogecable

faced, which the European legislation addressed, represent in an intricate way plenty of technological difficulties and political interests. Therefore, unlike pay television, which arose protected by monopoly, digital television by satellite burst directly into a competitive environment.

The Vía Digital offer opted rather more for variety and quantity than for specialisation in a certain type of contents. However, the marketing director of Vía Digital pointed out soccer and cinema, in this order, as the main thematic variables (Anuncios, 1997). The aggressive price strategy placed the product in a certain price range, which was rather cheaper than the one of Sogecable's platform. In addition to Telefónica, the state company of telecommunications, Vía Digital's shareholders included Televisión Española, the state owned television, Televisa, the Mexican television channel, the Recoletos communications group and some Spanish autonomous television channels.

However, all in all, both offers based their strategy on furnishing the exclusive contents which people seemed willing to pay for. Digital technology brought the combination of two types of direct payment: the subscription and the pay-per-per-view. On one hand, subscribers paid a monthly fee to access one or several packages of channels. On the other, they also had the possibility of accessing certain programmes through the pay-per-view system, such as soccer games and recent films.

Until the implementation of pay-per-view, the pay channel was the first "window" of cinematographic openings in television. Moreover, there were not any other exclusive sport matches offered but those of pay channels and those that public and free commercial channels were allowed to broadcast. One of the key concepts on which the pay channel based its offer, the exclusiveness of its corresponding "window," started to belong to the next stage of direct payment. A fair number of soccer games can only be enjoyed through pay-per-view and films are offered through this payment system three months before they appear on the film channels included in their subscription fees.

The subscription to packages of channels goes together with the idea of abundance, since their offer overcomes by far that of conventional television. On the other hand, pay-per-view grants the possibility of enjoying exclusive contents. Abundance and exclusiveness of the same type of contents represent the distinctive characteristics of the satellite digital supply in Spain, which are common to both platforms.

Despite the added advantages of cable, with regard to its supply of complementary services, such as telephone and Internet access, the process of infrastructure creation was considerably slower and more expensive than the installation of antennas and decoders for satellite television. All this, together with the noticeable local character of cable legislation, allowed Canal Satélite Digital and Vía Digital to spread more quickly in the market. The fact that their target was a national market gave them the opportunity to negotiate film and sport rights that were difficult to acquire for companies of reduced dimensions.

In the five years before the two companies merged, the increasing number of subscribers, together with considerable loss and indebtedness, defined the evolution of both platforms. Table 8.1 shows the evolution of subscriptions, the results before taxes and the indebtedness from 1997 to 2001 of Canal Satélite Digital (CSD) and Vía Digital (VD).

Table 8.1: Comparison between CSD and VD: Subscribers and Financial Results

YEAR	SUBSCRIBERS		RESULTS*		INDEBTEDNESS	
	CSD	VD	CSD	VD	CSD	VD
1997	260,168	77,000	-125,508	-82,594	3,83	1,74
1998	599,350	288,600	-160,248	-234,040	4,88	2,51
1999	813,490	440,100	-63,539	-291,500	3,61	4,15
2000	1,051,563	633,059	-24,583	-395,027	3,46	10,38
2001	1,230,038	806,379	-40,209	-484,568	3,22	-6,92

*Thousands of euros.
Source: *Noticias de la Comunicación* (October 2002).

These numbers present the market growth of digital television by satellite, which at the end of 2001 had more than two million subscribers. Nevertheless, this growth, which is accompanied by a remarkable increase of the gross operating results, runs parallel to losses and to a terrible financial position. In both platforms, the business is financed by a certain amount of borrowed capital, which is far superior to their own resources, and losses, especially in the case of *Vía Digital*, showed the difficulties of survival of the business. Therefore, the dreadful economic situation and the market growth of digital television by satellite laid down the necessary conditions for consideration of a merger agreement.

Monopoly as an Answer?

Nevertheless, in order to understand the fusion of the two digital platforms, it is also necessary to consider the development of other pay experiences through cable and satellite, from a content point of view. The mainstays of programming of any of the new pay television services continued to be the same ones that helped Canal Plus to spread in the market: popular contents which became exclusive, soccer and film premieres. In this sense, Sogecable went from monopoly to competition when it was forced to yield the broadcasting rights for soccer to the rest of pay television operators and when it had to compete with them for the films of Hollywood majors.

The slow development of cable and the failure of the first experience of digital terrestrial television let the two satellite platforms be the main competitors for the broadcasting rights of contents. As an inescapable consequence of the nature of the business and the legislation, the programmes which generate the subscriptions must be present in all the offers. The rest of the offer consisted, fundamentally, of specialized contents which consumers will never have time to enjoy because subscribers will never have enough time to enjoy more than about one fourth of the services for which they pay. Hence, exclusiveness and abundance. In such context, in addition to the losses of both platforms, it seemed that a single operator was able to satisfy digital television supply with these characteristics.

It was hardly surprising that Canal Satélite Digital and Vía Digital announced their decision to merge in May 2002. In September of 1999, two years after the launch, the first rumours about a possible merger began. However, they did not reach an agreement then. After two more years of losses, the public announcement of a company merger agreement was not surprising at all. On 8 May 2002, an integration deal of the two platforms was signed, but it had to overcome different legal barriers, and therefore, it had to be modified.

After receiving the approval of the Competition Court, the Cabinet authorized the merger agreement in December 2002, establishing 34 conditions in order to limit the operation. At the end of January 2003, the presidents of Telefónica and Sogecable modified the original agreement according to these conditions. Nevertheless, they decided to appeal to the Supreme Court with the intention to lift five of the 34 conditions, which according to both companies, would not hinder the fair competition among the operators but could make difficult the future of the resulting company.

These five conditions make reference to diverse aspects related to competition and the growth of the merged company. With regard to competition, the first condition establishes the obligation to open up 20 percent of the channels to third operators and condition 13 forbids the new platform to commercialise its television services together with Imagenio, the Telefónica project which includes Internet broadband access through ADSL technology. Concerning growth of the new platform, condition 19 prevents the companies of Sogecable from making strategic alliances with any corporation of the Telefónica group. The last condition that they have requested to eliminate makes reference to the five-year term of validity for the imposed conditions.

The merger is already a reality. More than 2.5 million subscribers will become clients of the new platform, which has been called Digital + and will start its operations during the summer of 2003. In a certain way, Telefónica got released from a business in which it had many expectations, but did not know well enough. Sogecable has overcome an important obstacle, its main competitor, in order to reinforce its leadership in pay television in Spain.

DIGITAL TELEVISION BY CABLE: A DIFFICULT DEVELOPMENT

Unlike what occurred in other countries, the regulation of cable television services in Spain dates from 1995 and its commercial introduction only began in 1998. However, many analogue local networks, of little significance, were already operating thanks to the existing gap in legislation until that time.

After the start of activities by several operators, which was slower than expected due to diverse problems related to the network lines, the number of subscribers was not very significant after two years of operations. There were about 350,000 subscribers in 2000. Despite this, the main three protagonists of this new business, Telefónica Cable, Retevisión (A.O.C., Association of Cable Operators) and Cableuropa (ONO), announced investments amounting to around 10,000 million Euros for the following decade. The introduction of cable brought up a great number of questions from its inception, in spite of cable's hope to win part of the telephone business and to compete for high-speed Internet access, and even though it was the technology with greater possibilities to commercialise interactive television services.

In principle, compared to other technologies of television distribution, the cable added value had to be associated with the offer of totally interactive services, thus standing out among the other means of television transmission. With this object in mind, the main operators designed their strategies. Nevertheless, the use of the distinctive potentialities of cable entailed an economic and commercial stake for a very long term, mainly because the experience in other markets showed that the penetration of cable services was slow and selective. On the other hand, *premium* channels and the most attractive contents for pay services, especially the rights of soccer and films from the main North American majors, were blocked by long-term contracts signed by the digital platforms by satellite. Finally, the telecommunications operators, which were in charge of the development of the sector, were faced with the possibility of developing other alternative communication networks whose concessions were given at that moment: the LMDS and UMTS licences.

In addition to this background situation, Telefónica, the only operator authorised by the law to offer its cable services nationally, decided to freeze its plans to operate in the year 2001. With the previous permission of the government, the operator announced that its Imagenio project, specially designed for cable, would become part of its clear commitment to ADSL technology, which will include interactive television services as well (according to plans, the present pilot experiences will be transferred to the main Spanish cities throughout 2003). Since the withdrawal of Telefónica, the cable market fell into the hands of two operators, which had a situation of single operator in their respective demarcations. One of them, Retevisión, with a strong presence in the most important regions, covering 80 per cent of households, ended up by integrating its share in different operators (A.O.C., the Association of Cable Operators) under the trademark of Auna. The other one, Cableuropa, has a smaller geographic range (20 per cent of households), and operates under the name of Ono.

As a result of this situation, the market remained shaped as an unbalanced duopoly. In addition, considering that the television business involved less of 20 per cent of the income of each one of the operators, "their strategy followed the British model, a strategy of utilities focused in telecommunications and high speed Internet access, with the television as a secondary element" (Bustamante, 2002, 243).

At the end of 2002, subscribers to cable television went up to around 750,000 and only half of them were subscribed to digital television services—the rest received an analogue multi-channel supply. As Table 8.2 shows, the

Table 8.2 Evolution of Pay Television Subscribers

	1999	2000	Incr. %	2001	Incr. %	2002*	Incr. %
Satellite	1,253,604	1,684,622	34.4	2,036,417	20.9	2,100,000	3.1
Terrestrial	760,424	998,682	31.3	920,483	-7.8	700,000	-24.0
Cable	103,785	298,176	187.3	587,829	97.1	750,000	27.6
Total	2,177.813	2,981.480	40.8	3,544,729	18.9	3,550,000	0.1

*Approximation to data corresponding to the end of the year.
Source: CMT (2002) and data from companies.

penetration of cable continued being low, although its growth rate overcame, by far, the other forms of pay television.

The distribution of subscribers between both main operators is reflected in Table 8.3, as well as the details concerning subscribers to telephone and Internet services.

Table 8.3: Subscribers to Services of Cable Operators

	AUNA/AOC	ONO	TOTAL
Phone	558,551	407,266	965,817
Internet	454,150	122,500	576,650
Television	476,000	274,300	750,300

Source: *Expansión* (November 27, 2002).

The uncertainty about the development of cable television services in the near future – even though it is accepted that there is a great potential in medium and long term – has become even more serious after the merging of the two digital platforms by satellite at the beginning of 2003. The green light given by the government to this operation, without satisfying limitations regarding the control that they have on key contents for pay television, has caused great discontent among cable companies. In fact, the position of control granted to Sogecable may well slow down the penetration of the digital television supply by cable operators even more. Besides, they fear that the new Sogecable—in which Telefónica maintains a significant participation—will favour the distribution of certain pay contents through ADSL technology. At the end of 2002, Telefónica had around 750,000 clients for ADSL, a market in great expansion which increased very quickly between 2001 and 2002 and reached altogether almost one million subscribers.

Considering that the pay digital distribution by satellite will tend to stay in a monopolistic situation, and that, after the failure of the main commitment for

DTTV, cable still is the only viable and possible competitor, the probabilities that integration between both leading operators, Auna and Ono, could take place in this market are increasing.

With a single digital platform by satellite, probably a single cable operator of national range and the clear commitment of Telefónica to develop audiovisual pay services through broadband, there is little space left for the last means of digital diffusion in the Spanish market: digital terrestrial television. Or in other words, after the failure of the pay model, the only option left is to develop access to multi-channel and interactive digital television under the category of free commercial television, with national as well as regional and local range.

DIGITAL TERRESTRIAL TELEVISION: CHRONICLE OF A FAILURE FORETOLD

In 2000, Spain was the third country of the European Union to introduce digital terrestrial television. The National Technical Plan for Digital Terrestrial Television (DTTV) of 1998 planned for five national multiplexes (four single frequency network (SFN) multiplexes and one multiple frequency network (MFN) multiplex) and one regional SFN multiplex. The multiplexes could carry at least four channels, except the national MFN multiplex, which would carry five channels. The plan also defined that 3 additional multiplexes and up to 2 additional local multiplexes will be reserved for later decisions. Finally, it was also established that, once the analogue switch-off takes place (the deadline was 2012), the existing analogue terrestrial television broadcasters would be allowed to operate a multiplex each. Meanwhile, the national MFN multiplex was reserved for the existing analogue terrestrial broadcasters, which will share the five Channels (two for the public television broadcaster TVE and one for each one of the three private companies which own the television channels Antena 3, Telecinco and Canal Plus). These private broadcasters had to start digital simulcasting broadcast before April 2002. With regards to the existing public regional channels when the plan was approved, each one had two digital channels in the MFN regional multiplex reserved. The rest of the digital channels which were not given to the existing broadcasters, in the national as well as the regional markets, had to be awarded to new companies, which should compete to obtain the public concessions.

From the economic point of view, the Spanish model of introduction of digital terrestrial television chose to expand the competition in the national market of audiovisual diffusion, making a commitment for the access of new operators, which were forced to yield to the concentration limits decreed by the Law of Private Television. This law prevents the already existing concessionaires from accessing the capital of new firms. At the same time, legislators and licences concessionaires had in mind the idea of creating a new national operator of pay television, which could compete with the already existing operators—essentially Sogecable and Telefónica—and without the intervention of the terrestrial analogue television operators.

The concession of licenses of national programmes created a leading operator, Quiero TV – with the second operator of telecommunications, Retevisión, as its main shareholder, which was entrusted with the management of 14 programming channels (3 multiplexes and a half). In the meantime, the two remaining free-to-air channels were granted to two new companies, Veo TV and Net TV, in which diverse journalistic groups participated. On the other hand, at the regional level, autonomous communities such as Madrid, La Rioja, Catalonia and Navarre initiated the adjudicating process of the programmes which were not reserved for the already existing autonomous channels.

The IDATE 2000 report about development of digital television in Europe referried to Spanish DTTV in the following terms: "The new entrants in DTTV will face a head to head competition with powerful 'multiplatforms' players and whether they will find any space in the markets remains uncertain" (IDATE, 2000). In fact, the situation for the new operators of pay services was very complicated. They entered a market which was already "skimmed," since their competitors had created huge entrance barriers, mainly the exclusiveness of premium contents and the property of reception systems, and because there were practically no workable advantages that could justify an Average Revenue per User (ARPU) around 17 Euros, which was similar to cable's and half of that of satellite. In addition, they had to face the cost and the shortage of decoders and entered a perverse spiral which started from the expectation of few users, followed by the discouragement of set manufacturers and finished with the costliness of each unit.

Quiero TV began its transmissions in May 2000 and at the end of year it had won 113,000 subscribers, with a strategy based on the promotion of Internet access through television. Thanks to an intense strategy of marketing and publicity and strong investments to acquire content, the platform reached almost 200,000 subscribers in 2002. However, the accumulated losses – nearly 400 million Euros – and the lack of confidence in the project by some promoters – mainly by the reference partner, Retevisión – ended up condemning the platform to closure, which took place in spring 2002.

On the other hand, private operators with concessions for free broadcasting services exhausted all the deadlines to start their broadcasting, by waiting to see what happened to the pay platform. As a consequence, later on, they just adjusted to the minimum broadcasting requirements, thus showing distrust in the possibility of leading the development of DTTV. In the case of traditional operators of free television, who initiated their broadcasting in April 2003, with such decision they also showed malcontent regarding the insignificant role which the law granted to them, in addition to the technical difficulties and the nonsense they felt since they have to share one multiplex where each one had only one channel. Thus, the technological and commercial incentives needed to accelerate the necessary transformation to progress towards the "analogue switch-off" were minimal. In this situation, the only way for free DTTV to progress would be through stronger investments—without almost any income expectations and by putting greater pressure on the advertising market.

Moreover, the new operators, Veo TV and Net TV, which had far fewer resources and less experience in the sector, could not drive the market either and their focus was becoming niche channels. In the meantime, while they waited to meet the deadline of June 2002, they were demanding better conditions for their unfolding from the government. These requests included: a broader bandwidth (they only had one channel each) to be able to develop interactive services; a deadline extension to begin their broadcasting; incentives to encourage the purchase of receivers, such as public subventions or moving forward the "analogue switch-off" closing date. The "invisible channels", as they have been named, entered 2003 in a truly precarious situation to such an extent that one of them, Net TV, was for sale without a buyer in sight.

Regarding state public television, the government did not reserve TVE a leading role in the unfolding of DTTV, unlike what occurred in other European markets, since it only received two channels in one shared multiplex. For that reason, public television did not start its digital terrestrial broadcasting until April 2002, together with the other channels which shared the multiplex, even though it could have done it long before.

Luckily, during the second half of 2002, the situation took quite a radical turn. After the bankruptcy of Quiero TV, the government announced that it would distribute the spectrum of channels from that platform among the four analogue operators – TVE, Antena 3, Telecinco, and Canal Plus. In addition to that, a proposal to merge the two platforms was put up for discussion, so the government was forced to evaluate the operation in view of the possibility that an excess of concentration in the sector could happen. Altogether, the bankruptcy of Quiero TV and the merging of Canal Satélite Digital and Vía Digital demanded a revision of the effective audiovisual policy and a determined boost to free DTTV, as a way of democratising the access of population to an interactive and multi-channel television service.

For want of knowing the new distribution of national multiplexes, it seems that the option for creating a leading platform is gaining in popularity—like the new British Freeview, in which TVE could have greater prominence. However, there is also a chance that the government may give a complete multiplex to each one of the operators. In the meantime, the Ministry of Science and Technology has announced its wish to shorten the deadline for the "analogue switch-off." Therefore, it is expected that the government will soon start an active policy to encourage the creation of a sufficient set of receivers and the adaptation of communal aerials, in such way that the spiral of shortage of receivers, shortage of attractive contents, shortage of demand, and lack of interest of the operators could be broken. Obviously, it will be necessary to adopt a standard of common reception once and for all, which so far moves towards the MHP regulation, which will finally lead toward the same API. Eventually, the development of regional and local digital services gains special relevance in this new panorama of an active promotion of free DTTV. As a matter of fact, the government has already announced that a Technical Plan for Local Television is being prepared. In this new plan for local television, each city with more than 100,000 inhabitants has a multiplex reserved. Furthermore, at the end of 2002, the government announced a new scheme of incompatibilities about the holding of television channels, including national, regional, and local channels, with the idea to preserve pluralism and competition.

Although the errors of the recent past do not give confidence to cherish special hopes, it seems without a doubt that it is the right moment to accelerate the development of DTTV to advance quickly with the democratisation of interactive television services. Just months ago, a report prepared by the Consell de l'Audiovisual de Catalunya (CAC, the Audiovisual Council of Catalonia) and the Commission for the Telecommunications Market (CMT) concluded with these thoughts: "DTT could represent for many households an alternative mean to access the services of Information Society.... All this justifies that an important effort should be made to introduce DTTV as soon as possible. The need of an immediate intervention in this field is reinforced by the possible development of other technologies, which could reduce the present competitive advantages of DTTV and cause a retreat in the motivation of citizens to participate in the ongoing migration process. Particularly, the unfolding of technologies such as ADSL or UMTS could affect the speed of the implementation process of DTTV" (CAC & CMT, 2002).

CONCLUSIONS

This chapter was completed as the audiovisual law of the Spanish government was on the verge of approval. Therefore, it is an especially crucial time, which will define the audiovisual panorama of the coming years. Nevertheless, the analysis made in the chapter allows some conclusions on the present and the future of digital television in Spain.

First, uncertainty defines the situation of the market, from a legal and technological point of view, as well as the answer of the different groups in view of the performance of their competitors. This uncertainty forced the government to take part directly in the implementation of digital television by satellite, led by haste and with little knowledge of the business. The launch of the satellite platform Vía Digital counted mainly on the economic resources of Telefónica, the state operator of telecommunications. Now Vía Digital is heading for disappearance if the merger with Sogecable does not save it. Behind this manoeuvre, there was the government's attempt to restrain the hegemonic power that PRISA Group was acquiring in the audiovisual territory. Nevertheless, Sogecable counted on more important assets: the know-how of the business of pay television, guaranteed by the seven years of monopolistic activity of the analogue channel Canal Plus.

Taking advantage of the wired network, Telefónica also played an important role in the development of cable television, since it was one of the two operators present in all the demarcations. However, the moratoriums for the beginning of their operations and the development of ADSL technology have moved it away from this business.

On the other hand, the government also took part directly in the implementation of digital terrestrial television, by means of the concession to Retevisión, under the name of Quiero TV. The first service of digital terrestrial television adopted the structure of a new pay television operation, competing with the two platforms by satellite and the incipient cable operators.

This has contributed to digital television being associated with pay television in Spain, at the expense of the development of digital terrestrial television. As a matter of fact, pay services are associated with the abundance and the exclusiveness of contents. Considering the present structure of the market, only those operators who have broadcasting rights to North American films and soccer matches can overcome the entrance barriers to the business. In addition to integrated telephone services and Internet access, digital television by cable has also needed the same supply of television contents to enter the market. In this sense, the television services represent the "killer application" for the cable operators as well.

Although digital technology presents manifold interactive possibilities, including the development of new products and relations with subscribers, the reality of the digital television business in Spain, five years after its launch, still corresponds to the content supply described above. Cable, satellite and terrestrial waves (with digital technology) have worked as distributors of a supply of television contents which, in order to be established, needed to be very similar.

When trying to force an enterprise structure like that described above in a television market that changes slowly, the digital television business had to support unsustainable losses that triggered a genuine reformulation of the sector throughout 2002. The new coordinates of competition go through the existence of a single digital television platform by satellite (if the merger is finally accomplished); the concentration of the cable sector (probably with a single operator of national scope); and the new awarding of multiplexes for digital terrestrial television to favour the future development of this technology by the free television channels (after the bankruptcy of the pay platform, Quiero TV). In addition, one of the main operators, Telefónica, ended up focusing on the future development of the diffusion of television through ADSL, after the government freed the telecommunications company from its duties to develop cable services in all the demarcations of the country.

However, in order to develop the sector completely, it is certainly necessary to give a clear boost to the introduction of digital equipment and the normalisation of an open standard of multimedia reception. Furthermore, it is also fundamental that the audiovisual policy of the government stops being such a continuous surprise and change. In this sense, it seems essential to reach a balance between the measures that tend to favour the competition and the need to let the market give shape to economically viable supplies.

REFERENCES

Alonso, Fidel, 1998. *Canal Plus. Aproximación a un Modelo Europeo de Televisión de Pago,* Madrid, Fragua.

Anuncios, 1997. Vía Digital en liza, *Anuncios,* 6-12 October, pp. 18-20.

Arthur Andersen, 2000. *El Futuro de la Televisión en España. Análisis Prospectivo 2000-2005,* Madrid, Arthur Andersen.

Bustamante, Enrique (Coor.), 2002. *Comunicación y cultura en la era digital,* Barcelona, Editorial Gedisa.

CAC (Consell de l'Audiovisual de Catalunya) y CMT (Comisión del Mercado de las Telecomunicaciones), 2002. *La televisión digital terrenal en España. Situación y tendencias,* Barcelona, CAC.

CMT (Comisión del Mercado de las Telecomunicaciones), 2002. *El mercado de las telecomunicaciones, audiovisual e Internet. Informe Anual 2001*, Madrid, CMT.

IDATE, 2000. *Development of Digital TV in Europe 2000 Report. Spain*, IDATE.

López-Escobar, Esteban, 1996. 'Expectativas del cable y del satélite', in Banco Bilbao Vizcaya (Ed.), *La Industria de la Comunicación*, Bilbao, Servicio de Estudios del BBV, pp. 221-236.

PRISA, 1997. *Memoria Económica Anual*, Madrid.

Sofres, A. M., 2002. *Anuario de Audiencias de Televisión*, Madrid, Sofres.

Chapter 9
Sweden: The Digital Threat
to Cultural Sovereignty

Allan Brown
Griffith Business School, Griffith University

With a population of around nine million, Sweden is a small country by global standards, but by far the largest of the Nordic nations. It has been governed by the Social Democratic Party (SDP) for most of the post-war period, usually with the support of one or more parties outside the government. The country has an extensive social welfare system, although it has experienced a weakened economy in recent years. Sweden has been a member of the European Union since 1995. Immediately following the September 2002 election, at which the SDP was returned to office, the government announced it would hold a referendum to determine if Sweden should seek membership of the Euro common currency zone. At the referendum held in September 2003 Sweden rejected the proposal to adopt the Euro.[1]

In examining digital television broadcasting in Sweden this chapter focuses mainly on the transition from analogue to digital *terrestrial* television (DTTV). Sweden was an early adopter of DTTV. It commenced digital terrestrial transmissions on 1 April 1999, being the third country wogrldwide to do so after the United States and United Kingdom which both began in November 1998.

The first section of the chapter outlines the history, structure, regulation and financial performance of television broadcasting in Sweden prior to the commencement of digital terrestrial transmissions. The second section describes the debate leading to the introduction of DTTV in Sweden. The next section relates the history of Swedish DTTV during its first four years, from 1999 to 2002. An examination is made in the fourth section of the state of play regarding Swedish DTTV at the end of 2002. Then what follows are some concluding comments.

---

[1] At present, the Swedish currency is the Krona. Throughout this chapter all money amounts are expressed in Euros at the conversion rate of 1 Euro equals 9 Swedish Krona.

TELEVISION BROADCASTING IN SWEDEN

History and Structure

Television was introduced in Sweden in 1956. It was organized as a monopoly of the public service broadcaster, Sveriges Radio (SR), which was also responsible for the country's radio service. In planning a second television service in the 1960s the government considered licensing a national advertiser-supported, privately owned channel. Instead, however, it decided that 'internal competition' between two public channels was preferable to 'external competition' between public and private channels, and in 1969 SR established its second television channel. The original channel was named Channel 1, and the new channel TV2. Swedish public broadcasting was reorganized in 1978 with the control of television separated from SR and placed under the responsibility of a new corporation, Sveriges Television (SVT). In 1996 the two television channels were renamed SVT1 and SVT2 (Weibull, 2001).

Both SVT1 and SVT2 are generalist channels and are transmitted nationwide. Programming for the channels is spread among six production units, two in Stockholm and four in regional areas. In 1997 the public broadcaster established SVT Europa, which is a satellite service transmitted across Europe and directed at Swedes and Swedish speaking viewers living outside Sweden. Most SVT Europa programming comprises in-house productions from SVT1 and SVT2 (SVT, 2001).

In common with much of the rest of Europe, the public service monopoly of television broadcasting in Sweden came to an end in the late 1980s. In 1987 legislation provided for the reception of satellite television and the (regulated) operation of cable systems in Sweden. However, it did not allow the licensing of commercial terrestrial advertiser-supported television channels. This situation gave rise to the operation of two free-to-air (FTA) commercial channels broadcast to Sweden from London by satellite – TV3 in 1987, and Kanal 5 in 1988. TV3 was established by the Swedish Kinnevik company.[2] Controlled by the Swedish multi-millionaire industrialist, Jan Stenbeck,[3] Kinnevik in 1997 placed its media activities into the Modern Times Group (MTG). Kanal 5 was launched by another Swedish industrialist, Mats Carlgren, who later sold the channel to the US-owned, Luxemburg-based Scandinavian Broadcasting System (SBS). For many countries direct-to-home satellite is a platform only for

---

[2] Kinnevik initially broadcast TV3 as a pan-Scandinavian, mixed language channel. In 1989 Kinnevik divided TV3 into three distinct language and content channels with the launch of TV3 Denmark and TV3 Norway, both also broadcast by satellite.
[3] Stenbeck died suddenly in August 2002.

subscription television (pay-TV). In Sweden, however, with the widespread reception of TV3 and Kanal 5, satellite was also a platform for FTA television.

The early popularity of TV3 and Kanal 5 resulted in significant amounts of advertising expenditure flowing out of the country. This prompted the government finally to allow the establishment of a commercial advertiser-supported terrestrial television channel. TV4 commenced operation in March 1992. It now comprises a network of one national and 15 regional channels. The TV4 network is controlled by the Bonnier Group, Sweden's largest media company, which has extensive interests in newspaper and magazine publishing, commercial radio and film production. Together with its Finnish partner, Alma Media, the Bonnier Group owns a 45 percent equity interest in TV4, while the next largest shareholder is MTG with 15 percent (Advanced Television, 2002).

The cable television industry in Sweden was substantially deregulated in 1992, as was satellite broadcasting in 1994. There are now approximately 70 cable companies in operation, with rival networks overlapping in many areas. Nevertheless, the industry is highly concentrated with the four largest systems—Com-Hem, Kabelvision, UPC Sweden, and Sweden On-Line—accounting for around 85 percent of total cable subscriptions. Swedish cable systems are in the process of being upgraded from analogue to digital (Media Map Datafile, 2001).

Recent years have seen fierce rivalry in the Nordic countries between the two satellite pay-TV services, Canal Digital and Viasat. Canal Digital is fully owned by the Norwegian telco, Telenor, and Viasat is a wholly owned subsidiary of MTG. Both satellite channels completed the conversion of their premium subscribers from analogue to digital in 2001 (those subscribing to the basic tier only still receiving analogue signals). By mid-2002 Canal Digital led Viasat in terms of market share with approximately 60 percent of the total number of subscribers, both in the Nordic countries overall and in the Swedish market (Sellgren, 2002b). According to one commentator (Naning, 2002), the two services have incurred losses of "several billion krona" and are likely to achieve profitability only by merger with each other. In addition to Canal Digital and Viasat, there are a number of other satellite channels transmitted into Sweden. These include the action and nature channel, TV6, and the business channel, TV8, both owned by MTG. Most of the satellite channels are also available on cable networks.

Approximately 44 percent of Swedish households subscribe to cable, 22 percent to satellite services, with 34 percent being 'terrestrial only.' The combined cable/satellite subscription for Sweden at 66 percent is significantly higher than the European average of around 47 percent. This is due partly to the licensing of only one national terrestrial commercial channel (prior to digital), as well as to the fact that most Swedes are fluent in English and can easily appreciate American and British programs available on cable and satellite. The combined national market share for SVT1 (26 percent) and SVT2 (17 percent) in 2002 was 43 percent. TV4 had 25 percent, TV3 10 percent of the total audience, Kanal 5 had 8 percent, while the remaining 14 percent was accounted for by cable and satellite pay-TV and other services (SVT, 2003). At the end of 2002, approximately 16 percent of Swedish television households were subscribers to digital satellite services, and another 5 percent received digital television via cable.

Regulation

The Ministry of Culture is primarily responsible for broadcasting in Sweden. It is the final decision maker regarding transmission technologies and the granting of licences for new terrestrial broadcasting services. The Ministry is advised by the Radio and Television Authority (RTVA), which also administers cable and satellite services. The Swedish Broadcasting Commission is responsible for the regulation of broadcast programming content across all platforms. The main legislation governing broadcasting is the 1996 Radio and Television Act.

In Sweden there are no statutory limitations on the foreign ownership of broadcasting companies. Licences are not issued for cable or satellite broadcasting, cable and satellite companies simply being required to register their operations with the RTVA. The three FTA terrestrial channels—SVT1, SVT2 and TV4— have 'must carry' status on analogue cable networks.

SVT is prohibited from carrying advertising, but is allowed to sell sponsorships of major international events. Advertising on commercial television, originally limited to 6 minutes an hour, was increased to 10 minutes in 1997. Advertising breaks within programs were originally prohibited. This ban was repealed in April 2001, however, to bring Swedish advertising regulation into line with that in other EU countries (Media Map Datafile, 2001).

Revenue and Profitability

In common with other Nordic countries, television's share of aggregate advertising expenditure in Sweden is considerably below the European average. Television accounts for around 31 percent in Europe overall, but only for around 23 percent in Sweden. Conversely, the proportion of advertising expenditure on newspapers in Sweden is much higher than the European average (Statistics Finland, 2000). This situation is largely the result of commercial television starting very late in Sweden. There has in fact been a substantial shift from newspaper advertising to television. Between 1990 and 2000 television's proportion of total advertising expenditure increased from only 2 percent to 23 percent, while that for newspapers declined from 78 to 54 percent (Carlsson & Harrie, 2001: 36,118).

All television households in Sweden are liable to pay an annual viewers licence fee which is set by the Parliament (Riksdagen). For 2001 the licence fee was €185. Licence fee revenues are paid into a Broadcasting Fund that, after the deduction of collection costs, is distributed to finance the operations of SVT, SR, the educational radio and television company Utbildningsradio, and the Swedish Broadcasting Commission. In 2001 licence fee revenues totalled €642 million, of which €360m (56 percent) went to SVT. The licence fee represented 90 percent of SVT revenues, the remaining 10 percent coming from the sale of sponsorships, programming rights, technical services and other sources (SVT, 2001).

TV4, Sweden's sole commercial terrestrial analogue television channel, pays the government an annual 'franchise fee' based on its advertising revenues and calculated on a progressive scale. For 2000 the fee for TV4 amounted to €49.8m, representing 17.8 percent of its total income. In the same year TV4 posted a record operating profit (after franchise fee) of €36m, 12.9 percent of total income. This was an increase of 150 percent on its profit for 1997 of €14.4m (7.0 percent of income). In 2001 the operating profit for TV4 fell to €25.2m (10.3 percent of income) (TV4, 2002).[4]

Data on the financial performance of TV3 Sweden are not available. The financial results of MTG, however, provide separate figures for the group's Viasat Broadcasting division that includes TV3 (along with several other satellite FTA and pay-TV channels in nine countries). The division recorded an operating profit for 2001 of €61.1m, representing 12.1 percent of net sales. The comparable result for 2000 was €55.6m, 13.2 percent of net sales. In 2002 the company advised that "free-to-air channels are the most significant contributor to the revenues and profits of the MTG Group" (MTG, 2002).

THE DIGITAL DECISION

In June 1995, the Swedish government appointed Lars Jeding as a one-person commission to investigate the possibility of digitizing the country's terrestrial broadcasting network. In his report, presented to the government in February 1996, Jeding asserted that the transition from analogue to digital was inevitable, and that it was not so much a matter of whether or not to introduce digital broadcasting, but the role the government should play in the process. Jeding

---

[4] These data are for the 'TV4 Group,' which consists of the TV4 national and 15 regional channels. Ten of the 15 regionals were wholly owned subsidiaries prior to 2001 when the group secured full ownership of all 15 regional channels (TV4, 2002).

proposed that the government make an immediate in-principle decision on the transition to DTTV. He recommended that the construction of the digital terrestrial network begin in 1997, that analogue broadcasting cease as early as possible but at least within ten years of the commencement of digital, and that an expert group be set up to work out the details and monitor the development of the project. He explained (Jeding, 1996: 28-29):

> The reason for starting digital broadcasting [sooner rather than later] is to provide the general public with terrestrial digital broadcasting as an alternative to digital broadcasting by satellite or cable... It is important to get many channels quickly into the terrestrial network which, it is intended, should become a 'super digital highway', supplied by numerous broadcasting companies.... What should attract commercial players to choose the terrestrial network is nationwide coverage, low broadcasting costs, reasonable rules regarding content, the right to send commercials and the opportunity, in a technically simple way and without onerous administrative costs, to charge and receive payment for the programmes they broadcast.

The Jeding report sparked off heated debate between supporters and opponents of DTTV. It has been claimed that opposition to DTTV in Sweden was stronger than in any other country (BIPE Consulting, 2001). The main supporters were the ruling Social Democrat Party, Sveriges Television and Teracom, the state-owned operator of the analogue terrestrial network.[5] They argued that DTTV would provide multichannel television to all Swedish households ('a democratic gateway to the Information Society') and provide strong competition to satellite and cable. An early start would favour domestic electronic equipment manufacturers and the digital software and hardware industries. They claimed further that DTTV would enable the government to promote cultural sovereignty by maintaining regulation of television programming. The Minister of Culture, Marita Ulvskog, said that digital terrestrial would bring the "regulation refugees" (TV3 and Kanal 5) back to Sweden into the terrestrial network and under public control (Brandrud, 1999: 136). Those against DTTV included the opposition Conservative Party, the national telecommunications carrier Telia, cable operators and MTG. They advocated a complete migration from terrestrial to cable and satellite broadcasting, closure of the analogue broadcasting network and the employment of the reclaimed frequencies for other communication uses. The issue was

---

[5] With Teracom not involved in either satellite transmission, cable television or telephony, its very survival was dependant on the adoption of digital terrestrial broadcasting.

resolved in November 1997 when the SDP reached an agreement with two parties in the opposition—the Liberal People's Party and the Centre Party—and the Riksdagen approved the government's proposal to establish DTTV broadcasting (Gröndahl, 2002a).

It was decided that Teracom would construct the digital network. Two profit-oriented companies were established—Senda AB and Boxer TV Access AB—both 70 percent owned by Teracom and 30 percent by the Skandia insurance company. The role of Senda was to manage the multiplexes and to set technical standards for interactive services. Initially, all DTTV signals in Sweden were encrypted, viewers thus requiring an access card ('smartcard') to receive digital programs and services. Senda has prescribed the Open TV system, but plans to migrate to the Multimedia Home Platform (MHP) standard "when technically and commercially possible". It estimates this migration will take two to three years from the time MHP set-top boxes (STBs) are introduced.[6] Senda also co-ordinates the electronic program guide (EPG). It has specified a common EPG for digital terrestrial channels. The EPG is to carry no advertising (EBU, 2002: 51).

Boxer was set up to promote and market the digital terrestrial platform. Boxer is the monopoly supplier of DTTV program packages and smartcards, and initially was the sole distributor of DTTV STBs. A notable feature of the Swedish DTTV model was that viewers needed to pay a subscription fee even if they wanted to receive only 'free-to-air' channels (but see below).

SWEDISH DTTV: THE FIRST FOUR YEARS

SVT first carried out digital terrestrial transmissions on a test basis in November 1995. The launch of DTTV was initially scheduled for January 1999, with two multiplexes to be operational from launch date. SVT applied for licences for no less than eight digital services: SVT1, SVT2, a new 24 hour news channel and five regional services. In addition, SVT requested capacity be reserved for a number of proposed pay-TV services to be established in co-operation with the British Broadcasting Corporation and other Nordic public service broadcasters. This request was not granted. The RTVA granted SVT licences for digital versions of each of its two national and five regional channels, and for SVT24, a news and current affairs channel.[7] With the introduction of DTTV, SVT adopted an 'all platforms' approach and transmitted all of its channels by satellite and

---

[6] Viewers with Open will therefore need eventually to acquire new STBs.

[7] From 2000 digital licensees were permitted to broadcast additional channels of programming if they had sufficient transmission capacity. In 2001 SVT established a 'supplementary' channel, SVT Extra, to provide occasional broadcasts of special events, for example, the Olympic Games.

cable as well as terrestrially. SVT and SR together were granted an additional
€66 million in 1999-2001 from licence fee revenues as contribution towards
their costs of digital conversion. The 'digital bonus' received by SVT, however,
fell well short of the amount it had requested of the government to provide a
secure financial base for the development of its digital services (Gröndahl,
2002a).

The expert group recommended by the Jeding Report for overseeing the
DTTV project has taken the form of an all-party parliamentary body, the Digital
Television Committee. This consists of nine members, three from the SDP and
one from each of the other six parties represented in the Riksdagen. Both the
RTVA and the Digital TV Committee are involved in the licensing of
commercial digital channels. Licences are allocated on a channel-by-channel
basis by means of a 'beauty contest' selection process. The RTVA advertises for
licence applications and carries out financial assessment of all applicants,
eliminating those considered financially unsound. The Digital TV Committee
examines all financially qualified applicants regarding their proposals for
programming and reports back to the RTVA. On the basis of its own appraisal
and that of the Committee, the RTVA makes recommendations to the Minister
of Culture who has the final decision on the companies to be awarded licences.
The formal selection criteria for commercial digital licences are vague and
imprecise:

> The range of programmes as a whole should appeal to different
> interests and tastes. Local and regional programmes should be given
> preference, as well as programmes that have a Swedish cultural
> background. The aim should be for several independent programme
> companies to take part (RTVA, 2000: 48-49).

DTTV licensees are required to use the Teracom network and to enter into
technical co-ordination agreements with both Senda and Boxer regarding
multiplexing, STB conditional access and the EPG. There are no special licences
for multiplexes. Instead, administrators are appointed by the RTVA to manage
multiplex operations.

The licensing of commercial DTTV channels in Sweden has been an
ongoing process since before the launch, and the government's experience in
dealing with licensees has been a difficult one. At the closing date for the first
round of licences in February 1998, 57 applications had been received. In June
1998 licences were granted to the following companies (RTVA, 2000: 53):

• Bonnier Group for the digital version of its national channel TV4;

- MTG Group for terrestrial versions of its satellite channels TV3 and TV8;
- SBS SA for the terrestrial version of its satellite channel Kanal 5;
- TV Linkoping Lankomedia AB for a regional channel named NollEttan TV;
- Landskrona Vision AB for another regional channel, Skånekanalen;
- Canal Plus Television AB for its primary pan-European Canal Plus service adapted for Swedish viewers;
- Knowledge Network AB for its K-World education 'e-learning' channel; and
- Cell ICD AB for an interactive channel, eTV.

By January 1999 there were no DTTV STBs available for viewers to purchase or rent. As well, there were complaints from some of the commercial licensees of delays by Teracom with digital transmissions, and by Senda with the conditional access system and EPG. Consequently, the launch was deferred for three months until April. In spite of the delay, on launch date four of the commercial channels—TV3, TV4, Kanal 5, and eTV—breached the conditions of their licences and refused to commence broadcasting. They claimed there was an insufficient audience for their programs. The government wrote to each of the channels in May demanding they commence their services. TV4 eventually went on-air in September 1999, and TV3, Kanal 5 and eTV in January 2000.

At the same time it was dealing with the defiant licensees the government authorized a third multiplex and the issuing of a second round of licences. Applications were called and 38 were received by the closing date in September 1999. In January 2000 new commercial licences were granted to the following companies (RTVA, 2000: 58):

- Bonnier Group for digital versions its TV4 regional channels;
- MTG for Viasat Sport, TV1000 movie channel and its ZTV music channel;
- Canal Plus Television AB for two additional movie channels, Canal+ Gold and Canal+ Blue;
- Malmo Media AB for channel DTU7 to provide Turkish and Middle Eastern programs; and
- Stockholm Lokaltelvision AB for a local programming channel.

Before the project had an opportunity to benefit from the newly licensed channels it suffered a further setback from MTG. With TV3 and its Viasat channels transmitted by satellite, MTG had opposed DTTV from the outset and was a reluctant licensee. The company considered that the success of DTTV would be at the expense of the satellite platform. In April 2000, just a few months after finally going to air with TV3, MTG imposed a monthly fee of €13 for the reception of three of its DTTV channels—TV3, TV8 and ZTV. The fee imposed by MTG for its three channels was just a few Euros less than the monthly fee for the entire basic (non-premium) DTTV package. Moreover, the three channels were available free of charge to viewers on both satellite and cable. MTG stated that it had decided to "compensate itself for the defaulting revenues from the [DTTV] operations" (Naning, 2001a).

Teracom responded by compensating digital viewers for the fee imposed by MTG. This represented a taxpayer funded subsidy to MTG of around €1 million per month (Gröndahl, 2002a). Teracom ceased payment of the subsidy in March 2001, and in June MTG announced it would completely withdraw from the DTTV project on 15 August. It made no move to hand back its licences and publicly discussed the possibility of 're-leasing' them to other operators. On the day of the 15th MTG faxed Teracom requesting it allow transmission of its channels to continue. Teracom had lost patience with the company, however, and at midnight it 'pulled the plug' on all five of MTG's DTTV services – TV3, TV8, ZTV, Viasat Sport and TV1000 (Naning, 2001b).

The MTG episode was not the only problem to afflict the project. SVT had withdrawn its five regional channels from DTTV in January 2001. In March 2001 the government authorized the provision of an additional two multiplexes and the issue of a third round of licences. Forty-one applications were received, and in August licences were approved for the following companies (Advanced Television, 2001a):

- MTV Networks Europe for three channels, MTV Nordic, Nickelodeon, and VH1;
- Eurosport Sales for two channels, Eurosport and EurosportNews;
- Discovery Communications Europe for two channels, Discovery Channel and Animal Planet;
- Bonnier Group for a TV4/CNN news channel;
- NonStop Television AB for its Entertainment/Style channel;
- Cinecinemas AB, a subsidiary of Canal Plus, for another movie channel; and
- Calico consortium for a regional programming service.

Most of the licences in the third round were allocated to non-Swedish companies and for channels already available on satellite and cable. In September the Minister announced that six of the selected channels (only) would be given direct access to the frequencies made vacant by the removal of the MTG channels, while the other channels would have to wait the establishment of new multiplexes. The channels to go on-air immediately were MTV Nordic, Nickelodeon, VH1, Eurosport, Discovery Channel, and Animal Planet (Advanced Television, 2001b).

Up to the end of 2002 there were a number of further developments regarding the line-up of digital channels. Three channels licensed in the first and second rounds had pulled out of DTTV, namely the Skånekanalen and Stockholm Lokaltelvision regional channels and the eTV interactive service. Also, the Bonnier Group decided against transmitting its TV4 regional channels on DTTV. The K-World e-learning channel proved to be financially unviable and ceased broadcasting in March 2002. The following month the RTVA issued a new licence to Bonnier to take over the frequency vacated by K-World. It immediately commenced a low-budget interactive youth service, called Meditv, with a focus on 'live chat' and games (Sellgren, 2002a). Bonnier was also permitted to provide a re-transmission of the CNN satellite signal on the DTTV platform. In September 2002 NonStop Television was permitted to commence DTTV transmission of its Entertainment/Style channel (Sellgren, 2002d), and just prior to Christmas 2002 SVT launched a new digital children's channel called Barnkanalen.

SWEDISH DTTV: STATE OF PLAY
FOUR YEARS AFTER LAUNCH

DTTV Take-Up

Table 9.1 sets out the Swedish DTTV channel offering of 21 channels (including the supplementary channel, SVT Extra) as at end of 2002. Multiplex A carries the five SVT digital channels, multiplex B the channels of Swedish-owned commercial companies, while multiplexes C and D carry those of foreign-owned broadcasters.[8]

As mentioned earlier, Swedish viewers were required to pay a subscription fee to receive any DTTV transmissions, even those of SVT1, SVT2, and TV4 that are FTA on analogue.[9] In December 2002 new DTTV subscribers were charged €44, comprising an €11 connection fee and €33 for one year's subscription for the basic package of 17 channels. The three Canal Plus movie channels cost an additional €24 per month, and the NollEttan regional channel €17 extra *per year* (Boxer, 2002). In that month, however, the government

---

[8] All commercial channels on the DTTV platform, except the Canal Plus premium pay-TV channels, earn income from advertising messages. The Meditv channel also generates fees from its interactive services.
[9] Some SVT1 and SVT2 programs are available in widescreen format on DTTV but not on analog.

Table 9.1: Swedish Digital Terrestrial Channels: 31 December 2002

Multiplex	Channel	Licensee	Programming
A	SVT1-D	SVT	digital version of SVT1
	SVT2-D	SVT	digital version of SVT2
	SVT24	SVT	news & current affairs
	Barnkanalen	SVT	children's channel
	SVT Extra	SVT	supplementary channel
B	TV4	Bonnier Group	generalist entertainment
	Meditv	Bonnier Group	interactive youth channel
	CNN	Bonnier Group	news
	NollEttan TV	TV Linkoping Lankomedia	regional
	DTU7	Malmo Media AB	Turkish & Middle Eastern
C	Canal Plus	Canal Plus Television AB	movie channel
	Canal Plus Gold	Canal Plus Television AB	movie channel
	Canal Plus Blue	Canal Plus Television AB	movie channel
	Kanal 5	SBS	generalist entertainment
D	Eurosport	Eurosport Sales	sport
	Animal Planet	Discovery Communications	documentaries
	Discovery Channel	Discovery Communications	documentaries
	Nickelodeon	MTV Networks Europe	children's channel
	VH1	MTV Networks Europe	music
	MTV Nordic	MTV Networks Europe	music
	Entertainment/Style	NonStop Television	celebrity/fashion

accepted a SVT proposal to release all SVT services from the Boxer agreement, thus making a FTA DTTV offer available to viewers from January 2003. It remains to be seen whether this change heralds the beginning of a greater shift toward free-to-air DTTV in Sweden.

At launch, the DTTV network covered approximately 50 percent of Sweden's population. In 2000 the Riksdagen approved expansion of the network to cover 98 percent. At the end of 2000 coverage was 70 percent, and by early 2002 had reached 90 percent (EBU, 2002). Despite this wide coverage, by the end of 2002 only some 140,000 Swedish households had subscribed to DTTV. This represented a mere 3.5 percent penetration level almost four years after launch.[10]

Teracom's Financial Problems

Not surprisingly, the poor consumer take-up of DTTV has resulted in low levels of income and substantial operating losses for the state-owned companies involved in the project. Teracom charges each DTTV channel €2 a month per activated smartcard, and has estimated that its breakeven number of subscribers

---

[10] Aulis Gröndahl, SVT, personal correspondence 17 February 2003.

is roughly 240,000, almost double the actual number so far achieved (BIPE Consulting, 2001: 125). In 2001 the government was forced to stand guarantor on a €220 million loan facility for Teracom.

In August 2002, in an attempt to stem its losses, Teracom embarked on a sweeping restructure and staff cutting exercise. It merged Boxer and Senda, and phased out the Senda brand name. Boxer ceased its business of selling (but not of renting) STBs. Viewers are now able to purchase DTTV STBs from retailers only. Teracom indicated that it was considering selling 19 percent of the shares in Boxer, thus reducing its holding to 51 percent (Sellgren, 2002c).

Proposals for DTTV Project

By the end of 2002, two alternative proposals had been put forward regarding the future direction of DTTV in Sweden. In a report issued in November 2001, the Digital TV Committee was critical *inter alia* of EU provisions that allowed satellite transmissions into Sweden to avoid Swedish regulation, and the process for the selection of DTTV licensees. The Committee made the following recommendations to the government in relation to these matters: in renegotiating the EU's Broadcasting Directive *Television Without Frontiers* the Swedish government seek a review of the country of origin principle; and "clear and unambiguous rules and criteria" be established for the selection of DTTV licensees.

The Committee also addressed the issues of DTTV coverage and the closure of the analogue system. It proposed that the digital terrestrial network be extended beyond the approved coverage of 98 percent to reach 99.8 percent of the population. The Committee considered such coverage a prerequisite for analogue 'switch-off' which it recommended take place in 2007.[11] To encourage greater DTTV take-up by viewers the Committee recommended that a two-tiered television licence fee system be introduced whereby digital households—including digital cable and satellite—pay €30 per year less than analogue households (Digital TV Committee, 2001).

A few months following the release of the Committee's report, the SVT put forward an alternative set of proposals for the future of DTTV and analogue switch-off. The SVT strategy is strongly associated with Christina Jutterstroem who was appointed Managing Director of the public broadcaster in June 2001. In April 2002 the SVT advocated the government use a combination of all three platforms—terrestrial, satellite and cable—to achieve a more rapid transition by viewers to digital and closure of the analogue system. The SVT argued against the proposal of the TV Committee to extend the digital network to 99.8 percent

---

[11] The government had not previously nominated a target date for analog switch-off.

coverage on the basis of "insurmountable costs." It claimed that it was more economical to attain universal digital coverage by employing all three platforms rather than focusing on terrestrial alone. SVT's claim was based on calculations by Teracom that extending DTTV coverage from 98 to 99.8 percent would cost roughly the same amount as to get to 98 percent, and that the most economical way to cover the additional 1.8 percent was by satellite (EBU, 2002: 53).

SVT points out that it pays a large sum each year for analogue transmission and that it would make substantial cost savings from an earlier switch-off. It estimates that the optimal switch-off date would be 2004, three years earlier than proposed by the TV Committee. SVT claims that its three years' savings on transmission costs could be used to finance access by all viewers to digital. The SVT proposes that an amount equal to the cost savings be paid into a 'distribution account' to finance a voucher system. Under this system *all* licence-paying households would be issued with a voucher equal in value to the price of a basic, easy-to-use 'people's set-top box' that would contain a smartcard providing access to national 'free-to-air' digital television channels (SVT channels and TV4). The voucher could be used as payment for a digital STB, regardless of it being terrestrial, cable or satellite. Viewers could then decide whether to subscribe to various tiers of pay-TV channels (EBU, 2002: 47).

In early 2003 the newly returned SDP government published a Bill setting out the future of DTTV in Sweden. It rejected both the TV Committee's proposal for a two-tiered television licence fee system and the SVT's plan for a people's STB. It did decide however to provide Teracom with a cash injection of €56 million (half a billion Krona) to avoid its bankruptcy and to finance the completion of the digital transmitter network. Also, it resolved for analogue switch-off to take place in Sweden on a region-by-region basis, with the transition to terrestrial digital to be completed by 2007. (Table 9.2 presents a chronology of digital television in Sweden.)

CONCLUSIONS

The decision by the Riksdagen in November 1997 to introduce digital terrestrial broadcasting was largely in response to the satellite transmissions from the UK into Sweden by TV3 and Kanal 5 that had commenced a decade earlier. The Swedish government had been concerned by the flow of advertising expenditure out of the country and its inability to regulate advertising and foreign programming on the satellite channels. It saw the early adoption of DTTV as an opportunity to preempt further inroads into the Swedish market by satellite broadcasters, and to protect national sovereignty by regaining regulatory control over the television programming watched by Swedish viewers. However worthy the government's intentions, the Swedish DTTV project has been seriously flawed, in terms of both timing and design.

The April 1999 launch date was clearly premature. Technical problems with the digital transmission network and encryption system had not been solved by the time of the launch, and the rental system for digital STBs was still being established: "The early start and great hurry caused technical problems, economic shortsightedness, uncertainty about the future and bad will among the viewers" (Gröndahl, 2002b: 6). The launch was also adversely affected by the recalcitrant attitude of the four commercial broadcasters that breached their licence conditions by delaying commencement of their DTTV transmissions. Their complaint of an insufficient audience tended to be self-fulfilling, as viewers were disinclined to subscribe to DTTV without the full complement of channels. It was more than a year after launch before the STB rental market was in operation and the full line-up of licensed channels available (EBU, 2002).

A major defect in the design of the Swedish DTTV project was that viewers were required to pay a subscription fee, even to receive programs that were available free of charge on analogue, including those of SVT for which they had already paid an annual licence fee. This anomaly was rectified in January 2003 for SVT digital channels (but not for TV4). The extremely poor take-up of only 3.5 percent after four years indicates that Swedish viewers consider the costs of subscribing to DTTV outweigh the benefits.

Part of the difficulty in attracting viewers to pay for DTTV—in Sweden as in other countries—is that because multichannel television was available first on cable and satellite, these platforms have a significant 'first mover advantage' over terrestrial. This has enabled them to gain long-term access to 'strategic programming,' especially movies and sport that are key to selling pay-TV subscriptions. Most viewers are likely to be more interested in the programming they can receive than in the form of transmission.

In an attempt to enhance the attractiveness and boost the revenues of the DTTV platform, the Swedish broadcasting authorities have been forced to grant licences to foreign broadcasters for mainly foreign programming channels that are already available on cable and satellite. This must be galling for the Swedish government that introduced digital terrestrial transmissions with the intention of protecting national cultural sovereignty in television broadcasting.

Acknowledgment
I am grateful to Aulis Gröndahl, SVT, for his valuable assistance in the writing of this chapter.

Table 9.2: Chronology of Digital Television in Sweden

1995	
November	SVT commences test transmissions of DTTV
1996	
February	Jeding Report recommends introduction of DTTV
1997	
November	government makes in-principle decision to introduce DTTV
	SVT Europa established to provide Swedish language pan-European satellite service
1998	
June	first round of DTTV licences granted
1999	
January	original date scheduled for DTTV launch
April	actual of date DTTV launch (1st)
September	TV4 commences DTTV transmissions
2000	
January	TV3, Kanal 5, & eTV commence DTTV transmissions
	second round of DTTV licences granted
April	MTG imposes €13 monthly fee for DTTV reception of TV3, TV8, & ZTV
2001	
January	SVT's 5 regional channels withdrawn from DTTV platform
April	Sweden brings regulation on advertising into line with other EU countries
August	Teracom disconnects MTG's 5 channels from DTTV network (15th)
	third round of DTTV licences granted
November	Digital TV Committee published report on future of DTTV project
2002	
March	eTV channel ceases broadcasting
April	SVT sets out proposed alternative strategy on future of DTTV
	Meditv channel commences DTTV transmissions
August	Teracom announces staff cuts and merger of Boxer & Sender
September	SDP government returned at general election
	E!/Style channel commences DTTV transmissions
2003	
January	SVT digital channels made available free-to-air
2004	
December	target date proposed by SVT for analogue switch-off
2007	
December	target date proposed by Digital TV Committee for analogue switch-off

REFERENCES

Advanced Television, 2001a. New DTT channel licences awarded, 29 August, http://www.advanced-television.com/2001/2001_newsarchive/24%20Aug-2%20 Sept.html#New%20DTT (accessed 14.08.02).

Advanced Television, 2001b. Swedish TV4 left out of DTT, 1 October, http:// www.advanced-television.com/2001/2001_newsarchive/1-8oct.html (accessed 14.08.02).

Advanced Television, 2002. Bonnier increases grip on TV4, 15 May, http://www.advanced-television.com/index.html (accessed 05.11.02).

BIPE Consulting, 2001. *Digital Switchover in Broadcasting: Annex – Country Profiles, Sweden pp. 121-136,* December, http://europa.eu.int/information _society/topics/telecoms/regulatory/studies/documents/annex_paper_country_pr ofiles.pdf (accessed 24.07.02).

Boxer TV Access AB, 2002. http://www.boxer.se/flowserver/ data.asp?fsUrl=c2l0ZUlkPTEmbWVkaWFFJZD1XRUJCUk9XU0VSX0FMTCZ sYW5nSWQ9c3dlJnBhZ2VVJZD02MjgmaXRlbUlkPTYyOA (accessed 16.12. 02).

Brandrud, Rolf, 1999. Digital TV and public service in the Nordic countries, in Jens F. Jensen & Cathy Toscan (Eds.), *Interactive Television: TV of the Future or the Future of TV?,* Aalborg University Press, 119-147.

Carlsson, Ulla & Eva Harrie (Eds.). 2001, *Media Trends 2001 in Denmark, Finland, Iceland, Norway and Sweden,* Nordicom, Göteborg University.

Digital TV Committee, 2001. *Final Report* (Summary in English), November, Stockholm, http://kultur.regeringen.se/propositionermm/sou/pdf/sou2001_90a. pdf (accessed 13.11.02).

EBU (European Broadcasting Union), 2002. *The Positioning of Digital Terrestrial Television in Western Europe,* May.

Gröndahl, Aulis, 2002a. Digital development in the Nordic region, published in German as Digitales fernsehen in den Nordischen ländern, *Media Perspektiven,* no. 9.

Gröndahl, Aulis, 2002b. A window of opportunity? Introduction of DVB-T in Sweden and Finland, paper presented at EIM Seminar, Sofia, 5 July.

Jeding, Lars, 1996. *From Massmedia to Multimedia: Digitalisation of Swedish Television*, SOU 1996:25, Stockholm, February, http://www.kultur. regeringen.se/propositionermm/sou/pdf/sou96_25b.pdf (accessed 10.04.02).

Media Map Datafile, 2001 (*6th ed.*). Sweden, CIT Publications, July.

MTG (Modern Times Group MTG AB), 2002. *Financial Results for the Period January-December 2001*, http://www.mtg.se/ (accessed 10.12.02).

Naning, Inge, 2001a. Overseas winners in Swedish DTT licensing, 21 August, http://www.advanced-television.com/2001/2001_newsarchive/20-27August. html (accessed 14.08.02).

Naning, Inge, 2001b. MTG returns Swedish DTT licences, 23 October, http://www.advanced-television.com/pages/pagesb/newsarchive2/October%20 22%20-%2029.html (accessed 24.07.02).

Naning, Inge, 2002. Pay television the Nordic way, 8 March, http://www.advanced-television.com/pages/pagesb/regnordic.html (accessed 04.11.02).

RTVA (Radio and Television Authority), 2000. *A Guide to Digital Television*, Stockholm, http://www.rtvv.se/english/pdf/digieng.pdf (accessed 10.04.02).

Sellgren, Goran, 2002a. Sweden's TV4 in iTV launch, 12 April, http://www.advanced-television.com/pages/pagesb/newsarchive2/april8-15.html (accessed 14.08.02).

Sellgren, Goran, 2002b. Sweden's digital interest declines, 16 August, http://www.advanced-television.com/index.html (accessed 16.08.02).

Sellgren, Goran, 2002c. Swedish Teracom's DTT merger, 23 August, http://www.advanced-television.com/pages/pagesb/newsarchive2/Aug19_27. html (accessed 26.08.02).

Sellgren, Goran, 2002d. E!TV joins Swedish DTT, 17 September, http://www.advanced-television.com/pages/pagesb/newsarchive2/sep16_23.html (accessed 17.09.02).

Statistics Finland, 2000. *Joukkoviestimet: Finnish Mass Media 2000*.

SVT (Sveriges Television), 2001. *Facts About Sveriges Television*, http://www.svt.se/svtinfo/inenglish/index.html (accessed 10.04.02).

SVT, 2003. *Mediebrev*, no. 156, 31 January.

TV4 AB, 2002. *Annual Report 2001*, http://www.tv4.se/imagesdb/t4i/files/ 2002513114640615_TV4_Ars_eng.pdf (accessed 04.11.02).

Weibull, Lennart, 2001. The Swedish media landscape: structure, economy and consumption, pp. 249-258 in Ulla Carlsson & Eva Harrie (Eds.), *Media Trends 2001 in Denmark, Finland, Iceland, Norway and Sweden*, Nordicom, Göteborg University.

Chapter 10
Finland: Uncertain Digital Future in a Small Market

Allan Brown
Griffith Business School, Griffith University

Finland gained independence from Russia in 1917, but is still influenced by its large eastern neighbour. It has also traditionally had close links with Sweden to its east, with Swedish being Finland's second official language. Finland's population of 5.2 million benefits from a strong economy, which is highly liberalized but with a large public sector. The information technology and electronics sectors make a significant contribution to the economy, with telecoms equipment manufacturer, Nokia, alone accounting for almost 4 percent of Gross Domestic Product. Voting for the Eduskunta (parliament) is by proportional representation. This has frequently resulted in the formation of coalitions, the current government comprising five parties headed by the Social Democratic Party. Elections for the Eduskunta will be held in 2003. Finland is the only Nordic country to date to have adopted the European Monetary Unit, with the Euro introduced in January 2002.[1]

Similar to the previous chapter on Sweden, the main focus of this chapter is the transition from analogy to digital terrestrial television broadcasting in Finland. Finland commenced digital terrestrial television transmissions on 27 August 2001. It was the sixth country worldwide to do so and the fourth European country after United Kingdom (November 1998), Sweden (April 1999) and Spain (May 2000). The first section briefly outlines the history, structure, regulation and financial operation of Finnish television broadcasting prior to the commencement of digital terrestrial transmissions. Then follows an account of the introduction of digital terrestrial television in Finland. The next section relates the experience of digital terrestrial television in Finland during its first year. The final section discusses the implications of the introduction of

---

[1] In this chapter all monetary data relating to the period prior to 2002 have been converted to Euros at the rate of 6 Finnish Marks equal to 1 Euro.

digital terrestrial television for each of the main players involved, namely, the government, viewers, the public service broadcaster and commercial broadcasters.

TELEVISION BROADCASTING IN FINLAND

History and Structure

Unlike all other European countries except the United Kingdom, Finland has traditionally had a dual public/commercial system of television broadcasting. The first national television channel, which commenced broadcasting in 1958, was shared by the public service broadcaster, Yleisradio (Finnish for 'all-round radio,' YLE), and a privately owned company, MTV Oy (MTV Limited).[2] MTV had its own 'block' of programs in the channel's schedule, earned its income from the sale of advertising transmitted with its programs, and paid YLE for the rent of its transmitters. In addition to rental income from MTV, YLE obtained revenues from audience licence fees.

YLE obtained a second channel in 1965. The original channel was named TV1 and the second TV2. The organisation of TV2 was the same as that for TV1, with MTV providing blocks of programming and selling advertising time on both channels. Although 97 percent of the Finnish population could access TV1 in 1965, TV2 did not attain similar coverage until the 1980s (Hellman, 1999: 110).

A third national television channel was established in 1986. Named TV3, the channel was funded entirely by advertising revenues. In a unique arrangement the licence for TV3 was held by YLE, while a separate company, Kolmostelevisio (Finnish for 'television three'), was responsible for programming expenditures and advertising revenues. The ownership of Kolmostelevisio comprised YLE (50 percent), MTV Limited (35 percent), and the emerging communications company, Nokia (15 percent). The arrangement for the third channel continued the public/private cooperation in Finnish television, with MTV continuing to provide programming and selling advertising on TV1 and TV2.

In 1991 MTV increased its stake in Kolmostelevisio to 80 percent by purchasing Nokia's 15 percent and 30 percent from YLE. In 1993 the arrangement between YLE and MTV came to an end with the transfer to MTV of the operating licence for the third channel. It was also decided that advertising

---

[2] Television broadcasting in Finland was actually introduced in 1956 by a private operator called Tesvisio. It could not compete against the YLE-MTV channel, however, and encountered severe financial difficulties. All Tesvisio equity was acquired by YLE in 1964 (Hellman, 1999: 106-110).

would no longer be carried on TV1 and TV2 thus giving MTV a national monopoly of television advertising. For its part YLE had to replace the MTV programming slots within its schedules on TV1 and TV2, which had comprised mainly popular prime-time programming (Hujanen, 2002). MTV obtained full ownership of Kolmostelevisio in 1997 by acquiring YLE's remaining 20 percent equity interest.

In May 1996 the Finnish government decided to establish a second national advertiser-supported television channel. The decision to licence a second commercial channel was made at the same time as the decision in principle by the government to introduce digital transmissions for terrestrial broadcasting (see below). In the following month it became clear that the two decisions were related. The terms and conditions of the proposed new analogy channel included the obligation to establish two digital program channels when digital transmissions were introduced. The licence was granted to Ruutunelonen (in English, 'Channel Four') Oy, which at the time was 50 percent owned by Sanoma Corporation. In May 1999 Sanoma merged with both Helsinki Media Company and Werner Soderstrom Oy (WSOY) to become SanomaWSOY. In 1999 and 2000 the merged company increased its holding in Ruutunelonen to 91 percent, and in 2001 the new channel was named Nelonen (SanomaWSOY, 2000; 2001).

Concurrent with the commercialisation and liberalization of terrestrial television broadcasting in Finland was the establishment of commercial satellite and cable services. The first analogy satellite service in Finland commenced in 1984. Finnish viewers can currently access two pan-European satellite services—Canal Digital, which is fully owned by the Norwegian telco, Telenor, and Viasat, a wholly-owned subsidiary of the Swedish Modern Times Group. Canal Digital started digital satellite transmissions in Finland in late 1998, and Viasat in mid-2001. In contrast with the situation in Sweden, Norway and Denmark, there is no satellite channel specifically dedicated to the Finnish audience. In particular, the satellite programs available in Finland carry no Finnish subtitles or dubbing. Similar to the Swedes, however, most Finns are fluent in English and appreciate British and American programming.

The first cable company started operations in Finland in 1975. There are around 50 cable companies operating in Finland with the two largest—Helsinki Television, a subsidiary of Sanoma, and Sonera, the national telecommunications operator—accounting for approximately 37 percent of total cable households (Media Map Datafile, 2001). By December 2002 all sizeable cable companies, except Sonera with 15 percent of total subscriptions, had upgraded their systems to digital. However, only a small minority of cable subscribers (about 5 percent) received digital services, the majority remaining with analogue. The cable companies in Finland are primarily networks for the transmission of satellite channels and domestic terrestrial channels, although there are around 15 local 'cable only' channels broadcasting in different cable markets. Under the 'must carry' rules cable systems are obliged to distribute all Finnish national analogy terrestrial channels without compensation. There is thus a symbiotic relationship between cable and terrestrial: The inclusion of the terrestrial channels on cable enhances the attractiveness of cable to viewers, and at the same time gives cable audiences access to terrestrial programming.

Approximately 43 percent of television households in Finland subscribe to cable television, and 11 percent to satellite services. The remaining 46 percent rely solely on terrestrial transmissions for their television reception (EBU, 2002). Most satellite households are also connected to the terrestrial or cable network. In 1993 licences were issued for four regional advertiser-supported terrestrial television stations, namely, Skycom, Nar-TV, KRS-TV, and Tampere TV. The combined average national audience share for TV1 and TV2 in 2001 was around 43 percent. MTV3 was by far the largest rating single channel with an audience share of about 39 percent. Nelonen had about 12 percent, with the remaining 6 percent accounted for by cable and satellite subscriber-supported (pay-TV) channels and the regional terrestrial services (YLE, 2002).

Regulation

The Ministry of Transport and Communications (MOTC) formulates broadcasting policy and drafts legislation, while the body responsible for the regulation of broadcasting (and telecommunications) is the Finnish Communications Regulatory Authority (FICORA). The operation of a cable network does not require a licence, but cable broadcasters must register with FICORA. The Finnish government reserves the power to issue television and radio broadcasting licences. The main pieces of legislation governing the broadcasting industry are the 1993 Act on Yleisradio Oy, the 1998 Act on Television and Radio Operations, and the 2002 Communications Market Act.

Since 1999, all commercial television and radio broadcasters with annual revenues of more than €3.3 million are liable to pay an operating licence fee. This is based on the amount of their advertising revenues and is calculated on a progressive scale. Until June 2002 the maximum rate was 24.5 percent for broadcasters with revenues in excess of €10 million (which included both MTV3 and Nelonen). Up to June 2002 operating licence fees comprised approximately 20 percent of total YLE income, with most of its remaining funding coming from the annual television fee payable by viewers. Proceeds from the operating licence fee and the television fee are paid into the State Television and Radio Fund, and passed on to YLE after deduction of collection costs.

The absence of ownership restrictions on Finnish media allows a high degree of cross-media ownership. SanomaWSOY, the 91 percent owner of Nelonen, is the largest commercial media company in the Nordic countries, and the publisher of newspapers comprising about 25 percent of total Finnish circulation. Sanoma also owns Finland's largest cable television operator, Helsinki Television. MTV Oy, the licensee for MTV3, is a wholly owned subsidiary of Alma Media, which is Finland's second largest commercial media group and the publisher of newspapers representing around 17 percent of total Finnish circulation (Statistics Finland, 2000). Alma Media, in turn, is effectively controlled by the Swedish Bonnier group, which holds a one-third equity interest in the Finnish media corporation.[3]

Television program regulation in Finland has historically been light-handed and imprecise. All three terrestrial broadcasters are subject to the 1989 Television Directive of the European Union, which imposes a 50 percent quota of European programs and a 10 percent quota of independent productions. However, they are subject to different Finnish content requirements: The YLE Act contains no specific stipulations regarding Finnish content; MTV3's operating licence requires only that a *sufficient portion* of MTV programming should be of domestic origin; while the operating licence for Nelonen requires that a majority proportion of *European* content shall be reserved for programs in *Finnish or Swedish* (Hellman, 1999: 172-73).

Revenue and Profitability

Television's share of total advertising expenditure in Finland is considerably below that for Europe as a whole, as is also the case in the other Nordic countries. Whereas television accounts for around 31 percent for all European countries, the figure for Finland is only around 21 percent. Conversely, the proportion of advertising expenditure spent on newspapers in Finland is substantially higher than for Europe overall. Nonetheless, there has been a steady trend in Finland towards television advertising at the expense of newspapers. Between 1980 and 1999 television's proportion of total advertising expenditure increased from 15 to 21 percent, while that for newspapers declined from 65 to 55 percent (Statistics Finland, 2000).

Data on the profitability of MTV3 are not available. The annual reports of Alma Media, however, do provide the financial trading results of its broadcasting division of which MTV3 is the "core business" (Alma Media,

---

[3] After Sanoma and Alma Media, YLE is Finland's third largest media company in terms of income.

2001).[4] Alma Media's broadcasting division earned sizeable and increasing profits up to the commencement of Nelonen. The profit (before provisions and taxes) for the 1998 year was €18.5 million, which represented 10.4 percent of net sales (Alma Media, 1999). The trading results of the broadcasting division were, however, adversely affected by competition from the second commercial channel. Although MTV3 accounted for 75 percent of total Finnish television advertising revenue for the 2000 year, the profit of Alma Media's broadcasting division fell substantially to €1.5 million. The decline continued in 2001 with MTV3's advertising share down to 73 percent and Alma Media's broadcasting operations actually incurring a loss of €19.7 million, representing 12.1 percent of net sales (Alma Media, 2002).

The financial results of Nelonen are disclosed in the annual reports of Sanoma. The fourth channel has been operating at a loss since it commenced broadcasting in 1997. It made a loss of €15.4 million in 2000, representing 29.9 percent of net sales (SanomaWSOY, 2001), and €15.3 million in 2001, again 29.9 percent of sales (SanomaWSOY, 2002). Both national advertiser-supported channels were thus making losses at the time digital terrestrial broadcasting commenced in 2001.

INTRODUCTION OF DIGITAL TERRESTRIAL TELEVISION BROADCASTING

The Digital Decision

Following the international allocation of the frequency bands for terrestrial digital broadcasting in 1995, the MOTC prepared two reports to assist it in the formation of broadcasting policy. The first of these, completed in December 1995, was a report on strategy for broadcasting in general (MOTC, 1995), while the second, completed in April 1996, dealt specifically with digital broadcasting (MOTC, 1996). The government considered these two reports at a meeting held on 8 May 1996. At this meeting the government adopted the main findings and recommendations of the two MOTC reports and made a decision in principle to introduce digital terrestrial broadcasting in Finland.

A wide range of considerations persuaded the government that Finland should be an early adopter of digital terrestrial television. It recognized that the transition from analogy to digital for terrestrial television broadcasting would, in the long term, improve the efficiency of spectrum allocation and reduce

---

[4] As well as MTV3, Alma Media's broadcasting division comprises SubTV (see below), Finland's only commercial nationwide radio station Radio Nova, and a 23.4 percent interest in the Swedish television channel TV4.

broadcasters' transmission costs. The government also saw the digitization of television as an element of its national strategy in the construction of the 'Information Society,' in particular by assisting Nokia in providing a local market for its digital television equipment. The early introduction of digital was considered a means to protect Finnish culture and the domestic television program production industry by promoting the terrestrial distribution platform and preempting further inroads into the Finnish market by foreign owned satellite broadcasters. Digital terrestrial would also provide multichannel television for viewers in Finnish Lapland who did not have adequate access to cable or satellite.[5]

At the May 1996 meeting the government also decided that: YLE was to establish a subsidiary company for the ownership and operation of the national terrestrial broadcasting distribution network; applications were to be invited immediately for the operating licence for a new national commercial *analogy* television service; and applications were to be invited in autumn 1996 for the operating licences for a national commercial *digital* television service (Wiio, 1999: 106-107).

In January 1999 YLE established a subsidiary company, Digita Oy, to own and maintain the terrestrial broadcasting transmission network, which carried the signals of the two national commercial channels, MTV3 and Nelonen, as well as those of TV1 and TV2. The purpose of separating the transmission network from YLE's other activities was to facilitate the sale of an equity interest in Digita. In November 1999 YLE contracted to sell 34 percent of Digita's shares to Sonera. However, Sonera withdrew from the contract in August 2000.[6] An auction to sell a part interest in Digita was then held in December 2000, which resulted in the sale to Telediffusion de France (TDF), at the time a subsidiary of France Telecom, of 49 percent of Digita's shares for €141 million.[7] The proceeds from the part privatization of Digita were to be used by YLE to help finance its costs of digital conversion. Digita is responsible for the construction and maintenance of the digital terrestrial broadcasting network, and all digital broadcasters pay Digita a fee for use of the network.

---

[5] Ismo Kosonen, MOTC, interview 11 April 2002.
[6] In July 2000, the Finnish Competition Council approved the contract but set as a condition that Sonera must not apply for an operating licence for digital television as long as it owns Digita shares. Sonera was not prepared to accept this condition (YLE, 2001).
[7] In June 2001, the European Commission approved the contract on the condition that TDF sell its Telemast Nordic subsidiary, which also provided broadcasting distribution services in Finland. The terms of the contract also give TDF an option, in force from 1 July 2003 to 31 January 2005, to increase its holding in Digita to 90 percent. It was announced in April 2002 that TDF would acquire a further equity interest from YLE in 2003 and become the majority owner of Digita (Advanced Television, 2002).

As mentioned above, the second national commercial analogy television channel was required as a condition of its licence to establish two digital program channels when digital transmissions were introduced. In the 'beauty contest' selection process for the license in late 1996 the final decision was between Ruutunelonen, then a 50 percent owned subsidiary of Sanoma, and a company partly financed by CLT, which in turn was 49 percent owned by the German Bertlesmann group. Hellman (1999, 159-160) explains that there was an assumption on the part of the government:

> ... that it would be more difficult to engage the multinational CLT in the construction of the Finnish digital television network ... than it would be to engage the national Sanoma group...Unlike CLT, [Sanoma] was considered a trustworthy and interested partner in accomplishing the digitalisation of the terrestrial network as a 'national project' in cooperation with the state, the YLE and MTV.

Accordingly, the licence for the new analogy channel was awarded to the Sanoma group.

In February 1997 the MOTC set up a working group, consisting of representatives from the ministry, YLE, MTV3, Nelonen, and Nokia, to prepare for the introduction of digital terrestrial transmissions. The group published its report in May 1998 (MOTC, 1998). The report set out some general principles and objectives for the implementation of digital broadcasting. It recommended that Finnish television should make a quick transfer from analogy to digital transmissions, and to that end work should commence on the construction of a digital distribution network to cover 70 percent of the population by the end of 2000. The working group proposed that initially digital terrestrial television in Finland should comprise of a total of 12 channels – the four existing analogy channels plus eight new channels – and should offer interactive supplementary services.

In May 2001 a parliamentary body, the Backman Working Group, published another report (MOTC, 2001), which effectively recommended that Finnish viewers should help finance the commercial television companies in the transition to digital. It recommended that: the operating licence fee for commercial *analogy* television channels be reduced by 50 percent from July 2002; the commercial *digital* television channels be charged no operating licence fee for their first ten-year licence period; and the annual television fee payable by viewers be increased in 2004 to account for the cost to YLE of its new digital services, and by 1 percent in real terms (allowing for inflation) each year from 2004. The government adopted these recommendations and new broadcasting legislation incorporating the changes, the Communications Market Act, came into effect in July 2002.

Digital Licences

YLE did not have to apply for digital licences as it was entitled to digital capacity in its own right under its 1993 act. The MOTC agreed for YLE to have five digital channels:

- TV1-D and TV2-D, to be digital versions of TV1 and TV2;
- YLE24, a news and current affairs channel;
- FST-D, a channel for Swedish language programming; and
- YLE Teema (Finnish for 'theme'), a channel devoted to culture, science, and educational programming.

In December 1998 the MOTC invited applications for commercial digital television licences. At the closing date in February 1999, 37 applications had been received from 27 applicant companies. The digital licences were granted under the same procedure used for analogy licences: The MOTC considered applications under a beauty contest selection process; the MOTC made its recommendations to the government for final decision; and the government allocated the licences to the selected applicants free of charge. The licence period for the new digital channels was set at 10 years, from 1 September 2000 to 31 August 2010, and licensees were obliged to make their programs available to 70 percent of the Finnish population by the end of 2002, and to 99 percent by 2006.

The successful applicants were announced in June 1999. Subsidiaries of the Alma Media group were awarded two digital licences:

- MTV Oy for MTV3-D, the digital version of MTV3; and
- the City-TV chain of companies for a generalist advertiser-supported service to provide regional programming to various areas of Finland.[8]

As well, a licence for a pay-TV sports channel was granted to Suomen Urheilutelevisio Oy, a joint venture between Alma Media (50 percent) and SanomaWSOY (35 percent), with the remaining 15 percent held by Veikkaus, the national lottery and pools operator.

Sanoma group subsidiaries obtained three digital licences:

---

[8] Four Alma Media subsidiaries comprised its City-TV chain, namely, City-TV Helsinki, City-TV Pirkanmaa, City-TV Turku, and City-TV Suomi.

- Oy Ruutunelonen AB for Nelonen-D, the digital version of Channel Four;
- Helsinki Media Company Oy for a pay-TV movie channel; and
- Werner Soderstrom Oy for a pay-TV educational channel.

There were only two licences awarded to applicants other than the incumbent broadcasters:

- Canal Plus Television for a proposed European Canal Plus pay-TV service to be adapted for Finnish viewers; and
- Wellnet Oy for a pay-TV health, fitness and lifestyle channel targeted mainly at senior citizens.

The digital licensing decisions of the government were influenced by a number of considerations. They clearly favoured the two major incumbent broadcasting groups, Alma Media and Sanoma. The government wanted to promote competition between broadcasters that were financially sound and with experience in providing a wide range of programming: "It would have been unreasonable to exclude Alma Media and Sanoma."[9] This criterion also resolved the issue of regional programming, with several separate applications for regional services being rejected in favour of Alma Media's chain of regional channels. Many of the applications were rejected because they were judged to be financially unsound. The government also considered that Finland already had a good supply of generalist channels, and the awarding of the digital licences was seen as an opportunity to introduce special interest terrestrial channels. As well, after granting licences to Alma Media and Sanoma, the government wanted to bring some new players into the industry.

In the preparation for digital terrestrial transmissions administrators were appointed for the multiplexes.[10] Each multiplex occupies the same amount of spectrum as a single analogy channel (7 megahertz). A major factor determining the choice of multiplex administrators was the need to facilitate the simulcasting of the existing terrestrial channels – TV1, TV2, MTV3, and Nelonen – in analogy and digital formats until analogy switch-off. Accordingly, YLE was appointed administrator of multiplex A in June 1999, and Alma Media and Sanoma of multiplexes B and C, respectively, in April 2000. Multiplex A was nominated for the transmission of YLE's five digital channels; multiplex B was to carry the signals for MTV3-D, Alma Media's regional channels, the sports channel and Wellnet; while multiplex C was for the carriage of Nelonen-D,

---

[9] Ismo Kosonen, MOTC, interview 11 April 2002.
[10] The 2002 Communications Market Act provides for the granting of separate licences for multiplex administrators.

Canal Plus, and the movie and educational channels. In addition, YLE, Alma Media, and Sanoma each has a supplementary channel—YLE Rinnakkainen, MTV Plus, and Nelonen Plus—for occasional transmissions (mainly sports events) on their respective multiplexes. (The licensed digital terrestrial channels and their respective multiplexes are listed in Table 10.1.)

Table 10.1: Licensed Finnish Digital Terrestrial Channels

Multiplex[a]	Channel	Programming	Principal source of funding
A: YLE	TV1-D	digital version of TV1	viewers' TV fee
	TV2-D	digital version of TV2	viewers' TV fee
	YLE24	news & current affairs	viewers' TV fee
	FST-D	Swedish	viewers' TV fee
	YLE Teema	culture, science, & education	viewers' TV fee
	YLE Rinnakkainen	supplementary	viewers' TV fee
B: Alma Media	MTV3-D	digital version of MTV3	advertising
	MTV Plus	supplementary	advertising
	Urheilukanava	sports channel	subscription
	Wellnet	health, fitness, & lifestyle	subscription
	SubTV-D[b]	regional	advertising
C: SanomaWSOY	Nelonen-D	digital version of Nelonen	advertising
	Nelonen Plus	supplementary	advertising
	Film Channel[c]	movie channel	subscription
	Werner Soderstrom[c]	educational	subscription
	Canal Plus Finland[c]	movies & documentaries	subscription

Notes:
    a. Each multiplex is also required to carry the signals of four YLE digital radio services—Radio Peili, Radio Aino, Ylen Klassinen, and Vega Plus.
    b. Name changed from City-TV to SubTV prior to digital launch.
    c. Licences withdrawn by government in January, 2002.

The introduction of digital broadcasting also necessitated the establishment of a number of technical and industry representative organisations. The first such body was the Digital TV Forum Finland, which was established in June 1998 to coordinate the development of Finnish terrestrial television. The Forum was replaced in May 2000 by the Digital Terrestrial Television League Finland. The DTT League consists of YLE, the holders of commercial digital television licences, and Digita. In February 2001, the three multiplex administrators established a joint non-profit company called Platco Oy to provide technical resources to assist them in the operation of the multiplexes and the development and implementation of interactive services.

In early 2001, following a recommendation of the Digital TV Forum, Finland became the first country in the world to mandate Multimedia Home Platform (MHP) interactive technology for digital terrestrial transmissions. The MHP standard was also adopted by Finnish cable systems, and satellite operators have agreed to migrate to MHP by 2005. The three Finnish multiplex administrators and the digital channels agreed to a common national electronic program guide (EPG). It will display information on the current day's programs on digital channels as well as those scheduled for the following six days, arranged according to time of broadcast or program type. The EPG will carry no advertising material. Finnish digital terrestrial channels will also carry 'superteletext'. It will have a common template, but, unlike the EPG, each individual channel will provide its own customised superteletext content. Finland has also adopted a common conditional access (CA) system for both terrestrial and cable television platforms. This means that digital viewers in Finland will need only a single card to access all pay-TV channels available on terrestrial and cable (A chronology of events relating to the introduction of digital terrestrial television in Finland is shown in Table 10.2.).

DIGITAL TERRESTRIAL TELEVISION: THE FIRST YEAR

YLE commenced test digital terrestrial transmissions in September 1997, and in September 2000 made digital broadcasts on multiplex A from the Sydney Olympics. Test simulcasts of the four terrestrial channels—TV1, TV2, MTV3, and Nelonen—were also broadcast on multiplex A from September 2000. In April 2001, when the two other multiplexes came into operation, MTV3 and Nelonen transferred their pilot services to multiplexes B and C.

In August 2001, the month planned for the launch of digital terrestrial transmissions, there were only basic (non-MHP) digital STBs available for purchase by viewers. Nevertheless, the MOTC decided to go ahead with the

Table 10.2: Chronology of Digital Terrestrial Television in Finland

1995	
December	publication by MOTC of *Strategy Report on Broadcasting: Radio & Television in 2010*
1996	
April	publication by MOTC of *Digitalisation of Broadcasting in Finland*
May	government makes decision in principle to introduce digital terrestrial broadcasting
1997	
September	YLE commences test digital TV terrestrial transmissions
1998	
May	publication by MOTC of *Digital Television and Finland*
June	Digital TV Forum Finland established to coordinate development of digital terrestrial TV
December	MOTC invited applications for commercial digital TV licences
1999	
January	YLE establishes Digita Oy to manage terrestrial transmission network
February	37 applications received for commercial digital TV licences
March	operating licences for MTV3 & Nelonen extended to 31 December 2006
June	eight commercial digital TV licences granted
	YLE appointed administrator of multiplex A
2000	
April	Alma Media & Sanoma appointed administrators of multiplexes B & C
May	Digital Terrestrial Television Finland replaces DTT Forum Finland
September	commencement of 10-year licence period for commercial digital TV licences
	test simulcasts commence on multiplex A of TV1, TV2, MTV3, & Nelonen
	YLE conducts test digital transmissions from Sydney Olympics
December	YLE sells 49% of Digita to TDF for €141 million
2001	
February	Platco Oy established to provide technical services to multiplex administrators
April	multiplexes B & C commence operations
August	official commencement of digital terrestrial TV transmissions (27th)
December	digital terrestrial network covers 70% of Finnish population
2002	
January	digital licences for educational channel, movie channel, & Canal Plus Finland withdrawn
July	Communications Market Act comes into force
2006	
December	target date switch-off of analogy terrestrial network

launch on the 27th as scheduled. The Minister's speech launching digital television (Heinonen, 2001) was appropriately low-keyed:

> The future of television will be digital. The road ahead is not straightforward but goes through trial and error, enthusiasm and disappointment—just like real life. Not all parts of television digitalisation have yet found their right place. Particularly equipment that is needed in interactive services has not yet been introduced.... Today we are taking the first steps along this road.

At launch date, the digital terrestrial network covered 50 percent of the Finnish population, mainly those living in the more populous areas in the south and south-west of the country including Helsinki, Espoo, Vantaa, Turku and Tampere. Coverage was 70 percent by the end of 2001. The analogy operating licences for MTV3 and Nelonen were due to expire in December 1999 and September 2002, respectively. In March 1999, however, the government extended both licences to 31 December 2006 to coincide with the planned analogy switch-off.The first year of digital terrestrial broadcasting in Finland was marked by difficulties and disappointments. Most notably, relatively few viewers accessed digital transmissions. An estimated 10,000 digiboxes (terrestrial only) were sold by the end of 2001, and 31,000 (terrestrial and cable) sold or rented by the end of August 2002. The latter figure represents only around 1.4 percent of total Finnish television households.[11]

The main reasons for the meagre digital take-up during the first year were the non-availability of MHP receivers, and the low level of interest by viewers in the programs and services offered by the new digital channels. Under the terms of their operating licences, the digital channels were required to be on air by the end of 2001. However, Sanoma's educational channel, Helsinki Media's movie channel and Canal Plus Finland had not commenced broadcasting by that time, and their licences were withdrawn by the government in January 2002 (MOTC, 2002a). As they were all subscription channels, they were critically disadvantaged by the non-availability of MHP-standard STBs required for conditional access.[12] As the three withdrawn channels had all been allocated to multiplex C it was left transmitting only Nelonen-D. In May 2002 the MOTC invited applications for licences to replace those it had withdrawn. By early

---

[11] In early 2002 the prices to consumers of digiboxes were around €335 for the Nokia model (without CA capacity) and €450 for the Finlux (with CA capacity) (EBU 2002). Sony launched its MHP integrated digital receiver ('Wega') on the Finnish market in May 2002 at a retail price of €4000.

[12] Sanoma may also have considered that the purpose of its proposed educational channel was somewhat pre-empted by the programming on YLE Teema.

2003 the MOTC seemed to have forgiven Canal Plus for its previous non-performance and announced the allocation of all three replacement licences to the French owned operator. The new channels, all pay-TV—Canal Plus, Canal Plus Yellow and Canal Plus Blue—have been available to Nordic satellite subscribers for a number of years.

At mid-2003 the fate of the other two digital pay-TV channels—the joint Alma Media-Sanoma sports channel and Wellnet—was uncertain. They were also adversely affected by the non-availability of MHP boxes, and had not commenced their subscription services. The sports channel was broadcasting free-to-air in prime-time for around 4-6 hours per day.[13] The Wellnet transmission consisted merely of the channel's logo.

The three new public service digital channels—YLE24, FST-D, and Teema—were all providing regular broadcasts, but for only a few hours daily, and with much of their content comprising simulcasts or rebroadcasts of programs shown on TV1 and TV2. Also available on digital was the new commercial channel, SubTV, which was created by Alma Media in its 2001 restructure of its City-TV chain of companies.[14]

A year after its launch the performance of digital terrestrial television in Finland fell well short of expectations. Digital transmission improved the quality of reception for the small number of viewers that had digital terminals.[15] There were nine digital television channels on air (excluding Wellnet and the supplementary channels), but four of these (TV1-D, TV2-D, MTV3-D, and Nelonen-D) were broadcast on analogy terrestrial. There were no digital pay-TV services on offer, superteletext was not available, and the EPG was in a rudimentary stage of development. Digital terrestrial television in Finland had a disappointing start.

---

[13] Although commercial digital licences are described here as 'advertiser-supported' and 'pay-TV,' in fact the licence conditions allow channel operators to be flexible in their sources of revenues. 'Pay-TV' channels can carry advertising, and 'advertiser-supported' channels can offer 'pay-per-view' services (Juha Mustonen, MTV3, personal correspondence 21 October 2002).

[14] In early 2001 Alma Media merged its City-TV chain into its cable channel, TVTV!, and called the new entity SubTV Oy. SubTV-D began broadcasting on multiplex B on digital launch date. Subsequently, the channel was reformulated into a youth channel broadcasting a high proportion of US drama and comedy series with no regional programming—a format substantially different from the original concept on which the channel was licensed.

[15] A significant proportion of the early digital adopters lives in areas of poor analog reception and thus particularly benefit from digital transmissions (Jaakko Harno, Platco, interview 3 May 2002).

IMPLICATIONS FOR THE MAIN PLAYERS

Government

As already indicated, a major problem throughout the first year of digital transmissions was the non-availability of MHP digiboxes, which delayed the commencement of terrestrial pay-TV and interactive services and caused consumer uncertainty. Governments cannot compel manufacturers to deliver products to the market by a certain date, but the Finnish government was over-eager to commence digital transmissions and failed to coordinate with manufacturers to ensure the availability of receivers by digital launch (an inexplicable outcome considering Nokia's involvement in the lead-up to digital broadcasting). When it realised MHP equipment would not be available in time it was forced by the conditions of the digital licences to keep to its August 2001 launch date in order to prevent a new round of licensing. In the event, three of the commercial digital licences had to be withdrawn, and viewers were left with a depleted digital offering.

Finnish policymakers consider it their role to provide a suitable regulatory environment that will allow broadcasters and viewers themselves to decide the extent to which digital terrestrial will be employed. The government wants to avoid influencing the operation of the market. At the same time, it has set 2006 as its target date for the switch-off of the analogy transmission system. While it has made universal *technical* coverage a precondition for analogy switch-off, it has set no criteria for the actual *penetration* of digital reception equipment.

Digital take-up may be boosted from 2003 with MHP boxes on the market and a full complement of digital channels and interactive services available to viewers. Nevertheless, it is questionable if market forces alone will be sufficient to allow the government to meet its 2006 target. A 2002 report prepared for the European Broadcasting Union points out that "... the consensus among broad-casters and other key players in Finland is that complete digital switchover by 2006 is not likely", and suggests that "... for the 2006 date to be realistic not only would the most optimistic penetration forecasts have to be fulfilled but also some sort of government intervention would be required" (EBU, 2002: 100-01). The government affirmed in May 2002, however, that it would not subsidize the purchase by consumers of digital reception equipment (MOTC, 2002b).

Viewers

Similar to the situation in Sweden, one of the motives of Finland to be an early adopter of digital terrestrial was to try to prevent the loss of market share to satellite and cable with their mainly foreign programming. As in Sweden and other countries, however, it is very difficult for commercial terrestrial pay-TV broadcasters to convince viewers to pay for programming on terrestrial when there may be greater variety and more popular offerings available on cable and satellite (Humphreys & Lang, 1998).

This points to a possible fundamental problem with the Finnish government's digital policy of granting most of the commercial digital licences for pay-TV services. The availability of pay-TV on terrestrial may not be a sufficiently strong incentive for viewers to invest in digital equipment. A proportion of viewers will be attracted to the improved reception quality of digital transmissions and/or the new interactive services. However, it may be that the necessary incentive for a majority of viewers to switch to digital will be additional *free-to-air* programming not available on analogy.

Yleisradio

YLE has been an enthusiastic proponent of digital and has taken a leading role in the Finnish transition from analogy to digital terrestrial broadcasting. It has assumed principal positions on all of the influential bodies involved with the development and implementation of digital transmission, and was the first broadcaster to put to air new digital television channels.

The proceeds from its sale of equity in Digita and the increase from 2004 in the television fee payable by viewers should provide a stable economic environment for YLE. Nevertheless, its finances are likely to be stretched for a number of years. It now needs to provide programming for five channels (six including Rinnakkainen) compared to its traditional two. In addition, from July 2002 it lost some 10 percent of its total income as a result of the halving of the operating licence fee payable by the commercial channels.

With its new digital channels YLE is making a strong attempt to maintain its key position in Finnish broadcasting. YLE's digital strategy is for TV1-D and TV2-D to be the core of its services. Both are to remain generalist channels offering a broad range of program genres and retaining pluralism and diversity in their output. They are now complemented by YLE24, FST-D and Teema, which are being developed as specialised channels, but representing traditional areas of public service broadcasting, namely, news, current affairs, programming for minority audiences, culture, and education (Hujanen, 2002). YLE is also developing educational and other interactive applications consistent with its public service broadcasting mandate.

In spite of more than doubling its number of channels, YLE seems unlikely to greatly increase its audience share, at least in the near term. Digital channels will not significantly affect analogy audience numbers until a sizeable proportion of viewers have digital receivers. Even then, neither YLE24 nor FST-D is likely to attract large audiences, and at least some of the audience for YLE's new digital channels will be traditional YLE viewers who will simply come across from TV1 and TV2.

Commercial Broadcasters

The licensing decisions of the Finnish government in 1999 largely favoured the incumbent commercial broadcasters, Alma Media and Sanoma: only six new digital commercial licences were issued even though there was spectrum capacity for many more channels (IDATE, 2000); five of the six commercial digital channels were licensed as pay-TV services (which can be expected to bring about less audience fragmentation and loss of advertising revenues than new advertiser-supported channels); and four of the six new channels went to subsidiaries of the Alma Media and Sanoma groups. In addition, the government provided financial assistance to the incumbents by halving the operating licence fee on commercial analogy channels and by waiving the fee on digital commercial channels for the initial 10-year licence period.

In arriving at these decisions the government was clearly mindful of the financial difficulties facing the incumbent broadcasters and the threat to their viability posed by the licensing of new advertiser-supported channels. As suggested above, the demand by viewers for digital reception equipment may have been stronger had it given them access to a greater number of free-to-air services. However, given the small size of the Finnish television advertising market, the government's decision to issue new licences for mainly pay-TV services is understandable, as is the granting of most licences to existing broadcasters. It is a paradox of digital television that its technological potential to bring about a substantial increase in broadcast ownership diversity is severely constrained by the harsh reality of broadcasting economics (Brown, 2003).

Incumbent Finnish commercial broadcasters will be hoping that the cost of digital conversion and potential loss of advertising revenue can be (more than) offset by the government's concessions in relation to the licence fee. All commercial digital channels will explore opportunities to make profits from interactive services. The new pay-TV operators will attempt to sign up digital terrestrial viewers who do not already have pay-TV, and to attract subscriptions from satellite and cable. The free-to-air commercial broadcasters will endeavour to continue the trend in favour of television advertising at the expense of the print media.

The transition from terrestrial analogy to digital broadcasting in Finland provides a challenge for all players involved. The government is primarily responsible for decisions regarding the transmission system, and a change in policy may be required to achieve analogy switch-off within a reasonable period. With digital television viewers can receive improved reception as well as an increased number of program channels and services, but most are not yet convinced that the benefits of digital exceed the costs. While YLE seems to have the most to gain and least to lose from the transition to digital, its finances are likely to remain tight for a number of years as it develops its new digital offerings. Commercial broadcasters are most at risk from the introduction of digital, especially the incumbents who face fragmentation of their audience. In Finland, as elsewhere, the transition from analogy to digital brings new services and greater competition, but increased uncertainty to television broadcasting.

REFERENCES

Advanced Television, 2002. Finnish licence financing "obsolete", 25 April, http://www.advanced-television.com/index.html, (accessed 27.08.02).

Alma Media, 1999. *Annual report 1998*, http://www.almamedia.fi/acrobat/alma media98eng.pdf (accessed 10.03.02).

Alma Media, 2001. *Annual Report 2000*, http://www.almamedia.fi/acrobat/ e_vuosikertomus2000.pdf (accessed 28.03.02).

Alma Media, 2002. *Annual Report 2001*, http://www.almamedia.fi/ vuosikertomus2001/eng/etusivu.html (accessed 10.03.02).

Brown, Allan, 2003. The digital future of terrestrial advertiser-supported television, *Prometheus*, vol. 21, no.1, 41-57.

EBU (European Broadcasting Union), 2002. *The Positioning of Digital Terrestrial Television in Western Europe*, May.

Heinonen, Olli-Pekka, 2001. Launch of digital television broadcasting, Press Release, 27 August, http://www.mintc.fi/www/sivut/english/digi_heinonen_ eng.htm (accessed 25.01.02).

Hellman, Heikki, 1999. *From Companions to Competitors: The Changing Broadcasting Market and Television Programming in Finland*, University of Tampere.

Hujanen, Taisto, 2002. Public service television in a digital multiplex: from coordinated universalism to channel profilization, paper presented at the European Science Foundation Programme conference, *Changing Media: Changing Europe*, Copenhagen, April.

Humphreys, Peter & Matthias Lang, 1998. Digital television between the economy and pluralism, in Jeanette Steemers (Ed.), *Changing Channels: The Prospects for Television in a Digital World*, University of Luton Press, 9-35.

IDATE, 2000. *Development of Digital TV in Europe: 2000 Report – Finland*, December.

Media Map Datafile, 2001 (6th ed.). Finland, CIT Publications, August.

MOTC (Ministry of Transport and Communications), 1995. *A Strategy Report on Broadcasting: Radio and Television in 2010*, 45/1995, December.

MOTC, 1996. *Digitalisation of Broadcasting in Finland*, 20/1996, April.

MOTC, 1998. *Digital Television and Finland*, 23/1998, May.

MOTC, 2001. *Improving the Operational Basis for Television Broadcasting* ('Backman Report'), 29/2001, May.

MOTC, 2002a. *Digital television*, http://www.mintc.fi/www/sivut/english/tele/massmedia/ index.html (accessed 22.03.02).

MOTC, 2002b. *Three new digital television programme licences will become open for application*, 2 May, http://www.mintc.fi/ (accessed 17.10.02).

SanomaWSOY, 2000. *Annual Review 1999*, http://kuvat.tietokone.fi/sanomawsoy/images/attachments/1918-Englanti.pdf (accessed 04.04.02).

SanomaWSOY, 2001. *Annual Report for 2000*, http://www.sanomawsoy.fi/vuosikertomus/pdf/In_English/Eng_a.PDF (accessed 04.04.02).

SanomaWSOY, 2002. *Annual Report for 2001*, http://www.sanomawsoy.fi/vuosikertomus_02/download/en/pdf/annual_report_2001.pdf (accessed 04.04.02).

Statistics Finland, 2000. *Joukkoviestimet: Finnish Mass Media 2000*.

Wiio, Juhani, (1999). *Managing Strategic Change in the Changing Radio and Television Market: A Finnish Example 1985-1998*, Yleisradio, Helsinki.

YLE (Yleisradio), 2001. *Annual Report 2000*, http://www.yle.fi/fbc/annual.shtml (accessed 09.04.02).

YLE, 2002. *Annual Report 2001*, http://www.yle.fi/fbc/kuvat/annual_2001.pdf (accessed 14.05.02).

Chapter 11
Denmark: Emulating Sweden, but Hesitating

Reza Tadayoni
Technical University of Denmark

This chapter provides a detailed analysis of the process of transition from analogue to digital television broadcasting in Denmark and on the development of the broadcast market. The Danish case shows that the increase in the number of broadcast services has been a major driver for transition to digital broadcasting. Satellite and cable solutions provided in Denmark are not radically different from other similar markets, but the Danish model regarding terrestrial broadcasting provides some new solutions that are discussed and analysed throughout this chapter

This chapter begins with a discussion of the broadcast sector including a short history of broadcasting and its current situation. Then a description of the transition from analogue to digital broadcasting in the Danish multi service, satellite and cable, market is offered, followed by plans for transition from analogue to digital terrestrial television. Ultimately some conclusions are drawn about the process and its current situation.

TV LANDSCAPE IN DENMARK

This section provides an overall picture of the Danish broadcasting market, in terms of its history, basic data on population, television households, market organisation, audience market share, and size.

A Short History of Danish Broadcasting

From the invention of radio broadcasting, the importance of this new medium was obvious both as a commercial product/service, which opened up for new business opportunities, and as a new platform for providing educational and information related services to general public. Denmark followed the European organisation model settled by the British Broadcasting Corp., namely a countrywide organisation of broadcast services, which was subjected to severe public service regulations (see among others Septrup, 1993, for information about history of broadcasting in the Nordic countries).

Danes, as in other Europeans, chose to regulate radio as a governmental property. This was in continuation of the European tradition of governmental organisation of infrastructures like railroads, post, telegraph and telecommunication – a tradition that builds upon the importance of national governmental organisations in Europe in the 1800's and the first part of the 1900's. Funding for broadcasting was based on direct license payment.

The result was the establishment of monopoly markets in Denmark and the market developed powerful incumbent broadcasters. The incumbent broadcasters have been challenged and diversity has been demanded during its history. This has been done both by way of pirate actions, like the broadcasting of Radio Mercur from international waters to the Danish audience in 1958,[1] and also through regular applications for commercial licenses by private actors. Later on the emergence of cable/satellite systems increased the available resources significantly and decreased the technological barriers for the number of actors on the market making the political barriers more obvious.

The development of different infrastructures like satellite and cable networks has changed the assumptions for the traditional regulation and organisation of the broadcasting market. In the last couple of decades, technological developments have further evolved toward using digital technology and interactivity in broadcasting. This development can be considered as the most radical innovation in the history of broadcasting since the invention of TV. This technological development along with the development in the political and economic set-up have created new conditions for the market for broadcasting services, which are described in the following having the point of departure in the Danish market.

Basic Data

Denmark is a small, Nordic nation that had a population of 5,358,000, living in 2,456,000 households in 2002. Its gross domestic product was €183 billion.

In terms of television, the country had 2.370,000 television households, including 1,112,000 households with more than 2 television sets. More than 80 percent of households with television had videocassette recorders/players. More

---

[1] To prevent such pirate broadcasting the Telecommunication by radio Act of 1949 had legislated that, "The setting up of, operation of, or use of broadcasting stations on the open sea or in the air space above it shall not be permitted." On that basis, radio Mercur was shut down by the government in 1963.

than 22 percent of households with television had satellite services available to them and more than 65 percent had cable service available if they wished to subscribe. Satellite and cable households may also use those services to view free-to-air (FTA) television.

Organization of Television Broadcasting in Denmark

Up to mid-1980s, the only Danish TV station was DR. DR is a public service station funded almost totally by license fees. It is terrestrially distributed and has a geographical coverage of about 100 percent. During this period it has always been possible to watch Swedish and German TV programs in the areas near borderlines. It has, for example, always been possible to see Swedish programs in the Copenhagen area.

From mid eighties another public service station, TV 2/DANMARK started. TV 2/DANMARK is funded partly (17 percent) by licence fees and partly (83 percent) by advertising and other incomes. TV 2/DANMARK also has a geographical coverage of about 100 percent percent and is terrestrially distributed. A real competition on the TV market in Denmark began with the introduction of TV 2/DANMARK.

In spring 2002, the Danish government decided to privatize TV 2/DANMARK, which had been partially financed by license fees since its beginning in 1988. Prior to 2006, TV 2/DANMARK is to be sold to a private concern. However, even though the station is to be privatized, it must still abide by certain public service obligations with respect to news and current events and a continued economic commitment to Danish film. Terrestrial broadcasting in Denmark is currently organized on three levels:

- *Nationwide coverage*, which consists of DR's nationwide radio and TV transmissions and TV 2/DANMARK's nationwide TV transmissions. DR and TV 2/DANMARK are both subject to the Danish public service regulation. According to the Ministry of Culture: 'Their programming must aim at quality, versatility and diversity and must aim for objectivity and impartiality in their dissemination of information to the public. Both stations are further obligated to programme for and broadcast to the entire population, including the transmission of programmes aimed at smaller target groups. Consequently, the executives and board of managers of the two stations are solely responsible for programming.' (www.kum.dk) DR and TV 2/DANMARK are each responsible for two television channels, one terrestrial and one satellite. From 2000, TV 2/DANMARK has operated TV 2 ZULU, which is distributed in the satellite network. From 1997, DR has operated DR2, which is distributed in the satellite network. By using some of the frequency resources allocated for local TV it has been possible to give a large part of the Danish population the possibility to access DR2 in the terrestrial network. DR has further 4 radio channels.

- *Regional coverage*, which consists of eight regional TV 2/DANMARK companies along with DR's nine regional radio stations.
- *Local coverage*, which consists of about 100 local TV stations and 250 local radio stations. The local TV and radio stations are private enterprises. Local stations are financed by membership and subscriptions and, to some extent, by municipal subsidies, sale of transmission time, and similar means. Companies, associations and others intending to establish a local broadcasting company must apply for an operation license from local boards organized at the municipal level.

Development and penetration of cable and satellite TV has opened the opportunity for other actors to access resources for offering TV programmes. Some new Danish TV stations are only distributed through cable and satellite networks. The important providers of Danish programmes in the satellite and cable are TV3/Denmark (with two channels) and TVDanmark (with two channels) funded partly by advertising and partly by subscription. Furthermore, as described in the following, several foreign TV channels like CNN, BBC, MTV, DISCOVERY etc. can be accessed through cable subscription or satellite reception. Premium pay-TV channels like TV 1000, CINEMA, and Canal Plus are also present—though with a low subscription base—on the Danish market.

TV Services

The Danish television stations are the public service TV stations, DR, DR2, and TV 2/DANMARK, a national advertising based channel (TV2 ZULU), two advertising based channels TV 3 and 3+ provided by VIASAT, and two advertising based channels TVDanmark 1 and TVDanmark 2 from SBS

DR and TV 2/DANMARK are public services stations and are obliged to follow Danish regulation. TV2 ZULU is transmitted from Denmark and is under Danish commercial TV regulations. TV3 and 3+ are not based in Denmark and transmit their services from UK; consequently they follow UK regulation of private TV. TVDanamrk 1 is also foreign based and need not follow Danish regulation but TVDanmark 2, due to its local TV licenses in Denmark is obliged to follow the Danish commercial TV regulation.

TV3 and 3+ and both TVDanmark channels base their programs on reality shows such as Big Brother, cheap and mainly American programs, including American movies, serials, etc, and as seen later their market share in Denmark is still much bellow the two public services channels.

Table 11.1 and Table 11.2 show the number and types of different services available in the satellite and cable markets.

Table 11.1: Satellite Service Types

Channel type	Number	Name
Non-subscription	7	DR2, Viasat Interactive services, TV2 Zulu, DR1, TVDanmark1, TVDanmark2, Canal Digital Interactive services
News	7	BBC world, Bloomberg, Sky News, CNN, CNBC, Sky News, BBC world
Entertainment	11	Four channels from TV3, Hallmark, TV6 Action, ZTV, Viasat Plus, Eurotica (also as stand-alone: DKR 69), Adult channel, Cinecinemas (also as stand-alone DKR 69), BBC Prime
Sport	3	VIASAT Sport, Eurosport News, Eurosport Nordic
Documentaries	10	History Channel, Travel Channel, TV6 Nature, Four from Discovery Channel, Adventure One, National Geographic
Kids	5	Nickelodeon, Fox Kids, Cartoon Network, TCC, TCM
Music	4	MTV, VH-1, Multi-music(10 channels), Music Choice (20 channels)
Premium movies	6	TV1000, Cinema, Playboy TV, Three channels from Canal Plus
Pay-per-view	2	Ticket, KIOSK
Stand-alone premium Channels	5	TV Finland NRK International Manchester United ORT International Two channels from Prime TV

Audience Market Share

In 2001, TV 2 led the market in terms of audience share with a 35 percent share, followed by DR1 with a 28 percent share. All others had shares of less than 10 percent. The market share of the Danish channels is still superior to the foreign channels and between Danish channels, the public service channels are the most popular. This popularity of national channels and public service channels is, however, a general phenomenon in the Nordic countries.

Table 11.2: Cable Service Types

Channel type	Number	Name
Non-subscription	8	DR1, DR2, TV 2, Two regional programmes, two foreign public service channels, Infokanalen
News	4	Bloomberg, WorldNet, CNBC, Sky News
Entertainment	5	[.tv], E!, TCM Classic Movies, Hallmark, Adult Channel, KIOSK
Documentaries	2	National Geographic, Travel channel
Lifestyle	3	Arte, Fashion TV, MCM International
Kids	3	Fox Kids, Nickelodeon, Cartoon Network
Music	4	MTV 2, VH-1, Muzzik, Performance
Stand-alone premium Channels	5	Three from Canal+, two from TV1000

TV Market in Denmark

Broadcast TV service market in Denmark, like many other countries consists of 3 main components: License fees, advertising revenue and subscription fees. Furthermore sponsorship and other sources of revenue are used by the public and private broadcasters. In the recent years revenues from Pay per view and T-commerce have emerged but the size of the market is very small and there is no data available on the size of this segment of the market.

In 2002, the television market generated about €953 million. Public funds provided €253 million, advertising expenditures were about €257 million and subscriptions approximately €243 million. The amount available in the market has been increasing.

The total market for broadcast TV in Denmark is about 1 billion €, that is, about 0.5 percent of the GDP. This is as mentioned only the amount of the market in terms of license fee, advertising and subscription fees market. In another work, we included the total broadcast industry and the size of the broadcast market in Denmark in 2000 was calculated to be about 2.8 percent of the GDP.

TRANSITION TO DIGITAL IN
SATELLITE AND CABLE NETWORKS

This chapter deals with the multi-service satellite and cable platforms. The subchapter contains a description of the roll out of digital cable and satellite. Furthermore the services available in these platforms and the business models and funding and access issues are discussed and analyzed.

Value Chain of Digital Broadcast Services

In this section the value chain of digital broadcasting is described with the aim of putting the content of the analysis of the Danish case, which is given in the following in a larger context and identifying the problem field and the focus of this chapter.

Figure 11.1 depicts the value chain of digital broadcasting. The links of the chain, listed at the bottom of the figure, involve the following elements:

- Content. Digitalisation influences on the content both regarding the content itself and regarding the new actors that will enter the market. By using the possibility of interactivity, the programs can evolve to involve the end-consumers actively in the programs they consume. Furthermore, new types of data services can be created and services known from the Internet can be provided in the broadcasting networks, and therefore new actors can enter in the broadcasting content provision market. The possibility for transmission of programmes in different technical qualities gives further the content providers new possibilities in their content creation and provision.
- Distribution networks will carry the MPEG-2 TS from content providers to service providers and from service providers to delivery networks. The distribution networks are of course only used if there is a distance between the content provider, service provider, and the delivery networks. Distribution networks were one of the first parts of the value chain that was digitised using different 'compression' standards, including MPEG-2 standard.
- The service provider is in charge of aggregating content, and maintaining Conditional Access, EPG and other functions relevant for the service package in different platforms.

Figure 11.1: Value Chain of Digital Broadcasting

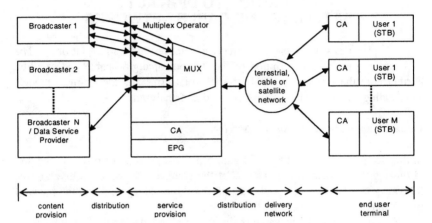

- The main delivery networks are satellite, cable, and terrestrial network that are going through digitalisation process in different speed. Different delivery networks have different characteristics putting them on a competitive position regarding some services and complementary regarding others.
- The end-user terminal will in a transition period be a digital Set-Top-Box eventually with a CA interface. In the long run integrated digital TV will replace the combination of analogue TV and digital Set-Top-Box. The interface to the end-user will be enhanced in digital TV as the programs give the end-user possibility for more active involvement in program production.

Delivery networks and service provision are most important regarding the objective of this chapter and are described in more detail in following sections.

Satellite

As mentioned previously there are approximately 530,000 satellite households in Denmark (22 percent of Danish TV households). The number of households who subscribe to satellite services are about 345,000 (14.7 percent of Danish TV households). The satellite market in Denmark is shared between Canal Digital and VIASAT. These two providers operate in all Nordic countries.

Canal Digital Danmark A/S is a part of Canal Digital AS, which was founded in March 1997 as a joint venture between the French pay-TV company

Canal Plus and the Norwegian holding company Telenor Plus. Today, Telenor owns 100 percent of Canal Digital. Canal Digital started its regular digital services in fall 1998. In the beginning of 2003, Canal Digital had about 1.2 million cardholders[2] and about 600,000 digital subscribers in the Nordic countries.

Canal Digital has no Danish TV channel itself but has a strategic cooperation agreement with SBS that owns TVDanmark. Canal Digital's premium pay TV channels are Canal Plus, Canal Plus yellow, and Canal Plus Blue).

Canal Digital turned off the analogue distribution of its main premium pay-TV channel, Canal+, in February 1999, and offered free digital set-top-boxes to its 15,000 subscribers for a one-year period. The only precondition was that the subscribers agreed to continue the subscription to Canal+ in 1999. At the moment (beginning of 2003), Canal Digital provides only digital services. The only analogue TV channel that is transmitted by Canal Digital is DR2, which is FTA.

VIASAT is owned by Modern Times Group (MTG) AB. VIASAT has about one million subscribers in the Nordic countries. VIASAT began digital transmissions in late spring 2000. This was a significant change in VIASAT's approach towards digitalisation—previously it maintained that the costs could not be justified by the marginal benefits in terms of more channels. According to VIASAT the change was primarily reasoned in the level of maturity of the market and the fact that introduction of digital satellite TV can now be done at considerably lower costs, as the price of set top boxes and satellite capacity has been reduced substantially. New interactive and commercial potentials may also have contributed to the change in opinion. VIASAT's advertising-based TV stations in Denmark are TV3 and 3+ and its premium pay TV channels are TV 1000 and Cinema. From June 2000 VIASAT stopped selling analogue subscription but they maintain parallel simulcasting to provide services to old analogue customers.

The satellite providers are eager to establish contracts with other popular Danish TV stations, including public service stations that are the most popular TV stations in Denmark. This has resulted in favourable contract conditions to make these channels available in their packages. DR and DR2 are, for example, available in all of the packages offered by Canal Digital and VIASAT with no cost for the consumers and no cost for DR.

Marketing of satellite services are intense and visible in the Danish market. Recently both Canal Digital and VIASAT have introduced programs for

---

[2] Cardholders are consumers who do not necessarily subscribe to the services but they acquire a card for minor expenses to access FTA channels, as, for example, major Danish FTA channels like public service channels are encrypted.

subsidizing set-top-boxes. The deal is that the consumers don't pay for the box but they must accept subscription to their premium services for at least one year.

Cable

As discussed earlier, the number of home-passed cable households in Denmark are almost 1.8 million, of which approximately 1.35 million (48 percent of TV households) subscribed to minimum one cable TV service.

The market for cable TV in Denmark is characterized by the two major network providers, TDC Kabel TV and SOFA, and a large amount of smaller independent operators who acquire their contents independently and offer services that vary considerably in terms of quantity and standards.

The cable operators do not have their own TV stations[3] and the packages offered by these operators are a combination of Danish and foreign TV channels. The public service and local TV stations are available in all cable TV networks due to 'must carry' regulation.

TDC Kabel TV is the largest cable TV provider, covering its 900,000 household network digitally. Although the network is digitalized, the numbers of digital subscribers are far below the expectations. Today there are about 100,000 digital subscribers in TDC Kabel TV network. This is very much due to the high expenses of digital packages and the lack of value adds services from consumers' perspective. At the supply side there are neither any strong incentive to put efforts in terms of subsidizing boxes to all subscribers to facilitate total transition to digital. TDC Kabel TV has, however, offered its premium pay TV subscribers free digital set-top-boxes and terminated analogue transmission of these services.

STOFA, the other major cable TV provider, is the Danish cable TV subsidiary of the Swedish tele-information group Telia. It has approximately 600,000 households in its network. STOFA does not have a centralised distribution network. Instead, services are provided through local head offices. STOFA's network is also almost partly digitalized but there are not so many consumers willing to go digital. STOFA started the digitalisation of its network in late 1998. In the areas where the network has been digitised, the premium pay-TV services are only transmitted in digital form and consumers' analogue proprietary boxes have been replaced by digital ones.

There are no indications of digitalisation of the remaining small and bigger SMATV networks, which count for about 300,000 households in Denmark. This is, according to FDA[4], due to the lack of economies of scale there is little

---

[3] TDC Kabel TV tried once to establish a sport TV station without any success.
[4] Source: Forenede Danske Antenneanlæg (FDA), Danish cable television organisation.

economic incentive for them to do so in the future. Another important reason is that the cable operators put their efforts in competing in Broadband market. Broadband cable systems are very much developed in Denmark and are in a good competitive position compared to other broadband operators.

Access Issues and Standards

Access to the services, especially in the satellite market has been subject to discussions in Denmark. The problem is that the two major satellite providers have chosen different Conditional Access (CA) and Application Program Interface (API), making it difficult for the consumers to change between the operators. As seen in Table 13.3, the majority of available boxes in the Danish market have Common Interface (CI) module that to some extent solves the CA interoperability problem, but the API problem remains unsolved. In the last couple of years, both Canal Digital and VIASAT have talked about migrating to MHP. There are so many problems in this process that is not realistic in a short term perspective. As a member of NORDIG, they are, however, committed to start conversion to MHP 6 month after the first NORDIG approved MHP box is available on the market. There will be a long period of parallel operation of the current APIs and MHP and exactly this long period is seen as a huge barrier in transition to MHP.

VIASAT deploys Viaccess as Conditional Access and Open TV as API. And Canal Digital deploys Conax as Conditional Access and MediaHighway as API. Table 11.3 shows the decoders available in the Danish market and some of their characteristics. As discussed, the majority of the boxes come with Common Interface module making them usable for reception of programs from other satellite providers.

Emergence of New Services

The majority of the channels available in the satellite and cable networks are traditional TV channels in digital form. The marketing and advertising of DTV in the Danish market has mainly been focusing on two qualities: 1) The variety of choices, and 2) The high technical quality of digital TV programs.

Better and easier navigation and the availability of easy access to programs have also been seen as arguments for the superiority of digital TV.

Emergence of new services, however, plays a secondary role in the marketing and composition of services in the cable and satellite networks. But digitalization of cable and satellite has expanded the possibility to subscribe to premium pay TV and Pay per view channels, such as:

Table 11.3. Characteristics of Set-Top Boxes

Name	Provider	CA	API	Compatibility		Integrated Modem
				FTA*	16:9	
Force Dmaster T	Force Electronic (late 2000)	Conax (+ DVB CI)	Media Highway	Yes	Yes	Yes
DVB-40S	TRIAX	Embedded Conax (+ DVB CI)	Media Highway	Yes	Yes	Yes
Philips digital box	Philips	Conax	Media Highway	Only by subscription	Yes	Yes
Force Duomaster 1030S	Force Electronic	Conax (+ DVB CI)	Media Highway	Yes	Yes	Yes
Force D-master 1133S	Force Electronic	Conax (+ DVB CI)	Media Highway	Yes	Yes	Yes
MediaMaster, S, C and T	NOKIA	Embedded Viaccess (+ DVB CI)	Open TV	Yes	Yes	Yes
MACAB (DBC-101)	MACAB/ SAGEM	Viaccess	Open TV	Yes	Yes	Yes
ISD 4150MTG	MACAB/ SAGEM	Embedded Viaccess (+ DVB CI)	Open TV	Yes	Yes	Yes
VACI-5350 & VA-OTV	Humax	Embedded Viaccess (+ DVB CI)	Open TV	Yes	Yes	Yes

*Free to Air Compatible

- The premium pay TV channels, Canal Plus, Canal Plus GUL, Canal Plus BLÅ[5] and Erotica
- The Nordic public services channels, TV Finland and NRK international
- Foreign language channels in TDC Kabel TV
- Pay per view channels such as KIOSK in Canal Digital service—in reality a NVOD channel

There are, however, offered new services in the TDC Kabel TV such as e-mail, chat rooms, advanced program guides, individual choice of camera angles, product information, and online shopping.

---

[5] Canal Plus BLÅ is a new service from Canal Plus. Canal Digital has announced that Canal Plus BLÅ will contain popular movies, some of them in 16:9 format

Interactive services in the satellite provision include e-mail, electronic programme guide, NVOD, and choice of camera angle for sport matchs.

Financing and Business Models

As discussed in the previous section of this chapter the satellite services in Denmark consist of:

- Danish TV services, which are owned by the satellite provider like TV3 at VIASAT or are in strategic alliance with like TVDanmark and Canal Digital. These are advertising and subscription channels and take part in both advertising and subscription markets.
- Foreign TV services, like CNN, Euro Sport, etc. These are primarily subscription based but also have some advertising revenues.
- Public service channels. There is no 'must carry' in satellite networks but the providers by themselves want to have Public service in all their packages, as these are the most popular in Denmark. The provision of public service does not give explicit revenues to the satellite providers but are important in attracting new subscribers.
- Premium Pay TV and Pay per view TV services, that are funded through subscription and pay per view.

The funding of satellite and cable operations consists of subscription fees from end consumers to basic and advanced packages and in some cases revenue from TV stations to make them available in their program packages. Furthermore they have advertising revenues through the TV stations they operate by themselves.

Next, some price examples of different packages are given in tables 11.4 and 11.5.

Table 11.4: Cost of Satellite Services.

Channels	€ per month
Viasat Basic	€ 53 (DKR 399) first 6 months, then € 24 (DKR 179) next 6 months
Viasat Gold	€ 27 (DKR 199)
Viasat Silver	€ 11 (DKR 79)
Canal Digital Entertain	€ 37 (DKR 278)
Canal Digital: Canal Plus	€ 27 (DKR 198)

Table 11.5: Cost of Cable Service Packages

Channels	€ per month
Basic entry	€ 7 (DKR 49) with subscription DKR 60 without
Canal Entertain	€ 11 (DKR 79)
Lifestyle package	€ 7 (DKR 49)
News package	€ 5 (DKR 39)
Children's package	€ 4 (DKR 29)
Family package (Canal Plus and Canal Entertain)	€ 35 (DKR 259)
Language package	€ 11 (DKR 79)

Subscribers need to have Viasat Basic in order to subscribe to Viasat Silver, gold or Ticket.

In addition to these, one should have subscription to analogue packages as well. The subscription fee is € 27 (DKR 199) for TDC Kabel TV. Part of the program package structure is outsourced to Canal Digital and so some of the program offers are identical.

THE DANISH MODEL FOR TRANSITION TO DIGITAL TERRESTRIAL TV

Terrestrial digital broadcasting does not yet exist in Denmark because there have been few available resources for digital broadcasting. There has, however, been an ongoing work to find new resources for digital TV by re-planning and harmonisation with the neighbouring countries in the last 5 years. This has resulted in 3 Multiplexers becoming available that will be deployed for digital Television. Work is going on to find a fourth Multiplexer by continuing re-planning and negotiations with the neighbouring countries. At the moment of analogue shut down, two additional Multiplexers will be released that currently are deployed to transmit DR and TV 2/DANMARK in analogue form.

Preparation studies are done regarding introduction of digital terrestrial TV in Denmark. Reports delivered in September 1998 by a working group formed by the Ministry of Culture (Ministry of Culture 1998) recommended the introduction of digital terrestrial TV in Denmark as soon as possible using frequencies reserved for this purpose by the political Media Agreement in 1996. At the time there was only one Multiplexer (MUX 1) available and it was reserved for digital transmission of DR and plus two new public service channels, one operated by DR and the other by TV2. Recommendations in the report included provision of a pilot phase to gain technical and organisational experience. Furthermore, it was suggested that the National Telecom Agency (now National IT and Telecom Agency) 'find' additional spectrum resources for digital television.

The focus of the political discussions following the report, however, shifted to a debate on the priorities in the use of the reserved frequencies (MUX 1), i.e., whether to use them for digital transmission or to expand the capacity for existing analogue services. This was provoked by a political disagreement on whether it is acceptable, that one of DR's second analogue services, DR2 was only transmitted via satellite and cable. Some political parties (mainly the Right Wing Opposition) wanted to give priority to terrestrial analogue distribution of DR2 above the introduction of terrestrial digital TV.[6]

In spring 2000, the Ministry of Culture formed a new working group including representatives from the parties involved, for example, consumer organisations, the IT-industry, the telecom industry, other public authorities and universities. It produced a report in August 2000 (Ministry of Culture 2000), which recommended that the digitalisation of the terrestrial network should proceed and that the necessary legal modifications should be made at the first given opportunity. Further, it recommended that there should be made room on the digital multiplexes for interactive digital services other than TV-programmes, such as e-mail, online shopping, and Internet-based TV channels.

Amongst others based on these studies, the Media Policy Accord 2002-06 (Ministry of Culture accord 2002) made a decision on putting the terrestrial digital television transmission rights out to tender (Ministry of Culture tender 2002) in order that a new terrestrial digital television platform gets established in Denmark. The tendering process is to take the form of an auction.

In the following first some of the argumentations for introducing terrestrial digital TV in Denmark are given, then an overview of available resources is given and later the content of the tender and the suggested model for a Multiplex/platform operator in the Danish market is given, at the end of this section the access and financing issues are analysed. The description of the tender is primarily based on (Ministry of Culture tender 2002)

Why Digital Terrestrial TV in Denmark?

One of the main arguments for digital terrestrial TV is connected to the coverage issue that is in close relation to the size of country; terrestrial networks can reach all TV house holds as it is possible to cover the whole country with digital TV.

---

[6] The problem of transmission of DR 2 in the analogue terrestrial network is partly solved by assigning some of the unused local TV frequencies to DR2. In this way the terrestrial transmission of DR2 covers the most populated areas in the country.

Denmark is a small country and the costs connected to covering the whole country are not high compared to, for example, further development of cable network or the users' cost for achieving satellite reception. Furthermore, portable and mobile reception is only possible in terrestrial networks. The later is seen as an important comparative advantage to satellite and cable networks.

Another technological advantage of terrestrial networks compared to, for example, satellite network is the simplicity of regionalising the signal. This is an important issue in Denmark as one of the Danish public service broadcasters (TV2/Denmark) has a regionalised structure in its program provision and it is politically decided to maintain this structure.

The terrestrial digital network will open for an alternative supply structure for information/communication. This infrastructure competitiveness aspect is very important as it is suggested that the terrestrial network is a cost effective way of transmitting digital TV signals. The costs at the end user side are seen as especially important. The fact that the signal can be received by existing roof (and by some indoor antennas) makes it easy to make the change to digital.

General reasons for transition to digital, like the quality issue, the expansion of number of services, interactivity, possibility for new services, digital TV as optimal platform for development of public service, etc. have also been used in the discussions.

One of the main argumentation against digital terrestrial TV is the lack of success in the markets where digital TV has been introduced. The lack of success in the Swedish market has had a negative influence on the Danish politicians. The liberal party, which is the biggest party in the government, still argues for use of reserved digital TV resources for distribution of analogue TV.

Available Frequency Resources

In the regional frequency planning conference of 1961, which was held by International Telecommunication Union (ITU) in Stockholm, Denmark obtained the possibility of establishing four countrywide/national terrestrial TV channels. These resources have, however, not been in use from the beginning and some of them are still unused due to different reasons described in the following. A countrywide TV channel in the following denotes a set of VHF/UHF frequencies that makes it possible to cover the whole country by one TV station.

The first channel, which has been in use from the beginning, has been operated by DR. It covers the whole population.

The second channel, which also covers almost the whole population, is operated by TV 2. The regional structure of TV 2/DANMARK makes it financially unattractive to distribute TV 2/DANMARK in satellite network.

The third channel (MUX1) has been reserved for distribution of digital terrestrial TV. According to the media agreement of 1996, DR and TV 2/DANMARK will have the possibility to simulcast their current analogue TV services in digital form. Regarding TV 2, the current regional division will be maintained in digital form. Furthermore, they will have the possibility for transmission of two new channels in digital form, one for DR and one for TV2.

The fourth and fifth channels resulted from efforts of the Danish Telecom agency to release more resources for digital TV in the framework of the Stockholm Plan of 1961, the subsequent Chester Agreement, and by coordinating frequencies with neighbouring countries. This has resulted in 2 more countrywide channels that will be used to establish two nationwide digital television transmission networks called MUX2 and MUX3.

The National IT and Telecom Agency is currently negotiating one more transmission network (MUX 4) with neighbouring countries. A time scale for these negotiations cannot be given at the current time.

Multiplex/Platform Operator Function

Multiplex/platform operator function comprises the operation of and management of a terrestrial digital television platform, including aggregating and distribution of content, maintaining Conditional Access system and providing the technology for Interactive services.[7] It is required that the whole digital terrestrial platform must be perceived as one platform in Denmark. The objective of the tender is to define this platform where the operator will get licences to operate the transmission networks, MUX 2, MUX 3, and possibly also MUX 4, subject to sufficiently close cooperation with DR and TV 2/DANMARK (which operate MUX 1).

DR and TV 2/DANMARK have been granted access, subject to the terms laid down by the Minister for Culture, to capacity on MUX 1 for transmission of their public service programmes and related services. The new public service contracts between the government and DR, TV 2/DANMARK, and the regional TV 2/DANMARK stations will specify which public service programmes and services are to be transmitted digitally in the first instance.

MUX2, MUX3, and Coming Multiplexers

The content available in the digital terrestrial network, that is, the right to provide TV services in the terrestrial platform has been a crucial issue in the

---

[7] In another case study of digital terrestrial TV in Denmark, different technological and techno-economic aspects of Multiplexes in digital terrestrial TV are analysed. If you are interested in the subject please refer to (Tadayoni & Skouby 1999).

Danish debate. According to the tender the operation of the terrestrial digital TV platform in Denmark might involve both transmission of programmes from programme companies, which operate on the basis of Danish or foreign programme licence or registration (primary distribution) and retransmission of programmes received from Danish or foreign programme companies, via terrestrial transmitters or satellite (secondary distribution). The digital TV platform operator must, further, prepare, maintain and transmit an electronic programme guide (EPG), as well as teletext services. Transmission of new digital services, such as e-mail, e-commerce, or games is seen as important.

According to the tender, the platform operator must maintain an access control and customer management systems in case of encrypted transmissions. The operation will further involve marketing the platform, including possible subsidisation of digital receiver equipment, and provision of technical support for viewers' reception of signals from the platform. Informing the population about the transition from analogue to digital television, including the phasing out of analogue transmissions, is one of the obligations of the platform operator.

Furthermore, the tender put specific obligations to the licence holder, mainly that the licence holder is obliged in the first instance to build and finance two nationwide transmission networks for the primary and secondary distribution of digital television and new digital services (MUX 2 and MUX 3). The establishment of the MUX 1 transmission network will be financed by DR and TV 2/DANMARK together.

Regarding the coverage issue, the licence holder is obliged to build the transmission networks so that it is possible for 99.9 percent of the population to receive digital signals via an outdoor directional aerial within 18 months of the award of the licence, assuming possession of digital receiver equipment. This corresponds to the percentage of the population that can currently receive DR 1 and TV 2/DANMARK analogue signals in this way.

As mentioned above regarding the content provided and distributed via digital transmitters, they must be on the basis of a Danish or foreign licence or registration. The licence holder is, further, obliged to ensure, partly through agreements with the industry, that viewers receive the best possible technical support in connection with the transition to the reception of terrestrial digital television signals.

A last point indicated in the tender is that the licence holder is obliged to meet the requirements laid down by the Danish authorities concerning the transmission networks' functionality and capacity for transmitting special messages in case of emergency, crisis, or war.

MUX1

Regarding MUX 1, it is further stated in the tender that the licence holder, DR and TV 2/DANMARK will be obliged to seek to establish mutual cooperation with the platform operator on the development of the digital transmission networks and the technical operation of the same.

Furthermore, cooperation with the platform operator is necessary regarding the establishment and operation of access control systems. This applies only if it is decided that transmissions on MUX 1 are to be encrypted. In this case it must be possible to receive the programmes and services that form part of DR and TV 2/DANMARK's public service activities as a "package" without any form of payment being required, including administration charges for the provision/updating of decoder cards.

Also EPG must be coordinated between DR and TV2/DANMARK and the platform operator. This includes at the very least all programmes and services broadcast via the terrestrial digital television platform. Programmes, etc. broadcast by satellite and cable may also be included subject to agreement with the operators of these platforms. The presentation of Danish public service programmes and services in the programme guide must at the very least reflect their share of overall viewing figures.

Another important issue is the coordination of the use of API. It is stated in the tender that the use of a common user interface for new interactive services, such as MHP must be coordinated with the digital platform operator.

Auction

The auction will be held on the basis of an order from the Ministry of Culture setting out guidelines for putting terrestrial digital television transmission rights out to tender.

One of the important issues is the timing of the auction, which is expected to be in spring 2003, and communication in connection with the auction, including publicity.

Another important issue is the application procedure, including who is entitled to apply, the information to be provided by applicants, minimum requirements for bidders (possible pre-qualification), requirement for bank guarantee, size of deposit, minimum price, publicity, etc.

According to the tender, the auction must further contain restrictions on the right to submit bids, the auction procedure (open or closed), the award and entry into force of the licence and the payment of the price for the licence.

General Terms and Conditions Regarding Licenses

According to the tender, it is intended that the licence will run for ten years from its award, without any guarantee of extension at the end of this period. It is further stated that the licence may be assigned to another party subject to the consent of the Radio and Television Board. Such consent will be dependent on whether the competition-related considerations underlying access to bid at the auction will still be met. Similarly, the licence may be withdrawn if the licence holder no longer meets the criteria for the auction due to ownership changes, etc.

Ownership Restrictions

According to the Media Policy Accord 2002-06, for competition reasons neither operators of another digital television platform in the Danish market nor programme companies with a dominant influence in the Danish market for the provision of television programmes may have a dominant influence over the company granted the licence to operate the terrestrial digital television platform.

Against this background, the tender suggests that the licence may not be awarded to DR, TV 2/DANMARK or TDC Kabel TV. Nor may the licence be awarded to legal entities that are related directly or indirectly to DR, TV 2/DANMARK or TDC Kabel TV. Related legal entities denotes legal entities that are controlled directly or indirectly by DR, TV 2/DANMARK, or TDC Kabel TV or that directly or indirectly have a controlling influence over DR, TV 2/DANMARK or TDC Kabel TV. The licence may neither be awarded to legal entities over which two or more of DR, TV 2/DANMARK, TDC Kabel TV, Canal Digital, and Viasat (or related legal entities) together have a controlling influence.

Regarding the satellite providers, it is stated in the tender that the licence may not be awarded to Canal Digital and Viasat together or to related legal entities that are controlled directly or indirectly by Canal Digital and Viasat together or that directly or indirectly have a controlling influence over Canal Digital and Viasat.

Access Issues and Standards

As seen next the tender does not put requirements on using specific standards but merely puts the overall framework. One thing is certain, namely, the public service channels must be accessed without additional costs. And if the signals are encrypted a decryption card must be provided without any cost to the users.

The tender specifies that the licence holder is expected to use standards approved by a recognized European standardization body for the distribution of digital signals, cf. article 17 of Directive 2002/21/EC (the Framework Directive). The licence holder is further to comply with the terms of applicable legislation, currently the Standards for the Transmission of Television Signals Act, on the use of access control systems. Regarding the API, the licence holder is expected to use an open application program interface (API) for new interactive services, cf. article 17 of directive 2002/21/EC (the Framework Directive).

One of the important issues in digital TV is signal accessibility, including access with indoor or out door antennas and mobile and portable accessibility. With regards to this issue it is stated in the tender that the licence holder is obliged to choose a protection level for transmissions that ensures that the vast majority of viewers who currently watch television using an indoor aerial will not be required to purchase an outdoor aerial. (The protection level has a bearing on the transmission capacity available for programmes, etc.).

Furthermore, the tender specifies requirements related to the quality and the number of services. It is stated in the tender that the licence holder is obliged to ensure that the picture quality of the television programmes broadcast is satisfactory. In addition, the minimum number of simultaneous television channels during prime time (5 p.m. to midnight) is set to six.

Non discrimination is guarantied by putting an obligation on the license holder to offer all broadcasters access to the platform on a fair, reasonable and non-discriminatory basis, cf. the current Standards for the Transmission of Television Signals Act (Act No. 471 of 12 June 1996), the National IT and Telecom Agency's Order No. 709 of 25 July 1996 pursuant to this act, and article 6 of Directive 2002/19/EC (the Access Directive).

Also development of new data services is seen as important. Here the tender specifies that the licence holder may use capacity not used for the transmission of television channels to broadcast to the general public both data, such as advanced teletext data, and new interactive services, such as e-mail, e-commerce, games and betting. The licence holder may also use this capacity to broadcast data, etc. to closed user groups.

Regarding the HDTV discussion it is obvious that neither in MUX 1 with 4 TV services nor in MUX2 & MUX 3 with the above mentioned, at least 6 simultaneous TV services in prime time, there is no place for HDTV.

The high number of TV services in terrestrial market is so important that it is unthinkable in the short term perspective to have HDTV on the terrestrial market. However, the discussion is raised it is interesting to see how far it will go, especially when the cost of flat screen large TV monitors become payable by the majority of people.

Financing and Business Model

No public grants or loans will be available for the establishment and operation of the transmission networks built by the licence holder, and they may not be financed by licence fee revenues. Furthermore, the licensee will be subject to the payment of a fee to the Radio and Television Board to cover the cost of supervisory work, etc. relating to the licence. The licence will also be dependent on the payment of a frequency fee to the National IT and Telecom Agency.

So the operation and maintenance of the network must be based on pure commercial mechanism. To what degree pay TV will dominate the Danish digital terrestrial market and to what degree the lessons learn from early adopter countries will be used to find another business model than satellite and cable is still an open question that is purely decided by the new platform operator. One thing is for sure and that is availability of public service channels with no additional cost, as the consumer pay license fee to the public service operators.

Analogue Shut Down

According to the Media Policy Accord 2002-06, it is intended that the transmission of analogue television will be phased out by the end of 2007. More detailed provisions on the timing of the phase-out will be laid down when the Minister for Culture sets out the main guidelines for the auction. According to the above mentioned tender, these provisions will be based on a balanced appreciation of the general frequency policy considerations, for the licence holder, whose business plan will be dependent on the phase-out date, and for viewers, who should be given plenty of time in the form of a lengthy transition period to replace/supplement their existing analogue television sets with new digital receiver equipment at prices that are reasonable for the individual household.

No decision has been made on the use of the frequencies released through the phase-out of analogue transmissions. The licence holder of the digital terrestrial platform cannot therefore assume that these will be made available for digital transmissions.

CONCLUSIONS

This chapter has given an overview of the Danish broadcast TV market with a primary focus on transition to digital. Like many other countries the transition to digital in the multiservice satellite and cable networks been driven commercially and by commercial actors, where terrestrial digital broadcasting is being formed by the government in close cooperation to the interests of the public service providers.

Regarding digitalization of satellite and cable there are no radical differences between Denmark and other Nordic countries. Digital satellite is almost introduced at the same time in different Nordic countries, and the same operators offer services to all Nordic countries. In a sense the satellite providers consider the Nordic market as one market, however, with minor differentiation between different countries. Digital TV is available in majority of big cable networks in Denmark and other Nordic countries. The subscription to digital cable is however far behind expected. One of the reasons for this is the lack of new digital service and the fact that expansion of number of services that have been important driving forces for digital TV in other platforms have not the same effect in the cable networks, with huge amount of analogue transmission resources. Regarding digitalization of terrestrial network there are, however, vital differences in the introduction and roll out strategies in different Nordic countries. Sweden was the first country that introduced digital terrestrial TV for 3 years a go, while Denmark is still in the preparation phase. From the beginning it was evident that the success or failure of digital terrestrial TV in Sweden would have vital impact on the Danish attitude to the problem. This has been shown to be valid. The lack of success of digital TV in Sweden is used massively to play against the digitalization process by different political parties in Denmark.

The two major digital satellite providers in Denmark have based their service on different and incompatible CA and API systems making it difficult for the consumers to change between the providers. However, the set-top boxes available on the Danish market include a common interface making it a bit easier to change but as the API cannot be changed, when changing from one provider to the other the consumers loose the new Interactive services. Both Canal Digital and VIASAT claim having plans to migrate to MHP, as member of NORDIG they are committed to start supporting MHP, 6 months after the first NORDIG approved box is available on the Danish market.

Regarding the content of satellite TV services, these consist of own TV services like VIASAT's TV3 and other services that are provided in different packages due to different agreements with the content providers. An interesting process in Denmark is the availability of public service channels in the satellite packages, without any 'must carry' regulations. The satellite providers distribute public service channels in their packages because these are popular and including public service gives the satellite providers better possibility to attract new subscribers.

Digital satellite providers in Denmark have been aggressive in their marketing and introduced favourable subscription services giving the end consumers possibility to get a free set top box if they subscribe to premium services for one year. Furthermore, both satellite- and cable-providers have offered free boxes to their premium subscribers and have stopped parallel simulating of these services.

In the terrestrial networks, major preparations for introduction of digital TV are done and the available spectrum resources make it possible to have 3 Multiplexes. More resources can be released in the on going process of re-planning and negotiation with the neighbouring countries.

The specific characteristic of the Danish model for introduction of digital TV is that one operator will gain license to operate the whole digital platform, i.e., both the current multiplexes and the coming one, except MUX 1 that is reserved for public service broadcasters. The platform operator will be in charge of composing its services and implementing a business model to drive the business on purely commercial basis. The platform operator will further decide on the Conditional Access system and the Application Program Interface. The government will only put overall framework for the operation and will not require the usage of specific technologies or in other ways to intervene in the operation.

According to the main actors in the broadcasting market in Denmark, the only successful business model is a total FTA operation of the majority of channels. Using satellite and cable business models are suggested to become unsuccessful from the beginning. This is among others based on experiences from other European countries.

Regarding the technical quality of the signal, that is, the HDTV/SDTV question, it is obvious that Denmark like other European countries have chosen the SDTV format, which gives the possibility for broadcasting TV signals in at least the same quality for current PAL signals. As reason for this, the bad HDTV experiences in the beginning of 1980s have been suggested. The problem has, however, other and more important aspect and it is the number of TV service in terrestrial network. A HDTV approach does not change the market of terrestrial TV in transition to Digital. Digitalization will only mean that the quality of current TV will be improved immensely, but the market and the number of providers in the market will not change. The only way digital terrestrial TV can be attractive is if there is room for new operators, otherwise the satellite and cable are so attractive that they will take share in even more part of the Danish TV market.

HDTV should be provided in satellite and cable network, where resources are available, and based on their experiences and when new spectrum is released in terrestrial network, for example due to analogue shut down, then it might be a case to consider HDTV programming on terrestrial network.

The result of the consultation process in the tender described in this chapter and the formation of final auction process are the interesting processes, which the Danish digital terrestrial TV is quite dependent on.

REFERENCES

Coase R., 1959. The Federal Communication Commission. *The Journal of Law & Economics*, October.

Falch F. & Tadayoni, R., 2002. An Economic Approach to Frequency Management. *Communication & Strategies*, Issue 46, 2nd quarter 2002, pp. 101-127.

Gallup, 2002. *Gallup TV-meter—årsrapport (annual report) 2002*. Gallup, Copenhagen.

Ministry of Culture, 1998. DVB the future of TV, CTI, Denmark, 1998.

Ministry of Culture, 2000. Digitalisation of the terrestrial TV (Final report from working group on digital terrestrial network), Ministry of Culture, Denmark, 8. August 2000.

Ministry of Culture accord, 2002. Media Policy Accord 2002-06 of 3 June 2002.

Ministry of Culture tender, 2002. Industry consultation on the establishment of a terrestrial digital television platform, 2002.

Noam E. M. (1991). *Television in Europe*. Oxford University Press, New York.

Septrup P., 1993. Scandinavian Public Service Broadcasting. The case of Denmark. In Avery, R.K. (Ed.) (1993).

Tadayoni R., 2001. Terrestrial Digital Broadcasting: Innovation and development or a tragedy of incumbents, *Communications & Strategies*, IDATE, Issue 42, 2nd quarter 2001.

Tadayoni R., & Skouby, K.E., 1999. Terrestrial digital broadcasting: Convergence and its regulatory implications. *Telecommunications Policy*, March.

Chapter 12
France: Attempting to Enhance Competition in an Oligopolistic Market

Marc Bourreau
Ecole Nationale Supérieure des Télécommunications
and CREST-LEI

Only 17 percent of French households received digital television in 2002.[1] Hence, for public authorities, digital terrestrial television (DTTV) is mainly a means to stimulate the development of digital television. However, cable and satellite operators (TF1, M6, and Canal Plus), which have been designated as leaders of the DTTV process, are reluctant, as they view DTTV as a competitor to their existing platforms.

TERRESTRIAL DIGITAL TELEVISION

In France, DTTV has been urged by public authorities. Its main goal is to increase the number of channels received by French households and to provide digital television to all. Indeed, in 2002, 52 percent of French households received only the five unscrambled free-to-air channels (TF1, France 2, France 3, ARTE/La Cinq, M6). 20 percent received an additional terrestrial pay television channel, Canal Plus. Only 28 percent received an extended choice of channels, through either cable (14 percent) or satellite (14 percent).[2]

For the Jospin government, the second goal of DTTV was to stimulate the development of public television (for instance, see Le Guen, 2001). Since the change of government, the role of public television on DTTV has been unclear, as we will discuss in the coming pages.

---

[1] Source: AFORM, TF1, Canal Plus, INSEE.

[2] On 30 September 2002, there were 3,433,731 cable subscribers (source: AFORM) and 4,788,000 subscribers to pay channel Canal Plus (source: Canal Plus). Mid-2002, there were 3,284,000 satellite subscribers (source: TF1 and Canal Plus). The total number of households is 23,808,000 (source: INSEE's survey, 1999).

Regulatory Framework

In France, the discussions about DTTV started in January 1996, when the Minister in charge of Culture and Information Technologies entrusted Mr. Philippe Levrier with the task of writing a report about the stakes of DTTV. The report concluded that DTTV was feasible. However, since then DTTV has met many political and regulatory hurdles and its introduction has been delayed many times.

The law of 1 August 2000 established the legal framework and the timeframe for the development of DTTV in France. The law introduced the following key principles:

- "simulcast" rule: according to this rule, incumbent analogue terrestrial television channels are allowed to be present on digital terrestrial television (Art. 30-1, III).
- "additional channel" rule: incumbent analogue channels have rights for an additional DTTV national service.
- private channels are allowed to control five channels *at most*, which implies that a provider cannot control a multiplex of 6 channels. Besides, companies outside the European Union cannot have a stake of more than 20 percent in a national DTTV service.
- The French communication regulatory authority, the Conseil Supérieur de l'Audiovisuel (CSA), should favour free channels over pay channels, and contribute to increase the diversity of operators and pluralism.

These four principles highlight the objective of the regulator and the government for DTTV to find a correct balance between the protection of incumbent operators (principles 1 and 2) and entry of new players (principles 3 and 4). Since the law of August 2000, decrees have been published to specify the legal framework.

Two decrees introduced production and diffusion quotas for DTTV channels. The aim of these quotas is to protect the French production industry. Decree n°2001-1333 of 28 December 2001 established production and diffusion quotas for DTTV channels. Different production quotas apply to different types of service providers: free channel, music channel, pay channel, pay cinema channel. First, all service providers except cinema pay channels are required to invest 3.2 percent of their net turnover[3] in the production or acquisition of European *cinema* programmes and at least 2.5 percent in French cinema

---

[3] Some expenses can be deducted from the turnover.

programmes.[4] The production quotas of cinema pay service providers are stronger: They are required to invest 21 percent of their turnover in the production of European cinema programmes and at least 17 percent in French cinema programmes.

Second, free service providers are required to invest 16 percent of their turnover in the production or acquisition of French *television* programmes. This quota is lowered to eight percent for music channels, that is, channels which offer music programmes at least half of the time.

To stimulate the development of DTTV, the CSA might decide to alleviate some of these rules in the schedule of conditions for an introductory period of seven years.

Decree n°2001-1333 of 28 December 2001 also introduced diffusion quotas: channels are requested to broadcast each year 120 hours of European or French programmes in primetime (i.e., between 20h and 21h). Other diffusion quotas are included in Decree n°2001-1330 of 28 December 2001, which modified Decree n°90-66 of 17 January 1990. In particular, service providers are requested to offer at least 60 percent of European programmes and at least 40 percent of French programmes. This rule applies to the annual schedule, but also during primetime (i.e., between 20h30 and 22h30).

Advertising constraints also apply to DTTV channels. According to Decree n°2001-1333 of 28 December 2001, channels will be allowed to introduce nine minutes of advertisements per hour on average per day, with a maximum of 12 minutes for one hour. Another decree, decree n°2001-1331 of 28 December 2001, regulates infomercials.

One of the most controversial rules is the "must carry" rule for cable operators. According to Decree n°2002-125 of 31 January 2002, cable operators are obliged to offer free DTTV channels in their digital television bundles.[5] This "must carry" rule concerns only cable networks, not satellite. One possible justification for this difference is that the must carry rule compensates the local monopoly power of cable networks, whereas the satellite television market is a duopoly. However, cable networks are strongly opposed to this rule. The French cable association (AFORM) and cable operator UPC have filed an appeal to the Council of State against the Decree. Besides, AFORM has asked the Prime Minister in December 2002 to abrogate the Decree. In its complementary report to the Prime Minister, Michel Boyon, a member of the Conseil d'Etat (the highest administrative body in France) and former CEO of the public radio group Radio France, stated that the Decree was transitory. According to Boyon (2003), in the opening phase of DTTV, the must carry rule will stimulate its

---

[4] "French programs" ("expression originale française") are French-speaking programs. Note that the rule applies only to "stock" programs (like films, series, documentaries, etc.).

[5] As for analogue cable television offers, only analogue terrestrial channels must be carried.

development. He also proposed to launch discussions about the cost of the must carry rule for cable operators, and hence its possible compensation.

Finally, some rules will be made prior to the implementation of DTTV. First, a decree will clarify the production and diffusion quotas for local television channels. Second, currently no person can own up to more than 49 percent of a national DTTV service, but this rule applies only if the "average audience" of the channel is greater than 2.5 percent. How the "average audience" is measured is still unclear; a decree is expected to clarify this point too.

DTTV Players

The French regulatory framework for DTTV distinguishes different types of players (see Fig. 12.1):

- *Service Providers or Channels* The CSA has first to select a list of advertiser- and pay-supported service providers for DTTV. Second, it shall establish a schedule of conditions for each service provider. As mentioned above, the conditions depend on the type of channel (advertiser or pay supported, cinema channel, music channel, etc.). Note that this selection process implies that both the business model (advertiser or pay support) and the 'genre' of the channel are fixed.

- *Multiplex Operators* There will be six multiplexes, each with five or six channels. Service providers have to join up to propose a multiplex operator to the CSA. If the CSA grants an authorisation to the multiplex operators, it delivers the frequencies for the multiplex. If not, service providers have a further period of two months to propose another multiplex operator.

- *Commercial Distributors* Commercial distributors commercialise bundles to end customers. They must make a declaration to the CSA.

Now, I describe who are or who could be the players.

Channels Compared to analogue terrestrial television, DTTV provides room for more channels. The main ideas in France were, first, to have both free channels and pay channels, and second, to take the opportunity of DTTV to introduce local television channels. In his report to the Jospin government, Deputy Jean-

Figure 12.1: Digital Terrestrial Television Players

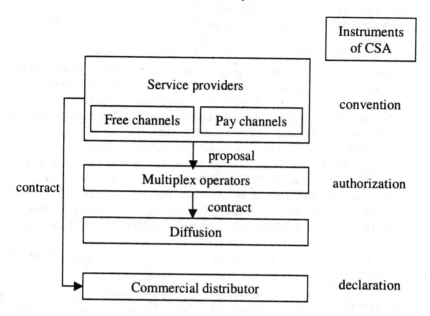

Marie Le Guen also suggested that one channel be reserved for associative television (Le Guen, 2001).

A third objective of DTTV was the introduction of "new" entrants. However, the number of available channels for new entrants was quite lower than the total capacity of 33 channels, as:

- Eight channels were earmarked for public channels and three for local television.
- Six channels were reserved for the three private analogue terrestrial channels (TF1, Canal Plus, and M6): three for their existing channels (simulcast rule) and three additional channels (bonus channels).

Therefore, only 16 channels were available for new entrants.

On 24 July 2001, the CSA launched a call for bids for national DTTV services. On 22 March 2002, 69 proposals were submitted to the CSA. On 9 April 2002, the CSA announced that 66 offers were valid, i.e., that they satisfied the basic conditions contained in the text of the call for bids. Since one applicant later withdrew, the CSA screened 65 proposals and conducted public hearings.

Three applicants resigned later on 18 October 2002 (TPS Cinétoile and TPS Cinéfaz) and 21 October 2002 (Odyssée).

The criteria for the selection were mentioned in the text of the call for bids. These criteria were related to *content* (ability to address large audiences and ability to stimulate the development of DTTV, pluralism, commitments in terms of production and broadcasting of programmes), *technical aspects* (geographical coverage, distribution), and *economic and competitive aspects* (experience of the applicant, financial aspects, fair competition, and diversity of players).

Among the 69 candidate channels, few were new. Actually, most channels were already offered on either cable or satellite networks.

On 23 October 2002, the CSA announced that it had selected 23 national service providers for DTTV (or 22 full-time services, as two services services— Cuisine TV and Comédie (Pathé)—proposed to share airtime on the same channel), out of which eight were advertiser-supported and 15 pay-supported (see Table 12.1). The selected service providers signed an agreement with the CSA in December 2002. Licences have been awarded for a period of ten years.

Table 12.1: The 23 Channels Selected by the CSA for DTTV (Owner in Parentheses)[6]

Free channels	Pay channels
TF1 (TF1)	Canal Plus (Canal Plus)
M6 (M6)	AB1 (Groupe AB)
Direct 8 (Bolloré)	Canal J (Lagardère)
i-MCM (Lagardère)	CinéCinémas (MultiThématiques)
M6 Music (M6)	Cuisine TV/Comédie (Pathé)
NRJ TV (NRJ)	Eurosport (TF1)
NT1 (Groupe AB)	i-télévision (Canal Plus)
TMC (Pathé)	LCI (TF1)
	Match TV (Lagardère)
	Paris Première (Suez and M6)
	Planète (MultiThématiques)
	Sport+ (Canal Plus)
	TF6 (TF1 and M6)
	TPS Star (TF1 and M6)

Source: CSA.

---

[6] In addition to these 23 channels (out of which two will share the same channel), there will be eight channels for public television and three channels for local television.

In the selection process, the CSA has followed different goals. First, the CSA has tried to select channels to address different audiences with different genres of programmes: young people (AB1 and Canal J), cinema programmes (Cinécinémas, TPS Star, Canal Plus), sport programmes (Sport Plus, Eurosport, Canal Plus, TPS Star), news programmes (LCI, I-Télévision), culture and lifestyle (Paris Première, Match TV), series (Comédie).

Secondly, the CSA applied equal treatment to each major player in the French television industry: Largardère (three channels controlled at 100 percent, two channels controlled at 50 percent), Canal Plus (three channels controlled at 100 percent, two channels controlled at 50 percent), TF1 (three channels controlled at 100 percent, one channel controlled at 50 percent), M6 (two channels controlled at 100 percent, two channels controlled at 50 percent), and Pathé (three channels controlled at 100 percent).

Thirdly, the CSA favoured "viable" channels, that is, channels controlled by large companies. In particular, associative candidate television channels were rejected. Similarly, existing channels were favoured, as their marginal cost of operating on DTTV is very low (it amounts only to the diffusion cost, which is around two million euros if 50 percent of the French population is covered).

Fourthly, if the CSA selected five new entrants in the terrestrial television market, namely, Groupe AB, Largardère, NRJ, Pathé, and Bolloré, only the latter is a real new entrant (with channel Direct 8) since the others already operate on cable or satellite networks.

However, the selection presents the following flaws: Despite the objective to improve the choice of programming available, the selection process has resulted in a duplication of channels. For instance, among the eight advertiser-supported channels that have been selected, three will offer music programmes: M6 Music, i-MCM, and NRJ TV. Similarly, four pay channels will offer a high proportion of sport programmes (or only sport): Canal Plus, Sport+, TPS Star, and Eurosport.

In addition, the CSA has favoured incumbents, but their incentives to develop DTTV are ambiguous, as some of them have invested in cable or satellite television. Indeed, 12 DTTV pay channels out of 14 are controlled by companies which operate satellite or cable platforms (TF1, M6, Canal Plus, Lagardère). For these players, developing DTTV means cannibalising their existing offers.

Besides, all pay DTTV channels already exist on cable or satellite; hence programme differentiation between cable/satellite and DTTV will be limited. This will be true in particular for cable and DTTV, as they will cover the same urban areas. However, the companies which control both DTTV pay channels and satellite and cable networks will have incentives to avoid cannibalisation of their existing platforms (as discussed above).

Finally, contrary to cable and satellite platforms, DTTV gave public authorities the opportunity to decide on the programmes. There will be only six new advertiser-supported private channels (out of which three will offer music programmes) and three public channels. Hence, the new "free" channels will be supported partly by an increase in public funding. However, if some channels fail to catch viewers' attention, the lack of flexibility in DTTV programmes will be an issue.

Public and local television Eight channels are reserved for public television, out of which five will be devoted to existing public channels (France 2, France 3, France 5, ARTE, and the Parliament channel). Therefore, three channels are available for new public channels. The idea was to try to maintain the audience share of public television, by increasing the number of channels. Indeed, in 2001, the report of Deputy Le Guen explained that the major issue with DTTV is that the increased channel diversity might result in a decrease of the audience share of public television (Le Guen, 2001).

France Télévision proposed three projects: a news channel, a repeat broadcast channel, and eight regional channels (on the same channel). However, the new government, the Raffarin government, has decided to wait before awarding the resources to France Télévision. Indeed, the Raffarin government thinks that the news programme channel project is useless, as two pay news channels have been selected by the CSA. Besides, it finds that the repeat broadcast project is unclear. Therefore, at the end of 2002, the government has decided to have further thoughts about public television before making any decision about public DTTV.

One implication is that it is not clear at all whether these channels will be awarded to public television or to new private companies. If the government does not use the three channels, the CSA will have to select new DTTV projects.

As for local television, it hardly exists in France. Public channel France 3 proposes regional programmes, but only for large regions. Only nine "real" local channels exist in France, which cover less than four million people. For public authorities, DTTV is also a means of developing local television. To that end, three DTTV channels have been reserved for local television channels. Since there are 110 planned diffusion sites, there could be theoretically 330 different local channels, each channel having a limited coverage area, but it is only an upper bound (Boyon, 2003). In particular, the 110 sites will be opened only in 2008 at the earliest; at the beginning, only 29 sites will broadcast DTTV.

The call for bids for local channels has yet to be launched by the CSA. However, the CSA is waiting until the legal framework for local channels is completed. Indeed, as already mentioned, the production and diffusion obligations for local channels are still undefined. These obligations will be published in a decree. Boyon (2003) suggests lifting production quotas for channels whose maximum audience is lower than ten million people, hence for local channels.

Advertising rules for local DTTV channels also have to be specified. Boyon (2003) proposes to allow local DTTV channels a larger share of advertisements in their programmes (15 minutes per hour), compared to national DTTV services. He also suggests lifting two anti-concentration rules which apply to local channels. The first rule (article 39-III of the Media Law of 30 September 1986) states that no person can have a stake of more than 50 percent in a terrestrial television company. The second rule (article 41 of the same law) forbids control of both a national and local television service.

Multiplex Operators DTTV will provide 33 channels. Three multiplexes will include five channels; the other three multiplexes will include six channels. Hence, quality of channels on the five-channel multiplexes will be higher than the quality of channels on the six-channel multiplexes. Service providers have to propose multiplex operators to the CSA by February 2003. In November 2002, the CSA proposed the following composition for private multiplexes (see Table 12.2).

Table 12.2: Composition of Multiplexes (Proposal of the CSA)

Multiplex R6	Multiplex R3	Multiplex R4	Multiplex R2
TF1	Canal Plus	M6	i-MCM
LCI	i-Télévision	M6 Music	Canal J
Eurosport	Sport Plus	TF6	Match TV
TPS Star	CinéCinémas	Paris Première	Direct 8
NRJ TV	Planète	TMC	AB1
		Cuisine TV/Comédie	NT1

Source: CSA.

In this configuration, each multiplex is led by one incumbent: TF1 (Multiplex 1), Groupe Canal Plus (Multiplex 2), M6 and Pathé (Multiplex 3), and Lagardère (Multiplex 4). Each multiplex includes both free and pay channels. The two five-channel multiplexes are given to the two major players (TF1 and Canal Plus).

The configuration proposed by the CSA aims at providing incumbents with high incentives to develop their multiplex. However, this configuration may also give rise to conflicts between incumbents and new entrants. Whereas the former have incentives to retard DTTV as it could cannibalise their investments in satellite or cable, the latter have strong incentives to make it develop fast. For instance, the NRJ Group has proposed that the six new free channels (Direct8, iMCM, NRJ TV, NT1, TMC, M6 Music) be rounded up on the same multiplex. On 30 June 2003, the CSA provided the final composition of multiplexes (see Table 12.3). Compared to its former proposal, there is a single change: NT1 and AB1 (Groupe AB) switch to multiplex R4 (M6), while TMC and Cuisine TV/Comédie (Pathé) switch to multiplex R2 (Lagardère).

Table 12.3: Composition of Multiplexes (Decision of the CSA)

Multiplex R1	Multiplex R2	Multiplex R3	Multiplex R4	Multiplex R5	Multiplex R6
France 2	i-MCM	Canal+	M6	Arte	TF1
France 3	Canal J	i-Télévision	M6 Music	La Chaîne	LCI
France 5	Match TV	Sport+	TF6	parlementaire	Eurosport
Room for 3 additional public channels	Direct 8	CinéCinémas	Paris	*Room for 3 local channels*	TPS Star
	TMC	Planète	Première		NRJ TV
	Cuisine TV/Comédie		NT1		
			AB1		

Source: CSA.

Distribution Operators The role of the distributor is to commercialise DTTV offers to end customers. However, how DTTV will be commercialised is unclear. Boyon (2002) proposed the following solution. On the one hand, large-scale retailers would commercialise decoders for the reception of advertiser-supported channels. On the other hand, DTTV distributors will commercialise bundles of pay channels.

The commercialisation of pay channels is still an issue today. The first idea was to allow Canal Plus to be the sole distributor for DTTV. Indeed, Canal Plus has acquired a large experience in the commercialisation of pay television. Besides, it was argued that Canal Plus would have an incentive to make its pay analogue subscribers switch to DTTV, which would stimulate the development of DTTV. However, this argument has a flaw. Indeed, Canal Plus already owns two digital television platforms: a digital satellite network (Canal Satellite) and a cable network (NC Numéricable). Hence, it could have incentives to favour its digital platforms by preventing the take-up of DTTV, which raises serious antitrust concerns (Gallot, 2002). Besides, since it has been awarded DTTV pay television channels, Canal Plus could also try to favour its own DTTV channels.

Gallot (2002) proposed another scenario, in which DTTV channels would create a joint company to distribute DTTV to end customers. However, the

French competition authority or the European Commission would probably have to endorse this joint company, which could take months, hence retarding the commercialisation of DTTV.

A last solution would be to allow two distributors or more. Boyon (2002) states that each distributor should have access to all DTTV channels to elaborate its bundle. However, exclusivity agreements between service providers and companies which commercialise satellite or cable bundles might make Boyon's non-discrimination rule difficult to obtain.

However, there were no candidates as of February 2003 to commercialise DTTV. Canal Plus withdrew and Orange (France Télécom's mobile operator), which announced mid-2002 that it would be interested in commercialising DTTV, is not a candidate any longer.

Diffusion of DTTV

Currently, Télédiffusion de France (TDF) has a de facto monopoly over the diffusion of analogue terrestrial television. Its monopoly might be challenged for DTTV. Indeed, new companies like Towercast (controlled by NRJ) or Motorola Labs have launched experiments to test the diffusion of DTTV. However, since diffusion sites are based on TDF diffusion sites, entry of new players will require that TDF allows competitors to install transmission equipment in its premises.

Technology and Spectrum Management

Technical aspects are dealt with by a commission of 150 experts from companies and public authorities. This commission, which has been set up by the CSA, examines the following aspects of DTTV: interoperability, transportability, signalling profile, unscrambled channels, update of terminals, and adaptation of joint antennas.

One the main technical issues today is the reallocation of analogue frequencies (i.e., those frequencies used by DTTV). The CSA estimates that 1500 reallocations are required for the roll out of DTTV. These reallocations will have two consequences. First, they will impose a cost on customers in some areas, as after reallocation analogue television channels will not be available on the same frequencies (this will be the case for areas which are covered by secondary transmitters). Between 850,000 and 1.7 million households could be affected by this problem. This is one reason why TF1 and M6 are opposed to frequency reallocations, as it will disturb their audiences.[7] In particular, TF1 has

---

[7] Another reason is that it delays the introduction of DTTV.

filed an appeal to the Council of State against frequency reallocations and M6 claims that new entrants should pay the reallocation cost. In March 2003, the CSA threatened to ask the Council of State to force TF1 and M6 to agree to these reallocations.[8]

Second, reallocations will be costly for the diffusion network. In his report published in October 2002, Boyon (2002) recommended that DTTV channels should pay the frequency reallocation one-shot cost. The French spectrum management agency (Agence Nationale des Frequenciés, ANFR) proposed that the government should advance funds for the first 500 reallocations which would cost 32 million euros. The DTTV channels will pay for the remaining 1000 reallocations (the total cost for the 1500 will be 64 million euros, that is, around two million euros per channel). The Ministry in charge of Culture and Communication followed this advice and decided to pre-finance the first reallocations. DTTV channels are supposed to reimburse these funds later. The funds will be provided by the Fonds de Reaménagement du Spectre, managed by ANFR.

The reallocation cost is the only frequency cost which the DTTV channels will incur, since they will not pay for frequency use, as was already the case for analogue terrestrial television.

The frequencies currently used by the six analogue networks will be freed up in the "long run", hence there will be a period of time in which analogue and digital terrestrial television will coexist. The 110 sites which are used currently to deliver analogue terrestrial television signals will be used for DTTV. According to the CSA, these sites will result in coverage of about 80 percent of the French population. However, according to a study made by ANFR, only four multiplexes will cover 80 percent of the population; the two others will cover only 60 percent of the population (ANFR, 1998). When analogue terrestrial television stops, 20 percent of the French population will not receive terrestrial television any longer. Besides, covering the last 20 percent of the population with DTTV would be probably very costly. Satellite-based solutions could be a better option.

Contrary to some countries, there is no commitment in France to stop analogue television after some date. The use of freed frequencies has not been planned yet. In 1999, Roger Chinaud from the College of the French Telecommunications Authority (Autorité de Régulation des Télécommunications, ART) proposed to allocate these frequencies to 3G mobile telephony, but this project is no longer mentioned. Some experts have also

---

[8] "Le CSA s'apprête à sanctionner TF1 et M6 pour leur refus de réaménager leurs fréquences", Le Monde, 3 March 2003.

proposed to organise a bid for these frequencies, whose revenues could be used to subsidise the switch of the last analogue subscribers to DTTV.

To stimulate the switch to DTTV, Boyon (2002) proposed to impose a progressive digitalisation of television sets. He estimates that with a renewal rate of 8 percent, all television sets will be able to receive DTTV within 12 years.

Another technical issue is that DTTV will generate interference with cable networks. This is because cable networks use some frequencies, which were left free by analogue terrestrial television, to broadcast both analogue and digital cable television to their customers. Since DTTV will also coexist at the beginning with analogue terrestrial television, interference problems will arise between cable and DTTV. This will be the case for customers whose connections with the cable network are defective. According to AFORM, the French cable association, this might affect between 20 and 30 percent of cable subscribers. Two solutions to this problem have been proposed (Boyon, 2003). First, cable networks might solve this problem on a case-by-case basis. Second, cable networks might change the frequency plan of their networks. Anyway, Boyon (2003) recommended that DTTV service providers should not pay for solving these interference issues.

Advertising

French Decree n°92-280 of 27 March 1992[9] excludes five industrial sectors from advertising on television: alcoholic beverage (i.e., beverage with more than 1.2° of alcohol), press, cinema, literary publishing, and large-scale retailing.[10] The rationale for this exclusion is to subsidise indirectly the national and regional press, in which these sectors can advertise.

In May 2002, the European Commission gave notice to France with regard to the exclusion of these four sectors from television advertising. In September 2002, the government launched a consultation about television advertising for the four excluded sectors. The government faces the following trade-off. On one hand, deregulating advertising on television would increase revenues of advertiser-supported DTTV free channels and/or local DTTV channels. On the other hand, it would hurt the press industry, in particular the local and regional press. According to Boyon (2003), the government is looking for intermediate solutions. For instance, it might allow advertising on television for small-scale retailing while maintaining the exclusion for large-scale retailing. It might also allow advertising at given hours. But no decision has yet been made.

---

[9] This decree is available online at http://droit.org/jo/19920328/MICT9200113D.html.
[10] When advertisements were introduced on French television in 1968, 29 industrial sectors were excluded.

Consumers

DTTV is supposed to provide viewers with higher quality for sound and images, and a wider choice of programmes. However, French authorities have favoured diversity (33 channels) over quality; hence, quality improvement over analogue television will be limited. Portability is another possible feature of DTTV. Portability means that with a single antenna inside or attached to the television set, viewers can receive DTTV signals everywhere in the house. However, offering portability requires the installation of additional transmitters, hence increases the cost of DTTV diffusion. In France, DTTV will probably not offer portability in the shortrun, as nothing has been planned yet.

The reactions of French consumers to DTTV, that is, their willingness to switch to DTTV, will depend on alternative television offers and on their switching costs.

A survey of 1000 persons made by Ipsos in France in September 2001 revealed that people who were planning to subscribe to digital cable or satellite were the most interested by DTTV (72 percent of them were). Half (54 percent) of existing cable, satellite and Canal Plus subscribers were also interested in DTTV.[11] Finally, 38 percent of those who had not subscribed to pay television and did not plan to were *not* interested at all in DTTV. Taking into account that approximately half of French population does not subscribe to pay television, it can be estimated that around 20 percent of French population (i.e., 38 percent of 50 percent) is not willing to switch to DTTV. It follows that the commercialisation of DTTV will be probably a difficult task. Besides, this survey suggests a paradox: Whereas public authorities targeted consumers who had not subscribed to pay television offers, the early adopters will be probably pay television subscribers or potential subscribers.

The second driver of consumer choice will be the cost of switching to DTTV. Switching costs will include:

- The cost of a new antenna (for some customers). According to a study cited by Gallot (2002), 32 percent of individual antennas will have to be upgraded to receive DTTV. The upgrade cost would be lower than 150 euros for 11 percent of antennas, lower than 275 euros for 18 percent of antennas, and lower than 380 euros for 3 percent of antennas. The same study estimates that 52 percent of collective antennas will receive DTTV without any intervention; 43 percent will have to be upgraded for a cost between 230 and 700 euros and 5

---

[11] Studies have shown that only half of satellite and cable subscribers are satisfied with the service.

percent for a cost of between 900 and 1800 euros. The average cost for collective antennas is estimated at 23 euros per household.

- The cost of a decoder. Many French studies state that the reservation price for a basic decoder is around 150 euros. Decoders could also be rented for a rental price around 7 to 8 euros per month. Decoders should be "plug and play." The upgrade of decoders should also be easy. For instance, consumers who purchase a decoder for free DTTV channels should be able to upgrade their decoder easily to receive pay DTTV channels.

Prospects of DTTV in France

In June 2000, the head of the CSA, Hervé Bourges, stated that DTTV would be launched in France at the end of 2001 or at the beginning of 2002. However, since then, regulatory delays have retarded the roll out of DTTV. In October 2001, the CSA announced that DTTV would be launched at the end of 2002. In its report to the government, Boyon (2002) estimated that DTTV might start in December 2004 over 29 diffusion sites which cover around 40 percent of the French population. In a second step, in December 2005, 50 percent of the population will be covered. It is only in 2008 that 110 diffusion sites will be used to cover 80 percent of the population.

However, a few regulatory uncertainties remain, which may further delay the roll out of DTTV:

- Three DTTV channels have yet to be awarded. They have been reserved for public television. However, the government is bringing the question up again. Besides, three channels are earmarked for local television. However, since the legal framework for local television on DTTV does not exist yet, the CSA cannot launch a call for bids. It seems difficult to launch DTTV in France, as long as these six channels are not specified.

- The CSA has to reallocate analogue frequencies, which may take time. Besides, TF1 and M6, two leading terrestrial channels, are opposed to the reallocation of analogue frequencies.

- Last but not least, there is no candidate today to commercialise DTTV. One is needed to commercialise pay DTTV channels and to stimulate the development of DTTV. The way decoders for free channels will be commercialised is also unclear.

In addition to regulatory uncertainties, there are market uncertainties. Since the beginning of the DTTV process, leading television companies have been reluctant about DTTV. They argue that DTTV is mainly another diffusion network and as such it is useless, as satellite or cable networks already exist. For instance, in an interview in *La Tribune* on 14 September 2001, Patrick Le Lay stated that he wished the French government would abandon the DTTV project. In June 2002, TF1, M6, Canal Plus, and producers joined in asking the French government to stop the DTTV process.

OTHER DIGITAL PLATFORMS

Cable and Satellite

In France, cable networks started to develop in the 1980s,[12] whereas the analogue Canal Satellite platform was launched in 1992. The two existing digital satellite platforms, Canal Satellite numérique and TPS, were launched later, in 1996.[13] Despite this late start, satellite has almost caught up with cable. In June 2002, there were 3.2 million satellite subscribers (2.1 million for Canal Satellite and 1.1 million for TPS) and 3.4 million subscribers to analogue or digital cable television (see Fig. 12.2).[14] The three cable leaders, Noos, France Télécom Câble, and NC Numéricâble, control 76 percent of cable subscribers.

Whereas satellite is 100 percent digital, only 22 percent of cable television users received digital television in September 2002. Besides, the digitalisation of cable subscribers is going slowly, as Table 12.4 shows.

The low digitalisation rate is not related to technical issues, as 85 percent of cable connections can receive digital signals. The reasons seem to be twofold. First, consumers find digital bundles too complex or too expensive. Second, cable networks have failed to generate higher revenues with digital cable than with analogue cable. Therefore, cable operators continue to commercialise their analogue offers.

---

[12] The first commercial cable network was launched in 1985. For an analysis of the French cable industry, see Perani (1999).

[13] Canal Satellite was launched in April 1996, whereas TPS was launched in December 1996. Canal Plus stopped its analogue satellite television service in 1997. Canal Satellite is controlled by Groupe Canal Plus, whereas TPS is controlled by TF1 and M6.

[14] Source: Canal Plus Groupe, Groupe TF1, AFORM.

Figure 12.2: Cable and Satellite Subscribers (Number and Penetration)

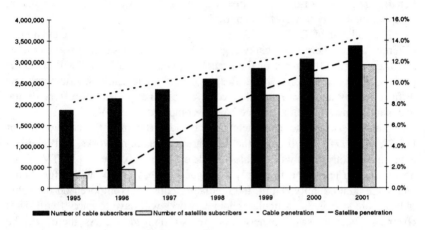

Source: ART (2003) and AFORM (www.aform.org).

Table 12.4: Digitalisation of Cable Subscribers

	1998	**1999**	**2000**	**2001**	**Sept 2002**
Number of cable television subscribers	2,580,830	2,819,840	3,020,418	3,239,411	*758,296*
Number of digital subscribers	219,297	380,976	517,191	664,212	*3,433,731*
Digitalisation rate (in percent)	8.5 %	13.5 %	17.1 %	20.5 %	*22.1 %*

Source: AFORM.

Competition Between DTTV, Cable, and Satellite

Cable and satellite platforms have failed to deliver digital television to end customers: only 17 percent of French households received digital television in 2002, though for instance satellite covers 100 percent of the population. Besides, growth rates are low.[15] Limited competition between cable and satellite players (in particular, there have been rumours about a merger between TPS and Canal

---

[15] For instance, the growth rate for satellite television is about 12 percent.

Satellite since 2001)[16] might explain the inability to address the mass market. For the French authorities, as I already stated, DTTV is a means of stimulating competition, hence the development of digital television.

The roll out of DTTV is likely to affect cable and satellite television in different ways. There is probably a geographic niche for satellite television, as satellite covers 100 percent of the French population and DTTV will cover 80 percent of the population at most. Besides, satellite television benefits from low diffusion costs and low regulatory constraints. Finally, satellite offers digital television, hence it is not at a disadvantage compared to DTTV.

Contrary to satellite, cable television could suffer from the competition of DTTV. First, DTTV will cover the same areas as cable networks, that is, urban areas, hence consumers will be able to trade off between cable and DTTV offers. Second, cable television is mainly analogue whereas DTTV will offer digital video and audio quality. Third, the regulatory constraints imposed on the cable industry are strong. In particular, cable networks will have to carry free DTTV channels (whereas satellite networks are not obliged to). As there will be between 16 and 19 free DTTV channels, possibilities of differentiation will be diminished for cable. The development of cable is also impeded by other regulatory constraints, which were set at the early stages of cable television.

The transposition of the Telecom Package in French law will provide public authorities with the opportunity to adapt cable regulation. In particular, currently, a cable network is not allowed to cover an area of more than 8 million inhabitants. This rule is probably not consistent with the new authorisation framework contained in the Telecom Package. If it were lifted, cable networks would have the opportunity to merge.

Television Over ADSL

In 2002, 38.7 percent of French households (i.e., 9,524,000 households) owned a personal computer. In January 2003, Médiamétrie estimated that 39.5 percent of the population over 11 had accessed the Internet in the previous month, compared to 33.5 percent in January 2002.[17] One of the main drivers of the growth of Internet access in France is ADSL, which is developing very rapidly (see Table 12.5). In particular, the number of ADSL subscribers nearly doubled in the last six months of 2002.

---

[16] In July 2002, the head of TF1, Patrick Le Lay, said to the media journal CB News that he 'did not exclude a merger between TPS and CanalSatellite.' In December 2002, daily newspaper *Le Monde* stated that Vivendi Universal, which controls Canal Plus, was thinking about a merger between the two satellite platforms.

[17] Source: Médiamétrie, *Baromètres Multimédia*, November 2002.

Table 12.5: Number of ADSL Subscribers

	1998	1999	2000	2001	June 2002	31 Dec 2002
Number of ADSL subscribers	0	35,000	220,000	430,000	650,421	more than 1.4 million

Source: Médiamétrie.

Because of high growth rates and because France Télécom plans to cover 80 percent of the French population by the end of 2003 with ADSL access (71 percent of the population is covered today), television over ADSL might represent a substitute to DTTV in the following years. For instance, Patrick Le Lay, the head of TF1, stated in a public hearing to the CSA about DTTV that the future of television was the Internet protocol.

There are different ways to offer television programmes over ADSL. Numerous French WebTV programmes are available on the Internet: local programmes (Issy Net TV, Chauds.net), associative television stations (Zaléa TV), thematic programmes (Monbébé TV, TV Mountain), etc. Television channels also have web sites which propose some programmes online. For instance, TF1 proposes its news programme on its website.

Television over DSL is more promising. TPS has started an experiment of television over DSL ('Dream TV') in Paris, Boulogne-Billancourt, and Issy-les-Moulineaux (for 200 households). TPS uses unbundled lines from LD Com, DSLAM from Alcatel, and digital decoders from Thomson. Dream TV offers a bundle of around 20 channels from TF1, M6, and TPS. France Télécom, together with France Télévision and M6, will also launch an experiment in Lyon in spring 2003. Free, an Internet access provider, plans to offer television services to its ADSL subscribers.

Finally, in February 2003, Monaco Telecom, Alcatel, and Moviesystem have launched a video on demand service over DSL, 'Sesame TV.' With this service, viewers can choose a movie for five euros from a catalogue of 400 films, which will be renewed every month.[18]

The current hype about television over DSL in France is supported by TF1, Alcatel, and Thomson. TF1 might view television over DSL as a means of retarding the launch of DTTV; Alcatel and Thomson propose technical solutions for television over DSL. However, the prospects of television over DSL are uncertain. First, for all players except the incumbent telecom operator France

---

[18] Cable network Noos also proposes 'NetCine,' a video on demand service, to its Internet users. NetCine proposes video on demand for prices about four to five euros per film for VHS quality.

Télécom, television over DSL requires access to unbundled local loops; but unbundling rates for co-location, unbundled lines, etc., result in higher diffusion costs than for cable and satellite, which questions the viability of this service. Second, the incumbent, France Télécom, is heavily indebted and will probably not be able to invest in television over DSL in the next five years, though television over DSL might be a viable service for it.

DVD Players

In 2002, 49.2 million DVDs were sold, compared to 32.7 million VHS cassettes. Besides, the number of DVD players doubled in 2002. There are now 5.6 million DVD players in France, which represent 24 percent of households (source: Syndicat de l'édition vidéo, SEV). If one takes into account consoles and personal computers which can read DVDs, roughly one third of French households own a DVD player.

CONCLUSION

In France, the CSA and the government have been influenced by DTTV experience in other countries, and in particular the UK case. However, a few French specificities remain. To begin with, the CSA decided to select channels and not multiplexes. This choice may have some consequences, as it will provide limited flexibility to multiplex operators. It may also be a source of conflict between channels. The reallocation of analogue frequencies is also currently an important issue in France, whereas it seems that it is not the case in other countries. Finally, diffusion and production quotas will apply to digital terrestrial channels, as to analogue terrestrial channels.

Though this is the expected schedule, DTTV will be launched in France in December 2004 at best. Indeed, three factors may retard DTTV further. First, the CSA chose leaders for its DTTV project, namely, TF1, M6, and Canal Plus, which were paradoxically strongly opposed to DTTV. Indeed, these three companies fear that DTTV could cannibalise their existing cable and satellite platforms. Whether DTTV can develop with reluctant leaders is unclear. Second, as Boyon (2003) notes, any delay in the DTTV process would postpone the launch of commercial services beyond December 2004. Hence, TF1, M6, and Canal Plus have strong incentives to retard the DTTV process. This is already the case (TF1 and M6 are opposed to the reallocation of analogue frequencies). Third, the government has not yet decided what the role of public television will be. DTTV cannot be launched before this delicate issue is resolved.

Last but not least, a few uncertainties remain about the French television industry. Will French cable networks merge? If yes, a major could emerge, otherwise the cable industry might suffer from the competition of DTTV (ART, 2003). Will the two satellite platforms (TPS and Canal Satellite) merge, as persistent rumours indicate? If they will, competition would be weakened. Finally, will Canal Plus, the French leading premium pay channel, disappear? If Canal Plus disappears, the question of the subsidisation of the French production industry will be brought up again.

REFERENCES

France: Autorité de régulation des Télécommunications (ART), 2003. *L'économie du câble en France : Contexte, marché et perspectives*, Etude réalisée par le cabinet JLM Conseil pour l'Autorité de régulation des télécommunications, January.

France: Agence Nationale des Fréquences (ANFR), 1998. *Etude sur la planification des fréquences pour la télévision numérique de terre – DVB-T.*

Boyon, M., 2002. *La télévision numérique terrestre*, Rapport établi à la demande du Premier Ministre, http://www.ddm.gouv.fr/rapports_etudes/documents/ RAPPORTBOYON.rtf (accessed 25.02.03).

Boyon, M., 2003. *La télévision numérique terrestre*, Rapport complémentaire établi à l'intention du Premier Ministre, http://www.ddm.gouv.fr/ rapports_etudes/documents/boyon_complementaire.rtf (accessed 25.02.03).

Gallot, J., 2002. *La télévision numérique terrestre : enjeux et modalités de mise en œuvre au regard des règles de concurrence, notamment au travers de la question de la distribution*, Rapport sur la mission confiée par le Ministre de l'Economie, des Finances et de l'Industrie, http://www.minefi.gouv.fr/ DGCCRF/consommation/telecom/tnt0202.htm (accessed 25.02.03).

Le Guen, J.-M., 2001. *Rapport d'information de M. Jean-Marie Le Guen, au nom de la commission des finances, de l'économie générale et du plan sur la télévision numérique terrestre*, document d'information de l'Assemblée Nationale n°2963, http://www.ladocfrancaise.gouv.fr/BRP/notices/ 014000294. html (accessed 25.02.03).

Loi n°2000-719 du 1er août 2000 modifiant la loi n°86-1067 du 30 septembre 1986 relative à la liberté de communication, http://www.legifrance.gouv.fr/citoyen/jorf_nor.ow?numjo=MCCX9800149L (accessed 25.02.03).

Perani, J., 1999. *Le pouvoir de monopsone: Une analyse économique de la télévision par câble*, Thèse de Doctorat de Sciences Economiques, Université Paris II.

Chapter 13
Germany: Large Free-to-Air Offerings Delay Digital Take-up

Nikolaus Mohr
Gerhard P. Thomas
Accenture GmbH

In comparison to other countries, there is a variety of reasons that complicate the digitalization process in the very special German television market. The main obstacles are: the situation and development of the technical infrastructure, a large free-to-air offering and domination of advertising financed broadcast stations.

The technical infrastructure for television in Germany is well developed. 82 million Germans in approximately 36.3 million households, make up the total television market in Germany. 20.6 million households thereof have cable and 13.8 million have satellite reception. In 2002, only about 1.9 million households still have traditional analogue terrestrial television reception (Statistisches Bundesamt, www.digitalfernsehen.de). The distribution of television reception by infrastructure is illustrated in Figure 13.1.

Different from other European television customers the German viewer disposes of a large offering of up to 30 free-to-air television channels via cable, more than 100 via satellite and approximately 10 channels via terrestrial. Almost everything from live soccer and Formula 1 auto racing to soft core erotic programmes can be seen on German free television. This situation leads to fastidious viewers and an almost saturated market. Only a limited number of customers are willing to pay for new services and programmes. Consequently, digital television offerings have a difficult starting point in Germany and were not able to flood the market, as it was possible in other European countries, such as UK, Italy and Spain, so far.

The majority of the existing broadcasting stations with nationwide reach pay large amounts of money for their analogue distribution through cable systems, by satellite and by terrestrial means. Their main method of financing is the advertising they offer. The total advertising revenues in the German television market amounted to €4.5 billion after deductions in 2001 (www.ard.de, Zentraler Verband der Deutschen Werbewirtschaft). There are also extensive restrictions on advertising, adherence to which is rigorously supervised by the 15 state media regulatory commissions (*Landes-medienanstalten*).

Figure 13.1: Distribution of Television Reception in Germany by Infrastructure Type

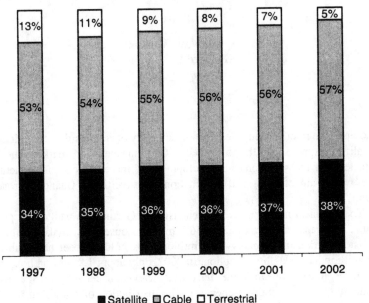

■Satellite ▢Cable ▢Terrestrial

According to Datamonitor (2001) highly cabled countries, for example Germany, which essentially rely on free-to-air programming, show the tendency to have less developed digital television markets. In these countries digital penetration and consequently also the average revenues per subscriber (ARPUs) tend to be low.

As far as digital television and the creation of new market models for the television industry are concerned, it can be said that Germany is behind other European countries. The prevailing form of television is still mainly advertising-financed free television. The pay television sector is dominated by the platform operator Premiere.

The future development of the digital standard for the communication and entertainment industry in Germany is planned and regulated in detail by the German government. By 2010, the digitalization of the television and radio networks is supposed to be completed. That includes the complete substitution of the analogue by the digital television submission technology. Today all major German broadcasting stations already provide digital and analogue broadcast streams. Digital penetration is expected to rise significantly during the upcoming years not at last due to the pending analogue signal cut off and the migration of free-to-air households.

OVERVIEW OF THE GERMAN DIGITAL TELEVISION MARKET

Regulatory Issues

The regulation of the German telecommunication and broadcasting sector is based on four central bodies of law. The telecommunication law (Telekommunikationsgesetz–TKG), the telecommunication service law (Teledienstgesetz–TDG), the media services treaty (Mediendienst-estaatsvertrag–MDStV) and the broadcast treaty (Rundfunkstaatsvertrag– RStV). TKG treats voice telephony, network infrastructure for broadcast and telecommunication, whereas TDG, MDStV, and RStV focus on content services. TKG and TDG are under control of the German federation; MDStV and RStV are controlled by the different "Länder."

The regulation has grown and is frequently referred to as obsolescent and often subject to criticism. According to J. Philipp Siemer (2002), finding criteria to differentiate the different services in order to assign them to the different regulations and laws is getting more and more difficult, if not impossible.

In addition, the separation that is currently being made is not stringent. Internet telephony and classical telephony are treated by different laws and fall into different areas of responsibility. The same happens for telephony and media services. The current division of responsibilities leads to various lacks of regulation or to opposed regulations, for example, in the areas of data and youth protection. Providers of new services try to sneak into the least controlled niche, but have no guarantee of the future developments of the regulatory situation.

The key problem leading to the inefficient laws in Germany is the divided responsibility between the federation and the "Länder;" contrary interests cannot be aligned and create obstacles: The German federation follows a more economic approach with focus on the telecommunication sector while the "Länder" tend to follow a more cultural-based approach.

Existing and potential providers of broadcast and telecommunication services are facing an uncertain regulatory situation. The missing competency and responsibility demarcation leads to insecurity about further and future legal developments and represses the progress in the telecommunication and broadcast sector.

A reform of the current regulatory situation, in order to support and push the development and spread of new digital services, is inescapable.

DTV Access Technologies

The market for access technologies is wide and is currently undergoing significant changes. In the Internet business, access via telephone line and modem has become a commodity and many people are now upgrading to broadband access. Furthermore, many of the newly emerging content types will need broadband. This presents two obvious challenges for those intending to offer the whole service/content spectrum: bandwidth and a return channel.

In this context, different access technologies are competing in terms of time to market and technological maturity. DSL in particular, is the recent star, and satellite will soon follow. Cable was positioned well, but is currently suffering because of huge investments, financial disasters of cable companies and the overall economic downturn. The mobile world will see new standards like UMTS in the years to come. W-LAN is supposed to be the technological star of the future, positioned between wire line and mobile—and seen as complementary to both. And within a few years, well-known terrestrial television will give way to interactive television. Therefore, the competition will increase and other upcoming and slower technologies, for example, power line communication (PLC) or wireless local loop (WLL) will continue to have a hard time gaining market share in the mass market. They are seen as niche players in a special segment (e.g. home networks, SME).

But not all of the described technologies above are suitable for accessing dTV. With respect to bandwidth, broadcast suitability and not at least the spread and development of the technology itself some technologies are more suitable than others. Among the most prospering ones concerning dTV are cable, satellite and DTT. DSL has potential but has just begun to develop dTV product offerings. The remaining technologies are Internet/PC focused and therefore will not be analyzed in detail.

Cable

The television cable infrastructure can be used for fast access to the broadband world including high-speed Internet access and voice-over-IP-enabled telephony. The cable network is currently being enhanced in terms of digitalization and back channel capability so it can be used for interactive and digital content and services. Of the 20.6 million cable households in Germany

1.62 million (7.9 percent) receive digital signals at the end of 2002 while 92.1 percent still receive analogue signals (SES ASTRA).

Players and Competition: In Germany, the largest European cable market, the cable network is divided into four network layers (NL); the structure is very complex and involves many different players.

NL 1 belongs to television stations, production facilities and dedicated operators. NL 2 is used for long haul transmission by Deutsche Telekom AG (DTAG) for terrestrial and by ASTRA/Eutelsat for satellite. NL 3 was recently sold by DTAG and is now owned by different investors.

Originally, Callahan acquired 55 percent of the cable network of North Rhine Westphalia (ish) and a 55 percent stake in Baden-Württemberg (Kabel BW) from DTAG, in the beginning of 2000. In 2002, Callahan's German subsidiary Callahan NRW filed for chapter 11. Currently, a consortium of Deutsche Bank AG and Citibank owns ish. Kabel BW is still owned by Callahan and DTAG. The cable network in Hesse (Iesy), a major stake of which was originally acquired by NTL, is now owned by a consortium of Apollo Management, L.P., and Pequot Capital Management.

The remaining regional cable networks (Bavaria, Berlin/Brandenburg, Hamburg/Schleswig-Holstein/Mecklenburg/Vorpommern, Lower Saxony/ Bremen, Rhineland-Palatinate/Saarland and Saxony/Saxony-Anhalt/Thuringia) were sold by DTAG in January 2003 to a consortium of Apax Partners Inc., Goldman Sachs, and Providence Equity Partners Inc. Additional owners of NL 3 are private operators, for example Tele Columbus, Bosch, PrimaCom, and municipal service providers.

NL 4 is owned by Kabel Deutschland GmbH successors (former DTAG), by professional providers like Tele Columbus, Bosch, PrimaCom, etc., and by a large number of small operators and independent housing associations.

Infrastructure: Some digital bi-directional cable platforms are currently being used in Germany. Especially PrimaCom in eastern Germany is the first company to offer a partially upgraded network, providing digital services. But in general cable operators are not able to meet their time and budget goals. Investments to upgrade the German network to bi-directionality are estimated at about €7.6 and €9.2 billion.

Demand: Despite the large investments especially into the NL3 in the different regions, the market in Germany is still weak. Investors hopes were disappointed and take up rates were low. Investors lost a lot of money; as can be seen in the case of Callahan NRW. The hefty investments for the purchase of the networks and its upgrades could not be refinanced. The economy's decline has also retarded development. Average revenue per user (ARPU)-based business models, which were basis of the business cases in the buying stage, were established on assumptions that seem unrealistic from today's point of view. Revenues lagged far behind expectations.

Whereas in other countries such as the U.S. and the U.K. the predominant cable business model is to offer a triple play product including idTV, high speed Internet (HSI), and telephony offerings, this is different for the German market. In Germany this offering faces a very difficult market situation in all three segments.

As can be seen at the example of Germany's constant struggling and only pay television provider Premiere, it is difficult to establish a pay television offering in the German market. In HSI as well as telephony, cable operators have to compete with DTAG. DTAG's DSL offering dominates the HSI market with a market share of some 90 percent. In telephony, DTAG still virtually holds its former monopoly status. Still, for cable services, demand is expected to rise significantly over the next few years.

In general the technical development did not become as widely accepted as expected, and the services did not live up to the expectations of the early nineties. Today only 5 percent of the network capacity is being used. Prices fell approximately 70 percent over the last three years.

Advantages of cable include the last-mile technology, high bandwidth, high transmission quality, residential and business customers, larger customer base than satellite, and that key players create economies of scale by implementing European rollout.

Disadvantages include bandwidth-sharing between users, time-to-market disadvantage compared to DSL, fragmented market structure leads to problems with fast service rollout, complex market structure due to separation in Germany between network levels 3 and 4, cable modem required (no standard modem), developments of a standard for set-top boxes are still in an early stage, and large up-front investments.

Future Scenario: The failure of the first attempt of DTAG to sell the 6 remaining NL 3 cable networks to Liberty in 2002, which was stopped by the German cartel office, paralyzed activities in the German broadband market and impacted nearly all players. Joint projects and investments that were planned among all regional network providers were postponed indefinitely. Only DTAG took this situation as an advantage to build up its DSL network.

The future scenario will depend strongly on the strategy of the new investors, the respective business cases and the regulations of the German cartel office. The success of triple play offerings in Germany is still being questioned.

Alternative business models with a limited network upgrade, focusing mainly on analogue television and only basic digital offerings are being discussed.

Efforts and activities for digitalization in Germany will be continued, so that the goal of having all households digitized by 2010 is expected to be met. The provisioning of full interactivity and back channel capacity of all households at that date is less probable.

Direct Subscriber Line (DSL)

Digital subscriber line (DSL) is a technology for transporting data through a twisted-pair copper wire from the local exchange to business premises or homes. Two-way communication can be established using the telephone line. At the current stage of development, DSL offers a bandwidth of up to 2 Mbps in synchronous mode (SDSL) and 8 Mbps in asynchronous mode (ADSL). To be suitable for dTV provisioning DSL still has some way to go. Although DSL offers the required bandwidth it is still mainly a high speed Internet access technology. Provisioning of dTV via DSL is still in its infancy.

Players and Competition: Today, DSL is the fastest growing market among the broadband access technologies. There are at least 40 vendors of DSL technology worldwide delivering the equipment needed. DSL has spread widely and is offered by nearly every telephone company. Market entry barriers for service providers are low. The market is extremely price-competitive and a shakeout is expected very soon. In the European DSL market the former incumbents tend to hold the dominant position.

There are more than 40 DSL service providers in the German market (DTAG No 1, QSC No 2, Arcor No 3). Today the "T-DSL" product of DTAG dominates the market with a market share of some 90 percent. Since May 2002, DTAG has offered two even faster DSL packages than the traditional T-DSL. T-DSL 1500 offers a download speed of 1.5 Mbit/s, and TDSL 2300 offers 2.3 Mbit/s.

T-Online/DTAG is currently planning a content, service and product offering especially designed for the television set. This product will combine services like VoD, EPG including features such as e-mail and messenger services. In addition, T-Online plans to offer an interactive television product in cooperation with broadcasters. T-Online Vision users will be able to directly interact with their television broadcast program, for example, participate in talk or quiz shows via an additional DSL stream.

As DTAG's market share shows, competition has not really taken hold and is currently being discussed by regulatory authorities.

Infrastructure: The network, running on the telephone cable, already exists, but the backbone infrastructure must be improved and new network elements in the main distribution knots must be installed. DTAG, for example, invested €1 billion to upgrade its DSL networks in 2000/2001. So far, QSC has invested about €250 million in upgrading its network in 40 German cities. Most of the DSL connections sold by QSC are based on line sharing with DTAG, QSC pays €4.77 per month for every line.

There are many variations of DSL (the most important are HDSL, SDSL, UDSL, ADSL, and VDSL, some of which are still being tested). The main differences are the proportion between fibre and copper, the transmission symmetry (symmetric vs. asymmetric) and the transmission speed. Fast Internet access (2 Mbps) is currently offered, but in the near future—using VDSL as a "download pipe"—up to 26 Mbps can be offered depending on the quality of the existing copper and the distance between the main distribution frame and the customer premises. This requires an extension of the fibre network to the curb.

In addition to DSL via the telephone cable, some telephone companies are also offering DSL via satellite. For details on Sky DSL, please see the satellite section in this chapter.

Demand: DSL is the leading broadband technology for high speed Internet, which is set to become a mass market. DSL subscription in Europe is expected to grow up to 15 to 20 million by the end of 2003. This means a growth rate of more than 200 percent from 4.6 million users in 2001, with Germany and Spain showing the highest growth rates. The German IT Association Bitkom estimates that 6.8 million DSL lines will be sold in Germany by the end of 2003. DSL offers an interesting broadband product, especially for residential customers, SoHos (small offices, home offices) and SMEs. In terms of revenue, residential customers will represent the most interesting segment. A real triple play consisting of high-speed Internet, interactive television, and telephony is still being tested and has not been launched on the market yet. Only short movie sequences can be seen so far.

The advantages of DSL include short time-to-market, no bandwidth-sharing (guaranteed bandwidth), potential access to all 37 million households in Germany and high coverage, the lack of need for Telco investment in copper infrastructure, lower costs for upgrading networks (€300 to €400 per subscriber compared to €600 to €750 per subscriber for a full cable upgrade), parallel transport of voice and data along one line (voice: analogue or ISDN data: ATM, frame relay, Ethernet, or IP), and secure point-to-point connection in comparison to the tree structure of cable networks requiring encryption.

Disadvantages are that the German market is dominated by former incumbent DTAG, that the rest of market fragmented, that DSL comprises many variations of different technologies and standards, that the backbone network to main distribution switches needs to be upgraded and, at present, only a fraction of potential customers are able to switch to DSL because of backhaul bottleneck. The final disadvantage is that performance is distance-sensitive, with maximum transmission speed up to a distance of 3 kilometres.

Future Scenario: DSL is expected to develop faster than other broadband technologies in the next few years. On the one hand, this is due to the wide coverage, ease of installation and the "time-to-market" strategy. On the other hand, it can be explained by the struggles of the other technologies. In contrast to cable where investments are huge, break-even with DSL should be reached earlier. Currently, DSL is very attractive and is penetrating the market in urban areas (due to range restrictions). In addition, the constantly growing number of service offerings is making DSL more attractive, especially for private customers.

There is a potential for DSL becoming a dTV player: New products and entertainment service, for example, dTV offerings will be offered via DSL in the near future. Campaigns will be launched to market the new service offerings triggering dTV demand via DSL within the next 3 to 5 years.

Digital Terrestrial Television

Using digital terrestrial technology—mainly known for multi-channel television and radio—idTV and interactive services (full Internet access) will be delivered to the home through an ordinary television aerial (no dish or cable). A back channel will be offered in the long run but is not automatically provided when DTTV is installed. Nowadays the telephone network has to be used as the return path.

DTTV requires a decoder (set-top box) or a new digital television set that has the required technology already built in. Digital Terrestrial in Germany, based on the technical standard DVB-T, is currently being developed.

In Germany currently nearly all of the 1.9 million terrestrial customers receive analogue television signals. Only about 200.000 customers located within the region Berlin/Brandenburg are receiving digital terrestrial signals.

Players and Competition: Berlin is the precursor of DTTV distribution in Germany. In the middle of 2003 analogue terrestrial television distribution will be stopped. Since October 2002, 250,000 households in Berlin and surrounding areas are upgraded to receive 24 channels via digital terrestrial. Medienanstalt Berlin/Brandenburg (MABB) the responsible institution, is currently planning the transition process from analogue to digital. Together with broadcasters, device providers and the institution for social benefits a model is being elaborated to guarantee dTV service provisioning (including the provisioning of a STB) to all parts of the population, even to those on welfare.

DTAG will operate the distribution infrastructure. Due to market entry barriers, the entrance of new market players will be sharply restricted initially. Compared to other European countries DTTV in Germany is expected to play a role in the broadcast area only.

Infrastructure: Digital terrestrial television will increase the number of regional and special-interest programs broadcast. This will be made possible by the underlying DVB-T (digital video broadcasting–terrestrial) technology standard which will exploit the transmission capacities to a maximum. The end users can continue using the same antenna as for analogue reception but setting up the required new net of masts is very complicated and costly.

DTTV has the advantage of pictures of excellent quality, crystal clear sound, and television can be watched in cinema-style wide screen format (using the latest television sets).

Demand: Forecasts predict further Digital Terrestrial penetration, with significant growth potential in the coming years although the total number of digital terrestrial homes will remain small compared with other broadband access technologies. The take-off and the success of the DTTV trial in Berlin will be decisive for DTTV's future in the German market. The dTV project "Northern Germany" a joint project of Lower Sachsony, Bremen, and Hamburg, as well as the dTV project "Central Germany" consisting of Saxony-Anhalt, and Thuringia, are waiting for the first outcomes of the Berlin dTV pilot, to proceed with or possibly adjust their plans.

Digital terrestrial television's advantages are that only digital set-top boxes or new TVs with built-in functions are needed for use, that the costs for the end user are limited, that it is not stationary and can therefore be used in different rooms, and that it is portable and mobile within a building.

It's disadvantages are that a new, higher quality television is needed, that there must be investment in new transmission and compression technology, that no return path is directly provided and there is no direct interactivity short term, that it requires a long time-to-market, that the number of receivable television programs is limited to 24, and that no other service offerings other than digital television will be available for the time being.

Future Scenario: Due to the late rollout of digital terrestrial TV, this technology will not play a significant role as an interactive and digital television platform in Germany. Traditional terrestrial distribution will develop into a niche market in Germany in the near future, since the majority of viewers will have already migrated to DSL, cable and satellite services.

Digital terrestrial television is not expected to sense a boom effect through the digitalization. In Germany the number of customers receiving terrestrial television is constantly dropping, last year by 26 percent (www.digitalfernsehen.de). The reason for the declining number of end customers can be explained not only with the limited number of programmes offered but also by end customers taking the chance of migration from analogue terrestrial to DTTV to switch to a different access technology, such as cable or satellite. As a result, forecasts project only limited growth of DTTV in the coming years according the most significant projections (Fig. 13.2).

Figure 13.2: Penetration Forecasts for Digital Terrestrial Television in Germany as Percentage of Total Number of Television Households

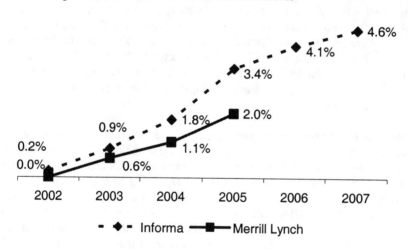

Digital terrestrial television is currently experiencing problems, caused by poor marketing, weak service offerings, and lack of governmental support. According to a report issued by the Yankee Group (2002), the DTTV players should begin by offering a simple DTTV product at a competitive price. Due to the current problems with digital terrestrial television, the analogue signal cut-off in the various European countries will be delayed.

Satellite

The current generation of satellite systems was primarily designed for broadcasting and offers mainly digital one-way high-bandwidth transmission. Most of the satellite systems still use different technical options as a narrowband return path. Two-way communication has been established as a bridge to the real two-way broadband communication. The new generation of satellite systems offers two-way, asymmetric broadband/ multicast capabilities (e.g. Tiscali, 130 kbit upstream and 400 kbit downstream). However, real two-way symmetric broadband/point-to-point communication capabilities are planned for 2004-2005 at the earliest. The advantages of satellite broadband technology are high bandwidth and only minor investments in infrastructure in rural areas. In Western Europe approximately 33 million customers are connected to satellite systems in 2002; 16.9 million European television households already received digital television via satellite by the end of 2001. This works out to 71 percent of all digital television households in Europe (Van Dusseldorp & Partners, 2002).

In Germany there are 5.1 million satellite customers who are enabled to receive digital signals; 2.1 million of them actually dispose of a set-top box (STB) and make use of the digital transmission. The remaining 3 million only need a STB to migrate from analogue to the digital world (www. digitalfernsehen.de).

Players and Competition: Currently, the market is still dominated by broadcast systems, but the situation is starting to change. The majority of satellite homes use their set-top box mainly for free-to-air reception. SES and Eutelsat are the two largest satellite Operators in Europe. Operating thirteen satellites, SES ASTRA offers the leading direct-to-the-home satellite system in Europe. Since May 2002 SES ASTRA, SES Global and DTAG are offering "T-DSL via satellite." This product also delivers DTAG's DSL to rural areas. It does not yet have a satellite back channel. Telephone lines must therefore be used to send data upstream. Moreover, SES Global, Gilat Satellite Networks Ldt., Alcatel Space and SkyBridge have formed SATLYNK, a new company that will provide two-way satellite broadband communications services throughout Europe. ASTRA's Broadband Interactive (BBI) Infrastructure offers service providers, application developers and value added resellers an asymmetrical IP-based high-speed two-way communications system via the ASTRA satellite system. BBI is capable of point-to-point and multipoint connectivity within the ASTRA coverage area.

Infrastructure: In the past, satellites have traditionally been used for television broadcasting and the telephony backbone. Both will remain the largest revenue sources over the next two to three years. More and more innovative services are now emerging in the narrowband (data services such as e-mail or paging, location-based services, telematic), and broadband (Internet access, e-commerce, tele-health, etc.) areas. Out of these different groups of satellite services, multimedia satellite services allow satellite operators to enter the broadband market. Recently, satellite technology in Germany has become more important as a substitute technology for the Level 3. In these cases data is sent by satellite receiver station to the head end of the Level 4, where it is fed in.

Demand: Two-way broadband communication is not yet offered in an acceptable price range. Demand comes mainly from broadcast applications (satellite TV). Beside pure television broadcasting there will be strong demand for digital broadcast applications (point to multipoint; transmitting digital files to several locations at a cost advantage compared to physical transport of CD-ROMs, tapes, etc.), satellite systems used as backbone backup solutions and combinations of TV-broadcasting and Internet activities where the user can shop or access information about TV, movies, etc. To use the satellite services customers need to have a satellite antenna, a satellite receiver, a universal LNB and a DVB satellite card.

The advantages of satellite broadcasting are that they provide last-mile technology, perfect coverage (nearly 100 percent coverage of the earth even in exotic areas and maritime enterprises), permit high-speed Internet access, file transfer and multicast content distribution–video, audio and data, data collection, backbone technology (due to high transmission rates), and innovative services (e.g., traffic telematics, object security, and ecology monitoring).

Disadvantages include bandwidth-sharing between users, long time-to-market for interactive services, long transmission delay (GEOs, geo-synchronous earth orbits), transmission quality is affected by bad weather, limited downstream bandwidth for current satellite system generation (due to limited transponder capacity), requirements of large up-front investments, and expensive satellite terminals.

Future Scenario: Broadband communication services via satellite will grow in Germany over the next few years and are expected to reach 8.5 million users by 2005. Most of these users will live in rural areas and therefore do not have access to cable or DSL services. Due to the satellite's total coverage, the gradual introduction of the back channel and the slow build-up of the cable network, growth looks promising for the satellite in the broadband realm.

However, applications relying on high bandwidth face a problem if transmitted via satellite due to bandwidth-sharing and limited transponder capacities. Satellite services will show an impressive market growth in the area of backbone/backup systems and digital broadcast applications. Bundles of satellite services with other access technologies (hybrid systems, e.g., DSL via satellite) will continue to be another growth factor. In addition, in terms of interactive broadband services, only some specific and appropriate (economical, technical) services are expected to be offered via satellite systems (e.g., B2B services, security or ecology monitoring and Internet access).

Digitalization in the satellite realm is currently being pressed ahead. The number of digital customers in Germany has grown by 51 percent in 2002 (www.digitalfernsehen.de). This development is expected to continue similarly during the next years. Satellite will remain the main competitor of cable in television transmission.

Technology Comparison

This section gives an overview and allows a direct comparison of the four technologies just discussed (Table 13.1).

Table 13.1: Overview of Technology Available

	Number of programs	Interactive services	Quality	Cost	Legal restrictions for end customer	Comments
Cable	Up to 90 channels (862 MHz) (Good)	Provides full back channel after upgrade (Good)	Excellent picture/sound quality (Excellent)	Ongoing cost (Satisfactory)	Dependent on HA (Good)	
Satellite	Up to 120 channels (Excellent)	Possible with back channel via telephone (Satisfactory)	Excellent picture/sound quality – weather influence (Good)	One time payment (Good)	Dependent on HA/other restrictions (Satisfactory)	Estimated 40% end customers can switch. Prominent position with 12 m households served (90% by Astra)
DTTV	Up to 24 programs (Poor)	Possible with back channel via telephone (Poor)	Depends on local reception situation (Good)	Set-top box (Excellent)	None (Excellent)	High mobility and portability
DSL	Limited VoD offer (Very poor)	Full capabilities (Excellent)	Software required (Good)	Access and usage/flatrate (Satisfactory)	None (Excellent)	Complimentary to cable, no full substitute. DTAG rolls out DSL aggressively

● Excellent ◕ Good ◐ Satisfactory ◔ Poor ○ Very poor

All four technologies have different exit points and different strengths and weaknesses. Cable's weakness is the relatively high ongoing costs and the fact that the network upgrade has to be completed to offer the full dTV and interactive television service spectrum. Satellite does not yet offer a proprietary back channel. DTTV's disadvantage is the weak starting point and the limited number of programmes that can be offered. DSL is positioned well but is limited to VoD services instead of programme offerings yet. Summing up, cable and satellite are positioned well and will achieve a high digital penetration beyond their users in the future. DSL is also positioned well but will not be able to offer the entire dTV product spectrum in the short term. DTTV will establish itself as a niche player in the German dTV market, significantly behind cable and satellite. Among the four technologies, DTTV is the one with less possibility to be a broadband success in Germany. The weak starting point and the weak position in the current market makes it fall behind the other three technologies in the long term.

DTV OFFERINGS

The German television market is dominated by two different kinds of players: public and private/commercial broadcasters. Each has different approaches to digital television.

Public Broadcasters

The digitalization process in Germany is pressed forward by many different players and interest groups. Each of them follow different short term interests but they are all longing for a common goal: a high and growing digital penetration in Germany for the analogue cut off in 2010.

The public broadcasters in Germany, ARD and ZDF, are supporting the transition process to digital by already providing digital content.

ARD DIGITAL Since 1997 ARD is offering a digital bouquet called ARD DIGITAL, which is aired in DVB standard via satellite. The bouquet includes the programmes: Das Erste, 3sat, Phoenix, Kinderkanal, arte, BR-alpha (learning channel) and ARD regional channels (Dritte Programme) free of charge and unencrypted. Additional EinsMuXx, EinsExtra, and EinsFestival are offered encrypted and against payment.

ZDF Vision Beside the ZDF main programme, the digital ZDF Vision offers special interest channels, numerous partner programmes, and opens the way for new interactive services. The customer can choose and put together its own programme package. Included are the channels: ZDF, 3sat, Kinderkanal, ZDF-Theaterkanal, ZDF.info, ZDF.doku, Eurosport, Euronews, and ZDF infotext.

According to ZDF's director Markus Schächter ZDF estimates, that despite the difficult current market situation, about 10 million German households are already enabled to receive digital television. Schächter assumes this number to reach 50 percent of German households by 2007. He sees his responsibility in providing and assuring free access to all offerings and services in a dynamic and changing media market. To be prepared for the future ZDF bases its offerings on the European standard multimedia home platform (MHP).

MediaVision   MediaVision is a neutral digital television provider platform owned by DTAG (formally publicly owned) that used to provide a joint offering of ARD DIGITAL, ZDF vision, and a variety of foreign language channels. Due to a lack of success MediaVision has stopped its distribution activities. In the long run, Kabel Deutschland GmbH (KDG) is planned to continue the business activities; the take over of the current contracts is constantly being negotiated.

Private/Commercial Broadcasters

Not only the public but also the commercial broadcasters offer their classic programmes in digital quality; some of them include other additional services into their offerings. A selection of the most important players follows:

RTL WORLD   RTL WORLD (mostly owned by Bertelsmann AG) is offering a digital package on ASTRA that includes the channels RTL WORLD, RTL TELEVISION, RTL II, VOX and Super RTL.
   Besides the provisioning of the digital program bouquet, RTL started airing its tele-shopping channel "RTL Shop" in digital on ASTRA on 1 July 2002. For RTL this means not only a gain of 1.4 million potential households, but also a strong positioning for the future. With €114 million RTL shop doubled its revenues in 2002. RTL is acknowledging the rising importance of the digital technology and the future potential of dTV and the new integrated digital services.

ProSieben Digital   The Digital television bouquet offered by ProSieben (formally owned by Kirch Media currently for sale includes the channels: ProSieben Digital, NEUN LIVE Television, DSF, Home Shopping Europe, SAT 1, N24, and Kabel 1.
   In March 2003, ProSieben introduced an interactive television product based on MHP, together with Sony. Parallel to the current television program the product offers news, weather, TV-tips, horoscope, and shopping. This offering is the first picture in picture offering in the German market. Together with this interactive television pilot ProSieben started interactive television advertising in cooperation with Mercedes-Benz (w&v).

Premiere Premiere, Germany's first pay-TV offering, is an important player in the German digital television market. Premiere, originally belonging to Kirch

Gruppe, has just recently been sold to the investment group Permira. Today's Premiere is the result of a merger between Premiere and DF-1 in 1999. It is available via cable and satellite and constantly counts with 2.6 million subscribers. The migration from analogue to digital was completed on February 28, 2003 with the disconnection of the analogue offering. Therefore all Premiere subscribers receive digital signals.

Premiere, was the first to offer pay-TV in the German market. Ownership of exclusive rights to movie and football allowed the platform to differentiate from the free-to-air offerings. Nevertheless, Premiere did not meet the financial goals, predicted subscriber numbers and ARPUs. Consequently it has constantly been revising its offerings and package structure. Premiere did not manage to build up a positive image and did not statute an example in Germany's digital television market. In 2002 Premiere got a new CEO and management, which seems to be able to realize the turn around. Rigorous cost cutting, a strong marketing campaign, and an easy packaging structure with a low cost entrance offering cause rising subscriber numbers. The current Premiere offering distinguishes between Premiere Start, Premiere Film, Premiere Sport, and Premiere Super.

Premiere Start includes one mixed channel offering entertainment for the entire family, a movie highlight every night, erotic movies at night and live soccer on Saturdays in a conference channel format. Additionally it enables the access to Premiere Direct, the VoD offering.

Premiere Film is Premiere's movie offering. It includes movie highlights every month, first time on German Television. Movies are shown on 7 channels without advertising. It includes Premiere Start and the access to Premiere Direct.

Premiere Sport broadcasts all soccer games of Deutsche Football League and UEFA Champions League, live and in conference mode. Additional Formula 1 racing with the ability for the subscriber to choose the preferred camera perspective. Other sport highlights broadcasted include boxing, golf, hockey, American sports, and others. It also enables access to Premiere Start and Premiere Direct.

Finally, there is Premiere Super that combines the content of all three packages just mentioned.

For the reception of Premiere a decoder (set-top box) is needed. The subscriber has the choice to either buy or rent a box. Customers that decide to buy a STB have the choice between the boxes HUMAX BTCI 5900 and Galaxis Easy World. Both can be used for satellite and cable reception. They also can choose the boxes Technisat Digibox Beta 1, Technisat Digibox Beta 2, and Galaxis Classic World that are for satellite reception only. For customers that decide to rent a box Premiere currently offers Kirch's proprietary d-box for €7.50 a month.

Cable Network Providers

The cable network providers play a special role when looking at digital services provisioning. Not only do they "transport and distribute" the digital offerings of the private and public broadcasters but they occasionally also add their own proprietary dTV offerings and services. These offerings and service include additional foreign language, special interest channels, pay television offerings ,and EPGs.

This section focuses on the description of selected important cable network providers that play an important role for the further development of dTV services in Germany. Besides the owners of the NL 3, which are already important due to their size and reach, also PrimaCom, a NL 4 provider, is worth mentioning: At the expenses of heavy debt burdens, PrimaCom was the first to offer a digital and interactive television product in the Germany market.

Ish/Iesy/Kabel BW The new owners of the former DTAG owned cable networks had great plans for digital and interactive television offerings, when buying the networks in 2000. In the course of the high financial burdens for the upgrade and the low take-up rates they refocused their planning and stopped the development of a highly interactive and digital television offering. The current strategy focuses on the development of a slimed down interactive dTV offering, including the provisioning of movies pay per view, and interactive services like email, SMS, and videogames. This offering is currently being developed.

Today, cable customers receive almost exclusively multiple analogue and digital broadcast channels in the high digital quality.

Consortium Apax, Goldman Sachs, and Providence Equity Currently the networks of the six German regions, which have just been sold by DTAG, are neither upgraded nor do they offer any additional analogue or digital content other than the traditional channels and programmes that are offered through cable. The strategy of the new investors, which has not been communicated yet, will be of major importance for the further development of the German television market, since the six regions make up the major stake of all German cable customers.

If the investors adopt an aggressive strategy, including the upgrade of the network and the installation of a back channel, digital television in Germany would feel a significant impulse and growing subscriber numbers.

PrimaCom As mentioned previously, PrimaCom applied a very aggressive strategy toward upgrade and product offering, at the cost of heavy debt burdens. The current digital offering includes a variety of the German commercial programmes, foreign language channels, as well as ARD DIGITAL and ZDF Vision.

In addition to the digital offering PrimaCom offers different packages: primatv Movies & More, primatv Family, primatv Life, primatv Wissen, MTV Paket, and primatv Maxi a joint offering for all packages. The navigation through the PrimaCom offering is facilitated by a proprietary EPG. It gives an overview of all the content provided and helps to sort for special interest content, genre, or a special time.

For the reception of the PrimaCom offerings a "PrimaCom Decoder," a STB based on the open television standard is required.

ADVERTISING

Digital terrestrial television does not only introduce a wider range of services offerings and a better and more sophisticate transmission quality but will also change the way television works today. The current business models, built on interruptive advertising, will change significantly.

In the world of interactive broadband media, permission advertising will replace or at least supplement interruptive mass ads, be targeted along customer habits and tailored to interactive content. The advertising challenge will be to offer customers what they want, when they want it.

Besides the fact that permission advertising will enter a new era, dTV and interactive broadband lead to innovative forms of interruptive and permission advertising. The new technology enables the bundling of television spots, commercial-based television programs, brochures, folders, catalogues, demo tapes, etc. This combination allows the creation of new forms of advertising. Examples include:

- enhanced and interactive ads: Interactive movie sequences (superstitials), product information by pushing a button (e-flyer), booking a test drive, making an appointment with a sales agent, follow-up, or direct transactions.
- Geo marketing: Every set-top box sold has a serial number, which is used to see where exactly (in which city) the box was sold. Using this information, ads are sent regionally, promoting a new store, sale, etc.
- Advertising in stages: Based on the serial number concept, advertising is sent very strategically. Customers who have ordered specific product information or interacted in advertising frequency can be provided with additional information the next time they use the service and will be shown a different spot the next time.

- Special target groups: Due to the existence of an increasing number of special-interest programs and channels, advertising is aimed more directly at its respective target groups.
- Situational addressing of the customer: Offering additional or related products or services when a service is used.
- Internet-like inventory: Home screens and programming guides feature banner-like spots.
- In-program sponsorships and interactive product placement: These elements counter the increased channel surfing, ad skipping and time shifting.
- Split screens with personalized ads.
- Theme ads within the EPG.
- Brand channel: also in combination with e-flyers.

A look at the examples just described reveals immediately that advertising as it works today will be completely overhauled. While in the past advertising has been used to "help the sellers sell," it is currently being revolutionized toward helping "the buyer to buy." Brand channels start playing an important role as well as new program formats such as advertainment—a mixture of advertising and entertainment.

Advertising on television starts to evolve with the change from analogue to digital television. Until this change takes place for the majority of television households, the only difference from today's advertising is that ads promote Internet pages with messages like: "For further information please visit our website www..."

After the transition from analogue to digital television, the platform for the development from broadcast to narrowcast will be created. idTV will then enable the direct link from traditional television advertisements to homepages and links. For example, distributors of special interest or brand channels such as hunting, fishing, golf, and cooking channels will be able to target their advertising in two different ways. First, the existence of these special-interest channels will allow direct contact to special interest groups. As a result, advertising can be very detailed and specialized due to the in-depth knowledge assumed about the people using that specific channel on a regular basis. Second, the information sent through the back channel enables the distributor and aggregator to track the customer's behaviour and interests, which then allows even more intense targeting to individuals. With this knowledge base, it finally becomes possible to combine traditional television with other links, for example, spots or brand channels will be offered on an e-flyer basis. This means that spots will only be shown or the user will only be led to the brand channel if the user clicks on the button for the flyer and therewith gives permission to be shown the "interactive" ad.

A vivid example is the concept of DaimlerChrysler that uses e-flyers to transform the customer from a low level customer to a high potential client. Through the flyer, the company provides customers with product catalogues and guides them to a brand channel that is broadcast on its own frequencies. This channel delivers background information on a specific car model or a movie with a car in action. These channels are pure advertising-oriented programs used to establish client contacts of all kinds.

END CUSTOMERS

All the new offerings and services enabled by digitalization will only be successful, if the end customer demands them and subscribes to them. Getting the customer into the boat is very difficult for a product new to the market, especially when its advantages and the added value are not seen immediately (like it is the case in Germany). When completely new products or services are introduced, understanding customer education and needs often reveals great potential for influencing their decisions.

In Germany, we have found strong evidence that most people only have marginal previous knowledge about digital television in general and interactive services in particular. A study conducted by Mediaedge CIA in Germany, for example, states that only 6 percent of all participants subscribe to digital free television or to Premiere. 77.2 percent state that they are not planning to get dTV or Premiere in the near future. Only 7.6 percent know and comprehend what video on demand (VOD) is and only 3.5 percent know about IdTV (Interactive digital television). This result shows that end customers do not understand what dTV and interactive services are and which advantages they offer. At the same time it explains why customers do not see the need to buy the new broadband offerings and they are not willing to pay the additional price for them.

Most Germans who already subscribe to Premiere or dTV or are planning to do so in the near future are mainly interested in specific interactive services such as VOD (61.6 percent) time-shifted television programs (50.5 percent) and different camera perspectives for sport coverage. Generally, whenever customer demand is evaluated by means of surveys, it is clear that the level of previous knowledge strongly influences the results, because customers can only demand products and services about which they have at least some knowledge. This "bias" effect may have influenced the result of other surveys that named for example video on demand and games as the most requested applications, partly due to their easy-to-understand and common names. As a result, other more sophisticated services might be more requested more often than they currently seem to be if they were better understood.

In consequence more customer education is needed to make dTV a successful product among the German population in the long run.

OUTLOOK FOR DIGITAL TELEVISION

Because Germany is under-developed when it comes to digital television and interactive services, there is a large market potential for dTV in Germany in the coming years. The targeted analogue signal cut-off in 2010 is an additional stimulus for the rapid and significant development of dTV services and infrastructure.

According to Datamonitor (2001), the German dTV market will gain 13.3 million digital subscribers in the period from 2000-2005, an increase of more than 550 percent. Cable and satellite are the primary distribution media for digital services; DTTV will start small but find its niche. Datamonitor believes that cable will dominate the digital market in the long term. The entering of new investors into the German cable market gives way to a prospering future with new, revised, and sustainable business models.

REFERENCES

Bear Stearns, January 30, 2002. *European Equity Research.*

BMWA, October, 2002. *Monitoring Informationswirtschaft Deutschland*

BMWi, 2000. *Digital Broadcasting in Germany—Launch Scenario*

Datamonitor, April, 2001. *Digital and interactive TV markets.*

Herbst, T. & G. Thomas, August, 2000. *Reinventing Cable TV.* Accenture publication.

HSBC, August 2001. *Cable TV in Germany.*

HSBC Trinkaus & Burkhardt, 2001. *The German Cable TV Market.*

Informa Media Group, 2002. *Global Digital TV*, 2nd Edition.

Jupiter, 2002. *European Digital Television: Rationalizing the Rollout of Interactive Services.*

Media Perspektiven, January 2002. Konturen des Digitalen Kabelmarkts

Merrill Lynch, 2002. *Media Handbook.*

Mohr, N., & G. Thomas, 2002. *Interactive Broadband Media,* 2nd Revised Edition. Frankfurt: Gabler.

Profound Market Briefing, 2002. *German Cable and Satellite TV Services Market.*

Siemers, J. Philipp., 2002. *Digitalisierung von Regulierung und Telekommunikation.*

VanDusseldorp and Associates, August 2002. *German iTV Overview.* Amsterdam.

WIK, August, 2002. *Förderung der Marktperspektiven und der Wettbewerbsentwicklung der Breitbandkommunikationsnetze in Deutschland*

Yankee Group, May, 2002. *ARPU comparison.*

Chapter 14
Italy: Slow Penetration, High Potential?

Francesca Gardini
Hernan Galperin
University of Southern California

This chapter analyses the development of digital television in Italy and examines how government policies, market forces, and demand factors are shaping the current restructuring of the Italian broadcasting industry. The Italian case is particularly well suited to discuss the opportunities and challenges that the transition to digital television presents to European market actors and policymakers in a context of rapid technological change and global industry consolidation. In particular, it clearly illustrates the changing location of the key industry bottlenecks in the digital television environment, and the new opportunities for strategic action by incumbent operators. As we shall see, the major commercial and regulatory battles associated with the development of digital television in Italy have been about control of soccer television rights and of technical standards for digital set-top boxes between vertically integrated operators. This case also constitutes a perfect scenario to study the evolution of the television industry in countries characterised by dual public—private broadcasting systems. Whether the transition to digital television will reshape the Italian broadcasting industry by reducing barriers to entry and democratising infrastructure access, or simply extend the existing duopoly structure into the digital era, largely depends on the outcome of the commercial and regulatory battles now unfolding.

The chapter is organised as follows. The first section provides a historical overview of the Italian television system: it examines the factors that led to a duopoly market structure in terrestrial television, the underdevelopment of cable networks, and a lack of a credible regulatory framework for local terrestrial broadcasting. The second section analyses the development of digital satellite television, focusing on the battle for the control of sports rights and set-top box standards between the two rival operators, and on the role played by European and national authorities in the regulation of this emerging market. The third section examines the transition to digital television in the terrestrial sector and the extent to which the introduction of digital services threatens the existing RAI-Mediaset duopoly. The conclusion discusses the lessons that the Italian case holds for the ongoing transition in other European nations and elsewhere.

THE FORMATION OF THE
ANALOGUE TELEVISION DUOPOLY

Television broadcasting began in Italy in 1954. As in most Western European countries, it was originally considered a public service that contributed to the nation's democratic and cultural life (Scannell, 1989). Concerns regarding the scarcity of the radio spectrum, the high costs of covering the entire national territory, and the socio-political functions associated with television led the Italian government to create a monopoly over broadcasting by establishing RAI, a corporation financed and controlled by the State.

Despite RAI's legal monopoly over broadcasting, the dramatic increase in the demand for television services during the 1960s and the beginning of the 1970s spurred the creation of numerous private broadcast stations. Although the government claimed that private broadcasting was illegal, in 1974 two Constitutional Court decisions established that cable networks and foreign-based channels did not infringe on RAI's terrestrial television monopoly. These provisions were included in the 1975 Broadcasting Act, which officially allowed cable and foreign-based channels to compete with the public service.

In 1976 the Constitutional Court took another step toward the liberalisation of the Italian television industry by legalising broadcasting at the local level, which resulted in the proliferation of local stations (Barca, 1999). However, the Court did not establish a clear definition of what constituted a local station. Moreover, the combination of a 'first come, first served' policy for allocating frequencies and the power restrictions that limited coverage to a small geographical area often made local broadcasting commercially unviable. As a result, many small television entrepreneurs actively bought and sold frequencies in order to achieve larger coverage, but only one of them became the real winner of this unregulated expansion of broadcasting services. This man was Silvio Berlusconi. By 1980, Berlusconi had consolidated his first quasi-national commercial network, Canale 5. To broadcast the signal to the entire nation and avoid infringing on RAI's national monopoly, each station was provided with a pre-recorded videocassette featuring programming that was aired almost simultaneously on his different local television stations around the country, giving the illusion of the existence of a national network (Poli, 2000). In 1983,

Berlusconi acquired control of a second network, Italia 1, and finally in 1984 he acquired a third, Retequattro (Grasso, 1992).

Although all private television stations were operating on a provisional legal basis, by the mid-1980s the Italian broadcasting industry had become a duopoly dominated by the three RAI and the three Berlusconi-controlled networks, now under the umbrella of Mediaset. This duopoly was legalised in 1990 by the so-called Mammi Law (Law 223/1990), which for the first time regulated private broadcasting. At the national level, the Law established that no single broadcaster could control more than three of the nine national channels licensed.[1] At the regional level, the Mammi Law failed to clarify the situation of local broadcasters, partly because of its omissions, and partly because the frequency allocation plan was never fully implemented due to the weakness of the responsible administrative body instituted by the Mammi Law, the Garante per la Radiodiffusione e Editoria (Barca, 1999). Some local television stations obtained temporary franchises, some never started broadcasting, and some never fully complied with the law. Aware of this chaotic situation, in 1997 the Parliament approved a new law (the so-called Maccanico Law - Law No. 249, July 1997), which set up a new regulatory agency (the Communication Authority), and established a deadline of January 1998 for the Authority to approve a new frequency allocation plan. The plan was issued on October 30, 1998, though it was not until July 2000 that the Authority approved the "Second Level Plan of Frequencies" for local broadcasters. Nonetheless, the lack of definition about coverage and the number of local stations within certain territories has left the local broadcasting issue so far unresolved.

Although RAI and Mediaset control more than 90 per cent of the Italian audience, a few commercial and legal attempts have been made to break their duopoly. In 1995, cinema producer and distributor Vittorio Cecchi Gori acquired two television networks, TMC 1 and TMC 2 (formerly Videomusic). His strategy to gather national audiences through the transmission of sport events eventually failed due to the lack of premium programming. A second attempt was made in 2000 with the acquisition of TMC 1 and TMC 2 by Seat-Pagine Gialle, a subsidiary of Telecom Italia (the former public telecom monopoly). The plan to launch a brand new television network called 'La Sette' (The Seventh) and become the third Italian broadcast operator was cut short as a result of the change in ownership of Olivetti, the majority-owner of Telecom Italia (acquired in July 2001 by the industrial groups Pirelli-Benetton). According to the Italian television ratings company, Auditel, La Sette's average market share is below three per cent.

---

[1] By implementing the Law, in 1992 the Italian government assigned three national licenses to RAI, three to Mediaset, one to Telemontecarlo (TMC), one to Videomusic, and one to Rete A (Berretta, 1997).

Regulatory action has also been ineffective to overcome the RAI-Mediaset duopoly. Although in 1994 the Constitutional Court declared Mediaset's dominance over commercial broadcasting illegal, a popular referendum held in 1995 validated it. The 1997 Maccanico Law also attempted to create more competition by entrusting the new Communication Authority with antitrust powers over media markets and establishing ownership caps. Each operator was allowed a maximum of 20 per cent of the total terrestrial frequencies assigned[2] and 30 per cent of the total resources in any given market.[3] However, the Maccanico Law did not result in any structural changes in the Italian television system. The Communication Authority did not require RAI or Mediaset to divest from any of their networks. The structure of RAI was left untouched, except for the commitment of RAI 3 to give up advertising revenues. Mediaset also kept its three networks, though it was required to broadcast one of them through digital satellite. However, this provision will only take effect once digital satellite reaches 50 per cent penetration, which is unlikely in the foreseeable future (it is currently at about 11.5 per cent, IDATE, 2001).[4]

Finally, pay-TV has represented only a small threat to the Italian duopoly so far, given its slow development. Several national networks and hundreds of local television stations offer Italian audiences a wide variety of free programming, thus reducing the incentives to pay a subscription fee for a service that has always been perceived as available gratis. Italian pay-TV started in the early 1990s when Mediaset launched Telepiù, a terrestrial pay-TV service that comprised three channels dedicated to film, sport, and culture (Poli, 2000). Since the company also controlled three free-to-air networks, regulators soon forced Mediaset to sell Telepiù, which was acquired by the German Kirch group (45 per cent) and the Swiss-South African group NetHold (45 per cent). Later, Telepiù was forced to relinquish part of its frequencies and broadcast two of its three channels over satellite, although the provision has not been fully implemented yet.[5] Telecom Italia also attempted to enter the pay-TV market

---

[2] Eleven national channels were allocated according to the National Frequency Plan approved by the Communication Authority in 1998. No national operator can thus own more than two terrestrial channels.

[3] 'Resources' comprehend all revenues from the financing of public service, advertising, telesales, sponsorships, revenues from agreements with public entities, and pay-TV subscriptions.

[4] At the end of 2002 the Constitutional Court ordered Mediaset to broadcast one of its channel though digital satellite by the end of 2003, regardless of satellite penetration. The enforcement of the sentence is in doubt, since the Parliament is discussing a new TV law (the so-called Gasparri law) that could change the antitrust limits set by the previous legislation.

[5] Although Tele+ broadcasts its three channel digitally via satellite, two of them can still be received as analogue terrestrial channels. In compliance with the Maccanico Law, which establishes that no single operator can hold more than one terrestrial license to broadcast encrypted programming, in 2001 the Communication Authority ruled that Tele+ must vacate frequencies by 2003, but only if digital satellite reaches 50 percent penetration (the same provision that applies to one of Berlusconi's channel).

with an ambitious and costly cable development project (the Socrate project). In 1993, it founded Stream, a company aimed at carrying programming produced by third parties via cable television (according to Italian law, telecom companies could not act as content providers). The roll out of the network, however, was extremely slow, and after the privatisation of Telecom Italia the project was suspended. To date, cable penetration in Italy remains minimal (about 0.3 per cent, IDATE, 2001), although demand for broadband Internet services has renewed interest in building a cable infrastructure.

NEW TELEVISION, NEW BOTTLENECKS: THE DEVELOPMENT OF DIGITAL TELEVISION

The advent of digital television in 1996 began a new phase in the Italian broadcasting industry, characterised by the arrival of the main European media conglomerates, the intense competition for premium content, and the adaptation of the regulatory framework to Community-wide rules. The first digital television service was introduced in 1996 by pay-TV operator Telepiù, which delivered a bouquet of channels through the Eutelsat/Hotbird II satellite. Two years later, rival pay-TV operator Stream followed suit with the launch of its digital service broadcast from the same satellite.

Regulatory activity has been particularly important in shaping the structure of ownership in the digital television market, as the introduction of the new services intensified two concerns among Italian policymakers. First, digital services could undermine the financial viability of established terrestrial broadcasters, which are viewed as playing an important socio-political role. Second, the market could end up 'colonised' by foreign players, thus foreclosing entry for the two Italian operators (RAI and Mediaset) in the new and more dynamic industry segment. The acquisition of Telepiù by French operator Canal Plus in 1997 and the attempts by the Australia-based News Corporation to take over Stream only fuelled these nationalist alarms.

In order to alleviate these concerns, Italian regulators left the door open for a partnership between RAI and Mediaset for the launch of digital television services, arguing that the high entry costs could only be afforded by a joint effort between the dominant local players. Nonetheless, the move was fiercely opposed by the European Commission.[6] As a result, the government shifted its

---

[6] "In larger Member States where pay-TV is less developed—notably Germany and Italy—a purely national approach to pay-TV is very unlikely to provide a firm basis for the development of DTV services until the effects of national oligopoly can be overcome. For instance, outside investors from other Member State—such as News Corporation Europe's efforts to enter pay-TV ventures in

strategy, using its powers to craft an agreement that balanced national and foreign ownership of the two existing pay-TV operators. In the case of Stream, which was 100 per cent-controlled by Telecom Italia, the Treasury Ministry employed its "golden shares" in the former telecom monopoly to influence strategic decisions about ownership changes. After months of negotiations, an agreement was reached in 1999 according to which Telecom Italia and Murdoch's News Corporation would each own 35 per cent of the shares. The remaining 30 per cent was divided between the Cecchi Gori Group (18 per cent), interested in exploiting its library of movie rights through pay television, and the Societa' Diritti Sportivi (SDS or Society of Sports Rights) composed of the Roma, Lazio, Fiorentina and Parma soccer clubs (12 per cent).[7] In the case of Telepiù, the government was able to negotiate the entrance of RAI in the French-controlled pay-TV operator. Though the stake was only 2 per cent, RAI kept the option of increasing it to 10 per cent in the future. The government welcomed this agreement as a way to boost national programming, given RAI's commitment to provide Telepiù with several themed channels.

The development of digital satellite services in Italy also set the stage for the regulatory debate regarding the rollout of digital terrestrial television (DTTV). Regulation had played an important role in the definition of the ownership structure in the new satellite services, and many Italian policymakers perceived the launch of terrestrial services as an opportunity to further reshape the competitive dynamics of the domestic television market. The new satellite services also provided the opportunity to understand how Italian audiences would behave in a multichannel environment. After decades of free television, information about demand preferences for content was considered critical to any plans for the launch of DTTV.

The Soccer Television Rights Battle

Like in most European countries, the development of digital television in Italy has dramatically intensified the battle for sports rights (in particular, soccer), given that the demand for such premium content is rather inelastic and a major subscription driver.[8] This has raised an important regulatory concern: how to

---

Germany and Italy—are one way to break the stalemate. The Commission will not permit the existing, highly regulated oligopolies that dominate national broadcasting to recombine in order to address pay-TV markets through a single platform since this would risk foreclosure" (EC, 1999, p. 14).

[7] In May 2000, the Cecchi Gori Group and SDS exited from Stream, which remained divided between Murdoch (50 percent) and Telecom Italia (50 percent).

[8] Soccer is the most popular sport in Italy and has a dominant presence on television. In 1998, it represented 61 percent of the total TV sports viewing, with 1,967 hours of coverage (more than 5 hours a day). Of the 20 most watched programmes in 1998, 18 were soccer matches. At the same

prevent the formation of dominant positions in the sale and acquisition of key television rights. Competition for soccer transmission was not an issue before 1993. Historically, the soccer league (Lega Calcio) sold the free-to-air television rights to the only possible buyer, RAI. The negotiation for the 1993-1996 seasons saw the entrance of a second player, Telepiù, at the time the only operator in the (analogue) pay-TV market. With no competition from Mediaset, free-to-air rights for the First and Second Division Championship (highlights, recordings and match summaries), as well as the rights for the live transmission of the fifteen Coppa Italia matches, were ceded to RAI for €69.7 million per year, while Telepiù was able to obtain the encrypted television rights of the live transmission of the First and Second Divisions' matches for €23.1 million per year (Poli, 2000). With the introduction of digital television in 1996 and the entrance of a new free-to air operator with the goal of breaking the duopoly RAI-Mediaset, the battle for the contracts for the next three seasons (1996-1999) became fierce. Telepiù was able to retain the pay-TV rights, but at a much higher price: €105 million per year (almost five times the amount paid in the earlier contract). With respect to free-to-air rights, two new players, Mediaset and the Cecchi Gori Group, entered the fray. Cecchi Gori made the highest bid but failed to present the guarantees requested by Lega Calcio, which then ceded the rights to RAI for €99 million per year (Poli, 2000).

Two events agitated the market when the television soccer contracts were up for renewal in 1999. The first was the change in the Lega Calcio selling procedures of sports rights. Following questions raised by Community regulators about the collective sale of rights by sports leagues (Temple Lang, 1998), the Italian soccer league allowed the individual teams to negotiate the rights for home matches directly with pay-TV operators. The second was the change in Stream's ownership structure, which strengthened the finances of the company and brought the exclusive rights of the four teams (Lazio, Roma, Fiorentina, and Parma) that shared in Stream's equity. Despite these changes, policymakers still feared that Telepiù could use its dominant position in the market to negotiate exclusivity deals with most of the soccer teams and leave Stream out of the game.[9] A combination of sector-specific legislation and competition policy instruments has been used to address this concern. First, legislation was passed in March 1999 establishing a 60 per cent cap in the amount of encrypted television rights to the First Division Championship

---

time, the sale of TV rights has replaced ticket sales as the main revenue source for soccer teams (Poli, 2000).

[9] At the beginning of 1999 Tele+ had an advantage over Stream both in terms of digital subscribers (520,000 vs. 120,000) and of soccer teams that had already signed exclusivity agreements with the company (7 vs. 2). See Esposito (1999).

controlled by any pay-TV company. Second, the Competition Authority began an investigation to ascertain possible anti-competitive behaviour in the pay-TV market. The investigation was started after Telepiù signed multi-year deals for the acquisition of encrypted rights for the First and Second Division Championships, and of numerous motion pictures produced by the Hollywood majors and the main local producers.

In mid-2000 the Competition Authority found that Telepiù company had committed an abuse of a dominant position under Article 82(b) of the EC Treaty, in that since May 1998 it had implemented a commercial policy for a period in excess of three years for the exclusive acquisition of the rights for the encrypted broadcasting of the most important Serie A and Serie B football championship matches. These rights related specifically to the broadcasting of the home matches played by the teams with the largest public following, such as Juventus, Milan, Inter, and Napoli (Competition Authority, 2000).

The ruling noted that Telepiù held a dominant position in the pay-TV market for various reasons: its large market share (82 per cent of total subscribers, but over 92 per cent of the turnover in 1999), its position as the sole competitor in the market for over six years (forcing television rights suppliers to deal with it), and its control of 60 per cent of the rights to the highest-grossing movies (in addition to its soccer rights). The agency also found that Telepiù had abused its dominant position by including several anticompetitive clauses in the contract for the cable distribution of soccer packages and programmes concluded with Stream in 1996 (which basically limited Stream to broadcast via cable only the soccer matches over which it had already acquired the broadcasting rights). The Competition Authority gave Telepiù six months to submit a report on the specific measures it would adopt to remedy these abuses.

The combination of sector-specific legislation aimed at creating competition in the acquisition of soccer rights and the intervention of the competition watchdog based on the application of general European competition law created the conditions for the growth of the second digital pay-TV operator, Stream. Between June and November 1999, Stream grew from 157,000 to 360,000 subscribers. In the following year the growth continued based primarily on three new programming categories: the 157 games of the Europe-wide Champions League soccer competition, the games of the popular Napoli soccer team, and the 2,400 hours of live and interactive transmission of the Italian version of "Big Brother," which is estimated to have brought at least 100,000 new subscribers.

Although the split of sports rights between two operators increased competition in the pay-TV market, it also created problems for consumers. Soccer fans could subscribe to the operator controlling the rights for the team of their liking. The subscription allowed them to watch all the team's home matches as well as those away matches the club played against teams that had also signed with the same operator. However, to watch the away matches played against teams that had signed with the rival operator, fans needed not just a second subscription but also a second home terminal, given that the two pay-TV operators deployed set-top boxes embedded with different security technologies (known as conditional access systems or CAS) and operating software. As discussed in the next section, this has prompted Italian regulators to intervene, although the room for regulatory manoeuvring was constrained by European legislation (EC Directive 95/47) regulating digital television standards and rapid technological change in the terminal equipment market.

The Set-Top Box Battle

The introduction of digital television dramatically raised the stakes associated with the digital television home terminal (Cave & Cowie, 1998). The main problem in the Italian context, as noted, has been the non-interoperability of the boxes deployed by the two satellite competitors that split the rights for the transmission of soccer games. The lack of Europe-wide standards for digital television home terminals is a result of the reluctance by European regulators to mandate common specifications, even though one of the main objectives of EC Directive 95/47 was to implement the principle that consumers need only one decoder to receive all the encrypted programming available on the market (Cawley, 1997; Levy, 1999). Italian policymakers found a legislative solution to this problem by forcing all digital television operators to make their boxes interoperable. This decision was the logical consequence of the adoption of a cap on the number of teams that each pay-TV company could sign. Consumers needed to be assured that with the same set-top-box they could receive all the matches of their favourite team, even if that meant subscribing to two different services. The same law that imposed the cap (Law 78/1999) also mandated the compatibility between CAS standards, and delegated to the Communication Authority the implementation of this provision within three months.

It was only after a year that the Communication Authority ruled that, in compliance with EC Directive 95/47, existing pay-TV operators could adopt either a multicrypt or a simulcrypt solution to the CAS interoperability mandate.[10] However, the lack of cooperation between Telepiù and Stream obstructed implementation. Telepiù used two different CAS: the SECA system (developed by Canal Plus) and the Irdeto system (used in the decoders deployed previous to the acquisition by Canal Plus). It transmitted its programmes in simulcrypt to allow both set-top box populations to receive the services. Stream

---

[10] The simulcrypt solution involves the simultaneous transmission of different encryption "keys" in the same broadcast signal, while the multicrypt solution involves a standard CAS interface for set-top boxes to which different decoding cards can be attached. See Cave (1997).

also used two CAS solutions, one provided by NDS (a News Corp. subsidiary) and the other by Irdeto. The July 2000 deadline established by the Communication Authority to make the two systems interoperable was ignored by the operators, which as a result received fines in September and October, and were ultimately summoned to reach an agreement or face suspension of their licenses. An agreement was finally reached and approved by the Commission in November 2000. According to the agreement, Telepiù and Stream would start simulcrypt broadcasting (i.e., using both the SECA and the NDS systems) in April 2001 (later postponed to August 2001), while the older Irdeto-based decoders would be replaced (Fontanarosa, 2000). However, the compatibility goal has not been fully realized. Although Telepiù and Stream did start symulcrypt transmissions, interoperability has been further complicated by the fact that the rival operators have deployed set-top boxes with incompatible APIs (Application-Program Interface).[11] As a result, despite the agreement on CAS, subscribers to one operator are still prevented from receiving the services of the other that depend on lower-level API functions such as pay-per-view (including soccer matches) and interactive television.

The Italian case shows the difficulties in balancing platform competition and consumer welfare in the regulation of standards for digital broadcasting. The attempts by the Italian Parliament to mandate decoder interoperability have faced the hostility of the commercial players. After two years, a final solution has still not yet been reached. Ironically, the ultimate effect of the government's efforts to sustain platform competition between the two digital satellite operators was to penalise pay-TV subscribers, at least in the short term. Both Italian and European regulators continue to believe that the market will eventually migrate to interoperable set-top box solutions such as the Multimedia Home Platform (MHP) being developed by the DVB group.[12] In the meantime, the two operators tried a different solution to this problem by announcing in April 2001 their intention to merge. While this solution would solve the interoperability problem in the short term, it posed obvious competition concerns, which were analysed in an investigation on the competitive effect of the merger conducted by the Competition Authority. According to the Authority, the monopolistic position of the merged company 'might significantly eliminate competition on a lasting basis, also in view of the considerable market entry barriers, that would damage consumers, by removing any incentives to improve the quality and the

---

[11] Essentially, the API is the operating system of the set-top box. Tele+ uses the MediaHighway API (developed by Canal Plus), while Stream uses an API developed by OpenTV.

[12] The DVB (Digital Video Broadcasting) group is a consortium formed by equipment manufacturers, broadcasters, content producers, software developers, and representatives of national regulatory bodies, which developed the European digital TV standards.

variety of the services and by doing away with price competition and other trading terms and conditions' (Competition Authority, 2001).

The merger would also create a monopsonist in the national market for the acquisition of premium sports broadcasting and film rights. In order to prevent an abuse of dominant position, the Competition Authority established that, should the two companies merge, the new operator could sign contracts with soccer teams for a maximum period of two years, and that soccer teams had the right to terminate contracts at the end of any season, if a new competitor entered the market. As a result of these restricting conditions, Telepiù initially pulled out of the deal, but in June 2002 Stream announced that despite the conditions it would acquire Telepiù for about €900 million.[13] The creation of a single operator in the Italian satellite television market, as was the case in the UK market a decade ago, will help realise the necessary economies of scale for the operation of satellite services, as well as alleviate the interoperability problems discussed. Yet, as the British example also shows, the creation of a dominant, vertically integrated pay-TV operator will require close regulatory scrutiny in the near future. In April 2003, the European Commission approved the merger between Stream and Telepiù. Interestingly, the merger conditions imposed by the Commission may also affect the introduction of digital terrestrial services in Italy. The new satellite monopolist Sky Italia has been banned from broadcasting digital terrestrial channels; therefore the new owners have agreed to dispose of Telepiù's national terrestrial frequencies. RAI has already expressed an interest in those frequencies to start DTTV transmissions, and other commercial operators could use them for the same purpose.

The development of digital satellite services in Italy offers some important lessons for emerging DTTV operators. Italian audiences seem to be willing to pay a subscription fee for a very narrow range of content, soccer being the most important. The commercial viability of the new digital terrestrial channels will therefore depend on the type and quality of content the operators will offer, and on the definition of a business model appropriate for that content. The pace of development of digital terrestrial television as a viable platform for free-to-air, as well as competitor in pay-TV, services is discussed in the next section.

---

[13] The new company, controlled by Rupert Murdoch (Telecom Italia retained 19.9 percent of equity control), will be renamed Sky Italia.

DIGITAL TERRESTRIAL TELEVISION:
A WAY TO OVERCOME THE ANALOGUE DUOPOLY?

Italian regulators have regarded the introduction of digital television as an opportunity to restructure the terrestrial sector and introduce competition in a market historically characterized by a duopoly between RAI and Mediaset. The first significant move in the launch of digital terrestrial services was the establishment of a DTT National Committee by the Communication Authority, which brought together broadcasters, network operators, industry players, universities and research and development institutes. The results of this committee were reported in the White Book on Terrestrial Digital Television published by the Authority in September 2000 and later submitted to the Parliament. After several unsuccessful attempts, in March 2001 the Italian Parliament laid down the basis for the transition to digital television for the terrestrial sector (Law 66/2001). The law establishes an experimental phase (until the end of 2002[14]), in which the holders of more than one television license (i.e., RAI, Mediaset, and TMC) can start digital broadcasting trials over their licensed areas. Given the high costs involved, operators are allowed to form consortia or alliances in order to achieve efficiencies in the management of tower sites and digital transmission equipment. Content providers are also allowed to participate in these consortia. To promote competition and entry of new operators, the plan establishes that license holders broadcasting in digital format must lease at least 40 per cent of their digital transmission capacity to third-party programmers on fair and non-discriminatory terms. In other words, dominant licensees would have to act as network operators and host independent broadcasters within the spectrum capacity they control. After the experimentation period, the temporary digital licenses will be converted into full licenses provided that the licensee has complied with the aforementioned obligations. It is expected that between four and five digital multiplexes will be created, one of which will be reserved to RAI. Interestingly, the law establishes that the licensing scheme will be based on the British model of legal separation between network operators and programmers. Network operators will manage the transmission network (the digital multiplexes) and lease space to programmers. According to the plan, this would reduce barriers to entry and increase the number of players in the terrestrial sector.

Due to the lack of available spectrum, the plan does not contemplate a simulcast period (a period in which the same programming is broadcast both in analogue and digital format). Rather, the turn-off of analogue transmissions is

---

[14] Although trials only started in the fall of 2003.

expected to take place on a market-by-market basis. The plan establishes a very short transition period: It calls for the complete switch-off of analogue transmissions by 2006. If this deadline were achieved, Italy would be the first country to complete the transition.[15] The key to this ambitious goal are the financial incentives provided by the State, which would amount to a decoder subsidy of about €76 per household (article 59, State Budget 2003). With 20.6 million households in Italy, the total cost of the subsidy would be about €1.5 billion. However, it seems unlikely that the transition could be implemented in such a short time frame, and the government has already announced that it is working on an alternative deadline because the original plan undervalued the costs and the resources needed for this complex task. Another question to be resolved is the identification of the frequencies to be used in the experimental phase. Although the 1998 Frequency Plan had reserved four channels for digital transmission (channel 9 in the VHF band, and channels 66, 67, and 68 in the UHF band), the uncertain situation of local broadcasting has tied up those frequencies. In order to alleviate this problem, legislators inserted a clause in Law 66 that facilitates the sale and acquisition of broadcasting stations when the purpose of the transaction is to promote the transition to digital television.

Many questions remain open about the plan for the launch of digital terrestrial services in Italy. On the supply side, the plan assigns a prominent role to existing analogue broadcasters, which will have few incentives to promote a transition that encourages new market entry and jeopardizes a comfortable duopoly structure. On the demand side, Italian consumers (90 percent of which still rely on analogue free-to-air television) will need to invest in new digital receiving equipment such as set-top boxes and integrated digital television sets. International experience shows that, where not heavily subsidised by service operators or the government, consumer equipment costs pose a major obstacle to the diffusion of digital terrestrial television (Galperin, 2002). The Italian government has been the first to announce an explicit subsidy to promote the take-up of digital set-top boxes by consumers. Yet, it is still unclear how the government will afford the projected subsidy, and whether equipment manufacturers will be able to produce decoders at or below the subsidy price. There is also the question of whether competition concerns will be raised by a plan that relies on public spending to stimulate the development of a particular delivery platform (terrestrial network) at the expense of alternative ones (cable and satellite).[16]

More importantly, it is also unclear whether there is enough political consensus to restructure the Italian broadcasting industry in any significant way.

---

[15] Although the U.S. is also scheduled to switch-off analogue television in 2006, it is clear that significant delays will occur (Galperin, 2002).

[16] Although the government announced a €75 subsidy for broadband Internet connections.

For decades the terrestrial sector has suffered from a lack of credible rules that promote competitive efficiency and pluralism. It took over 15 years for the government to approve a national plan for the allocation of analogue licenses that accommodates the demands of the different interest groups, and the resulting plan proved incomplete because it failed to define the legal status of many local stations. It is thus difficult to imagine that in a few years the recently created Communication Authority will be able to draft a plan for digital terrestrial television supported by the key stakeholders. The situation has been further complicated by the conflict of interests originating in the fact that Mr. Berlusconi's political party, Forza Italia, has become a dominant force in Italian politics, and Berlusconi was elected Prime Minister in May 2001. Therefore, while the plan outlined by the Communication Authority contains several provisions aimed at expanding pluralism and facilitating market entry in digital broadcasting (such as the separation between multiplex operators and programmers, and the requirement that 40 percent of the multiplex capacity be reserved for independent programmers), whether the deployment of digital services will overcome or ultimately reinforce the existing duopoly in the terrestrial sector remains to be seen.

CONCLUSION

The Italian case illustrates the new competitive dynamics and regulatory challenges associated with the transition to digital television in countries characterised by dual public-private broadcasting systems. Two issues have emerged as key determinants of the new television landscape: the control of premium sports rights (in this case, soccer) and the control of the digital television home terminal. Both Italian and Community regulators have attempted to shape the new industry structure by dictating the terms of competition among private and public broadcasters for these scarce resources, much like in the analogue world national authorities shaped the industry by dictating the terms of access to radio spectrum. In the case of programming rights, the decision to split the sale of soccer television rights among different operators in order to sustain competition between the two existing digital satellite platforms adversely affected viewers by forcing soccer fans to purchase two different set-top boxes and subscribe to two different services. To alleviate the situation, regulators required a certain degree of interoperability among the set-top boxes deployed by the satellite operators. This remedy proved inadequate given the rapid pace of innovation of digital television terminal technology and the lack of market incentives for operators to cooperate. This illustrates the delicate balance that exists between infrastructure competition and consumer welfare in information industries: Rules aimed at promoting platform competition have harmed consumers (at least in the short-term) by preventing attractive content bundling. The recent bankruptcy of the digital terrestrial operators in Spain (Quiero TV) and the UK (ITV Digital), largely due to overbidding for premium programming and generous decoder subsidies, is a reminder about the limited capacity of regulators to engineer the structure of the digital television market in a fiercely competitive environment.

It is interesting to note that in spite of active involvement by European regulators, Italian authorities have had significant autonomy to shape the evolution of the Italian television industry. This is well illustrated by the transposition of EC Directive 95/47 into national law. The single decoder solution mandated by Italian regulators contrasts with the implementation of the Directive in other member-states. In France, home terminal interoperability was left to voluntary agreements between market actors. In the UK, implementation has emphasized third-party access to the decoders controlled by the dominant operator (that is, BSkyB) rather than interoperability between rival operators. This different transposition of EC regulations begs the question of whether a more active Community involvement is needed to harmonise rules in a politically contested industry, over which member-states have typically resisted shifting much authority to European institutions.

The autonomy of Italian policymakers in shaping the evolution of the industry is also illustrated in the plan for the launch of digital terrestrial television services. While Community authorities have repeatedly acted against extension of market power by incumbent analogue operators into the digital television market,[17] the Italian transition plan as presented to date assigns a privileged role to RAI and Mediaset, the two companies that have dominated the Italian television landscape for decades. Community authorities may try to force changes to the plan, as was the case in the UK when the Independent Television Commission, under pressure from the EC Competition Directorate, forced BSkyB to exit the winning consortium in the race for the new digital terrestrial licenses. Yet, as discussed, multiple regulatory attempts to democratise infrastructure access and break the existing duopoly have been repeatedly bogged down by implementation delays and lax enforcement. This may change in the future as the rather young Communication Authority builds political resources and expertise in a country with little tradition of independent regulatory bodies. In many sectors once dominated by state monopolies—or in the case of Italian broadcasting, a public-private duopoly—formal delegation of regulatory authority is only the first step towards new rules of engagement

---

[17] Most notably in three cases involving Bertelsmann, Kirch, and Deutsche Telekom in the German pay-TV market (McCallum, 1999).

between government and market actors (Thatcher, 2001). However, the experience of other EU members shows that, notwithstanding Community action, the transition to digital television will only remove barriers to entry and enhance pluralism in the television sector if backed by a strong domestic coalition. It is yet to be seen whether such political coalition could be assembled in Italy. This is illustrated by the current debates over the new television legislation before the Italian Parliament. Looser antitrust limits have in fact been proposed to allow RAI and Mediaset to keep their three national television networks.

Finally, there is growing scepticism that the rollout of DTTV will proceed on schedule. In July 2002, government officials for the first time suggested that the projected switch-off of analogue services in 2006 may be too optimistic, in light of the considerable problems faced by DTTV operators in Spain and Britain. The president of the antitrust commission has called the 2006 target unrealistic, and the president of Fininvest (the holding company of Mediaset) has declared that the switch-off needs to be postponed for ten years. It seems difficult to believe that Italy will have a complete switch-off by 2006. As noticed, a political consensus that accommodates the demands of the different stakeholders is yet to emerge, DTTV trials have barely begun, digital receivers are not yet on the market, and consumers need to be persuaded to spend more money on television equipment and services: In short, too long of a list to be realized by 2006.

REFERENCES

Anania, F., 1995. 'Italian public television in the 1970s: A predictable confusion', *Historical Journal of Film, Radio and Television,* vol. 15, no. 3, pp. 401-406.

Barca, F., 1999. 'The local television broadcasting system in Italy: Too few resources for too many companies?', *Media, Culture & Society,* vol. 20, no.1, pp. 109-122.

Berretta, Giuliano, 1997. *Televisione dallo spazio. La TV via satellite e la rivoluzione digitale,* Milano, Il Sole 24 Ore.

Cave, M, 1997. Regulating digital television in a convergent world', *Telecommunication Policy,* vol.21, no.7, pp. 575-596.

Cave, M. & C. Cowie, 1998. 'Not only conditional access: Towards a better regulatory approach to digital TV', *Communication & Strategies,* vol. 30, pp. 77-101.

Cawley, R. A., 1997. 'European aspects of the regulation of pay television', *Telecommunication Policy,* vol. 21, no. 7, pp. 677-691.

Competition Authority, 2000. Press Release no. 21, Case Stream-Telepiù, Proceeding Reference no. A274, 21 June, www.agcm.it (accessed 10.10.03)

Competition Authority, 2001. Press Release no. 27, Case Group Canal Plus/Stream, Proceeding Reference no. C4754, 12 September, www.agcm.it (accessed 10.10.03)

Esposito, M., 1999. 'Calcio in TV, la rivolta dei club. No al decreto antitrust' 29 January, www.repubblica.it/online/televisioni/sat/esposito/esposito.html (accessed 25.04.02).

EC: European Commission, 1999. *The development of the market for digital television in the European Union,* Report in the context of the Directive 95/47/EC of the European Parliament and of the Council of the 24th October 1995 on the use of standards for the transmission of television signals, no. 540.

Fontanarosa, A, 2000. Accordo Stream-Telepiu: Arriva il decoder unico, 9 November, www.repubblica.it/online/economia/decoder/accord/accord.html (accessed 25.04.02).

Galperin, H., 2002. Can the US transition to digital TV be fixed? Some lessons from the European Union case, *Telecommunications Policy,* vol. 26, no. 1-2, pp. 3-15.

Grasso, Aldo, 1992. *Storia della televisione italiana,* Milano, Garzanti.

IDATE , 2001. Digiworld 2002, http://www.idate.fr (Accessed 03/01/2003)

Levy, David A., 1999. *Europe's Digital Revolution: Broadcasting Regulation, the EU, and the Nation State,* London, Routledge.

Mansell, R., 1999. New media competition and access, *New Media & Society,* vol. 1, no. 2, pp. 155-182.

McCallum, L., 1999. EC competition law and digital pay TV, *Competition Policy Newsletter,* vol. 1, pp. 4-16.

Poli, E., 2000. The revolution of televised soccer market, *Italian Journal of Modern Studies,* pp. 371-394.

Scannell, P., 1989. Public service broadcasting and modern public life, *Media, Culture & Society,* vol. 11, pp. 135-166.

Temple Lang, J., 1998. Media, multimedia, and European Community antitrust law, *Fordham International Law Journal,* vol. 21, no. 4, pp. 1296-1382.

Thatcher, M. (2001, August). Delegation, regulation and independent agencies in Western Europe. Paper Presented at the American Political Science Association, San Francisco, CA.

Chapter 15
Lessons and Conclusions

Allan Brown
Griffith Business School, Griffith University

Robert G. Picard
Jönkoping International Business School, Jönköping University

Digital technology for the production, transmission, and reception of television is clearly superior to analogue, and the eventual complete transition from analogue to digital throughout Europe, and indeed the world, seems inevitable. The main issues relating to digital television (DTV) do not concern whether to make the switch to digital, but when and how.

Digital simplifies, streamlines and reduces the costs involved with the production, editing, storage and transmission of television programmes and services. DTV transmissions generally provide improved picture and sound quality, and are much less susceptible to distortion and atmospheric interference. Because less power is required for digital transmissions, the energy consumption and broadcast cost for each television service is lower than for analogue. Digital is also more versatile. It facilitates 'enhanced' programming (multiple camera angles, additional information to complement programming, etc.) and interactive services. The development of digital compression techniques has reduced the amount of spectrum required for television transmission, and thus provides scope for a substantial increase in the number of television signals available to viewers. Digital terrestrial television (DTTV) creates the potential to reassign part of the spectrum released by the eventual termination of analogue transmissions to other communications uses, and provides the opportunity for national governments to generate revenue from the sale of part or all of this released spectrum capacity.

For European countries, the transition from analogue to digital needs to be seen within the context of the massive changes to which the television industry has been subjected since the mid-1970s. Most notable of these changes have been the introduction of multichannel television in the form of satellite and cable services, and the licensing of commercial, advertiser-supported terrestrial channels. These commercial services have provided strong competition to, and substantially reduced the audiences of, the incumbent public service broadcasters, many of which previously held monopoly positions in their national markets.

Another technical feature of DTV is that it allows choice of picture quality. In very general terms the choices vary from low strength signals which provide 'standard definition' (SDTV) pictures (about the same quality as current analogue PAL) to high strength signals providing 'high definition' (HDTV) images. Although the choice of digital signal strength is a decision for individual national governments and/or broadcasters, to date all DTV transmissions throughout Europe are in SDTV. Part of the reason for the uniform adoption of SDTV relates to the costly and unsuccessful attempt in the 1980s to develop a common European standard for analogue HDTV—the so-called 'MAC' initiative (see chap. 2). The European approach to digital picture quality contrasts with that of some other countries (for example, the United States, Japan, and Australia), which have provided for HDTV transmissions in their DTV systems. The significance of the SDTV/HDTV issue is that, because the transmission of HDTV requires much more spectrum than SDTV, a trade-off is involved for any DTV system between a greater number of SDTV channels and a smaller number of HDTV channels (currently 4 to 6 SDTV channels can be transmitted within the amount of spectrum required for one HDTV channel). This is of particular significance for DTTV where spectrum capacity, and therefore channel numbers, is much more restricted than for satellite and cable (Forrester, 2002).

Not surprisingly, a major difficulty in the transition to DTV across Europe has been the tension between the jurisdiction and powers of the European Commission (EC) and those of the national governments and regulatory authorities. The European regulation of DTV is examined briefly in chapter 1 and in detail in chapter 2. One of the main issues which emerges from these chapters concerns the unwillingness of the EC to impose uniform standards across the various DTV 'platforms' for digital transmission and reception equipment. This has resulted in the determination of different transmission standards for each of satellite (DVB-S), cable (DVB-C) and terrestrial (DVB-T), and the need for viewers to acquire separate set-top boxes (STBs) for each platform. This problem has been exacerbated by digital satellite operators employing proprietary and non-interoperable standards in order to 'lock in' their existing subscribers, rather than allow the market to be opened to new competitors by means of uniform standards. It was also noted in chapter 14, citing the experiences of France and the United Kingdom (UK), that national regulators have been inconsistent in their implementation of Commission directives regarding digital STBs. The lack of uniform standards has been at least partly responsible for confusion and uncertainty in the minds of viewers throughout Europe and has significantly impeded the development and take-up of DTV services. As quoted in chapter 1: "Standardization, compatibility, interoperability and application portability are essential pillars in the erection of a successful and competitive European digital television system" (Nolan, 1997: 610).

SATELLITE AND CABLE

In Europe, as elsewhere, satellite and cable television platforms have generally been converted to digital before terrestrial. One reason for this is that the broadcasting standards for DTTV were defined later than those for satellite and cable. The world's first DTV broadcasts commenced in the United States (US) in 1994 with the launch by DirecTV of its pay-TV satellite service. DTV was introduced in Europe in 1996 when three pay-TV operators launched digital satellite services—Canal Plus in France, Telepiù in Italy and the Kirch group in Germany. By 2002 all European satellite operators were providing services in digital and most cable networks in European Union (EU) countries had been partly or entirely upgraded to carry digital.

The UK was the first European country to introduce digital terrestrial transmissions. DTTV commenced there in November 1998 (the same month as in the US). Then followed Sweden in April 1999, Spain in May 2000, Finland in August 2001 and Germany in November 2002. Italy plans to commence DTTV transmissions in 2003, France and Denmark in 2004, and several other European countries by 2010.

Digital subscriber line (DSL) has been developed to distribute broadband communications over the telecommunications copper wire network. To date, its use has been mainly confined to high speed Internet access. Research is underway to develop technical solutions to facilitate the transmission of DTV over DSL. However, this work is still in its infancy, and the eventual technical and economic viability of DSL for television transmission remains uncertain (see chaps. 8, 12 and 13).

The proportion of European viewers receiving digital signals varies substantially across platforms and among countries. Although the main platform for analogue television has historically been terrestrial, the transition to digital has so far been driven by satellite and, to a lesser extent, cable. As indicated in chapter 1, the take-up of DTV in EU countries as a whole at the end of 2002 was:

- satellite, 13.9 percent of total television households;
- cable, 5.2 percent; and
- terrestrial, 1.7 percent.

Significantly, at the end of 2002 the proportion of television households in EU countries receiving *digital or analogue* television by satellite was 21.7 percent, and by cable 31.7 percent (CEC, 2002). This means that approximately 64 percent of European satellite subscribers had digital STBs, but only around 16 percent of cable subscribers. With the introduction of digital, some satellite broadcasters and most cable operators started to 'simulcast' in both analogue and digital. However, a much higher proportion of satellite households have migrated to digital than cable households. One reason for this is that most satellite households were subscribing to multichannel analogue pay-TV services, and migrated to digital via proprietary STBs subsidised by satellite operators (in many cases given to them free of charge). However, a much higher proportion of cable households subscribe to basic ('free-to-air') services only. Many of these cable households are not willing to pay a higher subscription fee for premium pay channels. In turn, cable operators consider it economically viable to provide digital STBs to high revenue premium subscribers, but not to low revenue basic subscribers who continue to receive their cable service by analogue (chap. 4).[1]

Another reason for the higher digital take-up by satellite is that digital conversion by satellite is a much speedier and less costly process than for cable. As soon as transponders are converted, digital signals can be immediately transmitted over the entire area of a satellite's 'footprint.' In contrast, the digital upgrade of cable networks tends to be carried out incrementally, with the sparsely populated and economically marginal areas converted only after the densely populated, more profitable areas. The slow pace of cable upgrade has been noted in Denmark (chap. 11), France (chap. 12) and Germany (chap.13).

The highest digital take-up rate across all platforms is in the UK with 41.4 percent of television households receiving digital signals at the end of 2002— 28.0 percent by satellite, 8.1 percent cable and 5.3 percent DTTV. This can be largely explained by the history of television broadcasting in the UK where the availability to viewers of only a small number of analogue free-to-air (FTA) terrestrial channels eventually led to a strong take-up of BSkyB's (analogue) multichannel satellite pay-TV service which commenced operations in 1989. Most Sky viewers migrated to digital when the service converted to digital in 1998 (chap. 7). A similar history of restricted analogue offerings contributing to

---

[1] In Germany, with a particularly high proportion of basic cable subscribers, at the end of 2002 only 7.9 percent of cable households received digital signals (chap. 13).

relatively high take-up of digital satellite services is evident in Spain (chap. 8), Sweden (chap. 9) and Denmark (chap. 11).

DTTV

Whereas arrangements for the commencement of digital transmissions by satellite and cable services are mainly determined by commercial operators, the transition to digital for terrestrial broadcasting primarily involves government decision making, and raises a wider range of issues and options. With DTTV national governments need to determine, among other things, the timing of the commencement of digital transmissions, the means to ensure that viewers can receive terrestrial FTA programming with their existing analogue receivers, the digital role for public service broadcasters (PSBers), the licensing of new commercial digital services, provision for digital interactive television (iTV) services, and arrangements for the eventual 'switch off' of the analogue transmission system. In general, commercial forces drive satellite and cable DTV, while DTTV is driven by the policies of national governments.

It should be noted here that one option for governments is to decide not to introduce DTTV at all, but to migrate all television transmissions within their national territories to satellite and cable platforms. This option has spectrum efficiency advantages, and was (unsuccessfully) advocated in Sweden by interests opposed to the introduction of DTTV in that country (chap. 9). To date, however, no country in Europe or elsewhere has indicated serious interest in abandoning terrestrial broadcasting.

The country case studies in Part II of the book explain how national governments in Europe have advanced various rationale for their decisions to introduce DTTV. Reasons common to most governments have been: to allow their populations to participate in the 'Information Society;' to expand opportunities for domestic manufacturing and programme production industries; to provide for a greater number of terrestrial television channels; and to bring about the eventual switch-off of analogue transmission networks to release spectrum for alternative uses. Another major motivation for introducing DTTV has been to facilitate increased competition, both by the terrestrial platform vis-à-vis satellite and cable, and among terrestrial broadcasters themselves (but see below). In Sweden (chap. 9) and Finland (chap. 10) the governments saw DTTV as a means to help prevent further loss of market share by terrestrial broadcasters to satellite operators (which are mainly foreign owned and transmit mainly foreign programming). The potential to generate increased competition in the respective national television broadcasting markets was cited as important in the decisions to adopt DTTV in each of Spain (chap. 8), France (chap. 12) and Italy (chap. 14). Other reasons for DTTV adoption have included the enhancement of cultural sovereignty by strengthening programming regulation (in Sweden), and the promotion of regional and special interest programming (in Germany).

With the introduction of DTTV most European countries have made additional spectrum available to existing terrestrial broadcasters and have required them to simulcast their programming in both analogue and digital during an interim period until analogue switch-off. Due to spectrum shortage, however, the simulcast model has not been adopted in Germany and Italy, where the transition to digital is being planned on a region-by-region basis with the analogue network to be shut down progressively as each region is converted.

Traditionally, with terrestrial analogue, governments have issued television licences on a channel-by-channel basis. With digital, however, it is possible for governments to issue licences for *multiplexes* consisting of a number of channels. In practice, both methods have so far been adopted in European countries: On a channel-by-channel basis in Sweden and Finland; in the UK licences have been granted for multiplexes; and in Spain both schemes have been implemented—one multiplex licence plus a number of licences for individual channels.

Consumer Take-Up

As just mentioned, DTTV penetration in the UK at the end of 2002 was 5.3 percent of total television households. Although a very modest level, this represented the highest take-up rate for DTTV in Europe (and indeed the world). The corresponding take-up rates for the other European countries to have commenced DTTV transmissions are 3.5 percent in Sweden, 1.5 percent in Spain, 1.4 percent in Finland and 0.6 percent in Germany (Berlin only). The reasons for these very low levels of DTTV take-up by European households are examined in chapter 6 and include:

- limited consumer knowledge of DTTV;
- 'technology fatigue' by consumers;
- high costs of DTTV reception equipment;
- consumer and industry uncertainty due to incompatible DTV technical standards;
- widespread consumer uncertainty and scepticism resulting from the failure of DTTV performance to live up to expectations and predictions; and
- restrictions on the development of DTTV services due to its uncertain business potential, high financial risks and limitations on capital availability.

A further reason for the poor take-up is the perception by consumers that DTTV provides few benefits by way of additional services. It is pointed out in chapter 6 that a major factor affecting the demand for new television services is the diminishing marginal utility of additional channels, that is, each additional channel or programming choice is less valuable to viewers than the last. DTTV is thus likely to have limited appeal to a viewer who has chosen not to subscribe to multichannel satellite and cable services, and is satisfied with the current range programming available on analogue terrestrial channels (the so-called 'Aunt Emily'). Only about half of European viewers subscribe to satellite and cable services, and only about one-quarter to premium services.

Digital interactive content, applications and services are examined in detail in chapter 5, and briefly in chapters 2 and 6. It is explained in chapter 6 that, similar to digital television in general, there has been to date a slow development and poor consumer acceptance of digital interactive services in Europe. Reasons for this include concerns about the ability and willingness of consumers to accept these new services (the 'chicken and egg' problem), and difficulties in integrating interactive advertising and sales processes. Chapter 5 agrees that interactive television has been subject to several false starts over the past few decades, but points out that many analysts and observers now expect that interactive digital television will experience a breakthrough in the near future.

Pay-TV or Free-to-Air?

For viewers who value multiple channels, both satellite and cable will retain a substantial advantage over terrestrial for the foreseeable future in terms of channel numbers. Moreover, because multichannel television was available on satellite and cable before terrestrial, they have a significant 'first mover advantage' over terrestrial. This has enabled them to gain long-term access to strategic programming, especially movies and sports, that is key to acquiring and maintaining pay-TV subscriptions. Most viewers are likely to be more interested in the programming they can receive than in the form of transmission. Thus the difficulty for commercial terrestrial pay-TV broadcasters is to convince viewers to pay for programming on DTTV, but not the greater variety and possibly more popular offerings available on satellite and cable (Humphries & Lang, 1998).

This raises the issue of the suitability of DTTV for pay-TV services. The most notable occurences in the short history to date of DTTV have been the collapses, both in April 2002, of ITV Digital in the UK (chap. 7) and Quiero TV in Spain (chap. 8). There were certain financial and marketing circumstances relating specifically to each of these corporate failures. What they had in common, however, was that they were both DTTV pay-TV operations, and were unable to overcome the incumbency advantages of their established satellite and cable rivals, and attract sufficient subscribers to become economically viable services. In Finland, all five of the licensed DTTV pay-TV channels experienced serious problems during the first year of digital terrestrial transmissions, and three of them had their licences withdrawn by the government (chap. 10). Furthermore, in Sweden a contributing factor to the low consumer take-up of DTTV was the requirement (until it was lifted in January 2003) that viewers pay a subscription fee for DTTV even if they wanted to receive only 'free-to-air' channels (chap. 9).

DTTV was relaunched in the UK in October 2002 as an all-FTA service, appropriately named 'Freeview'. At the end of 2002 it seemed likely that Spain would follow suit. And in France it is government policy to favour FTA over pay in the licensing of new DTTV channels (chap. 12). There are thus strong indications that, following the disasterous experiences of the UK and Spain, Europe is witnessing a swing away from pay-TV toward a primarily free-to-air model for DTTV.

DTTV BROADCASTERS

Public Service Broadcasters

European PSBers have traditionally broadcast terrestrially and FTA. Therefore, as explained in chapter 3, "As technology, the choice of [DTTV] represents for European PSBers the continuation of FTA broadcast television. In this sense, DTTV is a logical and the most natural choice for PSBers when switching from analogue to digital technology." In European countries PSBers have generally been strong supporters of DTTV. They have had two related motives for this: to expand the size and scope of their operations by providing additional programming channels; and to maintain and increase their share of the television audience which has been eroded by the advent of commercial FTA and pay-TV satellite and cable services.

The extent of participation by PSBers in DTTV is constrained by the amount of funding available to them. This perennial problem for public service broadcasting (PSB) has been exacerbated since the 1980s by the combined effect of the loss of audience share to commercial television, and the provision on commercial satellite and cable channels of many of the types of 'public interest' or 'merit' programming—news, current affairs, documentaries, children's, arts, and culture—traditionally the preserve of PSBers. After experiencing great difficulty over the past two decades in trying to convince governments to maintain their funding levels, PSBers are now seeking yet further resources to finance new DTTV channels.

This raises the issues of the amount of funding required by PSBers to set up and operate new channels, and the 'quality' of PSB programming with the transition to digital. Chapter 3 points out that in Finland (a small EU country) "digitisation means pressure towards more cost effectiveness and continued reduction in average funding per programme hour", and questions whether the response of PSBers to digital will be the same as that with the advent of multichannel television, namely, reduced domestic production and increased importation of foreign (U.S.) programming. It also notes that in the UK (a large EU country) the strategy of the BBC has been to avoid low-budget production for its digital channels, but this approach has come at the cost of restricted broadcasting hours (6 to 8 hours a day) and repeat scheduling of programmes (within individual channels as well as between channels).

It is further noted in chapter 3 that, to date, the dominant DTTV model adopted by European PSBers has been to maintain their existing, broad mixed-genre channels, and to complement them with new specialist channels. The new channels represent core areas of PSB programming such as news, education, science, arts and culture, and/or are targeted to special audiences, such as youth and children. In deciding on the types of new digital channels, PSBers are constrained by their public service mandates. The difficulty they face in trying to maintain and increase their audience shares with new digital channels is that specialist PSB programming may not appeal to large audiences, and at least part of the audience they do attract will be 'cannibalised' from their generalist channels. With limited new funding and the licensing of additional commercial channels in competition for audiences, there is no guarantee with the continued development of DTTV that PSBers will be able to prevent further declines to their audience share.

Commercial Broadcasters

Whereas European PSBers have been strong supporters of DTTV, incumbent commercial terrestrial broadcasters have generally been reluctant adopters of digital. Opposition to the introduction of DTTV by commercial broadcasters has been particularly hostile in Sweden (chap. 9). In the conversion to digital both public service and commercial terrestrial broadcasters are required to meet the cost of new production and transmission equipment and, in most countries, the expense of simulcasting in both analogue and digital until analogue switch-off. The major financial concern for commercial broadcasters, however, relates to *audience fragmentation*. It was explained in chapter 4 that, with an increase in the number of competitors brought about by the licensing of new digital channels, the average size of audiences for individual programmes is likely to decline. Advertising revenue per programme hour will tend to fall, while per hour cost of programming to channels will tend to remain constant, thus squeezing the profitability of commercial broadcasters.

The extent of this threat to incumbent terrestrial commercial operators largely depends on the decisions of national governments, in particular, the number of new commercial DTTV channels they decide to license, and to whom they license them. The granting of new DTTV licences to existing commercial broadcasters will enable them to operate differentiated channels and aggregate audiences across those channels, thus mitigating the potential financial harm of digital transition. Alternatively, the licensing of channels to new broadcasters will introduce new rivals, increase competition for revenues, and pose a greater financial threat to existing broadcasters.

To date, DTTV policies and licensing decisions of European national governments have generally favoured incumbent commercial terrestrial broadcasters. New DTTV licences have been granted to existing terrestrial broadcasters in the UK, Sweden, Finland, and France. In Spain, each of the three commercial terrestrial broadcasters were given a digital licence to enable them to simulcast their channels, although the main shareholder in the multichannel DTTV operation was the owner of a major cable network.[2] In Italy the incumbent terrestrial broadcasters seem likely to be assigned a "prominent role" in DTTV (chap. 14).

A parallel development has been the granting of licences for the terrestrial distribution of existing commercial satellite and cable services. Among the Freeview DTTV offerings in the UK are a number of satellite channels, including those of BSkyB (chap. 7). In the third round of allocations in Sweden in 2001 most of the DTTV licences went to (non-Swedish) companies for channels already available on satellite and cable (chap. 9). In Finland, all three licences issued in 2003 to replace those previously cancelled were granted to Canal Plus, again for channels already available on satellite (chap. 10). Similarly, in France the majority of DTTV licences granted were for channels already offered on either satellite or cable (chap. 12).

The implication of this pattern of licensing decisions in the early years of DTTV is that, while in theory DTTV has the potential to enhance diversity of broadcasting ownership throughout Europe, in practice it is mainly consolidating the position of existing commercial operators—terrestrial, satellite and cable. The main reason for governments and regulatory authorities granting new DTTV licences to existing broadcasters is the high cost of providing television

---

[2] As we have seen, the multichannel DTTV licensees in both the UK and Spain became insolvent in April 2002.

programming and the uncertainty surrounding the financial viability of new commercial outlets in an already highly competitive multichannel environment. As explained in the discussion of the licensing decisions in France, the advantage of existing satellite and cable channels as candidates for new terrestrial licences is that their marginal cost of operating on DTTV is very low.

The transmission of individual channels on more than one platform has been common practice in Europe since the introduction of cable television. Cable networks redistribute the signals of satellite channels and in many countries, under the 'must carry' rules, carry the signals of terrestrial channels. The granting of new DTTV licences for the terrestrial transmission of satellite and cable channels increases the ability of broadcasters to have their programmes distributed over multiple platforms and is leading towards an 'all platforms' approach to digital television. Nor is this phenomenon confined to commercial broadcasters. Chapter 3 considers the 'all platforms' approach within the context of the traditional universal service obligation for public service broadcasters, and suggests that for some countries it may be more economical to provide universal coverage of PSB channels by multiple platforms rather than by the terrestrial network alone. Since the introduction of DTTV in Sweden in 1999, the public service television broadcaster, SVT, has transmitted all of its channels by satellite and cable as well as terrestrially (chap. 9). It is also noted that in Denmark PSB channels are now available in satellite packages, without 'must carry' regulations (chap. 11).

ANALOGUE SWITCH-OFF

As already mentioned, the simulcasting policy for the introduction of DTTV provides for the transmission by terrestrial broadcasters of their programming in both analogue and digital during an *interim period* until the analogue terrestrial network is switched off. The key issue is what is the optimum duration of the interim period? The difficulty for national governments is that it is not politically feasible to switch off analogue transmissions unless and until a substantial proportion of viewers has digital receivers.[3] (The problem is further compounded by the issue of many households having second and third television sets, each requiring its own STB to achieve a complete transition to digital.)

It was stated earlier that by 2002 the level of digital take-up in EU countries was only 20.8 percent of total television households across all three platforms.

---

[3] In the US, Congress has directed that analogue switch-off not take place until at least 85 percent of households have access to digital television signals (Pepper & Levy, 1999). To date no European government has stipulated a minimum required take-up rate for DTV.

The take-up of DTTV has been particularly poor and below official predictions in each country where DTTV transmissions have commenced. National governments have nominated 'target' dates for analogue switch-off, ranging from 2006 (Finland and Italy) to 2012 (Spain). However, in the country chapters of this book it is noted in practically all cases that the target date is unlikely to be met and analogue switch-off will have to be deferred.[4]

European national governments do not appear greatly concerned about the prospect of delayed analogue switch-off, partly perhaps because the current demand for spectrum which would be released by the conversion to digital is not as strong as previously estimated (chap. 2). Nevertheless, switch-off should take place sooner rather than later. Simulcasting imposes costs in the form of additional transmission expenses for broadcasters to transmit in both analogue and digital, as well as the loss of revenue (opportunity cost) which national governments could earn from the alternative use of the analogue spectrum (albeit less than originally anticipated).

Although there have been DTTV transmissions in Europe for only a few years, from the pitifully low levels of consumer take-up to date, the market-based introduction of DTTV appears to be failing. There is a growing belief that market forces alone may not bring about sufficient consumer take-up of DTTV to allow the analogue networks to be closed down. The longer analogue switch-off is delayed, the greater will be the consequent private and social costs.

The potential exists for analogue switch-off to be deferred for several decades. Television sets are replaced about every eight years, their average life span. However, the significant proportion of viewers currently satisfied with the programming available on analogue FTA channels may replace the old set with a new analogue set, especially if it is cheaper than the 'equivalent' digital receiver. Such (rational) consumer behaviour will prolong the demand for analogue transmissions.

Without government intervention some technical innovations take a long time to be adopted by consumers, especially when the innovation is 'backward compatible' (old 'hardware' can continue to be used with new improved 'software'). Significantly, with the introduction of colour television transmissions, it took around 20 years for all European households to acquire a colour set. Without government intervention analogue switch-off could take at least that long (BIPE Consulting, 2002).

There are two main policies that European national governments are considering to facilitate and hasten analogue switch-off. The first is to make it

---

[4] The sole exception is Germany where, with a region-by-region system of analogue replacement rather than the simulcast model, the target date for analogue switch-off (2010) expected to be met (chap. 13).

mandatory for manufacturers to install digital tuners in all television sets. This approach has been adopted by the Federal Communications Commission in the US. The second, more radical, form of intervention would be for governments to subsidise consumers in their purchase of digital reception equipment. The Italian government has announced a subsidy of around €75 per household for the purchase of a DTTV set-top box. However, at an estimated total cost of €1.5 billion, this policy proposal may be modified (chap. 14). There are also concerns that governments may be in breach of European Commission competition regulations if they use public monies to favour the development of one delivery platform (terrestrial) to the detriment of others (satellite and cable). The Swedish public broadcaster has advanced a subsidy scheme which sems to avoid this potential problem. Consistent with its 'all platforms' approach to DTV, the SVT proposes that all households that have paid their television licence fee be given a voucher equal in value to the price of a basic STB, which could be used as payment for a digital box, regardless of it being terrestrial, satellite or cable (chap. 9).

In Europe, as elsewhere, the transition from analogue to digital broadcasting provides a challenge for all players involved. National governments are primarily responsible for decisions regarding the television transmission system, and changes to current policies may be required to achieve analogue switch-off within a reasonable period. With digital, viewers can receive improved reception as well as an increased number of programme channels, features and services, but most are not yet convinced that the benefits of digital exceed its costs. While public service broadcasters are relying on DTV to maintain their audience share, their capacity to develop new digital offerings appealing to audiences is largely dependent on the amount of additional funding available to them. Commercial broadcasters are most at risk from the introduction of digital, especially incumbents who face fragmentation of their audiences and reduced profits. The transition to digital brings more efficient transmission, enhanced reception, new services, and greater competition, but increased uncertainty to the television broadcasting industry.

REFERENCES

BIPE Consulting, 2002. *Digital Switchover in Broadcasting: Final Report,*http:// europa.eu.int/information_society/topics/telecoms/regulatory/studies/documents/ final_report_120402.pdf (accessed 24.07.02).

CEC (Commission of the European Communities), 2002. Eighth report on the implementation of the telecommunications regulatory package, COM(2002) 695

final, Brussels, December, http://europa.eu.int/information_society/topics/
telecoms/implementation/annual_report/8threport/finalreport/annex2.pdf
(accessed 30.09.03).

Forrester, Chris, 2002. "New thinking" on HDTV?, *Digital News*, no. 27,
October, 4.

Humphreys, Peter & Matthias Lang, 1998. Digital television between the
economy and pluralism, pp. 9-35 in Jeanette Steemers (Ed.), *Changing
Channels: The Prospects for Television in a Digital World*, Luton University
Press.

Nolan, Dermot, 1997. Bottlenecks in pay TV: Impact on market development in
Europe, *Telecommunications Policy*, vol. 21, no. 7, 597-610.

Pepper, Robert & Jonathan Levy, 1999. Convergence: public benefits and policy
challengers, pp. 21-36 in Christopher T. Marsden & Stefaan G. Verhults (Eds.),
Convergence in European Digital TV Regulation, Blackstone.

Subject Index

Contributors

MONICA ARIÑO is a doctoral candidate in Law at the European University Institute (EUI), in Florence. She holds a degree in Law from the Autónoma University of Madrid and has specialised in media and communications. Her research focuses on the interplay between competition and sector specific regulation in multimedia markets, particularly on access issues in digital broadcasting. She has been a visiting scholar at Columbia University School of Law in New York. Prior to starting her doctoral programme she worked at the Foundation of Regulatory Studies (Madrid), The European Commission Directorate General Information Society, and Steptoe & Johnson, LLP (Washington, D.C.). She is the author of several articles on audiovisual industry regulation.

ANGEL ARRESE is associate dean at the School of Communication at University of Navarra, Spain. He is an assistant professor of marketing and has been director of the Media Management Department. His main research interests are media marketing management and the economic and financial media markets. He is the author of two books and many articles on related topics.

ALAN BROWN is an associate professor in economics in the Griffith School of Business, Griffith University, Australia. His main research interests are economic and policy issues relating to broadcasting, telecommunications and the print media. Brown is the author of *Commercial Media in Australia: Economics, Ownership, Technology and Regulation* and he has authored several articles in international professional journals, including *Telecommunications Policy*, *Prometheus*, *The Journal of Media Economics* and *The International Journal on Media Management*. He has also acted as consultant to a range of private and public organisations and presented expert evidence to a number of inquiries into the Australian media. For 2002 he was Visiting Research Fellow with the Media Group at the Turku School of Economics and Business Administration, Finland.

MARC BORREAU is an assistant professor at Ecole Nationale Supérieure des Télécommunications (ENST, Paris) and a member of the laboratory of industrial economics (LEI) of the Center for Research in Economics and Statistics (CREST). His main research interests are economic and policy issues relating to broadcasting, telecommunications and the Internet. From 1997 to 2000, he served as regulatory economist in the Directorate for Public Affairs of France Telecom. He received degrees in engineering science, industrial organization, and economics.

HERMAN GALPERIN is an assistant professor at the Annenberg School for Communication, University of Southern California. He holds a B.A. in Social Sciences from the University of Buenos Aires, Argentina, and a Ph.D. from Stanford University. Galperin's research and teaching interests include international communications policy, global trade in audiovisual services, and regulatory reform in Latin America. His research has been published in article collections and journals such as the *Federal Communications Law Journal*, *Telecommunications Policy*, the *Journal of Communication*, the *Canadian Journal of Communication, and Media, Culture, & Society*.

FRANCESCA GARDINI is a Ph.D Candidate at the Annenberg School for Communication, University of Southern California. She holds a M.A. in Communication Management from the Annenberg School of Communication, USC, and a B.A. in Business Administration and Economics from Bocconi University in Milan, Italy. Gardini's research and teaching interests include strategic alliances and networks in the film and television industries, organizational structure of media and entertainment firms, organizational practices and processes in creative industries, and global trade in audiovisual services.

PETER GOODWIN is senior lecturer at the Centre for Communication and Information Studies, University of Westminster, United Kingdom. His research focuses on political economy of the media, media policy, media and politics, and the social and economic impact of media technologies. He is the author numerous journal articles and *Television Under the Tories: Broadcasting Policy 1979-1997*.

MÓNICA HERRERO is associate professor in media management and assistant director of students affairs at the School of Communication, University of Navarra, Spain. She holds a master's degree in media management from the University of Stirling (Scotland). Her research focuses on television economics, especially the implications of direct viewer payments to the economics of the television industry. Her doctoral dissertation analysed the pay television channel as a transition model towards the new television products and the new relationships in the digital era.

TAISTO HUJANEN is professor of electronic media and communications in the Department of Journalism and Mass Communication, University of Tampere Finland. He is co-ordinator of the joint Nordic network for PhD studies in Public

Service and electronic media. He is the author of *The Power of Schedule: Programme Management in the Transformation of Finnish Public Service Television* and co-editor of *Broadcasting & Convergence: New Articulations of the Public Service Remit*. His research interests include public service broadcasting, digitalisation of broadcasting and the history of broadcast journalism.

JENS F. JENSEN is professor in Interactive Multimedia and director of the research centre InDiMedia (Centre for Interactive, Digital Media) at VR Media Lab and the Department of Communication, Aalborg University, Denmark. His current research interests include interactive television, Internet and WWW, interaction and interactivity, the aesthetics of multimedia, and inhabited 3D virtual worlds. He is the editor of several anthologies, including *The Computer as Medium, Interactive Television: TV of the Future or the Future of TV?*, and *The Aesthetics of Television*. He has published more than hundred articles and papers on new media and the social and cultural implications of information and computing technology.

CHRISTOPHER MARSDEN is an independent consultant on broadband communications, with the Re: Think! consultancy network, a research associate of the CMuR at Warwick Business School, and a fellow of the Washington D.C.-based Phoenix Centre. He is the editor of two books *Convergence in European Digital TV Regulation* and *Regulating the Global Information Society*, and is the founder of the electronic *International Journal of Communications Law and Policy*. He has 12 years' experience in international telecoms and broadcast consultancy and has taught at the universities of Warwick and King's College, University College, and London School of Economics. Marsden received his LL.B and LL.M degrees in law from the London School of Economics.

NIKOLAUS MOHR is a senior manager for strategy consultancy at Accenture's Frankfurt office and concentrates on telecommunications and media entertainment. He focuses on organisational and strategic issues and advising companies entering the market for interactive broadband media. He received a master's degree in business administration and a doctorate in business studies. He is the author of several management books and numerous publications in management magazines.

PERTTI NARANEN is a researcher in the Department of Journalism and Communication at the University of Tampere. His research interests include journalism, interactivity, and the public interest. He is the author of a number of journal articles on media policy and technology issues.

ROBERT G. PICARD is director of the Media Management and Transition Centre and Hamrin Professor of Media Economics at Jönköping International Business School, Jönköping University, Sweden. He is one of the world's leading academic specialists in media economics and management. He is the author and editor of 17 books, a consultant to media companies and governmental agencies worldwide, and was editor of *The Journal of Media Economics* for a decade. He is currently editor of the *Journal of Media Business Studies*.

REZA TADAYONI is an assistant professor in the Center for Tele-Information at the Technical University of Denmark. His research focuses on policy toward new electronic technologies and the use of new technologies in media firms

GERHARD P. THOMAS is a managing partner for media and entertainment at Accenture, where he deals with strategic issues involving telecommunications and the media. He advises companies on establishing and expanding their business activities and oversees projects to optimising customer operations and create enterprise management solutions. He has specialist knowledge in designing and implementing customer information and settlement systems.